I0188801

Jewish soldiers in the Polish Army on Passover. Miechów, Poland, 1920.

Uniformed soldiers:
Top row, from left: Y. Gershinowitz, Unknown, Noah Gruszka.
Bottom row (from left) Y. Greitzer, M. Alschawski, Y. Kaminsky, M. Biltshuk.

Courtesy of Yad Vashem:
Archival Signature of the original photo in our collection - 12058_14.
Photo digitally corrected for scratches and tears.

Miechov Memorial Book, Charsznica and Ksiaz

This is a translation of:

Sefer Yizkor Miechow, Charsznica, Ksiaz

Original Book Editors: N. Blumenthal, A. Ben-Azar (Broshy)

Published by the Former Residents of Miechov, Charsznica and Ksiaz,

In Tel Aviv 1971 (Hebrew and Yiddish) 314 pages

Published by JewishGen

An Affiliate of the Museum of Jewish Heritage—A Living Memorial to the Holocaust
New York

Miechov Memorial Book, Charsznica and Ksiaz
Translation of *Sefer Yizkor Miechow, Charsznica, Ksiaz*

First Printing: January 2020, Tevet 5780

Translation Project Coordinator: William D. Cherny
Translators: Selwyn Rose and Gloria Berkenstat Freund
Cover Design: Nina Schwartz, Impulse Graphics LLC
Formatting: Joel Alpert
Indexing: Helen Rosenstein Wolf

Published by JewishGen, Inc.
An Affiliate of the Museum of Jewish Heritage
A Living Memorial to the Holocaust
36 Battery Place, New York, NY 10280

Printed in the United States of America by Lightning Source, Inc.

Library of Congress Control Number (LCCN): 2019934657
ISBN: 978-1-939561-79-4 (hard cover: 496 pages, alk. paper)

Cover photograph: Jews on the street in Miechów, c. 1932. Courtesy of the National Digital Archives of Poland.

JewishGen and the Yizkor Books in Print Project

This book has been published by the **Yizkor Books in Print Project**, as part of the **Yizkor Book Project** of JewishGen, Inc.

JewishGen, Inc. is a non-profit organization founded in 1987 as a resource for Jewish genealogy. Its website [www.jewishgen.org] serves as an international clearinghouse and resource center to assist individuals who are researching the history of their Jewish families and the places where they lived. JewishGen provides databases, facilitates discussion groups, and coordinates projects relating to Jewish genealogy and the history of the Jewish people. In 2003, JewishGen became an affiliate of the **Museum of Jewish Heritage—A Living Memorial to the Holocaust** in New York.

The **JewishGen Yizkor Book Project** was organized to make more widely known the existence of Yizkor (Memorial) Books written by survivors and former residents of various Jewish communities throughout the world. Later, volunteers connected to the different destroyed communities began cooperating to have these books translated from the original language—usually Hebrew or Yiddish—into English, thus enabling a wider audience to have access to the valuable information contained within them. As each chapter of these books was translated, it was posted on the JewishGen website and made available to the general public.

The **Yizkor Books in Print Project** began in 2011 as an initiative to print and publish Yizkor Books that had been fully translated, so that hard copies would be available for purchase by the descendants of these communities and also by scholars, universities, synagogues, libraries, and museums.

These Yizkor books have been produced almost entirely through the volunteer effort of researchers from around the world, assisted by donations from private individuals. The books are printed and sold at near cost, so as to make them as affordable as possible. Our goal is to make this important genre of Jewish literature and history available in English in book form, so that people can have the personal histories of their ancestral towns on their bookshelves for themselves and for their children and grandchildren.

A list of all published translated Yizkor Books in the project with prices and ordering information can be found at:
http://www.jewishgen.org/Yizkor/ybip.html

Binny Lewis, Yizkor Book Project Manager
Joel Alpert, Yizkor-Book-in-Print Project Coordinator

This book is presented by the
Yizkor Books in Print Project
Project Coordinator: Joel Alpert

Part of the
Yizkor Books Project of JewishGen, Inc.
Project Manager: Lance Ackerfeld

These books have been produced solely through volunteer effort of individuals from around the world. The books are printed and sold at near cost, so as to make them as affordable as possible.

Our goal is to make this history and important genre of Jewish literature available in English in book form so that people can have the near-personal histories of their ancestral towns on their bookshelves for themselves and for their children and grandchildren.

Any donations to the Yizkor Books Project are appreciated.

Please send donations to:
Yizkor Book Project
JewishGen
36 Battery Place
New York, NY 10280

JewishGen, Inc. is an affiliate of the
Museum of Jewish Heritage
A Living Memorial to the Holocaust

Acknowledgements

Special thanks to the National Yiddish Book Center in Amherst, Massachusetts and the New York Public Library for supplying the high resolution images used in this book.

Our sincere appreciation is due to Yad Vashem for the submission of the necrology for placement on the JewishGen web site.

The original authors were grateful to Genia Hollander for typing up the English text to facilitate its addition to this project.

Many thanks too, to the main translators, Selwyn Rose and Gloria Berkenstat Freund, for their careful attention to ensure that the original meaning is conveyed into English.

William Cherny, translation coordinator and sponsor of the translations wrote:

> The stories in this book provide a great insight into the lives of the people who lived there and a revelation of the support that they provided in the founding of the State of Israel and its academic institutions.
>
> Great respect should be paid to those who made the effort and took the time to have the stories originally assembled into this book. Especially, Shimshon Dov Yerushalmi, who is mentioned with in the story told by Shmuel Berger at page 270 and also those mentioned by Mr. Berger at page 408.
>
> I have nothing more to offer regarding this publication. I could not come close to the introductions and forward already in this book (see page 3). My financial support for the translation to English was made in memory of my father, Morris Cherny (Czerny), of Raclawice, Poland, who survived the war and settled in the United States as well as his parents and siblings, all of whom perished in the holocaust. I don't expect nor do I want any sort of recognition for that. I only expect that the Yizkor-Books-In-Print project volunteers will take the time and care to publish this book with due respect to those who contributed their remembrances. Their remembrances are facts that must be preserved for the generations.

William Cherny
Deember 28,2019

Notes to the Reader:

We apologize ahead of time for the poor quality of images in the book. Often these images had been scanned from the original Yizkor books which were of poor quality to begin with, being copies of old photographs. Each transfer results in loss of quality. We have done the best we could, given the original material and the resources and technology at hand. Even though images often appear of higher quality on computer screens, that does not transfer to high quality images in print. A reader can view the original scans on the web sites listed below.

Within the text the reader will note "{34}" standing ahead of a paragraph. This indicates that the material translated below was on page 34 of the original book. However, when a paragraph was split between two pages in the original book, the marker is placed in this book after the end of the paragraph for ease of reading.

Also please note that all references within the text of the book to page numbers, refer to the page numbers of the original Yizkor Book.

The original book can be seen online at the Yiddish Book Center web site:

https://www.yiddishbookcenter.org/collections/yizkor-books/yzk-nybc313887/blumental-nachman-ben-azar-sefer-yizkor-maikhov-kharshnitsah-u-kshoinz

In order to obtain a list of all Shoah victims from Miechov, the reader should access the Yad Vashem web site listed below; one can also search for specific family names using family name option. These lists are continually updated by Yad Vashem, so it is worthwhile to periodically search these lists.

There is much valuable information available on this web site, including the Pages of Testimony, etc.

http://yvng.yadvashem.org

A list of this book and all books available in the Yizkor-Book-In-Print Project along with prices is available at:

http://www.jewishgen.org/Yizkor/ybip.html

Index: Note that the Obituaries have not been included in the index, so please search these pages beginning on page 605 for any family names you might be interested in, for they are not included in the index. Also not included in the index are those in the list of "Jews of Wyszkow who fell, perished and died during World War II and later" on page 540.

Geopolitical Information:

Miechów, Poland
50°22' / 20°02'

Charsznica, Poland
50°25' / 19°26'

Książ Wielki, Poland
50°26' / 20°08'

Alternate names: Miechów [Pol], Miechov [Yid], Mekhuv [Rus], Mekhev, Myekhov

Alternate names: Charsznica [Pol], Charsnitza [Yid], Kharshnitza [Rus], Kharshnitse

Alternate names: Książ Wielki [Pol], Keshionzh [Yid], Ksyenzh-Vel'ki [Rus], Kshanzh Vyelki, Kshaz Vyelki, Kshanzh, Kshaz, Kshoynge, Kshoynzh, Książ, Xiąż, Xions

Period	Town	District	Province	Country
Before WWI (c. 1900):	Miechów	Miechów	Kielce	Russian Empire
Between the wars (c. 1930):	Miechów	Miechów	Kielce	Poland
After WWII (c. 1950):	Miechów			Poland
Today (c. 2000):	Miechów			Poland

Period	Town	District	Province	Country
Before WWI (c. 1900):	Charsznica	Miechów	Kielce	Russian Empire
Between the wars (c. 1930):	Charsznica	Miechów	Kielce	Poland
After WWII (c. 1950):	Charsznica			Poland
Today (c. 2000):	Charsznica			Poland

Period	Town	District	Province	Country
Before WWI (c. 1900):	Książ Wielki	Miechów	Kielce	Russian Empire
Between the wars (c. 1930):	Książ Wielki	Miechów	Kielce	Poland
After WWII (c. 1950):	Książ Wielki			Poland
Today (c. 2000):	Książ Wielki			Poland

Nearby Jewish Communities

Słomniki 9 miles SSE
Żarnowiec 11 miles NW
Wolbrom 12 miles W
Skała 12 miles SW
Wodzisław 14 miles NNE
Działoszyce 14 miles E
Sędziszów 15 miles N
Proszowice 16 miles SE
Skalbmierz 17 miles E
Pilica 18 miles WNW

POLAND - Current Borders

Map of Poland with * indicating location of all three towns

Hebrew Title Page of Original Yizkor Book

ספר יזכור מייכוב

כארשניצה וקשוינז׳

העורכים: נחמן בלומנטל
אביבה בן־אז״ר (ברושי)

ארגון יוצאי מייכוב כארשניצה וקשוינז
תל־אביב / תשל״א / 1971

MIECHOV MEMORIAL BOOK

CHARSHNITZA AND KSHOYNGE

EDITORS: NACHMAN BLUMENTAL
AVIVA BEN-AZAR (BROSHY)

IRGUN YOTZEY MIECHOV, CHARSHNITZA AND KSHOYNGE
TEL-AVIV, 1971

Table of Contents

Translated by Yocheved Klausner

D. Between the Two World Wars

Personalities and Families

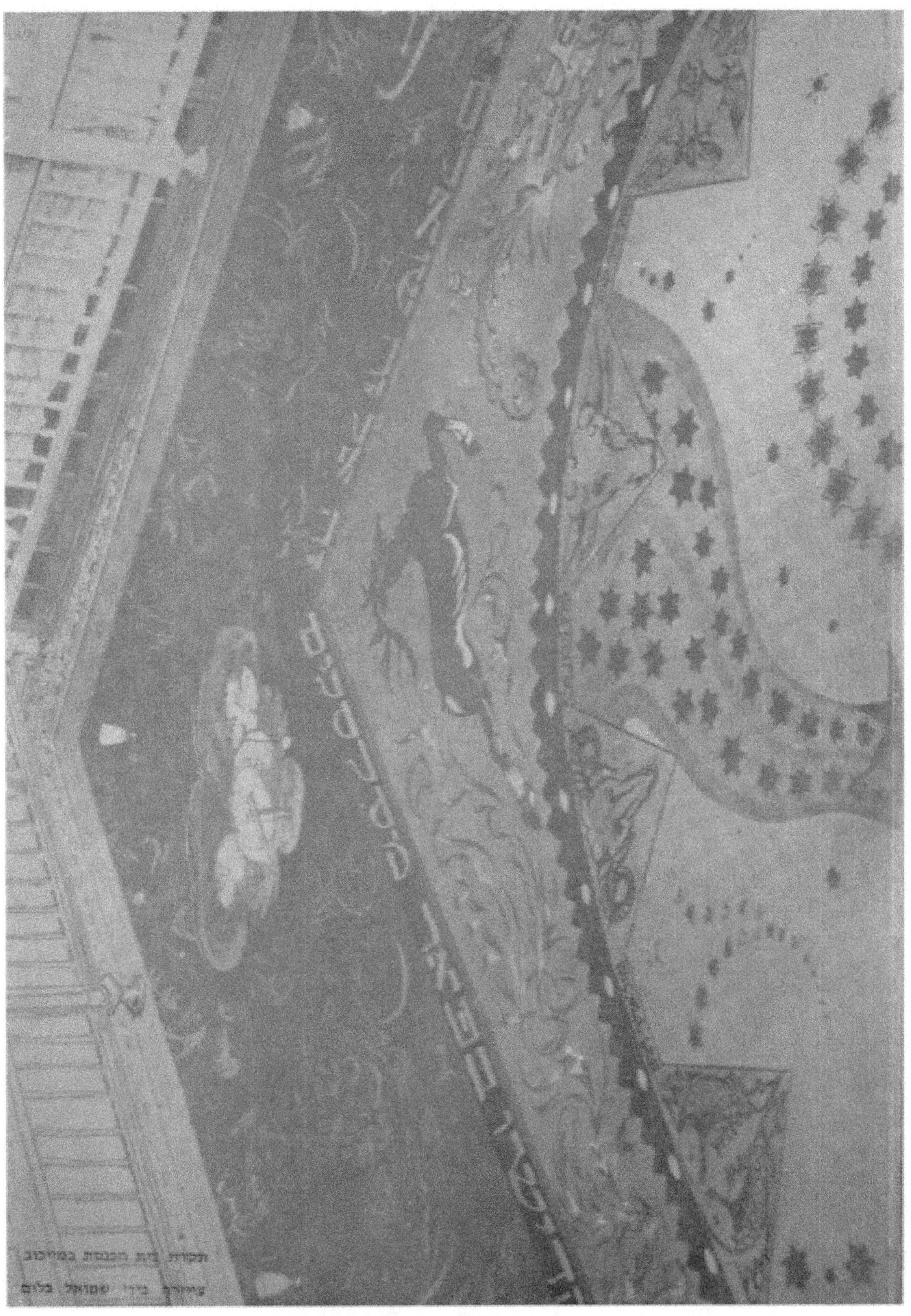

תקרת בית הכנסת במיכוב
ציור בידי שמואל בלום

[Unnumbered page]

The Book Committee

(l–r): Moshe Spiegel; Moshe Sabitzki, Treasurer; Shmuel Berger, Chairman; Michael Suknik, Secretary; Avraham Ya'acov Wlavromski

[Unnumbered page]

A Word from the Publishers

A. Ben–Azar

Translated by Selwyn Rose

A memorial book is, by its very nature a collection of subjective descriptions and experiences. The principal strength of the testimonies lies in their innate truth while at the same time they immortalize figures and events precious to the hearts of the writers. For this reason we were asked not in any way to compromise the tone of what is written without the involvement of the writer. We have preserved the popular style and avoided changing the style of the narratives. We have used, as written, local expressions whether they be in Yiddish or Polish as they occur frequently throughout such as: "Schloch" (untidy slob); "Rebbitzen" (Rabbi's wife); "Chodesh Gelt" (a financially good month {a wishful blessing}, etc.

Here and there we encountered varying versions of the same events, dates etc., and even opposing interpretations. We attempted in very case to verify and authenticate these details, either by historically reliable documents or even verbally clarifying with a number of the contributors themselves. Where it was impossible to make an unequivocal decision, we went with the majority opinion and even on rare occasions from force of circumstances, we have used two very different versions of the same event (as in, for example, the correct date for the installation of the first Rabbi of a town).

For the sake of easier reading – especially the Miechów and the surroundings children and their children's children who are unfamiliar or not fluent in Polish, we have partially introduced the Hebrew vowel system for the names of people and places and where possible the accompanying Polish name or expression in Hebrew.

The spelling system we have adopted is the non–vowel system according to the rules of the Academy of the Hebrew Language (April 1970); the transliterations from Polish and Yiddish are according to the accepted phonetic usages. We have made every attempt to maintain maximum consistency but since there are no clear rules for the spelling of names and places in Yiddish, we have been obliged to stay with the spellings used by the individual writers themselves.

A similar problem arose with family and first names that are written in many different ways in the monographs. We made strenuous efforts to be as accurate and as consistent as possible but it was not always possible. We rely on the understanding of the reader.

A. Ben–Azar,
Editor and publisher.

[Unnumbered pages]

Foreword

by Shmuel Berger

Translated by Selwyn Rose

We have succeeded in publishing the Memorial Book of the communities of Miechow, Charsznica and Kshoynzh. Throughout a long period of preparation we made the utmost efforts to collect all possible records and lists, material, photographs, documentary material and in particular we recovered and recorded memories as they were remembered by those of the communities who remained alive.

We wanted to resurrect on these pages the way of life of the Jewish people in our communities as they were throughout many decades and to implant a "memorial candle" to the memory of our dear parents, brothers and sisters and to all the Jews of the towns and villages, Torah scholars and traditionalists, business men and Zionists thousand of honest, simple folk and public benefactors.

We have tried to give a faithful picture of community life mainly between the two world wars until the liquidation during the Holocaust.

Most of the material in this book is the result of the writings of people who make no claim to be counted among authors of note. Each of them expressed his or her deepest thoughts as remembered and saved by them in memory. The unaffectedness, the good will and the soul-searching truth – these were the distinguishing excellence of those who assisted in this work.

These pages in this Memorial Book are a living testimony of the communities of Miechów, Charsznica and Kshoynzh, and in them we have per-petuated everything that was dear to us. From now on they will be the living only witness to us and our children.

This book will be used as a faithful, accompanying mourner for the remnants of our communities for the rest of our lives for the souls concealed within them were our families and dear ones who were cruelly exterminated and for whom there is no requital.

And if perchance our children will ask us what were these little towns and villages in which we were born and educated we will unfold before them these scrolls of our dear communities and they will see what a wonderful world sank into the depths of blood and fire.

In this book, the reader will find sketches, drawings, memories and lists of public businessmen, people and images, descriptions of public disputes and struggles for social rights and justice and the individual existence up until the day of destruction.

In a special article in this book I have detailed the story of the publishing of the book in full detail (see page 291).

In closing I must give thanks to all the survivors of our towns who answered our call and offered articles, lists, memories, pictures and documents, recounted their stories and helped in any way they could to reconstitute the life of the communities.

My grateful thanks go to the honorary president of the organization Mr. S. D. Yerushalmi (z"l) and the president A.L. Lavi , may he be spared for a long life, for their contributions to the book; and especially to the members of the national committee and the book's committee the honorable gentlemen Moshe Sabitzki the treasurer, Michael Sukenik the secretary and Moshe Shpiegel, all of whom worked with me throughout the whole period with eagerness and staying power in order to overcome all the pitfalls and difficulties in get-ting this book out; and also to Mr. Avraham Walbromski of Kshoynzh, on whose shoulders fell the burden of accumulating and editing the material from Kshoynzh and on his own wrote most of the monographs in this book concerning his community. The entire surviving community of Kshoynzh owe him their deepest thanks for perpetuating their community.

Lastly my thanks to the management of Yad Va-shem who took it upon themselves to publish the book; to the editor Mr. Natan Blumenthal for editing the material; to Mrs. Aviva Ben–Azar who, in effect, completed all the work working tirelessly and dedicatedly and faithfully in the final styling and editing of the book and brought it to press; the proof-reading was executed by Mr. Michael Broschi who coped successfully with all the special problems that arose in the publishing the memorial; and to the staff of the print-ing–house "Zohar".

Shmuel Berger,

Chairman of the Organization

And the Committee for producing the Book of Remembrance.

[Unnumbered page]

Waterfalls of time

by Y.L. Bieler

Translated by Selwyn Rose

My G–d, my G–d, my soul cries
Cry, daughter of Israel
Lament, and breathe
The fire consumed Israel
For destroyed communities
And for the catastrophe of the synagogues
Wood for fire
The beautiful cities of Israel.
For the generations who were cut down
Tears of fathers on tears of their children
In the valley of Auschwitz, they ended their lives
For the bonfires of the furnaces.

(Y.L. Bieler "Waterfalls of time" – excerpt).

[Unnumbered page]

Miechow – general view

The Church and the Monastery

The Town Square – "The Rink"

The Town Square – Sports Day

[Page 17]

On the Holy Communities of Miechów Charsznica and Kshoynzh

by Eliezer Lavi (Yazkirowitz)

Translated by Selwyn Rose

The northern entrance to the town

At the Gate

I do not aspire here to write a historical document on those communities for I am not qualified for such: neither is it in my mind to write about the events that occurred during those years of the Shoah – my family and I left Miechów six or seven years before the Second World War and arrived in Palestine late in the summer of 1934. But I cannot preclude myself from bringing to these pages some of the memories honoring and thus perpetuating their memory, in the very book dedicated to that cause.

The communities of Miechów–Charsznica were not among the long–established communities in Poland: It was founded only 100 years ago in the years 1864–66 and until that time only a few Jews would come there for trade fairs. Towards evening, the Jews would be obliged to return to their own nearby communities: Kshoynzh, Wodzislaw, Działoszyce, Wolbrom and Olkusz, all of which were ancient and long–standing. I remember, about 40 years ago they found a Jewish grave in the old cemetery of Kshoynzh dating back 600 years. In the folk–lore of residents of Kshoynzh and Wodzislaw they would relate from generation to generation that the first Jews who settled in Krakow described the town as "Krakow, near Kshoynz" or "near Wodzislaw."

From the time the Jews received permission to settle in Miechów and Charsznica the town expanded and they began to establish their own community. The Jews created small businesses and industries, traded with the local landowners, engaged in banking, construction erected windmills, indulged in logging in the surrounding forests and opened shops to which the local populace was drawn from the entire area which was rich with the produce from field and garden. The biggest windmill in Miechów, built to the latest technical standards was erected by Jews (Mordecai Greitzer, Alter Warshawski and Yosef Friedman). The windmill was also used to generate electricity and licensed by the authorities to supply all the municipal and government institutions and all the town's residents. It is interesting to think that it was therefore given to the Jews to illuminate the town and its streets. Somewhat later, another large windmill was built (by Mordecai Greitzer), in Charsznica.

The economic standard of the first Jewish settlers was stable and assured and they forthwith addressed themselves to organizing their community life. The Jewish community of Miechów–Charsznica was superior in its organizations and institutions compared to all the surrounding communities.

[Page 18]

The First Settlers in Miechów and Charsznica

(Family names in Alphabetical order).

As one who functioned as community secretary from 1922–33 and administered the membership lists, I take it upon myself to perpetuate the names of the first settlers whose families and grandchildren donated much to the development of the community. The number of souls in 1933 reached 2,600 and they are:

Adelist, Shmuel Leib; Olschewsky, Avraham Yosef; Olschewsky, Moshe; Eisenstein family; Issrowski, Shmuel; Itskovich, David; Buchner, Herschel; Borenstein, Michael and sons; Blum family; Blatt, Ya'acov Yitzhak; Brumer family; Brukner, Yosef Baruch; Bryn, Alter Ezrael; Bermann family; Brenner family; Goldberg family; Goldkorn, Dov Barish; Goldkorn, Moshe Schmelke; Ginsberg, Leibusch; Grossfeld, Aharon; Gertler family; Greitzer, Baruch and his sons, Mordecai and Yesheyahu; Greitzer, Yosef; Grynbaum family; Grynwald family; Gerstenfeld, Eliezer and Aharon; Horowitz, Yitzhak David (Itschel) and his son Avraham Mordecai; Huppert, Wolf; Hershliokowitz family; Weill, Moshe Yosef; Weissfeld family; Weizmann family; Wischlitzky, Elimelech; Waldliwerand, Zelig and his brother Reuven Shlomo; Wetfreund(?) family; Wanchdlowski(?) family; Wroclawski Simcha; Warschawski, Alter; Zelikovich family; Salzburg, Yoel and his son Shalom; Naphtali, Herzl and Haim; Jama, Avraham; Yaskiel, Herschel and his sons Yosef and Menahem Monish; Katzengold, Schmelke; Lederman family; Levitt family; Londner, Shimon; Lucki family; Liebermann, Emanuel; Lehreich family; Liesha, Avraham and Ya'acov; Langer family; Landsberg family; Lachs, Leib; Lishmann, Yehuda; Molstein, Mordecai and Yosef; Malinarski, Haim and his sons Menahem Manier and Yosef; Solewicz, Shlomo; Sukenik, Moshe; Stollik, Yehiel; Swirsky, Eliezer; Skowron family; Sereni family; Sercaz, Yehezkiel and Yisrael; Federman Eliezer; Fogel, Meir; Polski family; Posluszny, Avraham and his son Yitzhak; Feigenboim Bones and his sons David Yehuda Ya'acov and Haim Lev; Feigenblat, Alter (Charsznica); Feigenblat, Mendel and Moshe; Feureisen, Avraham Ya'acov and his sons Gedaliahu, Pinchas, Haim and Ze'ev Wolf; Pinchowsky, Shimon and his sons David Yehuda and Ya'acov; Pasternak, Avraham; Pacanowski family; Friedenberg, Shmuel; Zukerman, Aharon (Charsznica); Ziegler family; Zimmerman, Rabbi Moshe, ritual slaughterer and examiner; Koppelowitz, Fischl; Kupchik family; Kurland family; Kornfeld family; Katzurin family; Kaiser, Hanoch Ha'anich; Kleiner family; Klinger, Yudell; Knobel family; Rosen, Avraham; Rosenbaum, Yosef; Rosenblum family; Rosenberg, Alter; Rosencrantz, Kalman (the cobbler); Schechtman, Mordecai David; Sternfeld family; Scheinold(?), Elimelech;

Rabbis, religious leaders and cantors for the Miechów and Charsznica communities.

A. Rabbis

The first Rabbi installed as community Rabbi arrived in town in 1864. He was Rabbi Yesheyahu Scheinfrucht, the son of Rabbi Ze'ev Scheinfrucht (Z"L) a disciple of Gaon Rabbi Ya'acov Gesundheit (Z"L) the Rabbi of Warsaw. He was recommended by the well-known orthodox Rabbi of his generation Rabbi Shlomo Ha-Cohen Rabinowitz (Z"L) the author of "The Splendor of Solomon" just before his death on the eve of the month of Nissan, 1866.

He was extremely learned in the Torah and known for his righteousness, nobility of spirit and soul. He officiated as Rabbi of the community for more than 56 years and died at a good age in the spring of 1922 and buried with great honor in Miechów.

[Page 19]

His replacement was his own son, considered a genius, Rabbi Hanoch Ha'anich, who had previously ministered to the community of Charsznica. He was among the most recognized of Poland's distinguished teachers, wise and learned in the ways of life of the world and its customs and was referred to as an arbitrator throughout the region in major disputes between traders. His wife, Malka (May G-d avenge her blood), was the daughter of Rabbi Ya'acov Koppel Zukerberg (Z"L) originally from Przemyśl and the son-in-law of Rabbi Alexander Mendel Sender (May his Righteousness be Remembered for a Blessing), the eldest son the Holy Cabbalist Genius Rabbi Yitzhak Isaac of Komarno (May his Righteousness be Remembered for a Blessing), the son-in-law of Rabbi Avraham Mordecai Horowitz Komarno (May his Righteousness be Remembered for a Blessing), from Pińczów. He therefore was the brother-in-law of the Righteous Genius Rabbi Alter Shalom David Zukerberg – the last old Rabbi of Komarno (May G-d Avenge his Blood).

The Rabbinic genius Rabbi Hanoch Ha'anich married his only son, my dear friend, Rabbi Ya'acov Koppel (May G-d Avenge his Blood), with the daughter of the famous Rabbinic genius Rabbi Haim Posner (Z"L) – a member of the Rabbinical Committee of Warsaw, who functioned – like all the rabbis of the committee, one month of the year as the Chief Rabbi of the Warsaw Jewish community.

Rabbi Hanoch Ha'anich conducted his Rabbinate to a high degree and improved upon it by his participation, investing so deeply, that it could be said of him: "When a Man's ways please the Lord he maketh even his enemies to be at peace with him." (Proverbs 16:8), and all the parties and organizations respected him thus preventing much dissention within the community.

He perished in the gas–chambers and crematoria of Belzec towards the end of 1942 together with most of the community (May G–d Avenge their Blood).

B. Spiritual Leaders

Rabbi Joseph Kleinfeltz (Z"L) a great Torah scholar from among the Righteous of Radomsk; he died in 1924.

Rabbi Shlomo Ze'ev the son of Rabbi Ezriel Alter Bryn. He possessed a scintillating intellect and was considered a genius. He was a disciple of the master of the tractates "Agley Tal" and "Avnei Nazar". He was associated with the Righteous of Gur. He functioned as Rabbi and expounder in Charsznica after the death of his predecessor, the above mentioned first Rabbi and his uncle – the second of the community's Rabbis mentioned above – selected as the Rabbi, and Father of the Beth–Din in Miechów itself. He perished in the Holocaust with most of the community of Charsznica, May G–d Avenge their Blood. Of his family two sons survived – Avraham and Moshe Bryn and they live in Israel.

Also considered a genius was Rabbi Ephraim Fischl, the son of Rabbi Aharon Borenstein – an Expounder and auxiliary Rabbi in Miechów. He was an expert in the Mishna and knew the six tractates by heart. He was a family member of the Holy Rabbi of Sochaczew, the author of the above–mentioned tractates "Agley Tal" and "Avnei Nazar", May his Righteousness be Remembered for a Blessing. (His grandfather, Rabbi Yisroel Meir Borenstein (Z"L), was the brother of Avi, the Holy Genius of the above–mentioned Sochaczew); He perished with all his family in the Holocaust, May G–d Avenge their Blood.

C. Ritual Slaughterers and Inspectors

Rabbi Elimelech Spiegel (Z"L), a great scholar owner of many gifted attributes, from the "The Good Jew" of Neustadt and afterwards the Righteous of Khentshin,

Rabbi Moshe Zimmermann (Z"L), of Radomsk counted among the righteous of that community, of memorable demeanor, endeared by all and of a smiling disposition, righteous and just in all his dealings;

Rabbi Aharon (Urisch) Greenboim (Z"L), a learned scholar from among the Righteous of Gur, son–in–law of Righteous Rabbi Ephraim Fischl Borenstein mentioned above. May G–d avenge His Blood;

Rabbi David Burstein, distinguished scholar, a disciple of Rabbi David Goldman from Kalish May his Righteousness be Remembered for a Blessing, a man of many noble attributes and a noted prayer leader May G–d Avenge his Blood;

Rabbi Eliezer Wohlgelernter, (Z"L). He was the Patriarch of the family of famous Rabbis known throughout America, Canada and Israel. David was the fifth generation of the author of "Mishmeret Itamar" – and a visionary scholar from Lublin. A preacher from Kshoynzh and the Holy Jew of Przysucha; May his Righteousness be Remembered for a Blessing.

[Page 20]

Rabbi Ya'acov Yosef Lieberman a learned scholar from Radomsk, he was the grandchild of Rabbi Moshe Zimmerman – the ritual slaughterer and inspector mentioned above. He was also an excellent prayer leader. May G–d Avenge his Blood;

Rabbi David Fuchs, a scholar and disseminator among many, a recognized, precious G–d–fearing soul from among the Righteous of Gur, May G–d Avenge his Blood. One of his sons Rabbi Yosef Fuchs survived the Holocaust and settled in B'nei Barak. He was an exemplary G–d–fearing scholar, and a visionary and sponsor to our son. He died suddenly on 8th October 1965 and is interred in Kyriat Shaul close to Tel–Aviv;

Rabbi Leibusch Rabinowitz, a scholar, the offspring of the author of "Tiferet Shlomo" and the son–in–law of Rabbi Alter Rosenberg – the head of the Burial Society, May G–d Avenge his Blood;

D. Cantors

Rabbi Shmuel Issrowaski Ha–Cohen (Z"L) the Chief Cantor, spent his whole life occupied with the Torah and Hassidism, a polite and a pleasant conversationalist, among the elders of the Hassidim of Khentshin. He raised his son and daughters in the spirit of Torah and good deeds;

Rabbi Yisroel David Burstein, Ritual Slaughterer and Inspecto; survivors of his family include sons and grandchildren living in Israel and abroad;

Rabbi Ya'acov Yosef Lieberman, Ritual Slaughterer and Inspector;

Rabbi Tzvi Herschel Goldberg (Z"L), a G–d fearing man from among the Righteous of Gur. He was the son–in–law of the auxiliary Rabbi Yosef Kleinfeltz (Z"L) - considered a genius. Of his family a son survived, Avraham Goldberg, Living in Israel (Haifa).

E. Community Leaders in Miechów–Charsznica during years 1905–1933

Rabbi Simcha Wrotzlowski. It is thanks to his great toil a synagogue, theological college and additional Hebrew classes for children were built that were later used as a school (to replace the original huts that burnt down). These buildings were completed about 1906. He was murdered by robbers while travelling, May G–d Avenge his Blood;

Rabbi Mordecai Molstein functioned as community head up until the outbreak of the First World War, 1914;

Rabbi Yermiyahu Blum functioned as community head during the First World War for about three years;

Rabbi Avraham Friedrich was community head for about six years from 1917 until 1923/4;

Rabbi Avraham Sercaz functioned as community head from 1924 until 1939, until the outbreak of World War Two. During his term of office, the community acquired two additional houses, close to the synagogue buildings, from the above mentioned Rabbi Mordecai Milstein and from the family of Haim Bar Elyakim, Getzil Lewit (Z"L), with the intention of expanding the institutions, and many other activities for the benefit of the community that had been neglected for several decades. Community property, which was registered in the names of "guardians", was re–registered to the name of the community. It is worth noting that during the administration of the last two community leaders (Friedrich and Sercaz), that major community institution accepted with respect and esteem the decisions of these two functionaries.

F. Members of the Community Management

Avraham Mordecai Stern; Aharon Brenner; Aharon Leib Adler; Asher Antil Koppelowitz; Dov Barish Goldkorn; Haim Feureisen; Hanoch Ha'anich Kaiser; Yitzhak Fussloschni; Mordecai Greitzer; Moshe Koppelowitz; Nathan Borenstein; Reuven Shmuel Kleiner; Shmuel Fogel; Shmuel Leib Adlist; Shimon Dov Yerushalmi, May he be spared for a good life. Ya'acov Tzvi Nittler, living in Tel Aviv.

[Page 21]

G. Secretaries to the Community (in order of their administration).

An ideal personality and a staunch warrior for order in the community and the first of the community secretaries of Miechów–Charsznica, was Mr. Ya'acov Blum, the son of the head of the community. He began his appointment from 1917; until then the Secretariat had been run by a Christian official from the city council. Mr. Ya'acov Blum labored to organize the life of the community in an ordered and suitable fashion.

With his emigration to Palestine in 1920, his brother, Ephraim Blum was nominated and functioned, together with his second brother, Shmuel Blum – a known artist living today in France – until the end of July 1922. All the troubles and woes and fears of the Holocaust fell on Ephraim Blum and he survived and settled in America. He visited Israel thinking to resettle here but eventually decided to move to America and died in New York.

The writer of these lines was secretary of the community from August 1922, during the administrations of Friedrich and Sercaz until his own emigration to Palestine in September 1933;

My replacement was a dear student of mine, the noble spirited and gentle soul, Mr. Yona Bar Yosef Blatt who took over after he had completed his studies at the "Tachkemoni" school in Warsaw as a excellent student. After a few years, he suffered a heart attack while at work in his office at the community center. It was Wednesday 23rd August 1939, nine days before the outbreak of World War Two. May he be Remembered for a Blessing;

He was followed by Mr. Ya'acov Kornfeld until the Holocaust in which he perished. (I will have more to say of him below). The bursar of the community was Rabbi Avraham Liesha, the auxiliary Rabbi a Sochaczew Righteous Jew – May G–d Avenge his Blood.

H. Community Institutions

The Synagogue

The Miechów Synagogue's eastern wall painted by the artist Shmuel Blum

[Page 22]

The synagogue was financed on behalf of the community by the highly respected Avraham Goldberg and Shlomo Feigenboim who worked endlessly towards creating a fine synagogue for the community. During their period in office the community invested much money for re–painting and refurnishing the synagogue. The wall and ceiling paintings of the synagogue were created by the artist Mr. Shmuel Blum. All the institutions of the community and those supported by it were centralized in the community buildings and its offices.

I. Charities and Help Societies

1. "Achiezer" (brotherly help). – When, with the outbreak of World War One in 1914, the economic status of the middle–classes in general was disrupted and the poor of the town in particular was

aggravated, Mr. Ya'acov Blum with the help of the brothers Elimelech and Raphael Burstein (the sons of Rabbi Yisroel David, Ritual Slaughterer and Inspector) and Avraham Grossfeld, organized a help foundation called "Brotherly Help". No words can describe the toil and energy they invested in order to acquire cash, clothing, fuel, etc. to rescue souls in real peril, for those who had lost their livelihood. Especially vulnerable were those who were engaged in the trading of produce from the surrounding villages because all the produce was confiscated by the different conquering armies and transport by all the roads was dangerous. At first the general population showed little enthusiasm with the energetic young activists but after some time each individual suddenly became eager to be counted as a member of that foundation. Afterwards "Achiezer" became a permanent fixture of the community and on the initiative of this writer a second institution was created called "Gemilut Chesed Fund", which received permanent support from the American "Joint" and the Community. In the last years before this writer left Poland, interest–free loans of up to 1,000 Guilders were given per family, not only the poor but also the middle–classes, a sum that helped significantly. The functionaries in these institutions were: Avraham Mordecai Stern (Chairman); Haim Lewit (Vice–chairman); David Isskowitz; Aharon Berger; Avraham Goldberg; Yitzhak Tangwurtzel; Moshe Koppelowitz and Reuven Shmuel Kleiner. The secretary of these institutions was Mr. Ya'acov Liesha.

2. "Women's Society" – The women's society for the anonymous help of poor respectable families, especially widows and orphans, the leading women were: Fassili Feigenboim (Chairwoman), Raiyela Sukenik, Feig'eleh Borenstein, Feig'eleh Tenenwurcel and Feig'eleh Schoenthal. All of them very active in collecting donations from different sources, holidays and from other communal festivals in town. The activities of these ladies were a great blessing.
3. "Bikur Cholim" (Visiting the sick) – During same war our much respected Mr. Ya'acov Tzvi Gitler organized and instituted home visits and assistance for the many sick. The organization acquired suitable medical equipment costing large sums of money and which were difficult to obtain at the time. The medical assistance was given to all who needed it with devotion. Even in the case of an infectious

illness (e.g. Typhus). The devotion of Mr. Ya'acov Tzvi Gitler was indeed a great blessing.

The above organizations were famous throughout the entire area and a living example of giving aid to the individual in need.

- The Burial Society – A true selfless act of kindness – It is known that there were many complaints in many communities about the burial society in that they sometimes demanded fees that were exorbitant, an affront to both the living and the departed. Not so was the situation in Miechów–Charsznica. During the administration of the community chairman Mr. Avraham Sercaz May G–d Avenge his Blood, a decision was taken that no money would be demanded by the Burial Society for services rendered either for the burial or the erection of the tombstone and that all the expenses incurred and connected with the upkeep of the cemetery would be carried by the community and that close family members would be required to pay a sum equal to the community tax for that year and a similar sum at the time of the erection of the stone. A family that was exempt from the community tax was also exempt from any and all charges concerning the interment of the departed. This decision was greeted with much support and since then there have been no more complaints.
- The Burial Society was run by Alter Rosenberg (Chairman); Avraham Goldberg; Avraham Mordecai Stern; Yosef Baruch Bruckner; Yehiel Stollik; Yermiyahu Blum; Yisroel David Burstein; Mendel Goldberg; Pinchas Feureisen; Shlomo Meir Sheinfrucht – the eldest son of our first Rabbi (Z"L) and my brother, the last Rabbi, the above Rabbi Hanoch Ha'anich, May G–d Avenge his Blood. And may they be spared for a long life: Rabbi Ya'acov Leib Manele, today a senior official in the Tel Aviv–Yaffo Burial Society and the writer of these lines, until his emigration to Palestine.

[Page 23]

The Jewish Cemetery – Tombstone

Educational Institutions

1. Religious Seminaries

In 1917 a few young, learned scholars of the Torah, arrived in Miechów, married there and settled themselves in with the Gur Righteous group in the Community building. These young men gave group lessons in Torah mornings and evenings. At the head of the group stood Rabbi Moshe David Waxberg (Z"L), a noted Talmud scholar and a profound thinker. He had previously been one of the managers of the Zavirtcha Seminary and it was on his initiative that the Seminary was founded for students who had completed diverse study classes in the town. Every day one or other of the group (all of them without thought of recompense) lectured to the students and among them the writer of these lines. The students were obliged to deliberate on the lessons and learn by themselves a tractate decided upon by one of the group. Every Shabbat the students were examined by group and Torah scholars of the town. The Seminary developed and students came from other near–by towns. In 1919 a tenured and salaried head of Seminary was installed: the above noted Rabbi Moshe David Waxberg. The Seminary existed until the outbreak war between Poland and Russia in 1920, when all the scholars and some of the students were mobilized and inducted into the army.

[Page 24]

2. Schools

At the conclusion of the war between Poland and Russia "Agudat Yisrael" and the "Mizrachi" organizations were founded each one in Community buildings.

A. The "Foundations of the Torah" school of "Agudat Yisrael"–

Its managers were: The much respected Yisroel Eliyahu Krimolowski; the writer of these lines (from the summer of 1922 until he took the position of Community Secretary); Rabbi Moshe David Waxberg (Z"L). The members of the school committee were: My Master, Teacher and Rabbi, Rabbi Ya'acov Yitzhak Elhanan Rotenberg, May his Righteousness be Remembered for a Blessing and May G–d Avenge his Blood (he later transferred to replace his father Rabbi Shalom, (May his Righteousness be Remembered for a Blessing) in Chenstochov); Bezalel Harmatz; Moshe Avraham Melman and Moshe Mordecai Rosenblum May G–d Avenge his Blood.

Similarly, “Bet Ya'acov” school for girls came into being in the Community buildings. It was founded by the Haredi business-woman the distinguished Mrs. Sarah Shnirer (Z”L). She came to Miechów especially for that purpose.

B. The “Mizrachi” School –

The managers were: Yesheyahu Shmuel Hirshenhorn; Tzvi Kleinfeltz; Yitzhak Tzvi Weiner; the writer S.N. Kahanofsky; Yitzhak Hafter; Tzvi Yudkovitz (at times a teacher of the Mishna and Talmud in the school), and two hours each day the writer of these lines).

The school committee members were: Avraham Spiegel; Avraham Ya'acov Nyberg; Aharon Leib Adler; Gershon Gimlakwitz(?); Ze'ev Feureisen; Haim Feureisen; Hanoch (Handl) Zalmanowitz; Yehoshua Koppelowitz; Yehiel Shmuel Abramowitz; Ya'acov Gitler; Ya'acov Liesha; Yitzhak Tangwurtzel Yitzhak Schweitzer; Yisroel Spiegel; Moshe Yosef Spiegel; Shmuel Leib Adlist; Shmuel Fogel.

Absorbed by the “Mizrachi” was a school especially for girls under the management of Mrs. Fassia Teitelbaum, in which the students studied Judaism in Hebrew.

C. Teachers of Religion

The community concerned itself that there should be a teacher of the Jewish religion in Government schools for Jewish children. The first teacher was the writer S.N. Kahanofsky. On his death in 1926 his successor was the writer of these lines, in addition to his post as community secretary. With his emigration his successor was Mr. Ya'acov Kornfeld – a graduate of the teachers' seminary headed by the wise researcher Dr. S. A. Poznanski (Z”L) of Warsaw.

All the above institution received the warm support of the community which similarly supported the students who travelled out of town to study at senior religious schools.

Professional Organizations and Unions

All the above organizations also have offices in the Community buildings.

A. Associations

- "Agudat Yisrael" – among the founders were counted the above named senior members of the "Torah Foundation" school and in addition to them the much respected Gedalia Feureisen, David Yehuda Pinchowsky, Yosef Yaskiel, Yesheyahu Goldfreund, Moshe Mordecai Sereni and the brothers Shlomo and Zeinbel Blady.

[Page 25]

- The last mentioned succeeded towards the end of his life to immigrate to Israel and died in Haifa (Z"L). At the head of "Young Agudat Yisrael" were: Rabbi Issachar Ber Ha–Levi Rotenberg May he live to enjoy a long good life (who was later Father of the Beit–Din in Vodislov and is now living in Brooklyn and is one of the active leaders of "Ha–ADMOR" from Satmer May he live to enjoy a long good life) and the second Shlomo Goldfreund May G–d Avenge his Blood.
- "Mizrachi" – Among the founders were counted those mentioned above as members of the Mizrahi School and in addition the respected were Avraham Goldsobel and Avraham Grossfeld; my son–in–law Rabbi Haim Bar Elyakim Getzil Lewit (Z"L); the respected and generous Mr. Ya'acov Lewit – the well known industrialist living in Tel Aviv. At the head of "Mizrachi Youth" stood: the respected Yitzhak Bar Shlomo Meir Sheinfrucht (citrus fruit); Yosef Gross; Yesheyahu Burstein; Naphtali Hertzki(?), Bruckner; Pinchas Bryn May G–d Avenge his Blood; Haim Ze'ev Yuma, living in France; Eliezer Burstein, living in Canada; Yehuda Burstein and Avraham and Arieh Bruckner, living in Tel Aviv. At the head of "Mizrachi Girls – Bruriah" were Handel Yazkirowitz (neé Saltsburg) living in Jerusalem; Chaya Feigenboim; Feigel Unger (neé Yaskiel) and Miriam Gross May G–d Avenge her Blood. At the head of "Ha–Shomer Ha–Dati" stood Yitzhak Meir Shenker, graduate of the "Tachkemoni" in Warsaw; Meir Liesha; Meir Grunewald; Shlomo Kleinfeltz; Kalman Jama. Both of the above organizations and their youth offshoots, set up lessons for its members and supporters in Torah and lectures different historical topics and developed many public activities in all areas of life in our town.

- "General Zionists" – its founders in Miechów were the well–respected Avraham Sercaz; Ze'ev Dov Warshawski May G–d Avenge his Blood (the brother–in–law of S.W. Yeruzalimsky) he was the first delegate of the Keren Kayemet in Miechów; Ze'ev Dov Kaiser; Ya'acov Blum; Moshe Koppelowitz. Ze'ev while the head office was still in Vienna, during the First World War, for a few years. After he retired his place was taken by Mr. Ze'ev Dov Kaiser. Both of them were active and activators, and dedicated most of their time and efforts to spread the idea of redemption of the land. This organization founded a library with Mr Ya'acov Blum at its head, in Miechów with the name of "The Nightingale". It contained several thousands of books for reference and also for lending out. They also occasionally invited lecturers from out of town (Krakow, Warsaw). At the head of the library stood the respected lawyer Yerechmiel (Mitchell) Isskowitz, Ya'acov Buckner and Tsvi Lewicki - an accountant. There was also a branch of "The Zionist Movement" in Miechów. Its staff included Haim Isskowitz (Chairman); Elimelech Friedrich; Moshe Pinchowsky, May G–d Avenge his Blood; Hanna Zyngerman (neé Feigenboim) and Yehezkiel Dror (Friedrich), living in Israel.
- "The General Zionists" in Charsznica. The founders of the branch were The highly respected S.D. Yeruzalimsky (Chairman); the brothers Avraham and Nahum Gretler; Yosef Ehrenreich; Mordecai Kossowsky; Mrs. Rachel Kossowsky; Shmuel Ya'acov Gleitt; Mrs. Shifra Gretler (the granddaughter of the first Rabbi of Miechów and the sister of the Deputy Rabbi and scholar Rabbi Shlomo Ze'ev Bryn), living in Israel. This last was very active and founded a library for youth in Charsznica. "The Young Zionists" in Charsznica: The first activists were the highly respected Yesheyahu Bar Mordecai Greitzer and Zerach Bar Shimon Gretler (the writer Yisroel Zarchi (Z"L)), who went for training together to Grochowy and emigrated to Palestine as pioneers; After them came the brothers Eliezer, Aharon and Fischl Zukerman and they founded together a training school in the home of Rabbi Yesheyahu Greitzer (Z"L) in preparation for emigrating to Palestine and joining a Kibbutz. They also were concerned that the members of the group would receive work in the large metal–work factory of Mr. Dov Barish Goldkorn, May G–d Avenge his Blood, in the flour mill "Polonia" and in the storehouses

of Rabbi Mordecai Greitzer (Z"L). Many of the graduates of the training "camp" immigrated to Palestine and put down roots there.

[Page 26]

- "The Revisionist Zionists" At the head of the local branch were the respected David Burstein; Netta Kornfeld and Haim Eisenberg, May G–d Avenge his Blood. The main activities of the organization commenced in 1933. All the above organizations were extremely active especially during election times for the Community and the town, and the Zionist and Mizrachi organizations – also during elections for the Zionist Congresses. It is worth mentioning that all these activities took place in an orderly fashion with courtesy and relative quiet, without untoward behavior. Every one of the organizations was given the opportunity to express opinions from the Community platform without interruption.

B. Professional Organizations

- The Organization of Artisans whose founders were Shmuel Leib Adlist; Yermiyahu Blum; Aharon Berger and Reuven Shmuel Kleiner who also founded the "Cooperative Bank" for loans at low interest to artisans and small traders. The Bank was a branch of the center in Warsaw under the auspices of "The Joint". This organization out–reached to assist much help to Jewish artisans, at a time when the Government demanded a Certificate of Matriculation from a technical school from Jews who had never attended there.
- The Merchants Organization whose founders were Avraham Mordecai Stern; the brothers Ze'ev and Haim Feureisen; Asher Enzil Koppelowitz; Yitzhak Saltsburg; the brothers Yisroelczy(?), and Moshe Yosef Spiegel; Mordecai Rubin. The organization was also founded by the Bank as an example of the Bank as a supporter of the above enterprises.

Both the above organizations had representatives in the Community, in the town and in the local area Income Tax offices and protected the interests of its member–clients.

Jewish Representation in the Miechów Municipality

As a Jewish Community, Miechów was united with Charsznica and the local villages, although the Municipality was independent of them and separate. The Jewish population of Miechów was approximately 40% of the total population. Understandably the authorities didn't see that situation favorably and attempted from time–to–time to annex neighboring villages where there were no Jews in order to lessen the Jewish representation of the Jewish community on the Municipality. Nevertheless, the representation of the Jewish community on the Town Council was 30%. In the Council elections all the Unions and Organizations that I have mentioned above were represented on the Council.

At the head of the Jewish representation stood Mr. Avraham Sercaz and all the members acted in full harmony and took part in all the committees. The delegates influenced the choice of Mayor and the Council and on the election of Chairmen of the various committees and their members.

Jewish members of the Town Council were: The highly respected Avraham Sercaz; Avraham Friedrich; Aharon Berger; David Isskowitz; Haim Feureisen; Yermiyahu Blum; Lemel Katzengold; Mordecai Muhlstein; Moshe Koppelowitz; Nathan Borenstein; Tsvi Herzl Lubchi(?); Reuven Shmuel Kleiner and Shmuel Leib Adlist.

This writer was a member of the Education and Culture of the Municipality and also acted as Chairman of the Election Committee for the Town Council elections.

[Page 27]

The Pogrom in Miechów Charsznica

After the Passover festival of the 2nd and 3rd May 1919, a pogrom broke out against the Jews Miechów, on the eve of the intermediate Saturday of the festival and on the Saturday itself in Charsznica. During that pogrom my great uncle, the brother of my mother's father (Z"L), Rabbi Naphtali Herzl Salzburg, May G–d Avenge his Blood and dozens were injured some with serious wounds from which they never fully recovered.

Members of the Community and Jewish members of the Town Council, headed by Avraham Sercaz and Shimon Dov Yeruzalimsky from Charsznica, made strenuous attempts at the local and area level to get the authorities to stop the violence since there was a great danger present for all the Jews of the community. At the end of the Sabbath, Mr. Yeruzalimsky travelled to Warsaw and made contact the Jewish faction of the Sejm. They immediately tabled an interpolation on the situation. An "Investigation Committee" was dispatched to Miechów and Charsznica in which the lawyer, A.M. Hartglass of the Sejm faction took part. The Poles, of course, claimed the Jews were at fault. No words can describe the efforts made by Mr. Sercaz and Mr. Yeruzalimsky to prove the lie of the Polish claim. They accompanied the "Investigation Committee" the whole time the committee was in Miechów and Charsznica and visited all the injured people. In Charsznica Mordecai and Simcha Greitzer, Mordecai Tsvi Zukerman and his sons Joel and Isser, Motel Steinberger and Alter Feigenblott were all badly injured. Mr. Feigenblott broke down when visited and being questioned by the Committee, saying: "I have lived in this place many years, I beg you to invite all the Poles in the area and ask them if I have ever done anything wrong to any one of them during all my life; I'm already an old man, why did they beat me so cruelly and why did they spill the blood of my fellow Jews and myself? We are not guilty of anything!" The Hartglass faction said: "Please, members of this Committee, which one of you will answer the question posed by this injured old man?" Their faces reddened but they said nothing...

Afterwards, Mr. Yeruzalimsky led the Committee to the home of Mr. Dov Barish Goldkorn and showed how his home had been destroyed – his furniture and household goods, etc., etc. Finally Mr. Yeruzalimsky turned his face to the Police commander in Charsznica and pointing to him, said to the Committee: "If you want to know who is guilty for all this, here is the man! He came to every house after the rioters had finished their work...including the home of my son–in–law, Mordecai Greitzer, who had Government fuel stored in his warehouses: according to the contract with the Government, the Police were obliged to secure Government property when it may be endangered and provide active police protection. Although my son–in–law sent a message to him that there was a developing danger and indicated the legal reference on the contract itself, he took no action whatsoever. Even after the rioting began and my son–in–law and his neighbors were already injured, he promised to come immediately, and he did come but only after the rioters had completed their work." The Police commandant said not a word...The only result of the Investigation Committees visit was that the Police Commander was transferred to another post; a few rioters were arrested for questioning, but not one person ever stood trial.

After the Committee finished its work, Miechów town council convened a meeting at which Mr. Sercaz tabled a motion condemning the rioters and vindicating the Jews from all guilt in the matter; the motion was passed unanimously. At the time it was a great victory against the anti–Semites. It was achieved thanks to the hard, unrelenting work and dedication of Mr. Sercaz, May G–d Avenge his Blood, and Mr.Yeruzalimsky (Z"L).

[Page 28]

אגרת הברכה להמכללה העברית בירושלים

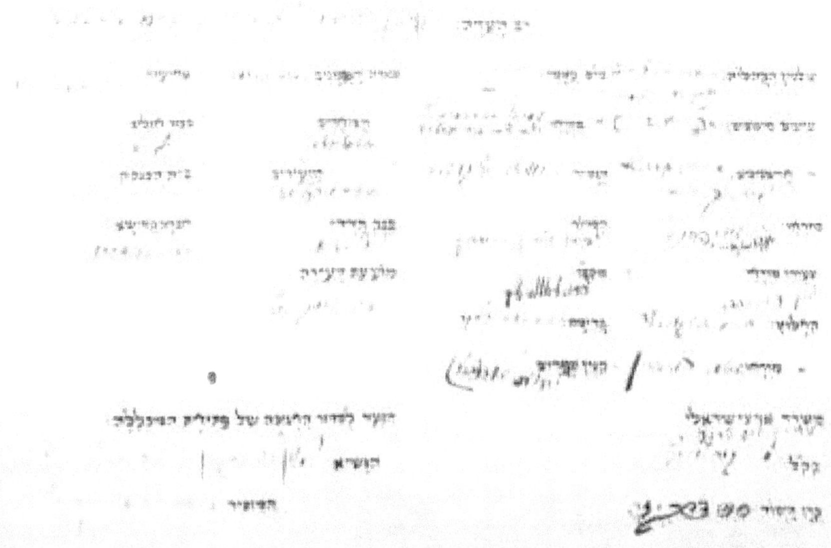

A Congratulatory Epistle sent to the Hebrew University of Jerusalem

On this most excellent historic day, in the life of the Jewish People of today – in an era of its rebirth in its National Home, a day of the consecration of this Temple of Wisdom, The Hebrew University on Mount Scopus.

On this joyous, splendid and heartwarming day of peaceful victory, for the Jewish People, for its Hebrew Language and for the Land of Israel, we, our little community of Miechów, one of the many dispersed throughout the five continents, find ourselves hard–pressed to express our great happiness in fitting words and to convey our congratulations and our deep feelings of this event and with soaring spirit, intense gaiety, commit our thoughts to this parchment.

To this Great House and those great ones of our people chosen to head the staff and pave our way forward, who have worked, are working and will continue to work for the benefit their People and its future and who are establishing this University. We pray that it may it be the will of our Father in heaven to enable this establishment to project its wisdom on its environment with sense of security and confidence among its students such that they will not need to seek abroad in the Diaspora and its foundations for knowledge and wisdom and spiritual nourishment;

that it should be open for all to study and learn without regard to religion, race, sex or creed; that it should radiate to the world the visions of Moses our Teacher and Law–giver (Deuteronomy 4, vi):

"Keep, therefore and do them; for this is your wisdom and understanding in the sight of the Nations, which shall hear all these statutes, and say, Surely this great nation is a wise and understanding people."

And the vision of Isaiah 2, iii: "And many people shall go and say Come ye, and let us go up to the mountain of the Lord, to the house of the God of Jacob; and he will teach us of his ways, and we will walk in his paths:

For out of Zion shall go forth the law, and the Word of the Lord from Jerusalem". May it be the will of our Father in heaven, that this House on Mount Scopus will shine forth as a Pillar of Fire that will illuminate the Universe with the light of Truth, Righteousness and Justice to open the eyes of the blind that they may find the way that leads to the happiness of Mankind and peace shall prevail throughout the world for a good and seemly life.

May it be the will of our Father in heaven that the founders of this House and their helpers will gather strength and courage to perform their sacred tasks for the sake of their people and that the memory of their toil shall not fade from the knowledge of Israel.
Amen!

The fourth day of the week, in the seventh month of the redemption, in the year one thousand eight hundred and fifty after the destruction of Jerusalem the Holy City 5685 (1925).

(Signatories):

Town Rabbi: (illegible); Aguda: (illegible): City School (illegible):
Community Council:
Miechow Zionists: Mizrachi: (Illegible); Eliezer (illegible): (Illegible)::
The Synagogue: (Illegible): (Illegible): Achiezer: (Illegible); Burial Society: (Illegible);
Bank Hadadi: (Illegible); Hadror Movement: (Illegible); Hazamir Movement: (Illegible);
Young Mizrachi; Maccabi: (illegible); Hechalutz Movement: (illegible);
Kadima (illegible); (illegible); Land of Israel Office: (illegible);
Keren Hayesod: (Illegible);

[Page 29]

Palestine – a Pillar of Fire to the Community of Miechów–Charsznica

Every occurrence that was connected with Palestine created a resounding echo in the community. Every happy event or festival, every negative edict from the Mandatory authority, found expression and a reaction in special sessions of the Community management, in cooperation with the delegates in the town Council, the Union managements and other organizations and also from the pulpit of the synagogue. Attempts were also made to take an active part in the life of Palestine by sending telegrams and petitions as seems appropriate and as directed by the highest national institutions.

The results of our drives and collections for Palestine by Miechów and Charsznica were an example to other towns.

In celebration of the dedication of the Hebrew University on Mt. Scopus, the Community sent the Chairman Mr. Avraham Sercaz as our delegate to the ceremony; he carried in his hand a laudatory epistle written on parchment, composed by the author S.N. Kahanofsky (Z"L), and was signed by all the notable personalities of the town (see the article in this book by Mr. Yeruzalimsky).

About the same time, a delegation under the auspices of "'Kibbutz' Miechów" headed by Mr. Mordecai Greitzer and Haim Feureisen, visited Palestine in order to purchase land for an agricultural settlement and the establishment of commercial enterprises. The delegation purchased a large tract of land in the vicinity of Afula for an agricultural settlement, from the "American Zion Commonwealth" (For the names of those who acquired plots of land seethe article by Shimson–Dov Yerushalmi).

These are the names of those who settled in Palestine during that period:

Rabbi Yesheyahu Greitzer (Z"L), Yosef Berger and Mordecai David Schechtman (May he rest in peace), and may the following be spared for a long and good life: my uncle, my mother's brother) Rabbi Ya'acov Saltsburg. Two of the purchasers, Rabbi Michael Wexler of Charsznica and from my family (my brother's brother–in–law) Rabbi Moshe Spiegel immigrated to Palestine intending to settle there but the project didn't materialize. They returned to Poland where they perished in the Holocaust, May G–d Avenge their Blood. Both of them had sons and daughters who live in Israel.

The community and its institutions generously supported those who immigrated to Palestine and were in need of financial assistance. The community budgeted each year for the national funds. A training 'Kibbutz' was based in the Community Buildings for those who were preparing for emigration. They received financial help, and places of employment, etc., the Community management and its institutions, Ha–Mizrachi and the rest of the Zionist organizations. Many of them immigrated to Palestine and settled there.

[Page 30]

Respected Personalities

These are the senior and elected residents – people who excelled in their qualities and way of life, scholars, righteousness, practical men and those of outstanding attributes:

Avraham Sercaz, May G–d Avenge his Blood, talented businessman and a fearless fighter for the rights of the Jews.

Avraham Goldberg, May G–d Avenge his Blood, of the Righteous of Khentshin; he was always ready to help anyone either physically or financially with the utmost he had.

Avraham Goldsobel May G–d Avenge his Blood, a scholar of note, highly educated, possessor of nobility of spirit, eloquent.

Avraham Spiegel, May G–d Avenge his Blood, a precious soul permeated throughout with boundless love for Palestine and his fellow–man.

Avraham Yama(?), (Z"L), All his life he donated to charities anonymously.

Avraham Waldliwerand, May G–d Avenge his Blood, Scholar of renown, from the Righteous of Gur. He was afire with Torah and ceaselessly working for the annuities for the righteous.

Avraham Ya'acov Nyberg, May G–d Avenge his Blood, a highly intelligent scholar of renown from the Righteous of Khentshin.

Avraham Mordecai Horowitz, (Z"L), he was the great–grandchild of Rabbi Avraham Horowitz (Z"L), known as the Sabah Kadisha of Pinchev, a man whose heart was dedicated to charity, benevolence and modest ways. He raised his sons and daughters in the ways of the Torah and good deeds. His offspring live in Israel and follow his ways.

Avraham Mordecai Stern, May G–d Avenge his Blood, a scholar of the Righteous of Kshoynzh, who gave his heart and soul for the good of institutions of charity and kindness.

Avraham Shimon Londner, (Z"L), A scholar and researcher of "S'fat Emess" and the son of Our Master, Teacher and Rabbi from Gur, May his Righteousness be Remembered for a Blessing; he was a benefactor to all men. He was generous to all who needed help and his home open to all. His forebears were all great Torah scholars. He raised orphans in his home and brought them up to the Torah and good deeds; he bequeathed them all his assets.

Aharon Grossfeld (Z"L). A scholar. He knew the entire Mishnah Berurah by heart.

Aharon Berger May G–d Avenge his Blood, a courteous man and a model of dedication to his fellow man. He was the Chairman of the "Bikur Cholim" committee from 1933.

Aharon Zukerman (Z"L). An honest, straightforward man, G–d–fearing. He was the founder of the Charsznica synagogue.

Elimelech Vislitzky, May G–d Avenge his Blood, a great scholar of modest demeanor; the Master Teacher and Rabbi from Ostrovtse, May his Righteousness be Remembered for a Blessing and his disciple also.

Asher Enzil Koppelowitz Rabbi Moshe Tversky, a scholar and possessor of many fine attributes from among the Righteous of Kuzmir and Rabbi Moshe Tversky of Lublin.

Benjamin Beinush Follman, May G–d Avenge his Blood, a great benefactor to his fellow–man and an accomplished speaker.

Benjamin Beinush Horowitz May G–d Avenge his Blood, a scholar and possessor of many noble attributes; he comes from among the Righteous of Kuzmir.

Bezalel Weizmann May G–d Avenge his Blood, from among the Righteous of Kuzmir and afterwards the host of Our Master, Teacher and Rabbi Moshe Tversky

Dov Brish Goldkorn, May his Righteousness be Remembered for a Blessing; his house was a house of charity and benevolence to all, from among the Righteous of Kuzmir and afterwards of Our Master, Teacher and Rabbi Mazurek, May his Righteousness be Remembered for a Blessing.

David and his brothers, Nathan and Moshe Borenstein May G–d Avenge their Blood. Scholars from the Righteous of Gur, coming from generations of good deeds and noble spirits.

David Isser Eisenberg, May G–d Avenge his Blood. A member of a charity and an anonymous donor to the above Rabbi Avraham Yama, he came from the Righteous of Krimilov.

Haashil Horowitz, May G–d Avenge his Blood Bar Orian, G–d–fearing from among the Righteous of Kuzmir and later of Lublin.

Zelig Waldliwerand (Z"L), a survivor of the Righteous of Kotzk and later of Gur, a very old man but clear headed and open–minded to alternative ideas.

Haim Salzburg (Z"L), (my grandfather). A renowned scholar, from the Righteous of Gostinin and later of Gur, Studying Torah and performing good deeds, he lived in poverty. He was a recognized specialist at circumcision which he performed freely. He held group classes in Torah in the house of the Gur Hassidim, among whom was Rabbi Yitzhak Gitler (Z"L), (His Name Will Live On). He also gave lessons after Sabbath prayers until late. I had the privilege of being examined by him on Rashi/ His image is always before me and brightens my ways. He was totally immersed in the Torah and righteousness, even during his last difficult illness. He had excellent ancestry.

Haim bar Elyakim Natsil Lewit (Z"L). he devoted most of his time to the "Brotherly Help" and "Bikur Cholim" institutions, he was from the Righteous of Our Master, Teacher and Rabbi, Rabbi David Goldman of Kalisz. He had sons and in–laws who were men of Torah and learning.

Haim Bar Saul Lewit May G–d Avenge his Blood. His home was a hostel for noted Rabbis, and he was privileged to marry his daughters with noted men of the times.

Hanoch Ha'anich Kaiser (Z"L). A scholar and a deep thinker of the Torah and righteousness from the Righteous of Gur.

Yehoshua Koppelowitz May G–d Avenge His Blood, possessor of fine attributes he received everyone pleasantly and with a smiling face.

[Page 31]

Yudel Gerszonowicz (Z"L). a man of great charity performed with heart and soul.

Yosef Yaskiel (Z"L). A master of the Mishnah from the Righteous of Gur, faithful to his Rabbi's house, satisfied with a little in all things and a soul–mate to all mankind.

Yosef Baruch Bruckner (Z"L). A scholar and a man of noble virtues and attributes , from the Righteous of Gur; he was head of the Burial Society for an extended period.

Yehiel Shmuel Abramowitz, May G–d Avenge His Blood, a scholar, and an expert in investigative literature and Jewish philosophy of Judaism.

Ya'acov Zimberg (Z"L). A scholar and a man of kindness and charity, of noble spirit, and the son of one of the well–known families of Warsaw.

Ya'acov Czernikowski, May G–d Avenge His Blood. A scholar of noble spirit from the Righteous of Gur he poured his soul into his work and prayers.

Ya'acov Yitzhak Blatt, (Z"L). A scholar and known as a keen intelligent arbitrator in commercial matters, the great grandchild of "The Prophet of Lublin" and he was named for him according to the Family Tree published in this book. He belonged to the Righteous of Khentshin.

Ya'acov Yitzhak Horowitz, May G–d Avenge His Blood. A G–d–fearing scholar, full of good deeds, he was the great grandchild of the Saba Kadisha

Rabbi Avraham Mordecai of Pinchev, May His Righteousness be Remembered for a Blessing.

Ya'acov Tsvi Gitler, May G–d Avenge His Blood. A scholar and from a Jewish home full of grandeur, he belonged to the Righteous of Gur, a businessman he soul longed for Israel and he immigrated with his family to Palestine – his heart's desire.

Yitzhak Hutner May G–d Avenge His Blood. A scholar. His entire person was the embodiment of respect and splendor, a member of the family of Rabbi Yehuda Sennal Huster (Z"L), considered a genius, a member of the Council of Rabbis of Warsaw.

Yitzhak Posluszny, May G–d Avenge His Blood. He was a G–d–fearing scholar who was a member of the Righteous of Gur.

Yitzhak Sheinfrucht, May G–d Avenge His Blood. An energetic businessman and a lecturer to the religious youth, he was grandson of the first Rabbi of Miechów

Yermiyahu Blum, May G–d Avenge His Blood. He was businessman, good–hearted to a fault, helping and financing all who were in need.

Yisroel David Spiegel,(Z"L), a scholar from Khentshin. His children and in–laws were all brought up in the Torah and righteousness.

Lemel Katzengold (Z"L). An advisor and help to all and of modest habits.

Meir Gitler, May G–d Avenge His Blood. A scholar of the Righteous of Gur, known for his generosity and grace. His wife, Yochaved, was the grand–daughter of "The Holy Jew", Remember the Righteous and Holy for a Blessing.

Meir Wallerstein, (Z"L). A scholar and a Righteous of Amshinov, related to the family of the author of "Tossofot Le–Yom Tov" and one of the sons of Rabbi Moshe May G–d Avenge His Blood, a scholar from the Righteous of Gur, known for his charity and kindness, who was from the family of the Great and Holy Rabbi Mendel of Pabianitz May His Righteousness be Remembered for a Blessing, May G–d Avenge His Blood.

Meir Fogel (Z"L). A scholar of many noble attributes, a Righteous of Khentshin and the regular host on his visits to Miechów of Our Master, Teacher and Rabbi, first Rabbi of Khentshin, May his Righteousness Remembered for a Blessing. He was able to settle many disputes.

Mendel Rogovski, May G–d Avenge His Blood. An extraordinarily charitable and welcoming host. (Charsznica).

Mordecai Greitzer (Z"L). A man of righteousness and kindness, well–known as an honest and truthful man. He had connections, through marriage with the world famous genius Rabbi Moshe Nahum Yeruzalimsky, (Z"L), from Kalish. He took part in arbitrations together with the Holy Genius from Ostrovtse. May his Righteousness Remembered for a Blessing and on occasion even got the upper hand in debate.

Mordecai Tsvi and his brother, David Zukerman, May G–d Avenge Their Blood, their main worry was to give help to the poor of Charsznica who were unable to fulfill the Passover rituals of Matzoth, etc, in particular which they did with dedication and faithfulness. Rabbi Zukerman succeeded in immigrating to Palestine his family, settled in Tel–Aviv and died 12th April, 1942 and was buried with honor in the cemetery in Nahlat Yitzhak.

Moshe Yosef Weill (Z"L). He was one of the first settlers in town and one of its important citizens. His sons and in–laws were men well–versed in the Torah and good deeds.

[Page 32]

Rachel Bornstein, the wife of Michael Bornstein.

Michael Borenstein May His Righteousness be Remembered for a Blessing. From among the first settlers and important residents of the town, from among the Righteous of Gur. He had eight children – all well versed in the Torah and good deeds.

Moshe Yosef Horowitz (Z"L). A straightforward honest man, he brought up his sons and daughters to the Torah and good deeds, he immigrated to Palestine with his family and died early morning, 3rd October 1965 and buried in the local cemetery of Holon.

Sandor Yosef Weintraub (Z"L) of Kshoynzh, a great scholar, from the righteous of Rodzin, who all the days of his life were dedicated to the Torah and to Hassidism.

Fischl Koppelowitz (Z"L). A great scholar and a Righteous of Chmelnik a resident of the town; his sons were Torah scholars and Hassidim.

Reuven Ziegler (Z"L). Possessor of many fine attributes. With the development of the Jewish settlement in Charsznica, he founded a second prayer–room in his home.

Reuven Dov Spiegel (Z"L). A scholar from the Righteous of Khentshin. His children and in–laws were Torah scholars. His son, Ya'acov Spiegel (my brother–in–law), and other offspring, live in Israel.

Reuven Shlomo Londner (Z"L). A scholar from the Righteous of Gur and among the important people in town (the grandfather of Rabbi Ya'acov Tsvi Gitler, May G–d Avenge his Blood).

Pinchas (Pincher) Eliyahu Gottlieb Bar Tsvi, born in Zarnovitza in 1897, the son–in–law of Rabbi Eliezer Gerstenfeld from Kurzeluv which belonged to the community of Kshoynzh. He was a Torah scholar and possessor of fine attributes. A member of the Community Council and Chairman of the "Gemilut Chesed Fund", which was very active in supporting the needy. He disseminated Torah among many. Three of his children live in Israel; Haim Meir (in Be'er Sheva), Avraham (in Kibbutz Netzer Sereni), and Shmuel (in Rehovot). They changed the family name to "Ahoviya".

[Page 33]

Shlomo Yama May G–d Avenge his Blood. A G–d–fearing scholar and the possessor of many fine attributes.

Shlomo Meir Sheinfrucht May G–d Avenge his Blood. A Torah scholar a welcome wise counselor and dedicated helper, modest in manner.

Shmuel Friedenberg, May G–d Avenge his Blood. His home was a house of righteousness and benevolence; he made anonymous donations an adherent of the Torah and those who studied it.

Shmuel Schmelke Katzengold (Z"L). An exemplary donor, among the notable people in town and married his daughters to esteemed scholars of the Torah and the elite of town.

Shimon Dov Yeruzalimsky (Z"L). The son of the noted genius of Kalish (see above), and the son–in–law of Rabbi Mordecai Greitzer (see above). A public figure and a vigorous fighter on behalf of the general public. He left Miechów and moved to Warsaw where he officiated as propaganda manager and publishing director of the central office of the "Foundation Fund" (the "Keren Kayemet") in 1925. He resigned from that distinguished position in 1935 and immigrated to Palestine in order to rear and educate his children in the Land of Israel.

Schrage Feivel Chencinsky (Z"L). A scholar from the Righteous of Gur; a businessman who concerned himself with needs of the public.

Schrage Feivel Lorek(?),(Z"L). An ordinary person but straightforward and honest. He himself fulfilled the verse "I will arise at midnight to offer Thee thanks". He was known as "The Psalmist Jew".

Righteous Women

Esther'leh: The wife of Rabbi Jonah Gretler (Z"L) (Charsznica); excelled in good deeds which were performed with intelligence and wisdom.

Bluma: The wife of Rabbi Michael Wexler (Z"L) (Charsznica); she was a mother to poor children, clothing them and providing shoes, thanks to the above average intelligence and understanding with which G–d had blessed her.

Chaya: The wife of Rabbi David Isser Eisenberg (Z"L), (Miechów) a charitable woman who donated anonymously and beyond her means. Her charity, modesty and intelligence were known far and wide.

Hanna: The wife of Rabbi Avraham Goldberg (Z"L). May G–d Avenge his Blood, a charitable woman concerned with compensation and pensions for retired teachers and Rabbis, etc. A great and modest woman.

Feiga–Lieber: The wife of Rabbi Mordecai (Z"L). Performed charity and kindness anonymously and was a treasure to worthy families in Israel. Her father, Rabbi Shmuel Silberberg, (Z"L), was the brother–in–law of the Master, Teacher and Rabbi, Rabbi Avraham Eger, from Lublin, May his Righteousness be Remembered for a Blessing, and her mother Mrs. Gittel (May she rest in peace), was the daughter of Rabbi Yesheyahu Lipchitz, May his Righteousness be Remembered for a Blessing, from Ogrodzona(?) and later from Warsaw. From the family of Rabbi Moshe Chalfin–Lipschitz, in–laws of the noted Rabbi Yitzhak Meir, May his Righteousness be Remembered for a Blessing, the author of "Khidushei Rabbi Yitzhak Meir" ("The Updates of Rabbi Yitzhak Meir") and later of "The Flying Seraph ", our Rabbi Menahem Mendel May his Righteousness be Remembered for a Blessing, of Kolchak.

Fassili: The wife of Rabbi Shlomo Feigenboim, May G–d Avenge his Blood. The Chairlady of the "Women's Society for Anonymous Help" (see above "Charitable Institutes and Societies "). She raised orphans in her home and supplied all their needs.

Kaila: The wife of Rabbi Menahem Maanieh Malinowski, May G–d Avenge his Blood, a shining example of righteousness and kindness, she was completely dedicated to helping others. She and her husband raised their children to good deeds and the Torah married their daughters to Torah scholars.

Raize'leh: The wife of Rabbi Avraham Shimon Londner (Z"L), A totally righteous woman in all senses, in cooperation with her husband.

Rayel'eh: The wife of Rabbi Moshe Sukenik, May G–d Avenge his Blood, a noble soul involving herself in matters of charity and especially the needs of preparation of brides for their weddings.

[Page 34]

On Closing the Gateway

I know full–well that with the best of good intentions I have not extracted in this my tale all the glory of the notables of our communities, and it is certainly deficient in general and particularly so regarding the honor and respect due to Charsznica and Kshoynzh.

Many of my colleagues know that 15 years ago I suggested and even pleaded in meetings of our organization, to apply ourselves and fulfill the hallowed obligation – to publish a "Memorial Book" of our town so that the remainder of us and our future generations will know the source of the tombstones, the pure treasure and honesty that is hidden in the archives of the souls of our fathers and our fathers' fathers; the nobility and purity of soul expressed in their faces and in their deeds. Unfortunately my suggestion has come to fruition only today. In the meantime serious illnesses have been my lot and several of the oldsters from our town, from whom undoubtedly we could have drawn much information, have gone the way of all flesh, and all I have written is only from memory. More than 36 years have passed since then and their memories and archives have gone with them and are no more.

I find it fitting to express my deepest thanks to the chairman of our organization in of recent years, Mr. Shmuel Berger, and to the rest of the members of the committee working without thought of reward, for their untiring efforts in saving what could be saved and bring it all to publication. They are the ones who encouraged me also to contribute my part in remembering our Holy Communities. Similarly, I must thank the Honorary President of our organization Mr. S.D. Yeruzalimsky (Z"L), who read this work and offered several observations which have been accepted. I close with the following Commandment among those that are obligatory to perform:

> *O, Earth, cover not their blood, and be not the place of their lamentation until the Lord looks down from the heavens and sees, and avenges them with His terrible vengeance; the vengeance for his People and for his Torah and for the blood that his servants shed like water, as Thou hast promised us: "Rejoice O, ye nations, with his people: for He will avenge the blood of his servants, and will render vengeance to his adversaries, and will be merciful unto his land and to his people."*

[Page 35]

History of the Jews of Miechów

by Nachman Blumenthal

Translated by Selwyn Rose

Statistical data

The Jewish settlement of Jews in Miechów is one of the youngest in Poland. Until 1862 – the year of the Great Reform in Congress Poland, concerning that part of Poland then belonging to Russia (since the Viennese Congress of 1815) and which included Miechów – Jews were forbidden to live there. The land was acquired by a Catholic monastery, as was emphasized in the Jewish Encyclopaedia[1]. Although no single document remains to bear witness to that prohibition on Jews entering the city (Judeais de non tolerandis), Jews were not permitted to live in Miechów or to be found there after sunset. However they regularly came into town when there was a fair or on market days from the surrounding villages in order to conduct business with the non–Jewish residents. Beginning in 1860 they were permitted to maintain their store–rooms and shops in town.

Only in 1862–1863 were the Jews allowed to put down roots there and they readily used that permission, as the census from those years show. A similar situation occurred in the 16 surrounding towns in Miechów's area[2].

A census carried out in Russia in the year 1857 demonstrates that there wasn't a single Jew in town[3]. The total population of the county was – according to that census of 1857, 109,877 souls made up of 105,582 Slavs (the Tsarist Government was not interested in emphasizing the large number of Poles in town that had become Russian so they were included together under the category of “Slavs”), and 4,295 in “The Ancient Religion” (“Israelites”). The next census from 1897 determined that the total population of Miechów reached 4,175 souls of whom 1,436 were Jews (34.4%). In the entire county there were then 115,000 people, among them 5,808 Jews, (5.5%)[4]. That represents a substantial rise in the number of Jews in the county.

The number of Jews continued to grow and in the first census conducted by the now- independent Poland, in December 1921, the number had grown to 2,383 in a total population of 5,699 (41.8%)[5]. In 1921 8,318 Jews in the entire county represented 5.6% of the total population[6]. Hand–in–hand with the growth of the Jewish population the population of the non–Jewish population was also growing as can be seen from the following table:

Population of Miechów as Shown in Official Tsarist Russian and Independent Polish Censuses

Year	Total Population	Number of Jews	% of Jews
1827	1,230	–	–
1857	1,427	–	–
1897	4,175	1,436	34.4
1921	2,383	5,699[7]	41.8

[Page 36]

During the thirty years when Jews were not present in town, the number of citizens grew by only 197 souls; while after Jews were allowed to settle in town the general population grew by 868 souls during 40 years and in the following 24 years after that by 1,021 souls. These figures prove that the growth in population during that period was not due to natural growth alone but an influx from without, seeking and finding improved sources for sustenance in that town. The settlement of the Jews in Miechów acted as an incentive, therefore, for the non–Jewish population and added to the development of the town.

A significant influence on the growth of the number of Jews in 1920–1921 was the pogroms carried out in the surrounding villages: the Jews sought shelter for themselves in the county seat – Miechów.

When we come to compare increase of the number of Jews in town with the number of non–Jews in the period from 1897–1921, we find that the Jewish community grew by 40% while the non–Jewish settlement grew by only 31%. But in the following years, until the outbreak of war, the numerical relationship changed negatively for the Jews. That is also true for the rest of the Jewish demographic factors.

We find for example, from Wasiutyński[8], interesting figures concerning children up to the age of 10, Jews and non–Jews, in the whole of the county of Miechów. In the year 1897 there were 1,859 Jewish children up to the age of 10 that comprised 32% of all the Jews; in 1921 the number was 2,224. From an absolute point of view the number indeed increased but compared to the growth of population their contribution lessened from 32% to 26.7% – a known trend among Jews when they become urbanized in large towns.

Regarding the census from 1921 onwards it is important to point out that the questionnaire provided by the authorities did not ask for the "Nationhood" or "People" of the resident but there were two other questions asking for "Religion" and "Mother–tongue" from which one can clearly draw precise conclusions regarding one's national affiliation. According to that census it was found that there were in town 2,383 persons of the Mosaic Faith (mojżeszowe wyznanie) but only 1,968 of them indicated Yiddish or Hebrew as their mother–tongue. These last were considered as belonging to the Jewish Nation. Regarding the others (415), it may be assumed that a small number of them were assimilated and the remainder were not familiar with the questions asked by the census officer who spoke only Polish. The official, the Commissar of Elections, was interested in proving the increase in the Polish–speaking citizens. He received official instructions directing him along those lines and sometimes exploited that authority.

By the way, the Jews also attempted, where possible, not to be included in the census for different reasons – (lack of identification papers, mistrust of the authorities, superstition, evasion of a "poll–tax", etc.[9]

No details were ever published of the last census undertaken in Poland in December 1931. It is only known that the town numbered 6,360 souls and there were 585 houses. Regarding the County the following numbers were recorded:

[Page 37]

The total number of residents in that year were approximately 154,000 of whom:

Roman Catholics	146,863
Mosaic Faith	7,271
Greek Catholics	32
Orthodox (Paraslavs)	67
Evangelicals	36
Others (Free thinkers)	305
Total	154,574

Distribution by language:

Polish speakers	147,738
Yiddish (and perhaps Hebrew)	6,762
Ukrainian	36
Russian	1
German	9
Lithuanian	2
Czechoslovakian	2
Other languages	24
Total	154,574[10]

Jews, who did not declare Yiddish as their mother–tongue represented about 7% of the number of Jews. It is doubtful if all of them were assimilated. (See comment above in re the census of 1921).

We have no official statistics for the later years. According to details supplied by "The Joint" in 1939 there were only 1,800 Jews in Miechów[11]. That number is less than the reality. It is true that an economic crisis overtook the Jews of Miechów, as it did on all the Jews of Poland during the years leading up to the Second World War. Following that emigration grew; but until then there was no emigration. In an article sent to Yad Va–shem in Jerusalem the ex–Mayor of Miechów, Julian Piwowarski, apparently taken from documentation in the hands of the authorities, gives the following numbers:

In 1895 : 665 Jews

In 1909 : 1,340 Jews

In 1939 : 2,448 Jews

These numbers seem reasonable.

He describes the Jews of Miechów as being steeped in the life–style of Western Europe rather more than those of the surrounding towns and villages, especially in the latter years. He says:

[Page 38]

"In 1939, only a small percentage of the town's Jews were distinguishable from the general population by their dress or language or their culture. The relationship between the Jews and the townspeople was normal, good and peaceful. Jewish traders bought and sold agricultural produce. They bought the produce from local land owners with estates and from farmers and exported them to various countries."

It is possible that before the war, Miechów was the only town in Poland where there were still Jews living from the previous generation, who remembered the generation of the first Jews who settled there. In this book are gathered the names of the founders' synagogue quorum: apparently they spoke about them and occasionally related incidents about them, their names passing from generation to generation until they reached us. The settlement of Miechów itself is very old. It was already known of in the 13th century when a group of monks of the "Order of the Holy Sepulcher" came from the Holy Land and founded there a monastery, named "The Holy Sepulcher" in which they built a model of the tomb of Jesus that they had seen in Jerusalem. Already in that century it achieved the status of "town" and was granted the right of self–government.

According to the modern Polish Encyclopaedia[12] by the middle of the 19th Century the whole town was already paved. It was an emblem of progress and European style of the day. In that period Miechów belonged to the region of Radom and included nine towns: Kshoynzh, Działoszyce, Slomniki and others.

[Page 39]

New Poland

It fell to the town of Miechów to play an important role in the history of the new, independent Poland. On 6th August 1914 the First Brigade of Pilsudski's Polish Legions left Krakow and marched to Miechów by way of Radslavice(?). It was the first appearance of the Polish Legions that came from Krakow (Galicia, Austria) and crossed the old Russo–Austrian border in the direction of Miechów (Russia), without military actions, since the territory had been previously conquered by the Austrian army.

The commander of the Legion, Josef Pilsudski, later to be the first President of independent Poland, together with the Chief of Staff Kazimierz Sosnkowski, was delayed in Miechów and remained there in the massive building of the alcohol manufacturing factory, destroyed by the Russian army before they left the town.

The following day, the well–known leader of the Polish Socialist party, Legionnaire officer, Ignaz Daszyński[13], later Chairman of the Polish Sejm arrived at Miechów. Daszyński took the apartment that had belonged to the doctor Jan Biali, who fled together with the Russians; he was appointed by Pilsudski as Military Vice–Commissar of the town and the county. As Mayor, Pilsudski appointed Gluchowski(?) and as Governor of the county, H. Zawarski(?), They organized a Militia and a hospital for infectious diseases; "Christians and Jews freely contributed 1,000 Austrian Kroner and gave it to the Polish army." (Daszyński). The last Polish military Commissar in Miechów was Dr. Richard Konitzki(?)

On 12th August 1914 a new Polish military commissar arrived in Miechów, sent by the Austrian army; he took over the responsibilities of the Polish Commissar who had overstepped his authority.

On the 13th of August Pilsudski returned to Krakow; his Staff Headquarters moved to Kielce, where the first regiment of the first brigade of the Pilsudski Legionnaires was raised.

On the way from Miechów to Kielce many legionnaires fell, among whom not a few Jews[14].

Persecution and Disturbances

With the establishment of Independent Poland in November 1918, Miechów was one of the towns in which the farmers from the surrounding villages together with soldiers from the new Polish army began to harass and persecute the Jews. In that activity they were "experts" – especially the subordinates of General Haller who had been brought from France – and also the Polish soldiers from the region of Poznan. The arrival of these soldiers always cast a the shadow of fear over Jewish residents.

These hooligans started by cutting the peyote and hair of the Jews; afterwards they "took" from the shops whatever they felt like taking and finally they would despoil their homes and murder the Jews.

Concerning these acts, the Polish–Jewish press of the day and also the Jewish factions of the Sejm protested. It was some time until peace and quiet returned and Jews began to be citizens of the new Republic, and to fight for their civil and national rights. Nevertheless after a period of relative calm the situation worsened.

Many and varied were the sufferings of the Jews in Miechów. At the time of the first elections for the Sejm, for example, the government created many difficulties for Jews who wanted to take part in the vote raising doubts

"....whether they are Polish citizens. And in as much as in Poland only Poles have voting rights, Jews who wished to take part in the elections are obliged to present a sworn statement that they are Poles." ("Chwila"[15] - 4th April 1919). Obviously, the Sejm factions were forced to become involved in the situation and not only that one.

The report of the Sejm Jewish representatives for the years 1919–1923[16] contain the following details incidents in which the faction saw need to act. Here are a few events from 1919: 8th March – 19th April – disturbances. In the first incident there were 7 injured and in the second – 60; concerning pupils in Polish schools who were forced to write on the Sabbath; in 1920 an event occurred involving the police: "The Jewish community is not permitted to work freely there..." In the month of June 1921, our factions were involved because of anti–Semitic incitement going on in town (name–calling in the streets, slogans, etc.).

[Page 40]

The "Chwila" edition of 21st May 1919 reports that at the railway station Miechów Jews were attacked and that Hartglass and Prilutzky of the Jewish faction in the Sejm were themselves witnesses to the event. The Jewish factions tabled a question concerning the event to the Head of State Pilsudski.

Larger attacks occurred in Miechów in local settlements in May of the same year. As a result the factions tabled a question in the Sejm. A special committee, created by the Sejm reported: "At the time of the disturbances in Miechów 3 Jews were seriously injured and 10 lightly so. In the county of Miechów: in Charsznica – 5 were seriously injured and 32 lightly injured, in Słomniki – 2 seriously injured and 8 lightly, in Kshoynzh – 2 seriously injured and 6 lightly injured. Many shops and the synagogue in Słomniki were ransacked. In connection with that event 40 people were arrested ("Chwila" 1st June 1919).

Later on the factions tabled a question concerning the anti–Semitic incitement orchestrated by General Latinik. In December 1921 the Factions received a reply according to which the Military Prosecutor of Posen had been commanded to investigate the matter...

Nevertheless, later on, as events and the world moved on and life returned to normal, the authorities in Miechów occasionally introduced anti–Semitic orders and from time to time there were outbreaks of anti–Semitic disturbances by individuals and organized gangs.

As an example "Der Heint" (the "Today" 28th May, 1930), information that an anti–Semitic inspector of schools Josef Schimkawitz at the time of the 3rd May festival, accosted a Jew named M. Heilig(?) and slapped him twice across the cheeks for no reason. Heilig referred the matter to the Chief Inspector of schools.

A questionnaire that was distributed among the survivors' organization included the following question: Which event from the years of your childhood is most etched in your memory? Very nearly all of them noted that the anti–Semitic riots that broke out in the first years of the rise of Poland in Miechów, Kshoynzh, Vilietchka, Charsznica and others. Understandably, each person recalled his own subjective memory, and each one recalled different details, but the overall picture was quite clear: violence against the Jews coincided with the establishment of the State.

Ya'acov Wildmann– Zlikovitz from Borzysko writes:

My memory of the pogrom of 1918 has never faded. It was Friday evening, and my Grandfather was reciting Kiddush. Suddenly there was a loud knocking on the windows and doors and there was shouting: "Open up!" The knocking and shouting grew unceasingly louder and louder. We stood trembling and dumb with fear. I was only a youngster but I could sense the danger and my heart filled with fear. The farmers broke down the door and the windows, gangs of bullies burst inside and began to beat my grandfather and grandmother with sticks. A woman neighbour somehow managed to smuggle us away and hid us in her home. We had a shop full of knitted goods and the hooligans took all the stock and destroyed everything. We couldn't continue to live there and moved to Miechów.

[Page 41]

Ya'acov Solnik wrote in his reply concerning the widespread anti–Semitism:

"The anti–Semitism in our town was very fierce, in every respect – physically and intellectually. More than once we had to defend ourselves against attacks from non–Jewish gangs, especially during excursions that the Young Zionist movement organized on Saturdays. Or we got beaten.

I remember in 1936 we heard that anti–Semitic pupils from the local school were planning a pogrom. I was among those that organized a self–defence program. We secretly notified all the Jewish youth. We divided them into groups according to where they lived and the night before the proposed attack we were prepared and on guard. We had also advised the Polish police who promised their help. It is impossible to know why – but the day passed quietly and without incident."

Another ex–resident of Miechów, named Yaffe recalls how, in 1937 gangs of bullies stood in front non–Jewish shops and blocked non–Jewish customers from entering.

Yet another Miechów resident, Yehezkiel Dror relates how he was given 10 days in prison because he had made propaganda during the elections to the Sejm, in favour of the national Jewish Front, Bloc Number 17, a stand which was unpopular with the authorities: the regime supported Bloc Number 1. (Sanacja).

The anti–Semitism caused population relocation within the Jewish settlements of Poland and strengthened the resolve of Jews to leave Poland.

Benjamin Goldberg indicates an additional phenomenon:

In the winter of 1939 – the last winter before the outbreak of war there was an outbreak of typhus (Typhus exanthematicus), in Miechów that affected only the Jewish population. About 30–40 heads of families were victims, mostly men, nearly all of them died. Among them: Gimelkovitz, Gershon; Goldberg, Mendel; Sarni, Hirsch Leib; Pintzevsky, Ya'acov; Rozenkrantz, Hirsch.[17]

The town was closed and quarantined – no one went out and no one came in; fairs and markets were cancelled. The peddlers who earned their daily bread wandering the streets and local villages, selling all manner of items for a chicken or basket of eggs, stopped going around; the non–Jews were fearful of getting too close to them, afraid of catching the disease.

Rabbi Alter

, the collector and sexton of the "Burial Society", found difficulties in mobilizing volunteers to carry out the last rites on the victims, because of the threat and fear of the plague was pandemic."

[Page 42]

Sources of Income

The sources of income for the Jews of Miechów were similar to those of all other Jewish settlements: Artisans, merchants, free professions. The Jews were very active in the areas of farming and economics. They established the mill "Marimont" (mainly owned by the Warshawski family), a generating station (owned by Avraham Sercaz and Hanoch Kaiser) and other small factories (bakeries etc.).

Undoubtedly, the seal of anti-Semitism made its impression on the lives and development of the town's Jews, perhaps more significantly than in other places (big pogroms in the years 1919/20 and offences against Jews – physical and otherwise – in the following years). The number of Poles in the town, who made a living from trade, was greater than in other towns. They represented 25.4% of Miechów's traders, while in other towns the percentage of Jewish traders exceeded 80%. These figures refer to the year 1897[18]). It is true that over time that situation changed but nevertheless the state of Jewish trade didn't improve. The reasons for that were: the rise of Polish trade unions boycotts against Jews, higher taxation implemented against Jews while Polish cooperatives were exempt, and more. The Polish traders would organize operations against the Jews in order to rid themselves of Jewish competition. The authorities also took a hand to destroy the economic status of the Jewish trade thus, for example, in 1922 the Jewish bakery was closed[19] on the grounds that sanitary conditions were inadequate and unsatisfactory.

The Jewish factions in the Polish Sejm would table questions and protests on the basis of conspicuous discrimination against the Jews – but uselessly. Both the open and hidden anti-Semitism of an overwhelming proportion of the Polish population, including the authorities, continued to increase and with it the economic destruction of the Jews.

The Jews searched for help against the economic ostracism: they organized themselves into professional unions (traders' union, artisans' union etc.), they founded cooperative banks for helping the needy and distressed, but none of it really helped because there was no widespread demand to support the Jewish market; the Jewish agent or intermediary became superfluous, because of the growth of the number of Polish merchants and also of anti-Jewish slogans that were heard even from ministers of state, like the Prime Minister General Felicjan Sławoj Składkowski, creator of the slogan: "Boycott the Jews – Forwards!".

With that policy Miechów preceded other towns significantly and was an "outstanding" Polish town. That policy is rather puzzling when one remembers that in the county of Miechów, battles were fought by Kościuszko (1794/5), as he preached equal rights for Jews and in his army there were Jewish fighters. Memories of that rebellion remain in the corporate psyche of the people. Racławice – the place where Składkowski defeated the Russians, not far from Miechów – became a symbol of freedom and equality.

It was here, also that the rebellion of 1863 against Tsarist Russia broke out in which Jews also fought and acted together with the Polish rebels. In memory of the rebels a memorial was erected in Independent Poland in the Market Square.

[Page 43]

Rabbis

The first town Rabbi to settle in Miechów was Rabbi Yesheyahu Shainfrocht. He officiated for forty years to the complete satisfaction of the entire community. He also represented the Jewish community in its external dealings in a seemly fashion. He died in 1922. He was succeeded by his son, Hanoch Shainfrocht who followed the same path as his father and didn't confine himself to religious matters alone. He was revered by many sectors of the Jewish community and took an active part in their social life. He perished, together with the community, which he refused to abandon, in September 1942. The reader will find many interesting details concerning him in this book from people who had direct contact with him during good times and bad, right to the bitter end.

The Rabbi Hanoch Shainfrocht was one of the founders of the "Mizrahi" school and supervised it throughout its existence; he displayed great understanding for the youth organization "The Hashomer Ha–Dati" which also included girls.

Social and Political Life

Miechów was a small town, nevertheless there was almost no Jewish political party that did not have a branch office in Miechów and didn't have some supporters. Each party attracted members to its side and that caused a very vibrant socio–political life. By the way, it is worth pointing out that the competition between the parties was carried on here in a quiet and orderly fashion more–so, in fact than in many other places in Congress Poland.

The strongest political party here was the Zionist party in its many factions. On its reach and growth we can learn from the results of the elections to the Zionist Congress. From the elections of the years 1929 and 1935, we have the following results:

	1929 Number of votes	1935[20] Number of votes
List 'A' (On guard) General Zionists)	57	196
List 'B' (Women's Party)	–	–
List 'C' Mizrahi	125	151
List 'D' Revisionists	3	6
List 'E' Hitachdut and Hashomer ha–Tza'ir	–	84
List 'F' Poalei Zion (left wing)	–	22
Total	185	459

We can see here a significant increase in the number of votes cast during the period under consideration. There was also a branch of the "Aguda" party in Miechów and a few supporters of the "Bund" and a small number of communists (the "Reds").

A large part of the Zionist youth movements belonged to the general "He–Halutz" party. Its members planned to immigrate to Palestine and prepared themselves at several training camps: Cieszyn, Czechowice (agricultural training–farm of the Zionist youth), Charsznica, Wolbrom, Kshoynzh–Vileyka, Proszowice, Łódź, Łuków, Zavirtcha, Vodislov, Galnika(?), near Góra Kalwaria, Olkusz, Bendin, Bystra(?).

There were Halutsim who, after five years of training were unable to obtain certificates, and they perished with the rest of the victims of the Holocaust.

[Page 44]

Youth Movements

During the twenty years of the existence of Independent Poland the following youth movements were active in Miechów:

National Guard later called the Young Zionists;

Mizrahi Youth;

Agudat Yisroel Youth;

Hashomer Ha–Dati;

Beitar.

In 1931 there was a convention in Miechów of all the regional branches of Hashomer Ha–Dati.

In all the youth organizations there were libraries and bulletin boards. Sometimes there were lectures. Drama circles were produced in Miechów and the local area. The income from these productions was always intended for national or social targets (The Foundation Fund, for the local poor and once even the Students' organization); once a year there was a "Flower Day".

In a comment published in "A New Day" (22nd March 1922) it was ironically reported that a writer from Miechów of the paper (whose name was not mentioned), reported that on Purim there was a production of S. Lanski's "The Dybbuk" by local players. A large number of people from the town and the surroundings came to watch the play but because the play was a drama rather than a comedy half the audience fell asleep during the performance...

On Purim they would dress up as leaders of the Zionists and stroll around the town from house to house, singing and playing music; the money collected was ear–marked for the Foundation Fund for Israel. (K.K.L.).

The Young Zionists played an important part in the collection of money for the National funds. In the evenings they would gather at their centers and pass the time singing songs and dancing the "Hora". The groups published a magazine in Yiddish (in 1924–1925), called "Torch". There were sections containing songs, critiques and information on the important events both in town and in Palestine. In total there were about 20 editions and it seems not one has survived.

There was also a public Jewish library in town called "The Zamir"; a children's library called "Dror" a drama society; a football society and a sports club called "Forward".

Schools

Jewish children in Miechów studied in the national schools – Polish government schools – in "Haderim" and the private Jewish school, "Ha–Mizrahi". Many Jewish children studied externally with private teachers in order not to have to sit bare–headed in Polish schools or listen to the Christian "Our Father" every morning or suffer the not a little the anti–Semitic taunts of the pupils and teachers.

The girls learned reading and writing (Hebrew and Yiddish) with Fassia Teitelbaum and Shlomo Solewicz.

Memorable from among the teachers are Av'eleh Lewit, Marsha Muncznik, David Staschower, Yisroel Eli Krymolowski, Yesheyahu Hirshenhorn, in whose class they played football on Fridays providing they knew the weekly portion of the Torah.

Among the managers of the Mizrahi school were Yitzhak Weiner, Tzvi Kleinarltz(?), S.N. Kahanofsky and others.

In the "Heder" "Torah Foundation" – the "Agudat Yisroel" stream, there were seven classes. The teacher of the top class was Moshe David Waxberg. In addition there was a school for girls from the same stream – "Beit Ya'acov".

[Page 45]

The Government Gymnasium

Miechów had a State–run Gymnasium named for Tadeusz Kościuszko. According to the report filed by the management for the academic year 1930/31, there were 275 pupils, all of them of Polish nationality; possessors of other nationalities were not accepted. These were the religious affiliations of the pupils:

262	Roman Catholics
1	Orthodox Christians
12	Mosaic persuasion

From the numbers it is possible to see that the numerus clausus was in operation. The Jewish pupils represented only 4.4% of the school population whereas in the town itself the Jewish population was almost 40% and it was known that the desire to study among the Jews was very strong. Clearly, therefore, in the State controlled gymnasium in which the school fees were minimal, especially for the children of officials, they weren't too hasty to accept Jews. Because of this the Jewish children studied in private gymnasia – Jewish or Polish – in other towns: Kielce, Chenstochov, Olkusz, Krakow and others. In the year referred to, there was, among 16 graduates of the gymnasium, one Jew – Sheintal Barak.

Among the staff there was one Jewish teacher, Sofia Kodlrowana(?) who taught natural sciences. Jewish religion was not taught at the gymnasium n spite of the fact that the curriculum specifies it. Only immediately preceding the matriculation exams, the pupils were sent to the Rabbi where they were examined in religion and the result registered on the matriculation certificate. The institute's doctor was Stefan Lehman, a relapsed Jew.

There was one Jewish member on the parents' committee, Avraham Sercaz, the community head; also taking part on the committee was the wife of the Jewish school's inspector, Burstein, who, according to rumor was also a relapsed Jew. In the national and primary schools, the religious teachers were Eliezer Lavie and Ya'acov Kornfeld.

Public Institutions

1. The Cooperative Bank

The Jewish cooperative society in Poland published annually mimeographed reports that included statistical details concerning the cooperatives included in that society. Following are details taken from the report of 1937:

The bank in Miechów, named Bank Spółdzielczy was founded in 1922. At the beginning of 1937 it had 153 members; during the year another 5 were added and 15 left; at the end of the year, therefore, there were 143 members. Their businesses were as follows: merchants and industrialists - 81, artisans - 46, others 16. The share value was 25 złoty. The financial involvement of the members, in addition to the share was 20 złoty. There were three clerks.

Almost all the artisans and merchants in town were affiliated.

Loans that the bank granted that year totalled 86,228 złoty about 756.39 złoty to each loan.

Only 19 of the share–holding members and ordinary depositors were in need of loans.

[Page 46]

A distressing and characteristic sign of the times can be seen in the fact that the total deposits that were withdrawn were greater than those deposited by 1,311 złoty: a relatively large amount if one takes into account that financial transactions of the bank were small.

A second cause of the bank's weakness was that it suffered from non–repayment of loans. No wonder therefore, that the bank made no profit.

As said above, the manager of the bank received no salary for his work, while the three clerks received the miserable sum of 1,631 złoty during the year or a monthly salary of 45.3 złoty. That is such a small sum that only a man in an economically deplorable situation, or a minor, still at living at home with parents and without prospects would be prepared to accept such a position.

From all these figures we can see that the bank was not considered to be one of the big banks and those who received its services were among the "Hoi polloi" of the population to whom the bank would extend a small loan at a small discount. All this proves how much the bank was needed by the masses of the impoverished toilers. The bank existed until the outbreak of World War Two and its situation certainly didn't improve.

2. The Merchants' Bank

The bank was founded early in 1929. On 24th March1929 the General Meeting of the Bank's members discussed changing the constitution and name of the Bank, a decision recognized and authorised by the Regional Court in Kalish, was changed to: Spółdzielczy Bank Kupiecki.

Avraham Friderich, Haim Feureisen and Moshe Koppelowitz were elected to manage the Bank, and as their deputies: D. Isskowitz and Shmuel Fogel.

At a congress that was convened on 23rd June 1929 in Lvov Moshe Koppelowitz was elected representative and member of the Regulating Board of the Central Society of all the Jewish cooperative banks affiliated to the Society of Banks, whose base was in Warsaw,. Moshe Koppelowitz also represented the General Cooperative Bank of Miechów.

The Merchants' Bank dealt with various banking issues and activities and existed up until the outbreak of World War Two.

There were also Jewish professional societies: The Union of Artisans and the Union of Merchants. There also existed charitable organizations such as "Visiting the Sick", "Sick–bed Assistance and Lodging for the Poor", "Brotherly Help" and so on.

The Community

With the elections to the Community in the offing the "Battle of the Parties" broke out, mainly between the Zionists and the "Aguda". There were small organized groups taking part in the elections, the Artisans' Union or one of the groups from a religious faction and so on. Similarly various "Blocs" sprang into existence, as was usual in Poland in those days.

The results of the elections for the years 1924 and 1931 show us clearly the atmosphere that spread over town and the direction of the national tendency.

The Zionists	2 places	(Avraham Sercaz, Shimson Yeruzalimsky)
Hamizrahi	1 place	(Yermiyahu Blum)
Aguda/Artisans/ Religious	1 place	(Hanoch Kaiser)

("Today" 3rd June 1924).

Also included in the Council was by law, the town Rabbi of Miechów

[Page 47]

The results of the elections in 1931 were:

General Zionists	4 places (among them 2 artisans)
Mizrahi	2 places
Religious non–party	1 place
Aguda	1 place

("Today" 28th May 1931).

The Community Chairman was for many years, Avraham Sercaz, who was also a member of the Municipal Council for an extended period. His replacement was Dov (Bernard) Goldman.

The Municipal Council

During the years 1932–1949, among the 12 members of the Municipal Council there were 5 Jews, while in the management the was just one alone – Mordecai Muhlstein.

In 1936, 9 Jews were elected among the 24 members of the Council and one to the town management. The Jewish members were: Hirsch Adlist, Moshe Aharon Gruszka, Reuven Shmuel Kleiner, Moshe Koppelowitz, Moshe Sosnovsky, Bezalel Weizmann, Avraham Sercaz, Haim Feureisen and Avraham Friderich; Yermiyahu Blum was in the management.

Zionist Activity

Among the important events on the national–State scene that caused excitement and arousal in the whole Jewish community that must be mentioned – apart from the Balfour Declaration – was the celebrations that took place after the San Remo Agreement. In the "Today" newspaper of 31st May, 1922 one reads: On Saturday 29th April 1922 there was great celebration in the synagogue in which all the Jews of town took part and even the supporters of the "Aguda". At the reading of the Torah, more than 50,000 Polish Marks were donated to the Foundation Fund.

That same day at 4 PM there was a big meeting in the synagogue and 1,000 Jews took part. On the next Saturday the amount donated by those called to the Torah exceeded 100,000 Marks. The dedication of the Hebrew University in Jerusalem at that time also echoed excitedly in Miechów.

In 1930 Alter Droyanov came on a visit from Palestine and appeared in a production. He wrote recorded a number of anecdotes that he heard from the youngsters and was much impressed by their personality. In 1933 a big demonstration took place against the regime of Hitler. All the shops and workshops were closed and the demonstrators marched past the Government building chanting anti–Hitler slogans.

The Second World War Years (1939–1945)

The town of Miechów was overrun by the Germans on 6th September 1939. The governorship then passed to the German civilian authority that at its head stood Dr. Hans Frank. On the 26th October 1939 Miechów was attached to the County of Krakow. The post of County Governorship of Miechów was created, that was much larger than the previous county (Polish): the new county included 6 towns (Wolbrom among them) and 871 villages and covered an area of 2,900 square kilometres with 410,000 residents[21].

The first County Governor was Dr. Zinser. The department for Volksdeutsche, propaganda, housing issues and Jews was administered by a graduate of the school for SS officers, Leutenschläger. They brought German–domiciled nationals to town and they had all the important administrative positions; less important tasks were given to the Volksdeutsche, including control of the rail (guarding the railway station etc.). The following offices were created and operated in town: German Inspectorate of Forests, German Police station in addition to the Polish one, a branch of the criminal Police (Criminal

Commissariat) and an office of the Nationalsozialistische Deutsche Arbeiterpartei (NSDAP). For the children of German nationals, two schools, in Miechów and Wolbrom were instituted in which there were 21 pupils and two teachers[22]. Schools for the local Polish population were not a consideration while the Jewish children were not considered at all in need of schools.

[Page 48]

Similarly a labor office was instituted in town that was directed towards putting the Jews to forced labor, the Poles to "obligatory works" and young Poles for building works on Polish project – "the front organized work camps". They built bridges and roads, drainage systems etc. For that purpose a branch office of the Krakow base – "Strassen und Brückenbau" was opened in Miechów. As a result of the stream of refugees coming from towns and villages, the population of Miechów grew by more than 10,000 (10,090 according to German sources[23]).

In October 1940 there were in the whole county of Miechów:

		%
Poles	421,324	92.7
State– and Volksdeutsche	496	0.1
Ukrainians	158	0.03
Jews	32, 497	7.1
	454,475	

In his advertisement of 1942 (p 15), D. Pearl states that such a number of Jews were alive at that time and that later the number of Jews was substantially reduced. In October 1940 – before the above statement – there were 2,788 work–places of Aryan artisans and 948 of Jews. From among them skinners represented 33% and in second place metal–workers, carpenters and others.

Among the increased number of Jews in the county were included 15,000 displaced Jews from Krakow, that had resettled in Działoszyce (5,000), Wolbrom (3,000), Miechów, Slomniki, Proszowice and Skalbmierz (about 1,000)[24].

On the 1st March 1943 the German authorities of the Generalgouvernement conducted a census of the civilian population according to which there were at that time in Miechow only 6,392 souls, many less than the number at the beginning of the occupation. The difference signifies the number of victims up until that time[25].

The Jews in town suffered from all the edicts that were laid on the Jews throughout conquered Poland. However, in Miechow the edicts were intensified in some instances, for example: from the festival of Succot, 1939 until Passover 1940 Jews were allowed out on the streets only from 9 o'clock in the morning until 3 o'clock in the afternoon. After the conquest of the town Torah scrolls were burnt during which the Jews were made to sing.

Miechów was different from the other towns in the General–gouvernement in that the head of the Judenräte in the whole County (eleven, all told), was a (German) government appointee, a Jewish commissar (Isaac Applebaum).

[Page 49]

His title was: ***Kommissar der Judenräte für den Kreis Miechów*** – Commissar for the Jewish councils in Miechów County. The official newspaper Gazeta Zydowska writes a short time after his appointment that the situation of the Jews has been bettered and that the Commissar makes many surveys accompanied by representatives of Government institutions But the Jews living in the Miechów ghetto had other opinions.

In the same edition the paper complimented the Judenräte and the Aid Committee whose field of activity encompassed the town and all the surroundings.

According to an official document of 30th December 1940, the Assistance Committee had the following members:

Freidrich, Avraham – Export merchant (Chairman);

Adlist, Hirsch – Articled artisan;

Sercaz, Avraham – Business owner of ”Marimant”;

Dr. Krieger, Leon – Lawyer'

Dr. Lancer, Moshe – Doctor.

In the same building where the Judenrat offices operated, a peoples' kitchen opened up and distributed 300 lunches. The Women's Committee distributed food to 150 children. There was also a kindergarten managed by an accredited nursemaid. 400 of the 800 lunches distributed in the region were financed by the Judenrat. The chairman of the Judenrat was Adlist.

The Judenrat supplied an oven for sterilization. The health committee supplied an inspectorate for examining living accommodation and the community doctor gave free medical assistance to the needy poor. The health Committee prepared medicaments. The bath–house was open to the public every Friday.

Shmuel Leib Adlist

[Page 50]

In an article from the above newspaper (vol. 88 10th October 1941), they continue to praise the activities of the Judenrat: in the 14 communities there are 14 kitchens operating without loss. The expenses were met by the activities of Jewish self–help and by monthly payments from wealthy circles. Of 3,300 souls in Miechów 1,000 required assistance from the kitchen; a payment of 40 groschen – that covered only a part of the Funds price – was collected from over half the diners. 200 children also received a free breakfast or paid 10 groschen. From the two reports of expenses that we have brought from the official Jewish newspaper we learn that the situation of the Jews had worsened significantly.

In August 1940 vaccines against Typhus exanthematicus were injected. The poor received the vaccine free. Because of the extremely congested conditions in the ghetto the Judenrat transferred 100 families to other communities, provided accommodation and a parcel of food for the journey.

In November–December 1940 there was an outbreak of Typhoid (Paratyphoid) in the ghetto (Gazeta Zydowska Vol. 31 5th November 1940 and vol. 44 20th December 1940). At that time there were 100 Jewish artisans working in their workshops in Miechów; the chairman of the Judenrat made sure that they received additional food and raw materials.

From the Jewish–Social help center in Krakow, the Council for help would receive essential materials from time to time. For the month of August, for example, 100 kgs. of oils, 150 kgs. medicines 200 packets of laundry powder 50 cartons of milk were delivered.

In the month of August the Jewish Ordnungs–Dienst was formed. The Polish police appointed Dr. Leffelholtz as Commissar of the Jewish police for the whole "great" area of Miechów, in which 11 branches of the Jewish Ordnungs–Dienst operated. The service waged war against beggars; foreign beggars were sent back to their homes. The Jewish commissar for all the Jewish communities in the area was also responsible for the distribution of food. The store of food that was supplied to him by the Town management for the whole area was distributed by him as he saw fit (Gazeta Zydowska Vol. 88).

The Judenrat instituted an arbitration council, a judiciary council which had 9 members (3 units) and other administrative departments.

For the 14 kitchens that operated in Miechów and the area the department of nutrition and agriculture of the area Governorship would from time to time portion out necessary commodities and fuel for heating. The portion was gradually reduced with time until it ceased entirely.

Thus, for instance, the Committee of Assistance for the Jews (***Jüdisches Hilfe–Komitée*** or, in Polish: ***Żydowski Komitet Pomocy*** for the month of September 1941 there was a special rationing (Sonderzuteilung) for the poorest of the county: 655 kg barley grits; 555 kg pasta; 655 kg sugar; 3,000 flour; 500 kg sugar; 700 kg spaghetti; 300 kg buckwheat.

The rationing for October of that same year was far less, while just before Passover 1942, Miechów received from the center 400 kg of potatoes and flour.

In March 1941 there was an outbreak of Typhus exanthematicus in virtually the entire County. Later the plague attacked Miechów as well. By order of the authorities a curfew was placed on the houses and residents that had become infected: for 8 weeks it was prohibited to enter or leave those houses.

It was even prohibited to introduce food into the homes. The Jews living there were expected to starve completely. The committee in Miechów organized correspondence to the Jewish central Help Committee in Krakow. The same harsh edicts were handed down for Pilica(?), Zarnovitza Wolbrom and others.

[Page 51]

In a letter from 18th April 1941 to the center, it was stated that in Miechów 23 cases of Typhus exanthematicus had been recorded. Members of the stricken families had been isolated and those Jews were forbidden to leave town. The Help Committee was obliged to assist those families. The German office would occasionally supply a little foodstuff for the isolated people like: 10 liters skimmed milk for the 43 isolated souls from Skalbmierz for the two months of August and September 1941.

Many facts prove that even in those dark years, the Jewish people managed to maintain the "Imago Deo" and made heroic attempts with all their strength to continue to live normal lives especially in the care of their children. Against the law, they insisted on educating their children in secret. The older children studied and read for themselves. They also took part in the children's section that appeared once a week in the ***Gazeta Zydowska***, the only Jewish paper in the Generalgouvernement that was published in Polish in Krakow. For instance: in vol. 30 (15th April 1941) and vol. 44 (3rd June 1941) we find a geographical and mathematical questionnaire for children set by Riva Warschawski of Miechów, to amuse and test themselves.

The Deportation and Destruction

On 26th September the Commissar of Miechów proclaimed an order demanding 300 Jews to leave the ghetto no later than 4th October and move to Działoszyce. There were 6,747 Jews living there at that time – 47% more than before the war (4,574).

On the 30th June 1942 another proclamation appeared creating a "Jewish living area" in Miechów (Jüdischer Wohnbezirk). Anyone found outside that area would be put to death. The order was signed by Kelpers as manager of "Police Matters" department in the offices of the County Governor.

Of course with no choice in the matter, the Judenrat could do nothing but acquiesce. On 25th August 1942 the head of the Gestapo Beierlein demanded cash payment of a fine, in gold and other valuable possessions. The demand was made separately to each town – and they had until 3 o'clock in the afternoon. There is no need to say that there was not the first "Fine" that had been levied on the Jews of the county. But this time it was levied – supposedly – to delay the deportation. At that time rumors were already rife about the extermination camps... so the Jews found it essential to pay the ransom in order to save their lives. The Judenrat therefore, fixed a price for each family and the Jewish Ordnungs–Dienst made moves to collect the money[27].

The payment didn't help in any way, and on Thursday 21th Elul, 3rd September 1942, the largest deportation of the Jews from the whole County of Miechów, went into effect. Much material on the deportation is to be found for the reader in this book, in which it is discussed from different points of view.

Jews from the surrounding towns were brought to Miechów. A "Selektzia" was carried out on the forecourt in front of the railway station and the young and healthy were separated and sent to work at the special camps; the remainder, the great majority, were jammed into the freight–cars and transferred to – as we learned later – the extermination–camp at Belzec.

In Miechów the main deportations began the same day. At 5 o'clock in the morning, the German Gendarmes woke all the Jews and commanded them to assemble within 10 minutes. The transported the Jews to the Railway station, separated the younger ones and sent them to the work camp at Plaszów near to Krakow. The women, the old men and the children were sent to Belzec, to the extermination–camp. There remained a small group of youngsters who had to remain behind to attend to the deserted ghetto; he left–behind Jewish property. The valuable articles and documents of the Community Office from before the war and the days of the Judenrat – especially the "Department of Jewish Population" – were transferred to the central offices in Krakow, in accordance with the orders of replacement County Governor, Schmidt, from 11th December 1940.

[Page 52]

A number of young Jews who escaped from the Plaszów camp joined the work–force platoon in Miechów. On 14th November 1943 the platoon was liquidated: 70 healthy young men were shot on the spot, among them: Moshe Koppelowitz, past–member of the town council; the son–in–law of Michael Lis, a member of the community council of Slomniki; Wolf Bar Kaiser, a member of the Community Council of Miechów and Chairman local Zionist party; Aharon Schweitzer, one of the respected residents, and others.

From among the Holy Community of Miechów, there remained only 34 Jews alive. Some of them because they lived on the "Aryan side", as it was called, some of them survived the camps and others joined the Partisans. Among those were Berger, Grynbel and Meyer Shalom, who perished later.

These are the names of the Germans whose bestial deeds are etched on the memories of the Jews: Beierlein – Head of the Gestapo; Kazak – his deputy; Josef Rittinger – Criminal Police; Hacket Dachowe, Schubert, Robert Biev, Dr. Schmidt – deputy County Governor; Bindt – Inspector of prices – all of them Reich–domiciled German nationals. Volksdeutsche: Kobalski – Gestapo; Micha Beckmann Gorniak – Labor office.

On the matter of resistance an important Polish source provides an example: At the time of the deportation from Miechów, Kalman Malinarski drew a knife from his boot and attacked the deputy County Governor, seriously wounding him.

Translator's Footnotes

1. Strasbourg 1913, vol. 11 pp. 440.
2. Bogdan Wasiutyński: Ludność Żydowska w Królestwie Polskim pp, 69.
3. In 1865 there were 3.9% Jews in the whole of the county of Miechów; that was the lowest percentage in the 19 counties of Congress Poland. See pp. 27 in the book by Wasiutyński quoted above (Note 2).
4. Wasiutyński states – in contrast to the Encyclopaedia – a different figure concerning the total number of residents in 1897, i.e. 3,731 alone; consequently he give a higher percentage of Jews: 38.5%. Compare: Bogdan Wasiutyński: Ludność Żydowska w Polsce w wieku XIX i XX, Warszawa.
5. Wasiutyński p.30.
6. Ibid p. 17
7. Ibid p, 30
8. Ibid p.181
9. Statistisches Gemeindeverzeichnis, Berlin 1939.

10. E Podhoritzer–Sandel: O ZagÅ‚adzie Żydów w dystrikcie Krakowskim Biultyn Żydówskiego Instytutu Historyczneo 1959, Nr. 30 pp. 88.
11. Published by Shmuel Argelbrand from 1859–1868 in Warsaw, in 28 volumes.
12. Pamiętniki, 1926 Vol.2, p. 162 et seq.
13. Glos Gminy Żydowskiej, Warsaw, 1938 No. 10/11
14. The Jewish–Polish newspaper that was published and distributed in Lvov
15. The provisional National–Jewish Council and Jewish faction in the Sejm from January 1919 until July 1923 – edited by Y. Greenboim. Warsaw, 1923.
16. The Miechów county Governor recalls the plague of February 1939, in his report of 5th July 1940 and adds that it caused the deaths of more than 100 people (Yad Va–Shem archives).
17. Dr. I. Schiper: Dzieje handle żydowskiego na ziemiach polskich p. 537, 1937.
18. See "The Jewish Artisans' Voice" Vol. 1 : 11.4.1922, the Journal of the Central Council of Polish Artisans.
19. Max Freiherr du Prel: Das Generalgouvernement, Würzburg, (second edition), p. 260, 1942.
20. Ibid: (first edition), p. 1943, 1940
21. Die Struktur des Arbeitsamptbezirkes Krakau, (The Katograph 1942)
22. Gazeta Zydowska, No.23 7.10.1940
23. Yad Va–Shem microfilm
24. The Ringleblum Archive, V. No. 448.
25. According to Avraham Tannenbaum: The Auszidlung in Miechów County, Our orld, Munich, No. 60 (142) 22.10.1948
26. The Observer: H. Menahem, 30.7.1945, p. 3, mentioning all the Jews by name, afterwards more Jews "appeared" – when they were saved
27. Machajek: ChÅ‚opcy z lasu. P. 122, 1950.

[Page 55]

From the Past

A. Anecdotes from the Town

Ya'acov Spiegel Recounts

Recorded by Moshe Spiegel

Translated by Selwyn Rose

Elimelech Spiegel, the ritual slaughterer and his wife Gila were among the first ten Jewish settlers in Miechów. These Jews arrived in the town in the 60's of the 19th Century together with Yisroel Kupchik, Bonham Feigenboim, Kalman Rabinowitz, Michael Borgestein, Yehoshua Posluszny, Shlomo Waciarz, Moshe Yosef Weill, and others.

Miechów's first synagogue burnt to the ground in 1898. The tragedy occurred on the evening of Hoshanah Rabbah, when one of the praying women accidently upset a lighted candle – one among hundreds memorializing the dead – on a pile of pages of old prayer–books. The congregation was in the middle of the "Amidah" prayer (which may not be interrupted by speech or movement) and the incident remained unattended for a few minutes and within those few minutes, the fire took hold not only on the dry, old pages and books but spread very quickly to the entire wooden building and the building became an inferno and the synagogue burnt to the ground.

A short time later two of the town's community leaders of the time, Rabbi Simcha Varoslowski and Rabbi Eliezer Siwirski erected a new elegant synagogue that was renowned throughout the district for its decorative paintings and colors. The decorations of the synagogue were executed by Shmuel Blum, the son of Rabbi Yermiyahu Blum, now living in Paris. It is said that the building still stands today and is being used as a municipal store–room.

The water drawer

In those days there was no installed water system in Miechów's houses but at some distance in Dziluczitza Street, behind the hospital and the municipal park there was a potable well known locally as "Stok". The well was used by our water drawers; they would fill a large barrel transfer it to a horse–drawn cart and distribute buckets of water to all the houses in town. One of the water drawers was an immense man nearly two meters tall whose feet were so large he was forced to order specially made boots. Compared to him his wife, Gitla was tiny gaunt and slim – a real "dried up fig" but for all that a treasure of a woman, righteous and generous. In that respect it should be mentioned that Rabbi Yesheyahu, who had never delivered a eulogy for anyone, even the most respected people in the community, eulogized Gitla on her passing and praised her many qualities for over an hour.

She kept about twenty mattresses in her home ready for any chance guests, beggars and wayfarers who passed by, moving from town to town, looking for alms, and delegates from seminaries donating money for all types of charitable foundations. There were even occasions when Gitla ran from house to house seeking an additional mattress for a lodger.

[Page 56]

There was no single sick person in town for which Gitla did not prepare food or support. She carried about a dozen cups on a tray which she filled with soup from other house–wives and distributed to "her" sick patients. On market days she would take buckets of water to give the farmers' cattle and horses to drink. approaching Passover she bought beets and pickled them to provide for the poor and needy.

The Fire

In 1905, there were two uprisings in Polish towns, which were bonded to Tsarist Russia: A general revolt against the Tsar and a workers' revolt to establish a socialist regime. The Russian authorities in Miechów arrested a number of people in the county offices whom they considered the ringleaders. The county offices were then in Karkobaska Street, facing the banqueting hall of A. Gerstenfeld. Quite quickly and spontaneously a crowd gathered of local Polish farmers armed with axes shouting in loud voices and demanding the immediate release of the arrested leaders. In reply the authorities brought in a Cossack platoon to protect the municipal buildings; neither had the Poles been standing idle: they set fire to the home of Shmuel Shenker thinking that would somehow cause the release of the leaders.

Ya'acov Spiegel, who was then a young boy, saw the blaze from the window of his house. His father stopped him from leaving the house but he somehow managed to sneak out to watch from close up what was going on.

In the meantime, Haye'leh, the daughter of Rabbi Yosef, the teacher, was giving birth. When he saw the flames approaching his house, he took the new–born baby from her arms while she, at a loss what to do, ran directly towards the flames. Then, the young Ya'acov grabbed her and ushered her purposefully into the home of Rabbi Yesheyahu, thus saving her life.

An Argument in Town

Recalling a dispute that once broke out in town at Rosh Hashanah 1910

It happened in the synagogue after the finish of the morning and additional morning prayers which concluded at about 3 o'clock in the afternoon. Two respected members of the community, Rabbi Yisroel David Spiegel and Rabbi Haim Levitt, suggested an immediate start to the afternoon prayer leading on to the evening prayer without the necessity of going home for a short break and then having to return. Two others, Rabbi Simcha Varoslowski and Rabbi Mordecai Milstein were strongly opposed to the proposal: “No! No, we will not pray now. We'll go home and return later.” Physical violence broke out between the two groups and blood was actually drawn.

Virtually the entire congregation of the synagogue, with very few exceptions, was drawn into the affray in that Holy place, and it eventually spread out into the street, from the water–well as far as the market place. It was impossible to separate the opposing groups until darkness fell and shrouded the street and the conflicting Jews; with torn caftans and broken limbs the exhausted participants were forced to return to the synagogue for the evening prayer.

For many years afterwards fathers told their children about the argument and pointed to it as a prime example of unfounded hatred or “a storm in a tea–cup”.

[Page 57]

The First Personalities

by Ya'acov Levitt

Translated by Selwyn Rose

The first Jews settled in Miechów in the 60's of the 19th Century although community life only started at the end of the 80's. In those days the community leader was Rabbi Simcha Varoslowski a respected Jew and multi–faceted businessman. All the formal arrangements, like ritual slaughtering, registrations in the municipality records, wedding formalities and ceremonies, divorces, were carried out in the home of the first Rabbi of Miechów, Rabbi Yesheyahu Sheinfrucht. It was during that period that the first synagogue was burnt down; it was rebuilt on the initiative of Rabbi Simcha Varoslowski in 1898 and the new synagogue, bigger and beautiful still stands today.

The cost to the community was quite large: the community numbered nearly two hundred souls and they were obliged to levy a tax per Jewish family to cover the cost. There were direct taxes, and the community leader appointed a special agent to collect them; there were other taxes that were collected and they financed items like slaughtering, grants for weddings, ritual baths, rabbinical arbitrators of disputes and other peripheral community services.

Some years later, my father, Rabbi Haim Levitt (Z"L), brought to our town the ritual slaughterer Rabbi Yisroel David Burstein (Z"L) from Iłża in the county of Radom, known in Yiddish as Driltch. Rabbi Yisroel David immediately made friends, and was liked by everyone in town by his generous nature, his distinguished learning and straightforward honesty. He settled into an apartment close to the synagogue and in the yard built a small wooden hut for slaughtering the chickens. He delighted the congregation with his renderings of the prayers accompanied by his sons who were also competent vocalists, with deep, rich voices.

The first banker, who helped the city merchants by granting loans and credit – was Rabbi Schmelke Katzengold (Z"L). They say that one fine day it became generally known that he had become wealthy and decided to open a bank in town to help small businessmen that began to flourish and expand. There was also another bank in Miechów with its center in Sosnowiec, founded by the Bergman Company and Partners (or Landau and Partners). In the same bank the chief clerk was Rabbi Moshe Sukenik, who arrived in town Miechów from Sosnowiec dressed in modern clothes like any non–Jew; nevertheless after he met the beautiful widow, Rey'leh, the daughter of Rabbi Nathan Bornstein and proposed to her, he repented and promised his in–laws to follow all 613 commandments and become a faithful G–d–fearing Jew. And indeed from that time Moshe Sukenik was a good, G–d–fearing Jew. His children were raised according to the Torah in addition to their secular education.

Also living in Miechów was Rabbi Mendel Kurland, owner of a large house in the Market Square. The house was later sold to Avraham Rosen (Holoschitzer) and Aharon Reinstein (the baker). Rabbi Mendel Kurland was associated with the Righteous of Kutchak and smoked a long pipe. He didn't have much pleasure from his son Noah because he didn't love the Torah. After he went missing from his lessons with his Rabbi, Rabbi Avraham Schwarzer, the Rabbi himself met him in the street and asked why he hadn't come to the lesson and this – by all accounts – was his reply: "I heard bells ringing in town and supposed it was because the Rabbi had died, so with no Rabbi, there was a holiday from classes...!"

Noah Kurland would travel from place to place, hither and thither and found different ways of amusing people and getting up to all sorts of mischief. When his father received complaints about him at one place, he simply moved him to another until he returned to Miechów. Here he stayed for a short while and when he got up to his old tricks and the seminary in town got fed up with him, he simply went wandering off again all over Poland's towns and villages.

[Page 58]

Rabbi Ya'acov Lewit studied under the learned instructor and rabbinical judge, Rabbi Yosseleh Kleinfeltz. Jewish farmers would come to him to announce the birth–date of new–born calves so that they could slaughter the animals ritually after seven days in compliance with Jewish law. A Jewish villager once came to him with a question: his wife had borrowed a saucepan from a non–Jew Mr. Maczik, and had cooked a stew in it for lunch. What is the status of the saucepan...?

Rabbi Yermiyahu Blum (Z"L), when he was young, would mingle with the Polish "intelligentsia" in town and make friends with the secretaries. When he needed to try and mitigate or cancel any punishment that might have been incurred, Rabbi Yermiyahu would go into the offices of the authorities and very often succeed in getting the judgement set aside.

March of the Generations

by Meyer Goldberg

Translated by Selwyn Rose

A town: its homes, its lanes, hills and its valleys. In this town people passed their half–forgotten childhood, in it they dreamed the dreams of youth and adolescence, here they matured and grew old.

A chain of generations, and here and there ghosts and stormy rattle their chains. She has many components: the first Jews who settled in Miechów; the magnificent synagogue erected here as if asserting "I am here!"; the assembly of members who gathered to found the local branch of "Ha–Mizrachi"; or the Jewish "Zionist Youth" movement, sworn for some reason to be faithful and true to the principles of Baden–Powell.

Two structures were established, as if symbolizing the conduct of the two streams of life existing at their feet: the one– the sanctuary of Jewish prayer and life and opposite it rising in pride, the round dome of the church.

I, a Jewish child, in passing by "there" in broad day–light, would slant my eyes towards to the mysterious dome with fear. The windows of the church glittered, green and red with pride, and I imagined to myself I could sense the burning hatred inside. Its yard was fenced in, steeped in trees and greenery, while around it reared the buildings of the government: the court–house, the government house, the Municipality and the town gaol. The incumbent military priest – I met him a few times on the street. He was always in a hurry, red–faced, his black, tight–fitting robes rustling in his haste as if to an unfinished burial ceremony. Tens of exciting stories, the fruit of youth's wildest imagination accompanied him to his house.

A few paces from there – is the "movie–house", the "house of dreams"; it was the fire–brigade's earlier base. If you're looking for a quick way to grow up then this is it; to sit inside on creaky chairs and feed your eyes on the heroes and dream to the background music.

For the likes of us, we were prohibited from entering but by bribing the usher we could sit quietly on the floor in the first rows and peek between the legs of those seated in front. In fact, most of the movies I saw were through a hole in the exit door. I was the lucky one because my house was quite close to the hut. I could sneak out of the house and if lucky find the slit "unoccupied"; there was no one happier than I: I clung to the hole like a lover.

Not far from there was the Starostrova: The building seemed very much out of place and a stranger to my eyes, what little we knew of it. I recall, at home, where very little use was made of alcohol, my father boasted “Me and the Starostrova are very busy today...”, and closing the side of the square was the government building, and next to it the church, with the sun's rays shining on its walls. That side seemed to me cheery with its colors perhaps because my friend Dziasek(?) lived close–by. I was unusual among my friends because of that friendly connection but I was not mistaken in my judgement of him. Later on I heard many stories about how he had helped the Jews during the dark days of the Holocaust and there are those who say he was eventually killed for protecting Jews.

[Page 59]

Not far away – but for all that far enough to be as if in another area – stood the synagogue, not as high as the church but wider with high, tall windows. The Star of David over the entrance caught everyone's eye. Inside was so much light on Saturdays and the eve of festivals, but gloomy and barren during the weekdays. Row after row of pews all facing east with the Rabbi's special alcove slightly hidden from sight. I remember how they refurbished and painted the synagogue and how we gazed, dumbstruck at the inscription over the entrance; there the names of Shmuel Blum and the non–Jewish artist were inscribed.

The faces of everyone were illuminated on Fridays, Saturdays and festivals with the colors, reminding me – in my eyes – like the smile of greeting my mother (Z”L), would bestow on guests arriving at our home. On the Day of Atonement, come the shadows of anxiety, and the majestic prayer of the Rabbi, permitting us to pray together with sinners and transgressors. For some reason I always searched for Buchner at that time: Ya'acov Buchner the erudite, the respected, the Epicurean. On the Day of Atonement the walls of the synagogue enclose the congregation in their warm embrace and who among us would be absent for Morning Prayer recital at the moment of the “The King”, when one faces east and the heart begins to pound. There from his prayer–shawl–enshrouded face comes one of the finest voices filling the sanctuary with sweetness and glory: “The King....” – It is the ritual slaughterer, that wonderful personality. With rolling eyes I am huddled against my father's prayer–shawl as if seeking support.

And what is that great wind that rushes through the streets during the closing prayer of "Ne'ilah"? Not a soul is to be seen in the street, as if all existence, Jewish and non–Jewish in the town has come to an end.

And the joyful festivals, everyone between the walls of the synagogue was joyously happy with smiles, and there was mischief everywhere. One's eyes are turned secretly upwards seeking the eyes of your heart's desire in the women's gallery...

Voices. The voice of the cantor Rabbi Yisroel David the slaughterer, and the voice of my father (Z"L) during Friday evening prayers.

There was not a lot of magnificence in the Rabbinical seminary or close to the lectern of the synagogue – but here, too, there were great moments: twilight at the end of Shabbat, the "Third Meal", "Escorting the Queen" (Shabbat), or when the Rabbi came to his disciples; but above all, especially when ordinary weekdays came to the Study House: the attractive warmth in the small house, the learned preacher with his dissertation, the orthodox wedding; all added to the walls of the synagogue and the Study House a sort of Jewish overseer: the "Mizrachi" school and above it "Agudat Yisroel"...and so on. An effervescent life in such a small area, always full of movement, as if nothing ever comes to rest in the house and its rooms...children, youths, young men, old men fading away, and even the dead – all are tied together by the umbilical cord of the four embracing walls of the house.

And who were these Jews of my town from the generation before mine?

Well, it was like this, they always walked as a family group to and from the synagogue, each man with his wife. And didn't the stride of Avraham Sercaz, resemble the elegance of his father, perhaps without the secular nature of the former, the fruit of his generation and his public standing; thus strode the father of Avraham Friedrich in his traditional appearance; thus strode the father of the ritual slaughterer Burstein, or the newly–wed Abrahamowitz, twirling his silver–decorated walking stick, or Rabbi Av'czi the match–maker – warm hearted and hot tempered. Thus strode the tribes: the Czajkowski's, the Pulaski's, the Pinczowski's, the Blum's, the Fogel's, the Feigenboim's, the Lewit's, the Goldberg's, the Spiegel's, Abrahmowicz's...where is the pen that will record these offspring, this proof that they are all part of one body, that is the character, the personality of the town...let the man, Polish or otherwise, come and weave together the tapestry as its witness, that it will be seen: A Jewish town, her sons and daughters.

Thus strode our fathers and thus they stride in our hearts and we accompany them in our loving memory.

The District-City Miechow – *Powiat* [*district*] Miechow

by Yosl Charif (Astri)

Translated by Gloria Berkenstat Freund

An association with the district-city Miechow is engraved in my memories of my deepest childhood years. I always remember in my deep old age the district city when I browse in my memories of my childhood years. They stand living before me and ask for restoration, and, although I already was a young boy of 10 when I saw Miechow for the first time, I had seen many pictures of it in my imagination many years before.

The wagons from Miechow would pass before our windows in the village of Piotrkowice Wielkie that led to the highway, a dusty Polish road from Slomnik to Proszowice and back. And on such roads, my brother, Feywl, a young man, left to become a trade employee in Reb Betsalel Grinbaum's business in Miechow. How did our mother, of blessed memory, say it? When the wings grow, one has to leave. We were the only family "on the road" and what serious opportunity could there be for the children in the village?

The "Days of Awe" and the losowania [drawing of lots] – appearing for the draft in Miechow – are very differently engraved in my memory. Hartske, the oldest brother, arrived from Bendin where he worked to appear for the draft. He hated Russia, was a revolutionary and yet he went to serve.

Another year cheerfully arrived. The old one was discarded. The first thing he did was throw his hat in the fire: "Burn Fonya [contemptuous Yiddish name for Russia]," he said and his hat with red stripes around the visor flamed in the fire. I understood that in the Miechow district] things were being done with which my brother Hartske did not agree.

That the lottery was not [a thing] for Jews I knew. I also understood from this what Jews would say, that non-Jewish recruits would get drunk and throw empty bottles at the heads of Jews, particularly doing this when they were [reporting] to their regiment. Jews on the roads were not very secure with their heads. Many emptied bottles of spirits were broken over them.

The customs duty official, who had a post in the village that was not far from the Austrian border, would also travel to the district city; the Russian Orthodox families also traveled for their holidays because there was a Russian Orthodox Church there. From time to time, the Blum family's daughters, whom my mother taught to knit and to embroider, came. They carried a sort of city manner into the village.

However, the image of Reb Yosef Soyfer [scribe], a Jew with a parchment-like face, is mainly engraved in my memories; a wide grey beard, a thin nose and sad, dark eyes that sat under his forehead in which the grooves undulated on him like a sea of sorrow. He, Reb Yosef Soyfer, would come to the village of Waganowice, where a minyon [10 men needed for prayer] of village Jews would come together in Rozenblat's and Shlomo Szajntajl's mill. He would come for all of the Days of Awe because the village minyon did not have a Kohen [member of the priestly caste]. There he had to give the priestly blessing, bless the congregation. Before Musaf [additional prayers on Shabbosim and holidays] on the Days of Awe, he would immerse himself, dive under the cutting white water, even in a downpour. His body was actually transparent and his skin seemed to put together with sheets of parchment, such a strange gentleness. His figure gave the impression of a trembling leaf. Despite his poverty and difficult life, a peaceful smile always floated on his thin lips; it can be said a satisfied smile of one who was content with his lot [in life].

[Page 61]

The first time I saw Miechow was on a Friday morning, when I was put in a wagon filled with Polakoshkes [baskets made of small branches soaked in water and woven in the small villages] in which Jendrusz, our friend, took us. We had left the village at midnight. This was right after Passover. Miechow, in its slumber, was revealed to me, a 10-year old boy, as a sleeping giant, the church, the Russian Orthodox Church not far [along], with the larger market, with the country inn and when the sun became lower over the roofs, we left Miechow on the road to the Charsznica station.

Incidentally, I am reminded of a story about a hare that had run before us on the road. Jendrusz said that we would have to come back. He was correct...

We settled in Slomnik [Słomniki]. In later years when I worked and lived in Sosnowiec, I would travel through Miechow to Slomnik to my parents for the holidays or just for a quick visit. After the First World War, it occurred many times that I spent the night in Miechow and I spent the night in Bunim's son Dovid's guesthouse. I remember the heavy, yellow, wooden beds, the small iron beds that took up an entire room, stuffed with bedding, large dark rooms.

Reb Bunim's son Dovid was a Jew with a friendly smile. The breath came from him with a certainty; he looked like a Jew who makes a good living, who himself came here to stay overnight. He actually spoke of Eretz-Yisroel, of Jerusalem and a longing flashed in his eyes. He finally went to the land [of Israel] and lived here for a while and found his eternal rest here.

Our venerable teacher, Maks Erik (Zalman Merkin), the great literary-historian and Jewish researcher from Sosnowiec, also did his military service in Miechow. Later he would remember his days in Miechow where he infected the young with Labor-Zionism...

Many years separate us from those days and it is hard to believe that Jews no longer travel to Krakow, not with the local train that goes to Dzialoszyce, which is almost complete empty of Jews. One does not travel through Slomnik and certainly not through my birth village of Piotrkowice Wielkie. The inns are no longer in Jewish hands; there is no one even to ask to be protected from gentile hands...

[Page 62]

The nearby Keshionz [Książ Jews] were called the Keshionzer corpses, a strange nickname. Today there is no one living and no corpses.

High Holidays in My Parents' Home

by Getzl Levitt

Translated by Gloria Berkenstat Freund

The Jewish heart quivered with the first sound of the shofar [ram's horn], the first day of Elul [Hebrew calendar month, late August to September]. An unending fear showed in everyone's eyes; this was the fear for the coming Day of Judgment. They ran to the cemetery, traveled to the rebbes for Rosh Hashanah and they got up early every day on the Days of Repentance for Selikhos [prayers of repentance recited before Rosh Hashanah]. They shouted, poured out tears, lamented – actually would have done anything. All in order to awaken favor from the God in heaven.

The approach of the Day of Judgment was felt in every corner of our home. Our parents tried to prevail on the children, each in their way. Our father, may he rest in peace, strongly demanded that we pray with fervor, arise every day for Selikhos and read a sacred book; our mother changed completely. Her gentle nature became gentler, quieter. Her voice had an echo of an internal tremble. She asked the children sincerely and quietly to remember how we behave in the world. We should plead and pray to prepare for the Day of Judgment.

Shabbos [Sabbath] at Minkhah [afternoon prayers] in the synagogue. The artisans, the ordinary Jews, not students, recited the psalms, chapter after chapter. They were those who regularly recited [the psalms] for the public. Each one recited a day [it is traditional to recite specific psalms on different days of the week]. Moshe Kasher, Kalman Szuster and others whose names have left my memory spoke quickly, full of errors with earnest faces. Although they understood almost no words, they knew they were reciting the holy psalms and they stood before the Master of the Universe for the congregation of Jews. The words rang more sincerely, particularly for the days of Selikhos. The voices shouted louder. The recitations came out even more incomprehensible because more often the words were swallowed by tears. However, I am sure that they reached the Divine Throne. When the recitation of psalms ended, Moshele Melamed [teacher], a small, agile Jew with lively eyes, stood and recited the Minkhah prayer, a sad prayer said with longing and sadness at the departing Holy Shabbos. It became dark outside; the week approached; the heavy toil for a piece of bread. It simply cut the heart to see how the Jews had changed. They went home for the third Shabbos meal. My father wanted all of his sons at the table. The house became full of mysterious shadows. That day, during the month of Elul, the shadows were frightening, full of secrets. We washed [for the prayers before the meal], the haMotzi [prayer over the bread] was said and we immediately began to sing Shabbos songs, sad moving melodies. My mother, may she rest in peace, secretly wiped her eyes and quietly murmured: God of Abraham, of Isaac and of Jacob. The words flowed with such melancholy; a plea to God for mercy for the family and for all of the Jewish people was heard, that the incoming week should be a healthy one and with income. Her lips only whispered, no voice was heard. Therefore, her tears flowed quietly over her face and hands.

[Page 63]

My father came back from Maariv [evening prayers] He poured the glasses of wine for Havdalah [ceremony concluding Shabbos]. The Hine el Yeshuati [Behold, God is my salvation] sounded quieter than usual. We sang Hamavdil [He who separates] after Havdalah.

My father took off his silk caftan and put on his bathrobe. His face was covered with a dark cloud for the entire time. His head bent a little, his eyes turned to the ground, he smoked a cigarette and inhaled. My mother with nervous movements busied herself lighting the lamps. Someone pushed the door and with a clear "Good week, Chaiml, good week, Miriam," Shmuel Pravda (Fridenberg) came in. He shook his broad, long beard, did not say a word, sat down at the table, moved toward the lead box of tobacco, filled the small [cigarette rolling] machine, took a rolling paper and filled a cigarette. Then he tore off the tobacco that remained on the cigarette, banged it on the table several times, smoked near the Shabbos evening light and inhaled deeply after a smokeless Shabbos day. He was a quiet man, mainly listened to another talk and his only reaction was a downward shake of his head as a sign that he agreed with the other one's talk or from right to left – a sign that he did not [agree]. And in both cases the shake was vigorous, energetic and his impressive beard also shook vigorously. He was an honest man, very truthful, did not tolerate any falseness, any lies. Therefore, he had the nickname Pravda [truth in Russian]. Visiting after him was Liber Brener, a very clever Jew, more than a wise man, a small face with a Mephisto–like beard, a Mephisto–like smile with small sly eyes one of which looked east and the other west and his running, floating gaze looked across, over you, to the side, but never directly and straight in your face as if he was afraid to meet your gaze. He spoke with a smile on his face and with a crooked mouth. His words were cynical and always aimed at someone, not God forbid, to insult someone or to hurt someone, but just to give a jab for his own great pleasure and for the pleasure of everyone around him. He was just the opposite of Reb Shmuel Pravda; he entered with a satisfied, laughing face, said a loud, "Good week, Reb Chaiml, good week, Miriam, good week, Reb Shmuel!" And he sat down at the table. He did not smoke – he immediately began to tell stories, usually about the village, of his trips during the week through the villages, of the male and female peasants, their bastards, about his transactions with them. [He] listed many names of villages and tens of names of gentiles with whom he traded. He knew the most intimate details of their lives. He told with exact [details] about the constant struggle that he had to carry on against the Jewish competitors who wanted to snatch away his little bit of goods, grains and sweets.

[Page 64]

And this he said: "I discussed the matter with Picze from Komorów, that God willing, I would come very early on Thursday and take the wheat from him. I woke up at two in the morning, hitched up Spayard and drove to Komorów. I knocked on every shutter and waited. Nothing. I knocked again – a little harder – quiet. I knocked even harder. Something moved inside. Picze came out. He asked [in Polish], "What do you want, Liber?" I looked at him and my heart beat quickly.

– What do you mean what do I want? Have you forgotten that I have to take the wheat today? That Amo had agreed upon it with us? – I was shouting.

– Do not shout, you will awaken my household – he answered quietly – Judka will take the wheat. He is a more honest Jew than you. He gave an entire zloty more per measure than you.

– Is this proper for you to do, Panie [Mr.] Picze? You do such a thing? You have deceived me. You had agreed with me and you sold the same goods again to Judka?

– And you are permitted to deceive me? – Everything was boiling in me. However, it was not the gentile's fault, but Judka, may his name be erased. He can expect the devil from me. Thus I thought and I will keep my word.

– He gave a zloty more, but he will cheat you with five zlotes along the way. I know him well. Come in to the room and we will reweigh [the wheat]; you will see yourself. He did not want to go, but he went, took a candle and entered the room. The sacks stood full of aromatic wheat. I grabbed a sack, placed it on the scale, put a foot underneath and lowered the trigger of the scale. The scale sprang up, 110 kilos instead of 100.

– See, Panie Picze, that I am correct?

– The gentile asked, And you want to take the sacks at 110 kilos?

– Yes, of course! I answered. I will even lose money, but let someone else – never!

Throughout Liber's story, my father sat with his head down and his head sunk even further. However, when he began to bestow curses, he shook his head as if wanting to reject an ugly thing. He moved his hand nervously, indicating that he should stop his story. Reb Shmuel Pravda roared angrily. You have to bring out your stories for the first Selikhos? You chose [this] time to curse a Jew!" Meanwhile, other Jews came in; these were our customary Shabbos night visitors: wheat traders who traveled through the villages, bought sweets and provided them for us. They came Shabbos night to settle accounts for the entire week. Acquaintances also came to visit for a conversation along with a glass of tea.

[Page 65]

Everyone took a place around the table. The Mameshi [mother] served tea with snacks. They sat, talked, sipped the tea and ate the cookies. And in the middle they smoked a cigarette. The Mameshi constantly poured tea as soon as someone had emptied his glass. What did they talk about? They usually lamented that era's sinning world. About the young people who had entirely left the road that God had commanded. It is any wonder then that there are such calamities here? That there is no income and the gentiles want to tear out the last bite of bread from their mouths, that almost no beard is seen, also no sheitl [wig worn be pious woman] and, we should not mention this, [no use of] a mikvah [ritual bath] – so how is this a wonder [that they were being persecuted]?

Yitzhak Zalcberg, the jajczaz (egg seller), spread his hands and said with his quiet, but penetrating voice: "Go to the market, you will see what is happening outside. Young men with girls walk together without shame, a disgrace." Reb Shmuel Pravda said: And we are better? Are we the same as our fathers?

We managed to leave the completely packed room that was filled with thick cigarette smoke. In the street I breathed deeper. At line A–B[1] at the market I met all of my comrades: Moniek Kocengold, Shimkha Zibenberg, Wolf Bladi and so on. They stood and exchanged gossip. I wanted to walk, not stand. Moniek left with me to march around the market. We spoke about literature and art. Our pace became faster, more impulsive. We forgot the entire world around us. We became more deeply involved in our conversation. The moon shown and covered the houses, the trees, the strollers with a muffled, intimate light. We floated to a higher world; we were torn away from the earth. Suddenly we stopped. We looked around. The young men continued to stroll. Young girls passing by threw thirsty looks at us. We retuned to earth. We were young. Our blood flowed in our veins. We sent passionate glances accompanied by suitable words – Selikhos with its crying and prayer was forgotten. Life goes on! Yet I instinctively looked at the city clock. It was already 11. My parents would be aggravated. I quickly went home and quietly entered the house. Because I wanted to do so more quietly, I imagined that the door had never scraped as loud as this time. The group already had dispersed. I took a few steps and got entangled in a chair and it fell. My father gave me an angry glance and said:

– Of course, if one, long may he live, comes late, is it a surprise?

I felt strong regret.

We began to prepare for Selikhos. There was a solemn mood in the emptiness of the house. The Mameshi rearranged her sheitl [wig worn by pious women]. Her eyes expressed complete optimism and goodness. She prayed with her soul, without words, and asked for mercy. Her eyes seemed to be covered by fog; these were the tears that she had tried to hold in. She searched the holiday prayer book and the woman's prayer book and the will of God for what to say and for what to ask. The Tateshi [father], his forehead wrinkled, put on his silk kaftan with the gartl [belt made of strings worn during prayer to separate the upper and lower parts of a man's body]. Meanwhile, he thought. A person needs to look inside himself, in his own heart, in the sense: "And purify our hearts to serve You in truth." One must purify his own heart so that he can reach the true level and be worthy and to attain the true taste of repentance and, thinking this, he already felt elevated. The clouds that had covered his forehead for the entire evening left; his look became clear.

[Page 66]

– Children, we have to go to Selikhos – his voice rang quietly, solemnly. The Mameshi could not control herself. The tears were stronger than her will. –

There already was a considerable crowd in the synagogue. The entire synagogue was brightly lit. The light covered everyone's face with a holiness and solemnity. This time it was another light, as if it had flowed and come from other worlds. And this created a holy, serious mood. The Jews, rested after Shabbos and dressed in their Shabbos clothing, talked among themselves with half muffled voices, as if afraid to disturb the holy atmosphere of the synagogue. –

The synagogue filled. All of the seats were taken. The passageways were full of worshippers. Young and old, several generations. The same for the women's synagogue [section]. A buzz as if from a beehive was heard from above. –

Twelve [o'clock] neared. Shmuel Khazan [the cantor], or Shmuel Szenker, already had come from the mikvah [ritual bathhouse] with his hair washed, with wet peyes [side curls]. [He] entered the synagogue with quick steps, with his large booted feet, his face in concentration, his eyes nervously squeezed together and did not see what was happening around him. Yosl Shamas [the sexton], or Yosl Shuster [the shoemaker], with his two–meter [6 foot 5 inches] height, stood and waited at the reading desk. Shmuel Khazan went to the cantor's reading desk and began to put on his talis [prayer shawl] and with open eyes looked at his assistants, the "choir," the Rozenkranc brothers, Kalman Shuster's sons. Yosl the Shamas banged the table. He said something with his toothless mouth. It was supposed to be: "A beautiful silence during prayer." But a strange roar came out. It became so quiet that the flying of a bird could be heard. It even became quiet in the woman's synagogue. The women prepared their handkerchiefs, ready for the struggle [with their tears]. As soon as Shmuel Khazan began to prayer, they would turn to the Master of the Universe; they would attack with so many tears and pleas that He would have no other recourse and would have to provide a good year. What then – would they let [a bad year happen]? They would be quiet? And Shmuel Khazan did immediately begin his Yisgadal v'yiskadash [Magnified and sanctified... the opening words of Kaddish – the mourner's prayer] with feeling and fervor, like an electrical storm had gone through the fully packed synagogue. The congregation moved like a cradle; a shout came out of everyone's mouth. Voices, high and still higher carried from their hearts straight to heaven. Shmuel Khazan had to wait until the congregation calmed itself to be able to end the prayer: "Oh, the soul is Yours and the body is Your handiwork" – so alas what is a person? So, forgive us, God, and [do not punish us] with suffering. "May God save us." Shmuel Khazan prayed with great rapture and religious ecstasy. His feet did not stay on the ground; his body moved from left to right and his hands were not still for a second. He brought new melodies of his own composition to the first Selikhos [prayers of repentance recited before Rosh Hashanah] and the congregation prayed heartily, with feeling and with tears like a river that flows downstream with noise and like a storm, without interruption, until little by little the storm was quieted. The congregation groaned deeply and a smile appeared on their faces. The first battle had ended and they were sure of a victory. Things would be good! The One in heaven would take pity on them and give them a good year. The congregation dispersed with this good feeling.

[Page 67]

In the morning: a Sunday like every Sunday of the year. The shops were closed; it was quiet and calm in the street. The gajes [gentiles] were in the Catholic Church, in the "tumah" [pejorative word for church, also meaning impure]. Groups of Jews, the so–called "shtekelekh Yidn" [Jews with canes or walking sticks] were in the streets walking back and forth.[2] They told stories or jokes and waited for their clients to leave the Catholic Church. The wild clang of a bell was heard at 12 o'clock. All at once, dozens of bells, coarse baritones, middle–altos and very thin sopranos, each alone, poured out their sounds into the void. And with the flood of ringing bells that filled the hearts of the Jews, particularly the Jewish children, with fear, a flood of people began to leave the Catholic Church. Hundreds and thousands of peasants in their peasant clothing that gleamed with dozens of colors, bright, shouting men in their long white [hooded] smocks – the sukmanes – of coarse wool with wide, brown leather belts. The women [were] in very wide, colorful dresses sewn with encircling colorful ribbons. The shops threw open their doors and windows. The village gentiles and their wives and children began to buy. A few gentiles from the villages also would come to us to receive payment for sweets they had delivered the previous week, entering, sitting comfortably in the kitchen until it will filled with them. One of them usually asked: How are you? And a conversation began to develop about real, political themes, mainly about wars. Meanwhile, my father brought in a bottle of whisky and small glasses, poured, offered it and my mother carried in cookies and snacks. Each [emptied] the small glass right into his throat and took a cookie. Thus a half–hour passed. My father sighed after their departure: "Even on the holy days of Selikhos [s [prayers of repentance recited before Rosh Hashanah] we have to to deal with the gentiles who come immediately from church. Everything for a livelihood! We are still in exile."

[Page 68]

And thus passed the days of Selikhos. During the day, ordinarily, there was the chase after income. At night in the synagogue and in the morning awakening from the best sleep, springing from a warm bed, rapidly and tremblingly they threw on their clothes and walked in the cool night through the dark streets to the synagogue.

Erev Rosh Hashanah [the eve of the New Year] arrived. Our hearts were full of expectation. People's heads were bent deeper in humility. The children tried not to laugh too loud and not to fool around too much. A cloud covered every face. My mother and sisters were busy in the kitchen. [They] busied themselves, cleaned, washed and prepared the traditional foods. {They] cooked carrots, worked so that there would be a fish head for each male, a fruit for Shekheyonu.[3] My mother, as usual, hurried and rushed us not to be late. Fear of the Day of Judgment was recognizable in all of her movements. All of the rooms were cleaned by nightfall; all of the foods were cooked, all of the children had had their hair washed and were dressed for the holiday. Everything was ready to welcome the distinguished and holy guest: the arriving New Year. It was solemn and earnest; it was not only a New Year that was coming, it also was the Day of Judgment!

My mother dressed in white, began to bless the candles. She lit the candles and all of the candlesticks and simultaneously the tears ran from her eyes. Everyone stood around the table and watched intently. A holy quiet reigned. We heard the candles tremble until they flared up. The candles did not look like simple candles this time, but like holy creatures, souls that shine with a secret flame. The Mameshi [mother] spread her hands and covered her eyes with them. The candles whispered quietly and through her fingers, quickly and quietly, flowed her tears, many, many tears, warm, erev Rosh Hashanah tears from a real, sincere Jewish mother. We all stood quietly and cried with her. We went to pray; at the door our father turned around and wished: You all should pray for a good year! Tears rang in his voice. It was clear, bright in the synagogue. There was a short pause after Minkhah [afternoon prayers]. The congregation heartfully recited the prayer [in Hebrew], "May the old year with its ordeals end and the new year with its blessings begin." And finally, may the old year with its ordeals end and may the New Year with its blessing begin. We began the Maariv [evening prayers]. We prayed with heart [in

Hebrew]. "(O God) cast your fear upon" – God, cast your fear on all of your creations, and rule over the entire world – [in Hebrew] "King, You alone [rule] over the entire world and let there be an end to all suffering!" – And let cruelty dissipate like smoke.

Having finished praying, they exchanged best wishes. There was a tumult, a clamor, everyone pushed and stuck out their hands: A good year and may you be inscribed [in the Book of Life]! A good year Reb Chaiml, Moshe, Shlomoh! Health, income and pleasure from the children! The children should be freed from gentile hands! They wished for everything, for every possible and impossible blessing. They entered the house with a wide "Gut yom–tov!" [good holiday] and again wished the Mameshi and one a good year and may you be inscribed [in the Book of Life]. We made the Kiddush [blessing over wine] loudly and solemnly. We sat down for the meal. My father loved to give his opinion of the holiday foods. Mainly, he praised the carrots and, perhaps for the thousandth time, said that in Karlsbad a doctor told him that if the peasant knew how much health is stuffed into each carrot, he would ask for 100 a piece. The cheerful mood that had reigned over the eating changed at the blessing [at the end of the meal]. They said the blessing with religious fervor; then their eyes began to stick together [from their tears]. The earlier tears, then the fat meal and wine had an effect. The children fell asleep at the table. The Tateshi [father] sat studying Mishnius [Oral Torah] – the Rosh Hashanah tractate. Despite being tired, the Mameshi sat and listened to my father's studying. –

[Page 69]

In the morning, the Mameshi woke up everyone. The congregation in the synagogue recited Psalms before the prayers. Mordekhai Mulsztajn began the blessing and recited verses from the Book of Psalms. Yisroel–Dovid the shoykhet [ritual slaughterer] called out HaMeylekh [The King] with heart and feeling and prayed Shakharis [morning prayers]. His sons, Elimelekh and Rafael, helped him and he prayed as the women had specified; it broke their hearts. "V'yeasu kulam agudah akhat" ["May we bound together in one bond"] – and everyone should be bound together – he asked in his falsetto voice. "La'asot ritzonkha b'levav shalem" ["To do the Divine will with a full heart"] – we should do your desire with our whole heart. After reading – a pause. It was a custom that many acquaintances came to us on both days of Rosh Hashanah between Shakharis and Musaf to drink coffee. The Mameshi cooked a large kettle of aromatic coffee for this purpose and served everyone however much one wanted and, in addition, she pleaded again: Drink another glass. The kettle stood on the stove and was warmed. –

The pause ended. The blowing of the shofar [ram's horn]! The congregation hurried and began to run back to the synagogue. A shiver went through the body. The congregation covered their heads with their talisim [prayer shawls]. The Shamas banged the table loudly: Lamnatseysekh [For the song master]! The congregation swayed and sang, enraptured. After the Tkies [blowing of the shofar], Shmuel the Khazan prayed Musaf with fervor, with passion, as was his habit. He sang many new melodies. After praying, there again were good wishes. They returned to the synagogue right after eating to pray Minkhah and for Tashlikh [usually the casting of crumbs, symbolizing one's sins, into running water as a symbol of atonement]. Everyone left for Chasznicer Street to the river. They recited prayers and shook out their pockets. Gentile boys stood opposite them, mocking and ridiculing the Jews and their customs. It was already dark on the way back. One must not sleep on Rosh Hashanah, so the majority of the congregation returned to the synagogue to wait for Maariv. Coming home from Maariv, they again wished Lashanah Tovah, made Kiddush and sat at the table. The mood was not as serious on the second evening, more of a holiday than like the Day of Judgment. After eating, my father went out for a short stroll. As usual there was no moon, and every time he said to me: "See, the moon is hidden because it does not want to be a witness against the Jews. The second day of Rosh Hashanah passed in the same way as the first. However, the ardor and fervor was a little weaker, cooler during the prayers. My mother repeated this fact every year during mealtime and, contented, she was covered in tears at the blessing, as support for the weak prayers of the congregation at the synagogue. After eating, my father said that we should not sleep on Rosh Hashanah, but instead of occupying ourselves with foolishness and speaking nonsense, it was better to sleep. But do not commit any transgressions.

[Page 70]

The days between Rosh Hashanah and Yom Kippur were outwardly similar to the rest of the days of the year. People worked. But it was still different. Jews protected themselves from arguing, stopped using curses and the like. "One should not open one's mouth for the devil." Even the teachers hit and cursed their kheder-yinglekh [religious primary school students] less. We would have compassion for one another and, in merit of this, may God have compassion for us. The days were mostly beautiful, bright, sunny. The heat had gone; the weather was warm and mild. It affected the mood and gave a person a moral lesson: it had just been the burning summer and now cool winds had been blowing. Everything in the world was ephemeral! Therefore, people reflected and did as much repentance as they could!

The congregation really did try to repent in their thoughts with prayers and also with deeds. They gave charity generously and with desire. Various Jews appeared with unknown faces, with long beards and peyes [side curls]. They entered with serious faces, loaded with various pamphlets with letters of recommendation, displaying their goods with a certain pride. They had [the goods] to sell! These were the pamphlets from various Yeshivus [religious secondary schools], societies, such as Hakhnoses Kalah [assistance for poor brides], and others. The goods were in demand then. The Tateshi gave to everyone, but it did not conceal a certain worry on his face. Every evening he would say to my mother: “God protect us from the evil eye, I separated myself [from them] as the Vistula [River] does from the entire world, and however much one gives they want more. Go and tell everyone that these are difficult times. Will they believe me? They think I am a rich man.”

My mother consoled him: “Do not worry. Is what you give yours? One does not become poor from giving. God will send more.

– Yes, it is easy for you to say, [ignoring] everyday promissory notes and payments. There are worries about everything.

There were Jews who were lively and joyful as they were the rest of the year despite the 10 days [between Rosh Hashanah and Yom Kippur]. When they entered, it became cheerful for the children. They were offered something [to eat]. Someone spoke. For a small glass of whisky they told beautiful stories and sang a cheerful song. My mother was not happy. – [They] found time for a foolish song. Yet it was erev [the eve of] Yom Kippur in the world! However, the children had not abandoned [foolish things]... Kalman the shoemaker was such a cheerful type. A Jew in his 80s, but lively, with a smiling face and full of humor. He came in, sat down, and after refreshments, he told stories about his long years of military service with the Russians. He played in a folk orchestra.

[Page 71]

Then he sang the children's favorite song. He sang with a hoarse voice, half Russian, half Polish and broke both languages:

Avram, Avram, Avram, Avram our father

Why do you not walk, why do you not fight, why, Pan [master or mister], do you not ask [to get us out of military service]?

Headquarters called us

Headquarters [sent] us

To where? Our country!

Finally, the song [turned to] Yitzhak and to Yakov Avinu [our father]. And he told a story woven with a song about Reb Ruvin Ber. The Jew was a respected businessman in the shtetl and a learned man. In his later years, sad to say, he became impoverished. For the lack of a choice, he bought a horse and a wagon, hired a young gentile boy who carried passengers from the train, from Charsznica to Miechow and supported himself with this. On the cold, frosty Shabbosim [Sabbaths], on the short days, it was necessary to leave a little before night to be there for the arrival of the train. The gentile boy was too lazy. It was warm for him in his boss's room. He could not just tell the gentile boy to go. It was Shabbos! But night was arriving and it was getting late. The gentile boy stood near the oven and warmed himself. The frost burned – but one had to earn a few groshn for oneself, for the gentile boy and mainly for the income provider, for the horse. It already was past Minkhah at Ruwin Ber's; he washed for the third Shabbos meal and instead of the Shabbos song Bnei Heikhala [The Sons of the Palace], he sang a song to the gentile boy in peasant Polish so that he [the boy] would understand what he (Ruwin] was talking about:

Kiedy Antek mandri bal

Tabi konia zapszangal

Na Stacie bi paiechal

Pare groszy i zarabial

Prędzej, prędzej ba puczna da paczangu.[4]

And in Yiddish it is:

If Antek would have had sense

He would have harnessed the horse

He would have gone to the station

And earned a few groshn.

Quicker, quicker, because it is late to go to the train.

We children laughed heartily at the story of the song. The time now came for [reading] letters with good wishes. These were not messages printed with three words that had been printed in advance years ago; they were letters that flowed right from the heart, from relatives, acquaintances, in–laws, usually short as opposed to detailed, with details about the worries and joys of the children who lived in various cities in Poland. Sometimes a postscript from a grandchild also appeared in a letter. My father would sit peacefully to read the letter, put on his glasses and comfortably read it aloud. My mother and the younger children listened. These were intimate letters, warm, with stories about various trivialities of daily life, but for us everything was interesting, real and spoke to the heart. Each letter ended with a request that my parents should [take a] few days and come to them and see the new grandchild who had entered the world, how beautifully it was developing. My mother, as usual, wiped her eyes. My father said to her – "Why are you crying, Miriam? Praise God that we have pleasure and we have good news from afar. Do you remember what I would say when the children were small? When we are old, if we live, I will not [be able to] take off the silk jacket with the satin hat. Here one child will invite me to a bris [ritual circumcision], a second to an engagement, a wedding. See, it is beginning to come true."

[Page 72]

Then they began to answer all the letters from the children with many details, with devotion, with motherly sincerity and fatherly thoroughness. [He] gave advice and instructions. [He] thought over every inquiry with his brain and heart and answered. No tears fell. It was erev Yom Kippur and what could be better at such a moment than a warm blessing from parents?

A separate chapter in my home was the best kind. How alive the radiant faces of my parents appear before my eyes when they did someone a favor and not just during the ten days of repentance but every day of the year. They were even ready at night to help everyone with an interest–free loan, a donation, advice, an intercession with the Jewish community where my father was a parnes [elected member of the community council] as well as with the head of the community where my father was a councilman (I think). Arbitration between spoiled partners – the trials took place at our home with force and cursing, conflicts between married couples for dozens of important and unimportant reasons. Mostly, the wives were victims of maltreatment by their heartless husbands. My father almost always decided for the women in the conflicts between husband and wife. He would say that she was the weaker one [and] needed to be supported. Even when the woman was not completely correct. Mainly, [he] tried to make peace between the couple. When he achieved this, he concluded by adding some strong words to the man!

I still remember my early childhood. This was in Tsarist times. My father was young then, full of courage, mature, carried on a great deal of foreign business, possessed a large mill and an estate. [He] was an eminent man and a community worker. And people sneaked past my eyes like a dream, deep, bizarre, detached, with a deep fear in their eyes. [On] dark, moonless nights, they came to us through the kitchen entrance. Many times – young women carrying tiny children in their arms. I later learned who they were, namely, the Jews were preparing to escape to Krakow, which then belonged to Austria. They were persecuted at the Tsarist–Austrian border. The path of the unfortunate ones led them into our house. They were given help. My father, as councilman in the city hall, issued false passports (they were called przepustkas) with false names, on his personal responsibility, and the Jews were sent to Krakow. There they were beyond every danger and could travel to work. My father hired a smuggler of renown, paid him and he [the smuggler] smuggled the person over to the Austrian side. My mother, wringing her hands, would beg my father: "Chaim, you are causing misfortune. Have mercy on your small children." My father considered this for a moment: It was hopeless; after a short deliberation, he said, "We must have mercy on them, they are Jews." My mother did not let it go, "And I and the children and you?" But it did not help at all. Telling them to go would have meant sending them back right into the mouth of the animal and the joy in the house was great when the agreed to sign was received that they had crossed the border and had successfully arrived. Eh, documents? Money? Such Chaim Lewits, Jews with warm hearts, who also cared, also were in Krakow. When we boys were grown up, our house was a meeting place for the young, mainly for the students and more advanced young people. Door and gate always stood open. Whoever left his home without a designated purpose came to us. He met someone here, a conversation started. They forgot when they came, why and when they needed to go home. Sometimes they went out for a stroll. During the day they went to Kamadower Road. Everything here was green and smelled of the freshness of a meadow, with rich earth, wheat and field flowers. It was a splendid landscape. We absorbed the amazing aroma of the singing and swaying around us and carried on discussions. What was there that we did not wrangle about and debate? About Kellerman's book that had just been published or about Ernberg who had just then written his anti–communist creations, or about other writers, looked all over for ideals, mainly those that were close to our own ideals. Everything interested us, every new idea, every new political direction and painting, art, philosophy grabbed us.

[Page 73]

A well of memories bubbles up in me. My heart is full; in my head is a desire to share it all. My desire is mirrored here, although in a small amount – the atmosphere that then reigned in our home and in thousands, thousands of Jewish houses in Poland 25–30 years before the annihilation.

I turn to the Ten Days of Repentance. We kept preparing for the real Day of Judgment.

[Page 74]

The heart was enveloped in a stronger fear on erev Yom Kippur: we had to stand before a court. We took part in malkos [the symbolic flagellation on the eve of Yom Kippur], we lay on the steps of the synagogue altar and the Shamas counted 39 small blows with a rod, counting up three times the verse Vehu Rakhum [He, the merciful one].

The women in the family were busy in the kitchen. They had so much to prepare. Two meals for today, erev Yom Kippur, and for the children who did not fast in the morning, and for the evening for the entire family after the fast they made kreplakh [small dumplings usually filled with meat]. I shaped them; this was my most beloved work.

We sat for the first meal. We ate quietly, without conversation. There was a nervous mood, a mood of waiting. After eating, my father went to the mikhvah [ritual bath], a cold [water] mikhvah. I loved to go along, without heat was without sweat. We soaped ourselves and poured buckets of cold water over ourselves – a delight!

After the mikhvah we went to the synagogue for Minkhah. Poor men of all kinds and all sorts of the world's cripples stood arranged in front of the synagogue and they demanded donations with pleas, crying, insolence, prayers and curses. This was the moment and they had to make use of it and all means were legitimate. In the synagogue the mood was one of half holy place and half market. Jews busily ran back and forth, exchanged money, borrowed, ran up to the dozens of plates, kayres [plates at the synagogue entrance for contributions on the eve of Yom Kippur] – for all kinds of charity institutions, for private people. shamosim [sextons] and among all of them, the plate for the community in Eretz–Yisroel – without an end. It was hard to put together a minyon [10 men required for prayer] for Minkhah. With the Minkhah prayers we were entering Yom Kippur. At the end of Shemoneh Esrei [18 benedictions recited three times a day], we recited al khet [Yom Kippur prayer of confession of one's sins]. People hit their hearts with enthusiasm and began the first Yom Kippur tears.

My mother, as usual, hurried and was afraid that she would be late, although there still was time. We sat at the table for the second meal. My mother pleaded: "Eat children, it is a mitzvah [commandment, more commonly translated as good deed] to eat today. The food today is counted as fasting." My mother ate very little and her mood was soaked in tears. Before the blessing after eating, we said that we should be permitted to drink right after the blessing. We recited the blessing and after the blessing we drank black coffee – a means so that we would not be thirsty at night – and my mother stood reciting the blessing on the candles. She recited the blessing enraptured, with the entire fervor of a deeply believing soul. Her tears quietly flowed; she prayed with ardor and poured out her heart to God and pleaded for her children and grandchildren, for her husband and for the Jewish people. This lasted a considerable time. The children stood in awe and waited, like one waits for the Khazan leading the collective prayer, for him to end the prayer. My father already was dressed in his kitl [white, linen robe worn by men on Yom–Kippur] over his silk kaftan and the white yarmulke [skull cap] on his head. When my mother finished lighting the candles, my father began to bless the children. One after the other approached, my father laid his hands on the children's heads and whispered, "May you be like [Ephraim and Menashe]"... and his eyes became full of tears.

[Page 75]

Everyone was ready to go to pray. Here Jews began to arrive with good wishes. Even before the blessing, Uncle Yekutiel arrived; [he was] my mother's brother, a tall and broad Jew with a pair of large and wide hands that rose in the air like a pair of oars. At the same time he turned on his seat with such power that we always thought he had broken it. He sat at the table for a while, said: "May it happen!" He stuck his giant hand in my father's and said in a coarse voice: "So, may you have a good year, G'mar Hatima Tova [May you be sealed in the Book of Life], a gut yom–tov [a good holiday]!" And he left. Then Yarme Blum, my mother's nephew, a short one, came in, came in with quick steps, his head a bit forward. On his face, a sort of doubtful cry, doubtful laugh; he went immediately to my father, said, “Uncle Chaiml! May you have a healthy year, Aunt Miriam! Have a good year.” More relatives and acquaintances came. Everyone gave quick, good wishes and everyone left for the synagogue. Walked and gave good wishes.

The synagogue was almost full. Everyone in kitlen [white, linen robes worn by men on Yom–Kippur], white yarmulkes, talisim [prayer shawls] – everything white, even socks. On the synagogue altar and on the windows stood long and small boxes filled with sand and stuck with burning memorial candles. They gave off an eerie luster, holy and secretive, something not of this world. The majority already were reciting the confessional prayer, not reciting, but crying out and moaning it deeply, singing with great fervor. They saw and felt as if the soul were squirming in great sorrow and regretted the sins they had done; [they] made a spiritual appraisal, a calculation of their body and limbs and the pain in the body and pain in the soul that was in the body! Then they asked one another for forgiveness for insults, for dishonest business, for each sin. There were Jews who cried in asking for forgiveness from someone. He must forgive him so that God would forgive him. – Yosl the Shamas [sexton] banged sharply on the table. Quiet. The respected ones in the synagogue went up to the Ark, taking out the Torah scrolls from the Ark, circled the reading platform with slow steps and the first one said and repeated the verse: “Light is sown for the righteous and for the upright of heart, gladness.” The Ark remained open until they returned. Shmuel the Khazan and the choirboys stood at the lectern. They began to sing the Kol Nidre [Aramaic prayer recited preceeding the Yom Kippur eve service]. A suffocating cry went across the congregation. An echoing lament was heard from the women's section. Shmuel the Khazan sang louder and louder. The men sang in an undertone with the same notes, each in his own way. And all of the voices blended together and created a powerful shout to heaven. There were not only pleas for mercy, but also shouts of pain from a tortured and persecuted people, a protest against constant insults and humiliations, for suffering, pains. Everything found an expression in these shouts and cries, the entire embitteredness of the tortured souls in the past and of the fear for the future. After Kol Nidre, everything was silent: Maariv was prayed more quietly, more calmly. After the silent Shemoneh Esrei [recitation of the 18 blessings], the Khazan [cantor] again presented his melodies for the liturgical poems. He created a fresh march for the Yeyles [Yom Kippur prayer – “Shall ascend”] and sang Ki Hinei [Behold] with courage with his choirboys. Then Ki Hinei Kakhomer Beyad Hayotzeir

["As clay in the hand of a potter"] crying and touchingly – Thus we are in Your hands, God, make of us whatever you wish. After Maariv, they wished each other a good year. Some went home, but most remained to recite Shir HaYikhud [Song of Unity], a long poem in stanzas that is especially dedicated to sing of the greatness, the powerfulness, the beauty and goodness of the Creator of the world. The mood at the crescendo of saying this was mild, excited, elevated. They did not ask for mercy, they did not lament about hardships. They sang a song of praise, an ode to the Creator – and why should they, too, not be elevated – when He is our Ruler? It was a mild, tender mood, an idyll between a couple, between the Creator of the World and his people, Israel.

[Page 76]

After Shir HaYikhud my father went home. My mother was waiting, sitting and smiling comfortably. Her eyes were still damp from her tears, but she felt like a victor after a struggle, although the struggle had not yet ended, but she was sure of final victory. He is still a merciful and gracious God.

In the morning, we again had to appear for the attack. We strode again. My mother hurried: "Children, time does not stand still." Everyone was in the synagogue. They again shouted, pleaded, said prayers of confession while beating their chests and the women's section with their weapon: a well of tears. And it flowed to heaven in self–accusation: we have sinned with eating, with drinking, sinned in watching, in walking, in speaking and with what [did we not sin]? But You, God, remember that we are weak creatures. We have come from the earth and to the earth we will return. We risk our lives for a piece of bread, we are compared to a shadow that disappears, to a dream that flies away and to a wind that blows.

Time moved slowly. Heads hurt from hunger, the eyes from tears. Small bottles of smelling salts appeared in the synagogue. One sniffed such a bottle; there was a strong twist in the nose and one woke up. The fathers told the small children to go home to eat. Although they were very hungry, they did not want to give in, but to strengthen themselves, and remain for a little while longer in the synagogue. They wanted to show that they already were big and would fast an entire day! Although they themselves did not believe this, they dreamed of the heroism with which they would have been able to boast to all of their friends. And with what pride they would have come home in the evening and sat at the table with all of the adults to "have breakfast" after the difficult fast! However, little by little they all went home and returned [to the synagogue] sated, but unsatisfied with their own weakness, disappointed.

It already was after the reading; they were praying Musaf [additional prayers for Shabbos and holidays], the spoken Shemoneh Esrei. The congregation proceeded with the greatest determination; we began to say Unsane–toykef ["Let us speak of the awesomeness..."]. We were hungry, we were thirsty, but who felt weak? Unsane–toykef flowed so that the walls shook; the day was frightening and terrifying; how could we calm ourselves when the angels in heaven were trembling and a fear enveloped them when the quiet call, "Here is the Day of Judgment!" was heard? Everything was being judged there, all living creatures: who would live and who would die; who in fire and who in water. But repentance, prayer and charity could save a person from the grave decree... Shadows began to appear in the synagogue. The candles lit for the dead began to tremble and flare and added a fear and otherworldly strangeness. The congregation sat weakened. Minkhah. My father prayed at the lectern. [He had a] claim on it. He said that every year before Minkhah he felt very weak, but when he went to the lectern, he felt an influx of fresh strength over his entire body – Neilah [the concluding Yom Kippur prayer]! The congregation woke up. They prepared with renewed strength. The last phase of the journey. They must obtain a good year through prayer!

[Page 77]

Yisgadal! {Glorified – the first word of the Kaddish prayer, in Aramaic.] Everyone jumped up from his seat; the special Neilah melody awoke and demanded its due: strengthen and gird your loins! The silent Shemoneh Esrei was transformed little by little into a shout – thus the quiet prayer flowed stronger and more powerful with rapture, fervor and loud shouts. They said the spoken Shemoneh Esrei, the congregation stood on their feet and thundered: [in Hebrew] "Open the gate for us now when the gates are closing!" Open, God, the gates of prayer, of mercy and grace; open them wide, before you close them. And thus continued the encounter without a break, without interruption, with tears, shouts and pleas, until the tekiah [the longest sound made by a shofar or ram's horn] and the Divine Presence departed. Hurrying through the Maariv [evening prayers] they again gave each other good wishes; they already had prayed for a good year, but were not yet home! They recited the blessing for the new moon! Finished, having reveled under the moon, they rushed home.

The table already was set with all kinds of good things. My mother had run home and prepared everything: wine, preserves, butter cookies and other baked goods. The coffee already was placed on the oven and was cooking and waiting for those fasting. They made Havdalah [prayer recited ending Shabbosim and holidays] and sat to have a quick snack; the hot coffee and baked goods smelled good. They had a little to eat and went out to the sukkah [booth or tabernacle, a temporary structure in which the meals for the Sukkos holiday – the Feast of Tabernacles – are eaten]. Even after such a fast! They hammered in a peg. They sat back down at the table. My mother's face beamed. They spoke about the problems of the past day, cheerful, in an elevated mood. Who had fainted; who had to leave right in the middle of praying because of weakness; about the Bale–Tefilus [readers of prayers on holidays] and their praying. This occurred at the close of every Yom Kippur. My mother, the great intercessor for the Jewish people, talking about Yom Kippur, always cried, saying: Looking down from the women's synagogue [section] one sees from above the Jews, all wrapped in talisim [prayer shawls], kitlen [white, linen robes worn by men on Yom–Kippur], white yarmulkes [skullcaps], standing in hunger and thirst, praying, crying and shouting. They look like angels. Could another people want to and do so, besides Jews? And why should not the Master of the Universe finally take pity on us and redeem us from bitter exile? And why should there not be an end to our troubles? Why is He silent and for what is He waiting? – thus she argued with the Master of the Universe after every Yom–Kippur.

[Page 78]

Thus were the Days of Awe for us and thus was celebrated the holy Yom Kippur that is exclusively and particularly for our people. The Yidishkeit [Jewish way of life] was not only a way of life, a form. It was a deep feeling, a holy flame that burned and warmed hearts and souls, flared up in a giant fire when the moment was suitable or drew in, but always smoldered and never was extinguished.

All of this no longer exists. A bloody flood erased everything. May these words, written with longing, sorrow and anger, be a bit of a matzevah [headstone] for that which has disappeared.

Translator's Footnotes

1. Line A–B refers to the designation of buildings about the perimeter of the market.
2. A man should not carry a cane or walking stick on the Sabbath under Jewish religious law. Shtekelekh Yidn were more assimilated and did so.
3. Shekheyonu is a blessing recited at each major holiday when tasting a fruit for the first time in the season in which the holiday falls.
4. The above is a transliteration from Yiddish of the song's broken, error–filled Polish lyrics.

Memories from Before the First World War

by Chaim Zalcberg

Translated by Gloria Berkenstat Freund

As was related by the esteemed elders of the shtetl [town], the first Jews in the 1870's were the following: 1) Naftali Hertsl Zalcberg, 2) Mendl Kurland, 3) Kupczik, 4) Lewit, 5) Bunem Fajgenbaum, 6) Milsztajn, 7) Moshe Josef Wejl, 8) Ruwin the watchmaker, 9) Mekhl Bornsztajn, 10) Yoal Zalcman. At that time there was no kohen [member of the priestly class] and when a kohen was needed he was brought from Kshoynzh [Ksiaz Wielki], where there was an old Jewish community. It should be understood that the kohen was brought on the holidays, when the priestly blessing was needed and he received his meals and a place to sleep from one of the Jews in Miechow.

There was a pogrom in Miechow in 1919 and my father, Naftali Hertsl, was severely wounded in his residence then and he died a week later. The entire shtetl mourned for a long time for this innocent Jew.

There was a district commandant, Arlof, in the earlier years, who was descended from a tsarist family and his line extended to Tsar Nicholai. It happened that this Arlof took the beautification of the shtetl as his purpose, that it would have a European appearance. He ordered that the statue of the Holy Mary, which had stood there for dozens of years, be taken from the market and he arranged to plant trees in all corners of the marketplace. He also decided to pave the remaining area of the market with stones.

The statue of Mary was brought to a special building, which had been built then in a side street, which extended past the small hill, and the Christians and peasants from all of the villages marched in their processions at the time of their holidays.

[Page 79]

In addition, the commandant, Arlof, built a church at the new market that was to serve as a gathering place for the Pravoslavna [Orthodox church] for the entire area.

Over many years Reb Natan Borensztajn, Reb Yitzhak Zalcberg, Reb Chaim Lewit, Reb Avrahamthse Fridrich, Reb Avraham Sercacz [and] Reb Moshe Olszewski were well–known members of the community council.

The author left Miechow in 1913 and emigrated to America. After the rise of the land [of Israel], he settled in Israel.

Miechow – general view from the northwest

[Page 80]

B. Cultural and Educational Establishments

The "Heder" and Teachers in Miechów

By Moshe Spiegel

Translated by Selwyn Rose

In 1913, one year before the outbreak of World War One, when I was a 3-year old child, my father, Avraham Spiegel (Z"L) decided to enroll me in Reb Aba'leh Malamud's "Heder".

I don't think there was a single child in those days that didn't pass through those first "Aleph-Bet" classes. Both my father and his entire generation learned there. During my time there, Reb Aba'leh was a man somewhere in his seventies. Nevertheless, he still had all his vigor and his wife bore him a son whom they named Hillel. Reb Abba Lewit a neighbor of Reb Aba'leh "Baby-face" Malamud was a short broad-bodied man with eyes expressing his good-nature. He habitually visited the homes of his little pupils and discussed their development and progress in "Hebrew" and "Chumash" with the parents. The little children of the Heder sat at a long table, learning their lessons together with their "Rabbi". During the long winter days we returned home with an enclosed lighted candle, to light the way home in the dark streets of the town. More than once Aba'leh's loyal helper, Reuven Lewit would accompany us home. Reuven survived the Nazi Holocaust and is here, in Israel with us.

Our studies continued every day from seven in the morning until the late evening hours but during the afternoon, while Rabbi Aba'leh had his afternoon nap, we were looked after by the "Rebbetzen" and she worked us very hard. The Rabbi had a few goats that he milked, providing him with a small additional source of income. Since they had no pasture available, we, the pupils would bring them old dry bread from home that we cut into small pieces with knives and that, for the goats, was virtually the only food they had, roaming around his yard.

The classes with Reb Aba'leh lasted for three years and when I was 6 he said to my parents that my knowledge of the Chumash and Rashi was greater than his own and that I should be sent to a more learned instructor.

So, I went to study under the "Litvak". We didn't know his name but everyone called him the "Litvak" because he came from Lithuania. As was usual with the Lithuanian Jews – whom we nicknamed "Tselem–Kop" – he was learned and a scholar, but easily angered and we occasionally suffered from smacks for minor offences or for any attempt to avoid working diligently. His gaze was piercing and penetrating so that we froze when he looked at us. His "Heder" was in Shlomo Scheintal's yard on Krakowie(?) street and in our haste to breathe a little freely and as a slight release from the heavy burden that the "Litvak" placed upon us, we exploited his little herd of goats and sneaked out. Behind his yard was the bakery of Yankel Becker, the father of Mendel Olshevski. In the few moments we had, we went into his bakery to see how he prepared the loaves of bread for the ovens. His work, in our eyes was holy work. At those times I felt a slight release from the atmosphere of the Litvak's "Heder".

[Page 81]

One fine day, I ran home and told my parents that under no circumstances would I return to his class because instead of teaching me Torah he made me feel mentally disabled. As a result, my parents sent me to the "Heder" of Reb Yisroel Eli Krymolowski. It happens that the "Heder" was a "university" compared to the "Elementary School" of Rabbi Aba'leh and the "Secondary School" of the "Litvak". In as much as with Reb Yisroel–Eli there were older boys – after their Bar–Mitzvah – and I was only 8, Reb Yisroel–Eli had to open another class for the younger pupils. Reb Yisroel–Eli was considered one of the teachers of the "Metukan" school movement. He introduced the study of the Gemara interpretations of the Torah into his lessons, like the explanations of Ibn Ezra and the "Radak" (Rabbi David Kimchi), et al...In addition he would also teach his pupils the "eight levels of giving" (Maimonides). He was tall and slim and loved to slap our fingernails with a ruler. His "Heder" was in Reb Salzburg's yard on Kshoynzh Street. We made a habit of going for a walk as far as Koyfetz Kushczushko to breathe a little fresh air in the open fields there.

These are the senior pupils that I recall from the "Heder" of Reb Yisroel–Eli: Mordecai Sultanik, Shmuel Bachmejer, Schmerl Isenberg, Hertz'ki Kornfeld and David Pinchawsky. The smaller children who learned with me were: Arieh Weltfreund, my brother Elimelech Spiegel, Elimelech Friedrich, Itcha Eisenberg, Haim Eisenberg, Moshe Pinchawsky, Moshe Shinblad, Yosef Grosz, Ya'acov Kornfeld and others.

During the first years after WW1 the "Mizrachi School" opened in our town and thus began a new era for the Jewish youth of Miechów.

Boy's Mizrachi School in Miechów

[Page 82]

The "Mizrachi" School

by Ze'ev Dror Friedrich)

Translated by Selwyn Rose

The imbuing of the youth with the spirit of Zionism, expressed itself in the founding of the "Mizrachi" school in town; the school was established in 1920. The founders, who maintained their concern and interest throughout the years of the school's existence, were: S.L. Adlist, the Chairman of the school committee, S. Abramowitz, the unofficial "inspector" of the school; A. Gottfeld, Y. Liesha, S. Fogel, A.Y. Nyberg, A. Spiegel and Y. Schweitzer.

The Haredim, the disciples of the Beit Ya'acov "Heder", tried to prevent the secular school's establishment and declared a boycott against it and more than once obstructed the supporters' right to be called to the Torah during prayers. Nevertheless, the grass-roots public support against their stand forced them at last to come to terms with the existence of the "Mizrachi" school and even to struggle for their own existence being such a tiny branch of the Seminary.

It should be said, the Committee members, to their credit, made sure to base the school's instruction on modern advanced methods and sound organization. Hebrew was the language of instruction except for one or two subjects where Polish was used. The social activities included parties as fore-runners to festivals, excursions, plays, activities in support of the Foundation Fund and participation in Zionist activities in town. The standard of cleanliness and discipline was in no way less than at any Beit-Sefer "Takin". I remember the atmosphere that spread throughout the school; the feeling of cooperation; the identical caps we all wore with pride, the ten o'clock obligatory meal-break (cocoa and the bread-roll that melted in one's mouth), the bubbly activity during recesses. Even now, recalling these memories, I live again events in school as if they truly happened just yesterday or the day before.

The first school manager was Yesheyahu Shmuel (Shyer Schmiel) Hirshenhorn. He ran a private "Heder" in his home. With his special, great understanding he devised new methods of management. His natural approach and affection towards children awoke trust and respect. In his twilight years we saw him sitting among peddlers selling woven baskets: it pained us much to see our beloved teacher thus. We passed by him and greeted him and he replied "Shalom!" with his usual smile as if all was well.

The vice-principal was Herschel Kleinplatz. He was always meticulously dressed. His work was carried out faithfully, with constancy and without too much business with the Committee or the parents and he even kept a certain distance from his pupils. His attributes earned him general approval.

Both of these head-teachers were still very much of the old Yiddish "school" of instruction. Those who came after them were already teachers of the modern style.

The appearance of the young teacher, Dov Goldenberg (today, Achihu, an academician in Israel), his behavior in class, his polished Hebrew, left a deep impression on us. His graceful and refined behavior towards the women in town was superior to that expected even in a progressive town like Miechów. About two years later, he left town and we, his pupils, deeply regretted his going.

Another teacher whose presence remains etched on our memories was the erudite old man, S. C. Kohanowitz. We learned much wisdom and knowledge from his lips. He lived his life in a sort of isolated splendor and accompanied us as one whom we all were obliged to respect. He was an enigma. Every verse that we quoted to him from the Tanach, he identified by book, chapter and verse; we were never able to fault him. His home was full of long memoranda and every corner that we could see in his house drowned in these notes in boxes or...a salad in the process of preparation for his meal. Even though at that time we were unable to evaluate adequately his personality – we took pleasure more than once from the Bohemian way of life he lived in the town where the fates had brought him.

[Page 83]

All the rest of our teachers left the mark of their personal touch on our school experience.

Yisroel Shai Krimolowski loved pedagogy and it was apparent to all that he had much pleasure from it and from his pupils.

Rosenberg. The teacher of secular studies, he liked wearing Rubashka–style clothes and walked very erect, like a trained military man. He was the only teacher who permitted himself to sit bare–headed in class.

Elimelech Spiegel: his room was full of Hebrew books; he was a very gifted teacher, with a noble spirit and soul. He earned much respect and prestige. We were proud of him as a secret writer of stories and hoped to hear great things of him.

The Head–teacher, Y.D. Weiner – he had vast pedagogical knowledge and was a very active man. He organized the school with great skill and raised the standard of education. He made sure that the first of the school's matriculation students would continue their education in the "Tachkemoni" school in Warsaw. His domestic life was not a happy one and after some of his colleagues on the committee began to constrain his activities, he left town and took up a position as Head–teacher at a big school in Katowice.

Finally, I cannot fail to mention Lipa Yazkirowitz, the community secretary, who was the religious teacher at the general public school (for Jewish pupils) and at our school taught Zionism and the love of Zion with great enthusiasm.

The first graduates, all of them, except Yehezkiel Unger (Z"L), went on to study at the "Tachkemoni" seminar of Mizrachi, in Warsaw. Two of them died untimely deaths: Yona Blatt (Z"L) died from a heart disease one year before the Holocaust and Yehuda Zalmanowitz (Z"L), survived the Nazi horrors of the Holocaust, arrived in Palestine, fought in the War of Independence and only a few years ago passed away after fighting a malignant illness contracted during his sufferings in the camps.

Girls' Public School; the religious instruction teacher, Eliezer Lavie and his girl students

[Page 84]

The "Mizrachi" girls' school; Manageress Fassia Teitelbaum (1926)

Standing (l–r): Yochaved Zarnowiecki, Haya Feigenboim, Hanna Salzburg, Esther Weltfreund, Gila Abramowitz, Zinda Szprynca, and Bashi Sheinfrucht;

Sitting: Fassia Teitelbaum, Founder and Manageress; Frieda Platzkovner, Teacher;

Kneeling: Selka Unger, Rahel Feigenboim, Timka Unger, Frieda Isskowitz;br> Sitting: Bloomer Unger, Rachtza Sheinfrucht, Dovila Abramowitz, Raize'leh Abramowitz, Platzkovner;

A stage production of the children presented in Miechówby the girl–students of Fassia Teitelbaum, directed by Herschel Lubetsky

[Page 85]

8th year students of Miechów Gymnasium, among them four Jews

Girl students in senior school in Miechów

Standing (l–r): Sarah Horowitz, Sarah Sukenik, Rosenbaum, Isskowitz, Gimelkovitz, Blum, Tamar Sheinfrucht, Hinda Shtolk

Sitting: Rafalowich, Assia Isskowitz, Rosa Ginsburg, Latovicz

[Page 86]

The Gymnasium in our Town

by Shmuel Berger

Translated by Selwyn Rose

Before the Second World War Miechów was a small town with a population not above 6,000 souls, Nevertheless, the town was notable in that its general level of education stood high for its day. The population of the town – Jews and Christians – was mostly cultured. Among the residents were many high-school, or higher, graduates and only a few were illiterate. In general terms the Jewish sector had a higher level of education than the Christians.

The educational framework in town played no little part in that achievement. There was no Jewish public school in Miechów, only "Haderim" in their various sects in which the children learned up until a certain age and since, in Poland there was compulsory education for children (up to fourteen years of age), the Jews were compelled to send their children to Government public schools where lessons were taught in Polish.

There were two public schools in town, for boys and for girls. In time another modern school was built for boys. In the public schools the Jewish children were not taught any specific Jewish topics, just "religious instruction". For many years our dear community president, Eliezer Lavie taught them – (see his monograph on Jewish education and its institutions, page 24).

Apart from those schools, there was a Polish Government gymnasium based on the humanities. The gymnasium earned a nation-wide reputation as one of the best in the country.

The Gymnasium carried the name of the bravest of freedom fighters of Poland, Tadeusz Kościuszko and that was because one of his decisive battles, which he won, was the battle of Miechów-Raclawice.

The gymnasium head, at the time I was accepted, was Mr. Tadeusz Lech. He was a member of the Andak Party, known for its intense hatred of the Jews and of course as one of them was himself a virulent anti-Semite. Nevertheless his attitude towards the children he taught in his school was fair and correct. He led the school's operations with exalted benevolence and kindness and it is thanks to those attributes and his courage that the school level of education was so high.

In 1927 only one Jewish child learned at the school. Not one Jewish family in town tried to register their child at the gymnasium believing that he wouldn't be accepted there; the perception being that the "Numerus Clausus" was in effect so far as "those of the Mosaic persuasion" were concerned.

My father, who wanted with all his soul to provide for his son an education as broad as was humanly possible, decided to try to enrol me in that institution.

Towards the end of my 4th year in public school I began to prepare myself for entrance to the gymnasium, and sat for the examinations at the appointed time. The examinations extended over three successive days. A few days later my mother went to the Head–teacher find out about the results. He answered her thus: "Your son has successfully passed the entrance examinations and is accepted as a student at the Gymnasium."

The news fell like a clap of thunder on the ears of the entire Jewish community of Miechów that was almost unable to believe what they had heard.

In the light of that success a few other well–off Jewish families thought to try their luck and send their sons to the Gymnasium. and at the second sitting that year two additional Jewish families succeeded and after them, slowly, slowly the numbers began to grow. In 1930/1 there were already 12 Jews studying at the school (according to the official report from the management of the school).

[Page 87]

The school concerned itself with as complete an education as was possible in fields different to the topics taught by teaching civil and social topics also. Among the themes were: literature, humanities, history, sociology, drama, a department of philology, a sports organization, scouts, chess and others.

In addition there was an orchestra of wind– and string–instruments that took part in school festivities of one kind or another including different parades – both national and religious.

All the Jewish students at the school helped one another and we were like one family: we studied together and played together.

It is impossible to deny that there was anti–Semitism in the school, and a number of the Christian pupils conspired against their Jewish colleagues. But they were in the minority. Officially the Headmaster and Staff were against the incidents, reacting strongly and with severe punishments to every complaint. I have already mentioned that the Headmaster, who behaved negatively towards the Jews in the different institutions in which he was active, especially those of the municipality but here, within the walls of this academic institution he would not permit any instance of negative behavior, verbal or otherwise against the Jewish pupils and was extremely strict on that issue.

He related with all due respect towards our parents and whenever they approached him and received them gracefully and courteously. We were all children of fervent, Zionist parents and from time to time we compelled to defend our honor as Jews. It occurred most frequently in the lessons on Polish literature in the senior classes. The literary analysis of Polish writings from different periods, showed the anti–Semitic strain quite conspicuously. Our colleagues in the class exploited the opportunity to attack the Jews. Clearly we did not remain passive under the attack and very often gave back twice what we received in bitter and unrestrained arguments. The teacher was obliged on more than one occasion to justify our stand on the debate.

It is true that not all the Polish writers were anti–Semitic. There were among them lovers of Israel – Righteous among the Nations (not in the modern post–holocaust context – Trans.), such as Eliza Orzeszkowa, many of whose works dealt with the Jewish question. Her writings pictured the Jew in a positive light, as a lover of his homeland, working and living from the toil of his hands.

In other contexts, too, we fought with pride as Jews but it wasn't always easy.

As students of the school we were forbidden to belong to any youth–movement except those approved of by the Gymnasium itself. Nevertheless and in spite of it all, we, the Jewish pupils, interested ourselves in everything going on in the Jewish youth movements and from time to time secretly took part in various activities, and helped wherever we could.

On the 1st of February 1931, Mr. Lech was relieved of his post because of his affiliation to and with the Andak Party and in his place as Headmaster a supporter of Marshal Pilsudski and his governing party was appointed. I must point out that the headmasters that followed Mr. Lech did not succeed to the same degree as did his predecessor and as time went by the school began a downward trend both in terms of administration and level of instruction. Mr.

Lech was a headmaster and manager par excellence: he loved his school and his pupils.

In closing I must emphasize that the Gymnasium was for me first of all a place of learning and widening of horizons in all the subjects taught there, and an excellent preparation for my future life. I acquired a sound basic education – general and social, and that advantage is still with me today.

[Page 88]

Gymnasium students

From r–l: Simcha Silberberg, Yisroel Yitzhak Lewit, Getzil Lewit, Moshe Katzengold, Shmu

List of Jewish students who studied at the National Gymnasium in Miechów in the Academic Year 1930/31:

1. BERGER, Shmuel: Graduated from the Hebrew University of Jerusalem, lives today in Israel.
2. GERTLER, Alexander.
3. WDOWINSKI, Aharon.
4. ZILBER, Eliyahu.
5. MALINROWSKI, David.
6. ZIVANBERG, Aharon.
7. SERCAZ, Yehezkiel: living today in Israel.
8. CZERBONOIGOTTA, Haim.
9. KOPPELOWITZ, Yehezkiel: Graduated from the Technion, Haifa as an engineer; today senior engineer in one of Israel's top companies.
10. KOPPELOWITZ, Mordecai.
11. SCHEINTEL, Dov.
12. SCHEINTEL, Michal.

(From the official administrative report of the gymnasium)

I have no information to hand concerning the remaining students; most – if not everyone of them perished in the Holocaust, May G–d Avenge their Blood.

[Page 89]

The "Dror" Youth Library in Miechów

by Moshe Spiegel

Translated by Selwyn Rose

Education began earlier in Miechów than in other towns in the county. The town's Gymnasium opened in the days of the Russian Government. A few families sent their children to that gymnasium and they were the ones who founded the "Zamir" library at the end of the First World War Among the founders were Avraham Sercaz, Wolf Ber Warschawski, Reuven Shmuel Kleiner, Ya'acov Buchner, Yerechmiel Itzkowski and others. The erudite and the Zionist youth of our town were always to be found around the library. There was also a drama group which staged their first shows in the flour silo of my grandfather Mr. Yisroel David Spiegel (Z"L): "Shulamit" and "David's Violin". Later they produced and staged Ansky's "The Dybbuk", Gordin's "The Slaughter", Peretz's "A Night in the old Market" in the fire brigade's hall, and others.

In the meantime a few of us other pupils from Mr. Yisroel Eli Krimolowski's "Heder" had joined and we became good friends. We exchanged secular books among ourselves and had conversations about them. We were six friends, Ya'acov Kornfeld, Moshe Pinczowski, Haim Eisenberg, Ya'acov Friedrich Elimelech Friedrich and the writer of these few lines. This how it really began: On Lag B'Omer in 1921, we six of us went on a picnic to the Chodowi Forest. We took a picnic hamper, eggs painted in different colors and each a book to read. After we had eaten our lunch, we all sat down in a quiet spot and were soon deeply immersed in our books. After a few hours, when we had finished reading, Ya'acov Kornfeld stood up and said: "Since we all want to be educated and we have no possibility from any source, let's all of us pool our books and then try to get some more books from among our seniors. In that way we can create a library for the young people and we can provide a little education from among those without means to buy books." We all expressed agreement with Ya'acov's idea and we gave him our books. In the fullness of time we collected more books and when we had collected about 20 books we opened the library in the attic of Ya'acov's house.

A few months later we met in the attic and named the library "Dror". At the start we were a very small daring group. In addition to learning Torah we dedicated ourselves to reading and increasing the number of books in the library. Eventually we managed to penetrate different sectors of the youth and guarantee some income for the library by making a monthly payment for the loan of books.

From among the pupils studying in the Gymnasium some joined the library: Shlomo Katzengold, Barish Scheintal, Yehezkiel and Herschel Solewicz and others. In the second year of our library we rented accommodation in the Rabbi's yard near the Scheinold family's house. The library expanded and already had 70 members and about 400 books in Yiddish.

It was during this period that the struggle between our parents and the religious sector on one side and us the operators of the library on the other side. It was a real intense fight. There were times when the owners of the premises, honored citizens, would come in while we were having a meeting and dragged us outside by force. We were young and had to give way to our seniors. I have to point out there was one element very much to our disadvantage: in the same courtyard lived the local Rabbi Yankeleh Rotenberg (Z"L). It was in this courtyard that all the orthodox zealots would congregate and exert much influence on the residents who would obstruct us in trying to operate the library in an orderly fashion. Nevertheless we were not deterred. With the increase in the number of our readers the library and its activities we opened other pastimes for seminars on our own initiative.

We began a drama group led by Ya'acov Friedrich, Eliezer Lewit and myself. Our work based itself on scrutinizing a play together, reading excerpts from it in the group and exchanging ideas of how to stage it. In the years 1925–1928 we produced and staged the following: "The Jackpot", by Sholom Aleichem, "The Slaughter", "G–d, Man and Satan" and others...our "Prime Donne" were Sarah Federman, (now Sukenik) and Malka Lubchi. The younger members were: Ya'acov Friedrich, Eliezer Lewit, Aharon Brukner (Z"L) (he died after a brief illness at 19), Aharon Blum, Moshe Scheinold and others.

[Page 90]

Similarly, we created a literary group that functioned in two areas: A) a lecture organization for Saturdays in which we featured well–known lecturers. Many of our youths took part in these and they were an excellent vessel for disseminating knowledge and acquiring literature in Yiddish. B) Publication of a news–sheet for review and for literature. During two years we published a news–sheet named "The Torch", not by print and not by stencil – but hand–written. Lack of funds and experience were the cause of making this extremely tiresome work. The news–sheet mostly covered reviews on newly published books, on different plays, poems, and feuilletons. However we were forced to stop publication in order to travel to other localities in Poland to continue our studies or to start to work.

In spite of it all, it was by that initiative that the first awakening of education for the youth in Miechów as a ground–breaking activity causing strong waves in our entire social framework.

The Drama Society

by Sarah Friedman (Sukenik)

Translated by Selwyn Rose

The young Jews in Miechów lived an unworried life and with no plans for the future. Most of them were employed in the family business and – as was usual, the business would be inherited by them, so for most of them there was little ambition to go out into the big, wide world. Every day they would walk around town to the center and the city square. The principal route was "from A to B" and there, there was a lot of congestion so they would walk down to the gardens near the church for some seclusion.

The social life among the youngsters was lively. There were two active libraries in town: "The Dror" and "The Zamir", which was under the management of academics. A drama group was organized and in time became a lively living theater. For every festival a new production was prepared. The direction was undertaken by the members Isskowitz, Liptscher(?) and Buchner. The success of our production awoke an echo throughout the area and we travelled to nearby towns as well. There is no need to add how much toil and sweat our work cost us, and how much we struggled to overcome the disapproval of our parents, the conditions of our work–place and our miniscule budget.

Obviously everything we did was on a voluntary basis: sometimes for the benefit of the "Zamir" library, sometimes for the "Women's Society" and sometimes for the Histadrut. The productions in which I myself took part were: "Motke the Thief" by Sholem Asch; "The Jackpot" by Shalom Aleichem; "God Man and Satan" by Ya'acov Gordin; "Moshke the Pig" by I.D. Berkowitz;

“Herschel the Nobleman” by Moshe Richter; “The Slaughter” Ya'acov Gordin and “The Scoundrel”. In the production of “God Man and Satan” Aharon Bruckner (Z”L) played the lead. He invested his heart and soul in the theater and I remember that immediately after the show he fell ill, took to his bed from which he never rose again. After that they related how, though he was ill and running a temperature he went on stage. It was one of the examples of the complete and utter enthusiasm and sacrifice for the sake of the success of the social activities of Miechów's youth.

The memory of Aharon Bruckner (Z”L) will not fade and his image will forever be before our eyes.

[Page 91]

The Youth of Miechów

by Gershon Charig (Katolyk)

Translated by Selwyn Rose

I remember clearly the period when I was a pupil at the “Mizrachi” school in Miechów. We learned in the synagogue building, on the second floor while the pupils from “Agudat Yisroel” learned on the third floor. I think it was probably 1922. I was then 8 years old, and most of the children were older. The animosity then and always, between the “Aguda” and “Mizrachi” didn't pass over us unfelt and frequently fights broke out between us – real fights. We both received and returned significant blows. Even stones were used, clubs, iron bars, belts – whatever came to hand.

Most of the young people belonged to one or other of the parties that had branches in Miechów starting with the extreme right – “Agudat Yisroel” – and finished at the extreme left – the Communist Party. This last was always under a false name out of fear of the authorities. Among the parties that were well organized were also “Agudat Yisroel Workers' Party” and the “General Zionists” party. At the head of the Betar group was David Bornstein, an ideal organizer. Also active was the youth group “Hashomer Hatza'ir” who organized many excursions and trips. My young sister Adel–Edna was a member of the National Guard. The “Young Guard”, mostly not from local youth, underwent training in Miechów before immigrating to Palestine. The members of

"Hashomer Hatza'ir" organized weekly meetings where members of different parties attended. Debates and arguments took place on many interesting and topical subjects. We also had in Miechów a few unorganized members of the "Bund". I was an active member of the left–wing "Poalei–Zion". We had a library that included books in Yiddish and Polish and we tried to bring culture to those, some of whom, could barely read and write. Most conspicuous among the leaders of our party were Meyer–Fischl Gertler and Ozer Bornstein.

From time to time lecturers would come from party headquarters to speak on different topics, political and literature. The appearance of Zerubavel in our town was greeted as a great event and he made a tremendous impression on us, both as an orator and a leader–figure.

I should point out that in Miechów, unlike many other places, there was a certain closeness between the Jewish youth of all the parties. Nevertheless at times there were indeed some stormy arguments although they never reached the point of a brawl. It may be said that our youth was cultured and devoted most of its spare time to reading. In addition to the party libraries, there were also general libraries. The "Zamir" library was excellent and richly stocked with good books, and also served as a meeting place for us all.

[Page 92]

Cultural Activities

by Moshe Spiegel

Translated by Selwyn Rose

In the period before the First World War, one could already see in the Jewish streets of Poland the buds of the various streams of political parties. But in Miechów the strongly conservative and devout community held sway, on the one side the various orthodox dynasties and on the other. The group of "Mitnagdim" from the Rabbi Ya'acov Emdin Beit Hamidrash – the "mid–point" between them, was not permitted to inject their new ideas into the younger generation.

During that period the main spokesmen for the Miechów community were: Mr. Nathan Bornstein, Mr. Yermiyahu Blum, Mr. Avraham Yama, Mr. Fischl Koppelowitz, Mr. Yisroel David Spiegel, Rabbi Yisroel David the slaughterer,

Rabbi Shmuel the Cantor. All these "stood guard" lest the young men get caught by the "new spirit" blowing on the wind from Warsaw in the newspapers "The Siren", "Today", "Heint" and "The Moment".

But despite all that, things began to change in the minds of the young seminar students. At that time Russia was fomenting on the eve of revolution against the Tsarist regime that found expression in the great Yeshivot, in mass demonstrations of workers and tithed farmers and their fight to liberate the people.

The Jewish youth founded a society called "Unity", an initiative of the "Bund". In Miechów, the idea caught on with the young people: Yosef Brukner, Ya'acov Blum, Shmuel Fogel, Avraham Spiegel, Moshe Sukenik, Yehoshua Koppelowitz, Haim Feureisen, Yishai Shmuel Hirshenhorn and Moshe David Blum.

These young men continued with their education normally without any discernible outward change in their behavior, but in the background they met nearly every day for special meetings where they received reports on the progress of the revolution throughout Russia and Poland. They identified with the revolutionaries in many of their definitions, but their heritage withheld them from taking an active part in the rising tide. An additional element to their hesitation should be pointed out: The patriarchal society to which they themselves belonged and honored in the homes of their parents and families and their deep connections with their parents and teachers in the study of the Torah represented a significant constraint on their behavior. When the Revolution (of 1905), failed and most of the revolutionaries were arrested, accused and imprisoned by the Tsarist police, the youth of Miechów continued to dream of a world where all was good, with social equality for all.

The hatred of the Jews by the Russian authorities grew in the years following the suppression of the revolution. Edicts were promulgated that restricted the Jews in the economic field, even more so their choice of where to live, and the areas where they already lived were further reduced, the blood libels were revived, like the historic trial of Mendel Beilis, accused of the murder of a Christian child to use the blood in a Jewish ritual.

All this brought the Jewish youth to an even deeper learning of the Torah and the Talmud. But the national knowledge and awareness caused waves between the pupils studying in the Yeshivot, and the call for auto emancipation by Leon Pinsker strengthened within them the need for general education and the drive towards a personal upright stature in every one of its meanings –spiritual and physical.

Also in 1913 the "Zamir" library in Miechów was opened by Ya'acov Blum, Reuven Shmuel Kleiner, Avraham Sercaz and Moshe Koppelowitz, who placed before themselves the lofty target of disseminating knowledge and education, the injection of good books to every home, the creation of extra–curricular activities like drama and literature, lectures by specialists in all fields of knowledge. And indeed many of the youngsters from all levels registered themselves at the library and enjoyed all the cultural activities programmed by "The Zamir". The drama group presented to the general public the best of our writers and those taking part were: Tsvi Lubczi, Mendel Olshevski, Ya'acov Buchner, Yerechmiel Itzkowski, Zussia Itzkowski, Shmuel Blum, Haya Buchner and others, staging the shows of Goldfaden, "The Dybbuk" and other productions.

[Page 93]

There was full identification between the plot being shown on stage by the actors and the audience; once the play stopped in the middle of "Sale of the Orphan Girl" because of the "objection" of one who shouted out with all his might:" Jews, Jews of Miechów would never permit such a thing!!"

Lecturers were invited from Krakow and Warsaw. All these activities increased the general awareness of the real existing problems among the Jewish public.

The education of the younger generation also took on a new character. In the place of the "Heder" and the strict teachers, there arose and were founded by the leaders of the "Mizrachi" (see above), the "Mizrachi" school with a staff of educated teachers. Hundreds of children registered for that school. Girls from families of means entered the Polish Gymnasium and received a general education in addition to the traditional Jewish teaching they received from the teacher Shlomo Solewicz or Mrs. Teitelbaum.

Those same years several charitable and communal societies were set up like: "Leinat Tzedek", "Sick visits" and "Brotherly Help". There was also an "Artisans' Society" a sports society "Kadima" and a youth library "Dror". In short, the cultural and social life of the small Jewish youth community was comprised of skin, bones, sinews and all and a broad network of activities was woven in all the fields mentioned above.

The great advances that occurred in the Jewish organizations and parties in the Poland of the twenties of the present century influenced Miechów as well and the first buds of organization, growth and development began to appear. In Miechów an excitement appeared in the ranks of the younger generations where they were taking the first steps within the framework of the organizations which they individually chose as the way forward for the people. There was a mutual struggle to convince the other of the spirit of the ideals that had developed from extensive study of the significance of the ideological streams that pervaded the Jewish street and found expression in the Jewish literature and newspapers.

Many of the simple folk, who grew up under straitened circumstances, were caught up in the ideologies of the left–wing parties and a few of them even left the town where they were born and grew up to move to one of the larger urban centers and in time became conspicuous because of their political activities.

During that same period, changes and transformations occurred in the Polish government, once it was the Andak party in power, then it was the farmers (PIAST party) holding the reins of power and once the socialists (P.P.S.) held the State "rudder". All these transformations failed to weaken the cultural activities of the various Jewish streams, rather the opposite is true, and they increased their presence in the struggle for its rights in all possible ways. Many young Jews, who had completed their obligatory education in high–school, in spite of the numerus clausus, operating in Poland, joined the leadership of the various streams of the parties and brought fresh blood into the new, Jewish society that had been created following the special circumstances of the new era, the springtime of peoples and nations.

During the thirties, the right wing held sway in Poland, anti–Semitism shot up and the hatred of the Jews increased. The Andak party publicized their slogan:"Don't Buy from Jews!" and "Haters of the Christian State".

In the wake of that policy, the small businesses suffered greatly, the economic status collapsed and many layers of the Jewish society became impoverished. The leaders of the Zionist movement warned the public that the time was coming to leave anti–Semitic Poland and immigrate to Palestine.

Debates commenced in the Zionist party on how best to move the idea forward to action. There were those that claimed that it was forbidden to abandon the struggle in the Diaspora and there was a need to struggle for the national and cultural rights of the Jewish people in all the places of its dispersion – and there were those who said there was no future for Jews in the Diaspora and that a great economic and physical disaster awaited the Jewish people without a territory and without a homeland of their own.

[Page 94]

These arguments received a tangible presence in the light of the various decrees enacted by the Polish authorities. The growing younger generations saw that there was no future for them in the slowly deteriorating economic life and joined the ranks of "Hechalutz", went to training camps of the various parties of their youth movements and increased their activity for the Zionist funds – "K.K.L." and "The Foundation Fund". They also became active in broadening clarification meetings to capture the hearts and minds of their parents, to generate a change in their lives too, and get them to obtain a profession and immigrate to Palestine.

In 1927 I left Miechów, the town of my birth and began to roam. I first went to Warsaw and afterwards to Sosnovitza. There I joined "Hechalutz" went through pioneering training in Suchedniev and in 1931 immigrated to Palestine. All those who fulfilled their vision and emigrated from Poland moved around for days and months before their immigration amidst the sense of the impending, growing and approaching disaster.

Cultural and Social Development in Miechow

by Moshe Savitzki

Translated by Gloria Berkenstat Freund

Right after the First World War the young people began to take part in cultural and community work. A much smaller number did so openly. The majority was secretive because of the negative attitude of their parents.

In addition many helped in the founding of the Hazimir [choral society] library that in time developed into a large, valuable library with books in three languages. The majority of books were in Yiddish, then Polish and a much smaller number in Hebrew.

The library leaders gave everyone instructions about what everyone should read; the directors changed often.

The daily press, such as Der Heynt [Today], Der Moment [The Moment], Hatzfira [The Siren] could be read on the spot.

An amateur theater was founded at the library that carried out very successful performances of the then current repertoire. Among others, Anski's Dybbuk was staged very successfully.

[Page 95]

The founders of the library and of the amateur theater were: Klajner, Bachner and Itskowicz. The also were the directors of the presentations.

A sports club was founded later that, alas, did not develop.

Thanks to the organizations mentioned, there was a coalescence of intelligent, aware young people who later founded a halutz [pioneers] and Zionist youth movement. The same society also began to organize the young in the Miechow area. Elimelekh Fridrich, who perished in a German camp, carried this out with great success. The first hakhshara [agricultural training centers] location in the area was founded in Miechow and later, they also appeared in other locations in the poviat [county or district].

The shtetl was divided politically into an organized Zionist party that was led by Avraham Sercaz, at the head of the Mizrakhi [religious Zionist] Party, organized by Adler, Yehoshua Kuplubic, Avraham Szpigel, Abramowicz, Fojgler and Joskerowicz.

The Mizrakhi Party organized everything first for the young, a carpentry school that Yehoshua Kuplubic led along with Yakov Szpigel, a carpenter by trade. Alas, Mizrakhi was not successful with the school. The very pious Jews and the Hasidim in the shtetl were not organized.

[Page 96]

C. Organizations and Youth Movements

From my Memories of the Youth Movements in Miechów

By Yitzhak Polska

Translated by Selwyn Rose

When one comes to survey the youth movements in our town one hesitates and asks oneself: How did it all begin? A small town huddling round its town square, in whose center flutters the Polish emblem – the eagle with spread wings – symbolizing every "turbulent" breathing soul in town.

Were there youth movements in town? Apparently, yes. The fact was mostly felt before conventions or elections to the Sejm.

Today, when you speak about a movement, you know its political platform or the names of the leaders. In our town even these things were hard to define clearly. Figures like Greenboim, Jabotinsky or some unknown person – were mixed up in the consciousness of the town's young people. The "Mitnagdim" could not always define whom they were opposing: were they against a political ideology or against a particular personage? But one institution was very certain – The Jewish National Fund.

Its paths were very clear and simple to us: pennies were collected in the little "Blue Boxes" at events and those pennies were the building–blocks of the Homeland.

I remember Yehezkiel sent me a picture of Palestine: he was on a wall laying bricks. The "message" was as clear as the K.K.L., itself – as clear as the eagle with spread wings in the town square.

And who would be the members of the Movements?

The girls were still learning spelling and writing Hebrew with "The 'Frau'"; the boys, wearing "kippot" or peaked caps: Elimelech Friedrich, of the Yiddish–Polish intelligentsia from the "Zamir", Yosef, his little brother, a fluent avid reader of "Heint"; Ya'acov, Bruckner's brother, and others, staging plays of

Peretz, at the same time as "Hagonsher" and his company of artisans were staging a production of Goldfaden's " Bar– Kokhba".

Peretz Lejzorek, he of the flattened nose, worked in a butcher's shop; Phini Gerszonowicz the son of Yidel the mighty blacksmith, dreaming of his status as a Ladies' Man, like his big brother. The Reinsteins were bakers. Hanna P. Was a simple girl, not much is known about her. The sister of Gershon Katolyk dreamed the dreams of all girls' ideal man. Netta Kornfeld looked for a suitable "uniform" to suit the pained creature within him. Buckner the intelligent and Maizel Mitzkowitz(?) – Who knows anything about them? Yehezkiel Ze'ev, P. Meir, P. Scherl, Yona Blatt and Zalmanowitz, will go to the "Takhmoni" School in Warsaw. The sons of the ritual slaughterer will accompany their father, the acclaimed cantor, in the synagogue New Year and the Day of Atonement.

[Page 97]

Elimelech P., Bornstein, Koppelowitz, Gerstenfeld and Meir G., played their roles of being detectives and their dreams, still in the bounds of reason: "If all the goyim die – whose shop will I take?" Yitzhak Sheinfrucht, the thick–headed one; he who wears the hat of the Seminary students, one far too small for his head but whose little blond sister was so nice. The small boys used to trail after the big girls as they walked along.

Krymolowski, adorned with his peyot was a brilliant Yeshiva student, dressed in his Sabbath finery with his Jewish determination, dances with his friends at the wedding of the Rabbi's daughter with wild enthusiasm. All of these later constituted members of the Movements – mostly "Mizrachi" except the last one – "Agudat Yisroel".

Elimelech Kornfeld will go to Łódź and one fine day will return to wear the uniform of the "National Guard". Will he be the first? In which Movements were Yehezkiel and his brother Ze'ev Elimelech then? And was Meir Fogel "defined", was Itze Polski and his brother already members of the Miechów Sports Movement "Kadima" with Simcha Koziol at its head?

Will Peretz Lejzorek ever be ready to hit his brother, because they oppose each other's political views? One thing is quite clear: there was a surprising integrity among everyone. Not one expressed extreme "self righteousness", never raised his hands and never disrupted a meeting. And that integrity lasted right up until the end. "The wolf shall lie down with the lamb" and no one knew which was the "wolf" and which the "lamb". The lack of bitterness between, and in the awareness of, the parties in our town and the innocence, was conspicuous in the tolerant behaviour of divisions within the families: Peretz Lejzorek was a confirmed and fiery "National Guard" and his brother Netta similarly "sold" on "Beitar"; Elimelech K., in one party and Netta his brother the other and it was the same in many families. The first to display openness in political opposition was, it seems to me, Mr. Lipa Y. It was in a meeting in the synagogue before the elections to the Sejm. In his address he brought a parable from the "Book of the Khazars" where he presents the Zionists and the Zionist left opposing "Mizrahi" as a parallel to the famous debate between the Rabbi, the Priest and the Pagan with the King choosing the Pagan by default – meaning the "Mizrachi". Opposition occurred. As I remember, Yehezkiel foamed with anger in public and we rushed to hold him back. But I'll admit that the adage pleased me and I sensed in that, that there were many like me. Then, one day it became clear to me, there are indeed youth movements in town: there are youth camps, excursions of all the youth movements to the forests on Lag B'Omer, parades in the streets, special uniforms.

Peretz Lejzorek dreamed the dream of the Land of Israel in the uniform of the "National Guard". He didn't know that he would not live to see it: Elimelech Friedrich and his younger brother influenced the Goldbergs, the Feigenblatts, the Firisens(?), the Feigenboims, the Zyndermans, the Tchaikovskys and many others. They took on another character and identity through their activism in the K.K.L.: affiliation to the "National Guard".

Elimelech F. convinced a young girl, his future wife, to join the "National Guard", both of them destined for extermination. Haim Isskowitz would also return to town only to perish there.

And still the confused mixture of political awareness of ours held sway. I remember I was in the "National Guard" when Jabotinsky came to Poland – a dream–figure – and spoke on the radio. A legend said he learned Polish in two weeks. I would listen to his speeches, they full of intensity and indeed from a mastermind; Moshe Stavski was also spoken of in the Movements but was somewhat remote and misty. What characterised the Movements were their meeting place and their learning classes: the Tanach, Homeland, Principles and love for the Land of Israel.

The rush to the Movements was age–related and not connected to the seniorities of the boys in the "National Guard" and older boys in "Beitar" and the even still older ones in "Mizrachi". Only here in Israel did I come to know that Gershon Katolyk was in the left wing Poalei–Zion.

[Page 98]

Activities for the Keren Kayemet

Keren Kayemet le–Yisroel convention with the participation of Alter Droyanov

Standing L–R: Yehuda Burstein, Golda Blatt, David Burstein, Sarah Sukenik, Leibusch Hirshenhorn, Hillel Sercaz, Leah Poslushny, Elimelech Friedrich, Hava Isskowitz, Hirsch Leib Gerstenfeld, Shmuel Sukenik

Sitting: Yitzhak Sheinfrucht, Bluma Kashubo(?), Droyanov, Wolf Ber Kaiser, Ya'acov Poslushny, Joskowicz.

The Flower Festival in Miechów (1927/8)

Standing R–L: Wolf Lejzorek, Pella Rosenboim, Mindel Feureisen, Paula Feureisen, Ha'anich Schweitzer, Haya Isskowitz, Wolf Ber Kaiser, Hendel Lubczi, Freidel Poloczyk, David Pinchowsky, Rachel Yama

Sitting R–L: Yitzhak Sheinfrucht, Tuvczi Rosenboim, Haim Isskowitz, Sarah Sukenik, Arieh Bruckner

Kneeling: Elimelech Friedrich, Leibel Kleiner

[Page 99]

There was one big party, a roof–party! The "Kaisers" and their like ruled there and at the events of the K.K.L., you could find them all.

The thread that tied all the Youth Movements together, a simple thread and characteristic attribute of our town: the love of the Land of Israel.

Before my eyes I see a picture from my days in town in the last years before I immigrated to Palestine. Purim in town: Youngsters from all the different Movements – youngsters of my own age, carrying giant K.K.L. boxes moving from house to house and singing a Yiddish song:

"The money goes for the Land of Israel,

Make a "Mitzvah" and throw it in the box!"

The "Mizrachi" and "Young Mizrachi" in Miechów

by Arieh Brukner

Translated by Selwyn Rose

From within the mists of time I am reminded of the earliest steps in the organization of the "Mizrachi" Movement in Miechów. After the First World War, we had a visit from Rabbi Yehiel Yitzhak Rappoport of Mniszew(?) in the Beit Ha–Midrash. The hall was filled from wall–to–wall; he spoke about the sanctity of the Land of Israel and of resettlement there.

At that time, when the Haredi Jewish community was opposed to Zionist activity which it rejected a priori, and that we must wait for the coming of the Messiah, it required enormous courage on the part of a Rabbi in Israel to preach active resettlement of Palestine in the spirit of the Torah and the tradition, and to create a synthesis between the study of the Torah and the keeping of the Commandments and the physical toil of redeeming the Land of Israel. Rabbi Rappoport (May his Righteousness be Remembered for a Blessing), excited his listeners and his words encouraged the establishment of the first group organizing the "Mizrahi" in our town. Even my own father and teacher (Z"L), who was a disciple of the Gur Yeshiva, was caught up in the idea of "religious–Zionism". He was among the first to register as a member of "Mizrahi" and took part in the courses organized by the founders. His affiliation was expressed in deeds: he decided to arrange his passport for Palestine. And in order to perform the Mitzvah: "Torah together with 'The Way of the Land'" he taught his sons the weaving profession in order to prepare them for immigration.

Enthusiasm caught the students in the Seminaries as well. Whereas until now they were steeped only in the teachings of the Torah they, too, were now harnessed to work for Zionism.

The Zionist idea that found root in the vacuum of our world bonded together the religious youth organizations in the framework of Mizrachi youth, whose slogan was "Torah and work". We will mention here the names of the first founders of that federation: Yitzhak Sheinfrucht, who was the living spirit and spur of its operations throughout the movement's existence until the Holocaust; Yesheyahu Burstein; Moshe Lewit; Ze'ev Horowitz; the Lishmann brothers; Mordecai Sultanik; my brother Naphtali Hertz Bruckner, who later became the head of "Hamizrahi" in Działoszyce and other places.

The federation of "Young Mizrahi" placed before itself two roles: a) To inject the idea of working the land by studying the Mishnaic order of "seeds" and b) To impart the youth with a profession and to instil within them a love of the work.

[Page 100]

Histadrut "Young Mizrachi" in Miechów

Standing R–L: Arieh Bruckner, Reuven Shinitzky, Sandor Stein, Aharon Bruckner, Yosef Gross, Moshe Pinchowsky, Moshe Spiegel, Yehuda Burstein, Haim Isenberg

Sitting: Yesheyahu Burstein, Yitzhak Sheinfrucht, Lipa Yazkirowitz, Tsvi Hirsch Wiener

"Young Mizrachi" Congress (1928)

Standing R–L: H. Poslushny, A. Bruckner, Yosef Gross, Leibel Bladdeh(?), Y. Burstein

Second row: Sandor Stein, Moshe Pinczowski, David Sukenik, Reuven Shinitzky

Third row: Ya'acov Kornfeld, Moshe Spiegel

[Page 101]

Training Carpentry–shop (1921)

"Bruriah" section of "Young Mizrachi" (1933)

Standing R–L: Rivka Fisch, Ruhama Katolyk, Miriam Gross, Shoshanna Brandstetter, Hindel Salzburg, Rachel Fisch, Frieda Rosen Sitting second row: Paula Feureisen, Yitzhak Sheinfrucht, Chairman of all the "Mizrachi" Movements, Hermann Machrachow(?), Hindel Walberg, Chairlady "Bruriah", Ethel Malinarski

Sitting first row: Rachel Lechai, Hanna Feigenboim

[Page 102]

Because of that, the orthodox students from the Beit Hamidrash started giving special, early–morning courses every day, in the cellar of the synagogue. All the members of the association would take part and even young men from outside if the topic was close to their heart. Some of the members started to learn different professions, such as knitting (with the Spiegel family), carpentry and so on. This activity drew many youngsters from among the town into our organization. Our members demonstrated great activity and diversity in all the Zionist institutions, like "Keren Hayesod" and " Keren Kayemet". In the beginning Moshe Koppelowitz (Z"L) was the first administrator of the K.K.L and Eliezer Burstein was secretary. Then came others: the very active Mr. Wolf Ber Kaiser (Z"L), who dedicated virtually his whole life to the Zionist idea in general and to the K.K.L. in particular and attracted all the youngsters in our town by his dedication and faith. After him came David Burstein (Z"L). During their time I was functioning as secretary and after me came Yehuda Burstein.

Thus the work continued, until we reached a pinnacle of real significance and that was delegating a team of ten members from the organization to the agricultural training farm at Marianów near Wolbrom, under the patronage of the Pacanowski family. Ten members from Wolbrom itself also joined us – members of the "General Zionists" – for agricultural training.

Both groups worked in complete harmony, in spite of differences of viewpoint.

The day's full agenda included instructional lessons on working the land – both theoretical and practical, by the farm manager. Also Tanach studies, Hebrew, the history of Zionism and knowledge of The Land of Israel. Members of the Zionist organizations of both Wolbrom and Miechów came to listen to the lectures.

In that training group, which was the first one of its kind in our town, the following took part: Elimelech Spiegel, Sandor Stein, Reuven Shinitzky, Aharon Bruckner (who died in the prime of life in Miechów at 18), Yosef Gross, Dov Scheinwald, Haim Isenberg and spared for a long life were Yehuda Burstein and the writer of these few lines, who are alive today in Israel.

Yehuda Burstein is the one who continued to be active after I left my family in 1928. He activated the next generation in all fields of Zionist activity.

The Youth Movements in Miechów

by Ze'ev Dror (Friedrich)

Translated by Selwyn Rose

The Youth Movements in Miechów were populated by young people who learned in two schools: "Mizrachi" and "Torah Foundation" – a foundation of "Agudat Yisroel". These two schools were different in their approach and mentality of learning, but in both of them was a fundamental Jewish education which took root and blossomed in the youth movements

The training in carpentry under the tutelage of Ya'acov Spiegel was the first sign of the organization of youngsters in town. That seed was enthusiastic in its devotion to the idea of productivity and even sent a few members for agricultural training but didn't continue for long; that generation has still not been trained. Yitzhak Sheinfrucht (Z"L), and spared for a long life Yehuda Burstein, who were the living souls of that organization, and were afterwards activists in the youth movements, lecturing on the problems of Zionism and Judaism and their influence on all the youth streams was significant.

[Page 103]

The "National Guard" was founded in 1928 by graduates of "Mizrachi" who had gone to Warsaw to study at the "Takhmoni" school. In that Movement there were already all the attributes that typified the youth movements in those days: uniforms, flags, scouting activities, ceremonies on festivals and Zionist events, the obligation of fulfilment, and so on. We recall with honor from among its founders: the brilliant Yona Blatt, Yehuda Zalmanowitz, who loved the quiet of academia rather than the stereotyped manners of scout ceremonial, Getzil Lewit, with a popular and practical approach always hewing to the point, and spared for a long life the impulsive Meyer Fogel, full of life and inventiveness, Ze'ev Dror, the "ideologue", and also Yehezkiel Dror the most active of them all, who was dedicated to the Movement, bearing the yoke of responsibility for the cell and even the first to go for training and immigrate to Palestine. For years Yehezkiel was the group secretary and activist, delegating staff–positions and directing the activity of everyone.

With the "changing of the guard" came Elimelech Friedrich, (Z"L), Haim Isskowitz, (Z"L), Moshe Pinchowsky (Z"L) and Esther Sheinfrucht, (Z"L), all of whom perished. Even though they were all very different types from beginning to end, what united them all was the enthusiasm for the interests of the Movement and their total dedication to the work. Each and every one of them was graced with some special quality: Elimelech with his intellect, Haim with his leaning to scouting, "order" and "militarism" (an ex–army officer), Moshe with his practicality and dedication to his aims and Esther with her essential vitality and sensitivity to the life of the cell: everyone loved her warm smile and her relationship with people. The cell represented content and the center of life for the young people. It directed their energy towards Zionism and their entire life became a foretaste of the future reality in the Land of Israel. Much of the happiness of life and their freshness would have been stifled had it not been for the attraction of that distant world on the youngsters, beyond the palpable reality of the Diaspora.

Zionist activity in town such as collection of donations, Flower Days, festival events and Purim with its parties, Zionist meetings, organization of bazaars, receiving lecturers and delegates, the sale of agricultural products, etc., all were found in the young people of the movements as faithful and moral activists. Their spiritedness sometimes infected the entire young, Jewish population of the town. The Lag B'Omer excursion – a parade, in effect – with scout uniforms and flags at their head, turned the event into an experience for the whole town. The town, which was Zionist obtained satisfaction from the scouts and looked upon them with paternal affection.

The entire cell breathed life. The youngsters found within it a place for social activity, everyone according to his personal taste. Peretz Lejzorek (Z"L), obtained his basic primary education in the cell. He was a sort of miniature Rabbi Akiva, he read voraciously, zealously and with great understanding. For him, the cell constituted his natural environment. For youngsters like Elimelech Kornfeld, Yosef Friedrich and others, the cell was the complement to the social development and education they received in school. The Polish middle school operated on Saturdays as well and was therefore inaccessible to the young Jews. Spared for a long life are those who immigrated to Palestine and established stable families; they owe a lot to the Movement that gave them considerable spiritual satisfaction; a sense of freedom and belonging, content and purpose in life, moments of joy and ennoblement of the soul. We will mention a few of them: Haaneh Feigenboim, the "Rebbetzen" of the girls, loved and supported by everyone; Tova Zinder, who in spite of the difficulties at home always maintained a good mood and inspired with her nobility of spirit everyone around her (everyone participated in her dramatic "doubts" concerning her love for Ashl Tchaikovsky; Hela Rosenblum, through whose influence the Movement took on a life of fulfilment and immigration; Meyer Goldberg, who infected so many with his clowning; Dov "the Pest" who had a finger in everything; Moshe Gerstenfeld, who brought to the atmosphere of the cell the deep–rooted popular spirit of his father, Antasha – a sort of Hershel of Ostropol from Miechów whose jokes, opinions and sayings were much sought after in town. Tsvi Greenboim and Munik Koppelowitz both of pleasant appearance, both always feeling at home; Kalman Sultanik, today a Zionist agent in America, already then he was active in forming his own faction in the cell.

[Page 104]

The "Hashomer Ha–Dati" group

The "National Guard" group

[Page 105]

The cell in Miechów radiated its influence and spread its activities all over the area, was in contact with Działoszyce and promoted the creation of cells in Zaverezshye, Żarnowiec and Kshoynzh.

The Miechów cell was counted among the five central counties of the "National Guard" in Poland and was even represented in the central leadership by Ze'ev Dror.

It is impossible to write about the Miechów cell without mentioning also the Charsznica cell which, officially, was the core of the Miechów cell, began and operated a many–branched operations in the movement of its own thanks to the activity of the Pulaski brothers (today Pulas(?)).

The cells of Miechów and Charsznica arranged mutual visits and on Shabbatot would generally arrange an excursion as a hike, which they saw as a sports activity, to the cell at Charsznica. The Charsznica cell was known for the effervescent life of its branch, the few families in the town were all Zionists – among them the Rabbinical delegate Yeruzalimsky – Yerushalmi; every visit of the Miechów group to the Charsznica group became an event.

The second movement in size and organization was the "Beitar". It was founded in 1929 by David Burstein, (Z"L), Nathan Kornfeld (Z"L), and Haim Isenberg (Z"L).

The group numbered about 150 members. The founders were enthusiastic followers of Jabotinsky; they spared no time or money to establish the cell and to broaden its influence on the Miechów youth. That same year Yona Blatt (Z"L), who represented a significant and serious strengthening personality, joined them in the active leadership of the group and even broadened his activities in the area as representative at the central command of "Beitar" Poland.

That movement did an excellent job of uniting internally its membership around the revisionist ideology; the cell held many meetings with its members debating the problems of the Movement on Zionism and the reality of the Jews in Poland. For the ordinary folk classes were arranged to provide basic education, arithmetic, and literature. On Friday evenings "Beitar" held meetings to which were invited members of all the Movements for an exchange of views and opinions. As speakers and lecturers, activists from other parties in town were also invited.

Conspicuous among the members of "Beitar" were Hirsch Leib Gerstenfeld, (Z"L), Tsvi Steinitz, (Z"L), Mendel Lewit, (Z"L), David Millstein, (Z"L), Golda Blatt, (Z"L), Bella Gerstenfeld, (Z"L), Haya Gittel Lewit, (Z"L) while saved for a long life were: Yitzhak Polski, alert and active; Yochaved Blatt, who "mothered" the members of the cell; Moshe Burstein who was active in leadership and social activities of the cell.

The third of the Movements was the "Religious Guard". That movement resembled very much the "National Guard" except that its members in the main came from orthodox families and their activities contained a strong essence of traditional religious orthodoxy. Active in the cell were: Yitzhak Sheinfrucht, (Z"L), and spared for a long life Yehuda Burstein who was also attached to activities in other Movements and a student in the "Religious Guard", and both were close to the members of other cells, from the "National Guard" and "Beitar".

The fourth Movement was "Poalei Zion" (both left and right).

Also active was the "Agudat Yisroel" Movement. Its members formed a separate quorum within the Seminary of the Gurer Rabbi's Yeshiva and devoted themselves daily to studying a page on Charity. Among these young students was Yosef Avigdor Polski, who had been nominated as rabbi in Vodislov and still today is known by that name in one of the English cities; Leibel Bladdeh and others.

[Page 106]

It should be mentioned that in spite of the different opinions between the Parties, tolerance reigned among the opposition. Unlike in many other places in Poland, the struggle between the Movements in Miechów was on an ideological basis alone and there is no recollection of any incident moving beyond the bounds of civilized debate and moving into personalities and personal accusations.

While speaking of "Movements" one must mention also the sports section "Kadima". Although most of its members were counted among the youth movements in town it also took part in other activities besides its sporting ones. It existed essentially as a Jewish football team and challenged Polish teams and discharged themselves honorably even, on occasion, winning. It was a sort of demonstration of self-respect and cultivated a feeling of pride putting themselves as Jews on an equal footing with the Goyim. The man who made every effort for the success of "Kadima" was Simcha Hirshenhorn (Z"L).

Himself no sportsman in practice, even wearing his Kippa and caftan, he found himself caught up in the idea of a Jewish football team and no effort was too great for him if it was connected to the team; he worried about training, care of the football pitch, its fences ("Kadima" was the only team in the town with its own playing–field) and on more than one occasion laundered its own team shirts.

Conspicuous among the players were: Herschel Steinitz (Z"L) and Hershel Solewicz (Z"L). Spared for a long life were: the Tchaikovsky brothers, Shamke Schweitzer, Yitzhak Pulaski and Benjamin Feigenboim.

A very special and unique group assembled in the hut of Sister Zinger. It was a group of sort of "salon" youths who were not disgusted – heaven forbid – by "Salon–dancing". (Whoever was caught in the "sinful" act was immediately expelled from the party without mercy). Among those who came to the hut were two Polish girls and it was a new phenomenon in town to see these two walking together with Jews on Saturdays in the Market Square.

The Kadima Sports Club

Mendl Alszewski

Translated by Gloria Berkenstat Freund

The idea of creating a Jewish sports club was born among several young people when the shtetl [town] was transferred to the Austrians by the Russians in 1916.

The founders of Kadima were: Berish Salewicz, Yehezkiel Salewicz, Mendl Kajzer, Mendl and Mordekhai Leib Olszewski, Fintsha Czajkowski, Leibl Mlinarski and so on.

The first time the young men learned and practiced at the targowiska [markets], at the spot that was the cattle market, they played football [soccer] in their regular clothes. Later, after Poland's liberation, when the club grew and began to arrange matches with other teams, they made blue and white uniforms and moved to the sports field of the Polish club, Unia, near the military barracks. There were times when Kadima defeated the best sports clubs from Zaglembie and Kielce.

[Page 107]

Left Poalei-Zion

In 1919 a military man of high rank came to Miechow, Mirkin and Sosnowiec and looked for contact with the Jewish young people from the working classes.

Later we learned that he was a literary researcher with the pseudonym "Maks Erik" and simultaneously he was active in the Left Poalei-Zion [Workers of Zion – Marxist-Zionists] party. Yekutiel Grajcer and I were the first ones to meet him. He carried on an animated conversation with us about communal work among the young in the shtetl. He urged us not to be passive, but to take an active part in fashioning the political resolve of the Jewish working young and this was only possible within the framework of the Poalei-Zion Party. We informed him that there were two dramatic circles in the city, one for the young intelligentsia, who were grouped at the Hashomer [the guard] Library, and the other from the working class.

After the meeting he began regular activities with a cycle of lectures about general socialism and Jewish socialism. He was negative about the Bund. Because of clandestine themes, the lectures took place each time in another apartment. The following comrades provided their apartments for this purpose: Yekutiel Grajcer, Noakh Gruszke, Eidl Kowal and Moshe-Chaim Olszewski. Only young men took part in the group and no young women.

In later years all of the young men left the shtetl for the great world and other active workers arose from the upcoming generation of young people.

Dramatic Circle

In about 1916 several young men created a dramatic circle and in a short time they attracted the following participants: the Lawcze family, the Grajcer family, both Skawran sisters, Yeshaya Tarnowski, Mate Krzesiwo, Shmuel Blum and Yerakhmiel Ickowicz.

We staged the following plays: Dovid's Fidele [David's Fiddle] by [Yosef] Lateyner, Moshe Heyt – Moshe Richter, Di Neveyle [The Carcass] – Peretz Hirshbein's, Di Ganevim [The Thieves] – from Bimka and from Ben-HaDor – a historic operetta.

The Ben-HaDor play was directed by Mendl Olszewski and the musical compositions were created by Alter Yosef Danciger. The creator of the scenery was Shmuel Blum and the costumes were put together from household clothing.

The performances were held at Yisroel Dovid Szpigl's flour warehouse. The actors themselves hammered together the scenery from boards. The seats for the public were also made of boards placed on sacks of wheat. We rehearsed at Yekutiel Grajcer's.

We traveled to the surrounding shtetlekh [towns], such as Slomniki, Kziaz [Wielki] and Wodzislaw.

[Page 108]

Founding members of "The Young Zionists"

Standing: Meir Fogel; Ze'ev Dror; Ya'acov Poslushny; Yehezkiel Dror

Sitting: Yehuda Zelmanowicz; Yona Blatt; Getsil Levit

Training groups of "The Young Zionists"

[Page 109]

The Rise, Development and Destruction of the Cooperative Movement in Miechow

by M. Sbitcki

Translated by Gloria Berkenstat Freund

In 1912, before the First World War, "the Second Cooperative Credit Bank" (Drugiego Towarzystwa Wzajemnego Kredytu) was founded in Miechow by the local merchants and respected middle class of the city, Nusen Borensztajn, Moshe Sukienik, Lemel Kacengold, Mendl Kornfeld, Yitzhak Posluczni, Yosef Brukner, Ahron Sercaz, Faywl Cenzinski, Ahron Leib Adler and bookkeeper, Maurici Zilberszlag. The premises of the bank were with Nusan Borensztajn at the market on the first [meaning the second in Europe] floor in the front. The activities of the bank consisted of giving loans to small merchants and artisans, as well as taking in deposits and savings from the Jewish community, as well as dowries of poor brides, with interest. The bank developed very rapidly and benefited from the trust of the entire Jewish population. It carried on widespread activity in Miechow as well as in the entire area.

When the war broke out in 1914, all of the assets of the bank were threatened. Only a few books, stamps and the iron cashbox remained of all the assets. A few years after the war, when economic conditions began to stabilize and trade relations became normal, it was necessary for the Jewish community to reestablish a cooperative bank that would be able to help and support the retailers and artisans in daily life.

In 1922, a Cooperative Bank in Miechow (Bank Spółdzielczy [Cooperative Bank]) again was created by the merchants, retailers and artisans, with the help of I.K.O. [Jewish Colonial Organization].

The founders of the bank were Nusan Borensztajn, Moshe Sukienik, Moshe Koplowicz, Enzil Koplowicz, Yehosha Koplowicz, Yitzhak Posluszni, Betsalel Wajcman, Lemel Kacengold, Chaim Walberg, Yerimyahu Blum, Ahron Berger, Hershl Edelist, Ruwin Shmuel Klajner, Yosef Lancberg and others. The bank was involved in all things that remained from the first finance society, as well as the same location and began to accept members in the bank. Each member bought a share for 25 zlotes to be able to have voting rights and to receive a loan. In a short time, the bank reached several hundred members; the majority consisted of artisans. A majority of artisan members actually were elected to the managing committee and council at the voting at the general meeting.

Nusan Borensztajn, Shlomo Fajgenbaum, Moshe Koplowicz, Ahron Berger, Betsalel Wajcman, Ruwin Shmuel Klajner, Chaim Walberg and Yosef Lancman were elected as council members; Yerimyahu Blum, Hershl Edelist and Maks Manela were elected as managing committee members. Y. Blum was the director of the bank. Its representative was H. Edelist; treasurer Moshe Sukienik; chief bookkeeper Maks Manela, chief personnel Moshe Finczewski, Moshe Szajnwald and Mendl Szenker. In time the chief bookkeeper, Maks Manela, left his post and his place was taken by Moshe Finczewski, who remained until the outbreak of the Second World War. Through the years of the bank's existence, the following people worked and functioned at the bank: Ruzia Adler, Pola Wdowinski, Zisl Gladna, Sura Mlinarski, Chaim Ejzenberg, Berish Salwicz, Yisroel Salwicz, Shlomo Kacengold, Ahron Blum, Chaim Prajs, Shmuel Berger, Meir Lisze, Lemel Ejznfeld. The number of members from every strata of the population grew and reached up to 300 people, with a share capital of several thousand zlotes.

The bank carried on all banking operations, such as giving long- and short-term loans, promissory note collections, bills of lading and savings as well as various accrediting and uncertain promissory notes of freight and train supplies in various branches.

[Page 110]

The bank grew larger from day to day.

The bank benefited from long-term credit of as much as 30,000 zlotes from I.K.O. (Warsaw) and also a credit from the Central Cooperative Bank in Warsaw. Therefore, an auditor from the Jewish Auditors Union of the Jewish Cooperatives in Poland would come from time to time from Warsaw, Rimarska 9.

The auditors from Warsaw, Dr. Chaim Szaszkes, Michelson and others often would visit. In 1926 there was a split between the merchants and the artisans at the annual meeting of the members of the bank. The majority elected the artisans to the council and the managing committee: Comrade Ahron Berger as chairman of the council; Comrade Hershl Edelist as chairman of the managing committee and artisans as other [managing committee members]. After this, a second bank of merchants was created in Miechow, Bank Kupiecki [Merchants' Bank]. The leaders were Moshe Koplewicz, Chaim Fajerajzen, Chaim Lewit, Avraham Fridrich, Avraham Sercaz, Yosef Blat, Shmuel Ulmer and so on.

The personnel of the bank consisted of Berish Salewicz, Eliezer Lewit, Pola Fajerajzen, Meir Yehiel Milinarski and Avraham Rozenkranc. The bank operations were only among the merchants and retailers. The two banks existed until the outbreak of the Second World War on the 1st of September 1939. When the German Nazis occupied Poland, all of the resources were completely looted by the Germans, who stole all of the Jewish possessions and then created a ghetto. In 1942 they deported the entire Jewish population and no trace remained of everything that the Jews had created with sweat and blood in Poland.

[Page 111]

D. Between Two World Wars

No. 1 Krakowski Street

by Sarah Ilan

Translated by Selwyn Rose

When I recall the big house where I lived forty years ago, with its entrances from three side–streets, I see each and every one of the people living there, standing before me as they did in their daily lives, Shabbatot and festivals. The tenants were many and varied: tradesmen, artisans, Torah students and those for whom the Torah was the very source of their livelihood. The house was not communally shared; each apartment was owned by the resident and the house itself was owned by another person, sometimes changing ownership, while the tenants were much more permanent and lived there for years and knew one another as if they were one large family. They reared their children and married them in the same courtyard and it could happen that the same son or daughter would then continue to live after the marriage and parents, children and grandchildren all living under one roof.

Among the tenants were widows whose children had flown the nest to distant parts and every day they awaited the postman in the hope that he would bring a letter from one of the offspring from abroad. I recall one of them who would come to visit us frequently. She left her children in America and returned alone because she was unable to adjust to life among strangers. Here, in this house, were people whom she knew. She would open our door and come in without even knocking and say: "Ah! Being here with you refreshes my soul; warm and plenty of light. May it be that the "light" of Shabbat will never dim." Her reference was to my father (Z"L), the "Man" of the family. She always had stories and jokes from the time she was in America.

As for the women in the courtyard, one could see some of them standing or sitting in front of the front door of the house. There were among them a mother and daughter who, from the few words and snatches of phrases one could catch, one would learn that no event, even the smallest of details, escaped their eye or attention. From the front door one could see the town spread out and humming with peddlers, shops and people just enjoying wandering slowly about the streets. Another mother and daughter used to come to our house, greeting my mother – may she live long – with advice for all, while they, themselves were at a loss all their lives.

The Cantor's House

His was the neighboring apartment, above ours. I would go there because they had a daughter about my age. Who can describe Friday evening? When Cantor Yankeleh (May his Righteousness be Remembered for a Blessing), was in front of the Holy Ark, intoning the melody of the Kiddush and "Woman of value...", with his two sons accompanying him, their deep, rich voices were like musical instruments ringing in my ears until this day. On the eve of the Day of Atonement people would come from all over town to hear his "Kol Nidrei" – even non–Jews would stand outside the synagogue listening to his rendering and telling each other: "Aah! He and his two sons could be opera–singers!"

[Page 112]

Even Jews, who never came to the synagogue throughout the year, would come to the concluding service to hear "Ne'ilah" from the Cantor.

There was a very pleasant ritual enacted every Rosh Hashanah after the evening prayer and the sanctification of the festival, the congregation would rush to greet the Rabbi with the blessing "May you be inscribed in the Book of Life," to which he would immediately reply "Le–Haim!" From the Cantor's house to the house of the Rabbi: whose apartment was also in the same courtyard. They would first greet the Rabbi showing the respect due to the Father of the Beit–Din and afterwards to the Cantor who was known far and wide for his simple popularity and welcoming expression to all he met.

Many people would visit the Rabbi every day of the year, some to obtain advice, some to receive encouragement or for one reason or another, others for condolences and some just for a secular conversation.

For the "Third Shabbat Meal" many people would congregate at his home to hear the prayer "Yadid Nafshi" and cantorial pieces from the Sabbath that were sung on Shabbatot between the afternoon and evening prayers. Often we would sit, his daughters, me and another girl, a good friend of Gold'eleh, in the Rabbi's wife's room and quietly hum the melodies we could hear coming from the other room, receive a slice of chalah and salted fish from the Rabbi's table and wait to hear the "Havdalah" prayer. The Rabbi would deliberately stretch the prayer signifying the end of the holy day of Shabbat, by half-an-hour to keep Satan from coming close to the Sabbath.

The Purim festivities would extend until daylight; musical instruments would play the dances of the orthodox, but sad songs were also heard, to remind us of our exile even in times of pleasure.

The preparations for the forthcoming Passover would commence in the Cantor's home immediately after the conclusion of the present one. Every year one of our Jewish congregants who owned fields and resided in town would bring a few sheaves of wheat in order to prepare Matzo Shemurah.

This was how it went: On one of the days when there was no rain and reaping took place, the Jewish owner of the field would come with his horse and cart and invite Cantor Yankeleh to be present at the reaping. The sheaves were stored until the next Hannuka, in a dry barn where no rain or moisture could reach them. They were then brought to the Cantor's house. We, too, the children, had a part in the preparation – to help sort the wheat from the chaff. All our spare time throughout the holiday was devoted to that purpose. When we had completed the selection all the wheat grains were again stored by the Cantor in a dry secure place where they remained until just a few days before the Passover festival. The grains were milled in the Cantor's house on millstones and the day before Passover eve the Matzo was prepared. At dawn the Cantor and his two sons, together with a couple of their closest orthodox associates went to bring water from the well to bake the Matzoth. On coming down the steps leading from his house the Cantor would approach the window of our apartment and call out to my father (Z"L): "Reb Herschel, Reb Herschel! Are the shovels ready"? And my father would reply: "Ready – but I am waiting until the last moment to flatten the dough as close to the time as possible so that they don't become contaminated with hametz."

Cleaning the house for Passover and the urgent consultations about what is Kosher and permissible and what is not, was in itself like a tractate from the Talmud. Every year, on the last day of Pessach, the Cantor loved to tell the popular story about eating "kreplach":

A woman named Fassia prepared kreplach on the last day of Passover. Her husband ate them with great gusto, having looked forward to them all the eight days of the festival (in an orthodox Jewish home it is not customary to eat them except on the last day). When he finished eating he felt a little uncomfortable. His wife warmed a saucepan–lid and placed it on his abdomen in order to ease the discomfort. Intermittently the husband would cry out

“Fassia! Bring me a kneidle;” ”Fassia – Bring me a “Pokrivka” ...because how can one forgo “Kneidlach” on the last day of Pessach?

[Page 113]

Cantor Yankeleh was always ready with a wise comment or words from the Torah. He knew to walk with his creator. He would say: “In today's world of lying, a man is obliged to clothe himself in a lie in order to get to the truth.” In his acceptance concerning those who failed to keep the Sabbath in those days, he would say: “The time has come for Jews to ride publicly on the Sabbath and a few in town will remind them: ‘Gentlemen, today is the Shabbos.’ And they would think the orthodox ones the minority.” On Selichot, when the congregation came to the synagogue and the Study House, they came also to hear the Cantor's rich voice. The younger generation would gather in our house and the conversation flowed on this and that. When the service had finished and our parents returned one of the group would jump up and say: “Reb Hershel! We made the prayer for Selichot here in your house, we heard every word...” and my father would reply with forgiveness: “I believe you, I believe you,”

The Wedding

One morning we got to know that the eldest son of the Cantor was engaged to be married and the wedding was to take place in the bridegroom's house because the bride was from abroad. It would be easier for her family to come to Poland than for the extended family here to travel abroad.

The owner, who had the biggest apartment in the block, vacated his house to enable the guests to use it for a week. Other tenants also made rooms available in their own homes in order to accommodate the many guests who were coming to the wedding from all over Poland as well as from surrounding countries.

There were many people from both sides dressed in Streimlers and silk caftans and the women in elegant decorated hats with gold necklaces round their throats. On the night of the wedding everyone congregated: musicians, comedians and entertainers, orthodox and just ordinary Jews. After the bridegroom's speech one of the comics stood up and began to make humorous comments, as is usual, about the various presents that were being given to the newlyweds and after the actual ceremony and the festive meal everyone went out for the traditional “Dance with the Bride”. For the first time I had the opportunity to see this event taking place among those who keep up the traditions with exactitude. And now the announcement is made: Honored "Mr. So–and–so" will please gladden the heart of the bride and groom with the Bridal Dance; the "someone" takes a kerchief at one corner and the bride the other corner and start dancing surrounded by a large circle of the other guests, the bride's "partner" changing from time to time, for over an hour, accompanied by the musicians and singing until the long list of dancers was completed and all the honored guests had danced. At the end of the dance the womenfolk, in a long chain, would accompany the bride to the previously prepared courtyard, while the men accompany the groom – accompanied by music, singing and good wishes to the newlyweds and blessings for creating a new home under the Torah and Good Deeds.

Every evening other guests were invited for each of the "Seven Blessings", as was the custom and the only thing missing from previous meetings was the actual ceremony.

On one of the evenings a man arrived, known throughout Polish towns by the nickname Reb Reuven "Come here". In a very original fashion, acting like a scholar of the Torah, he would tie some sort of a belt round his hips and hang upon it a large copper container filled with water on which was written "Fresh well water" and on his other side he hung a cup on a chain and thus adorned he would shout to all: "Let all those who thirst, come and drink from fresh well water!". And with that he would serve water to all who were thirsty. The man was tall, good–looking and had a long white beard. He would stroll all evening with a pleasant expression, and with faith in his place in "the world to come", because he was a Torah scholar. At all these events he had a list was so that not one of the participants, neighbours or children was missed out.

[Page 114]

The last landlord of the house that I knew before I left there was Wenchdelowsky. He and his family were good–hearted people with not many like them. They were our closest neighbours, with facing doors; we were like family members. When a tenant was unable to pay the rent in time he was likely to pay an embarrassing call on the family and say: "Maybe you haven't even got with what to live. Here, I'll give you something to get you by and when things get a bit easier you can pay me back together with the rent." Later on the family immigrated to Palestine and joined the Moshav Kfar Baruch. They loved agriculture and the farm and they loved the people they came into contact with. We made great friends with them in Palestine as well for many years. May they be remembered for a blessing.

Thus I remember the festivals, the joyful days and the ordinary days and the tenants in the house I lived as a child. Those I have mentioned, and to those I have not mentioned, please do not be hurt.

Shabbat gave flavour to the six–days of toil, which for most people was a daily struggle for survival under pressures of one sort or another – persecution, the acquisition of means to survive. But Shabbat made it all worthwhile: a day of rest, a walk to the synagogue, visits to neighbours and acquaintances, studying the Torah, visits with friends, a little freedom from the materialistic world and a little time to breathe, each one according to his taste and ability.

Our House

by Sarah Wertheim

Translated by Selwyn Rose

Our house was constructed in three sections and to each section there was an exit onto another street. There was a large courtyard that united all three buildings. The house belonged to Wenchdelowsky. The courtyard of the house resembled somewhat a small neighborhood in a city: There were people who had many professions and trades. Jews and non–Jews lived there together side by side.

Most of the tenants worked at their professions or trade at home, or opened a small shop in the courtyard. The charcoal–maker and a welding–shop opened on to the courtyard and the street while the jeweler, textile merchant, the feather seller and others – their apartments were their shops...

The relationships between the Jews and the non–Jews were not good and there was much open anti–Semitism. In the apartment beneath us was a tax–collector, Komornik, a Christian. When we needed to wash our floor, which was made of wooden planks, if a few drops of water seeped through the cracks, he would knock on the ceiling with a broomstick, shouting and cursing.

On our floor was another anti–Semitic family with five older daughters and a younger boy with a limp, named Stefek. The boy would often scare us and surprise us with blows. Once when he was hitting us and we called for help, our mother quickly came to help and coming down the stairs in excitement, she burst a vein in her leg.

The concierge of the house, Yana, was also anti–Semitic. She chased us regularly with a stick or broom and hit us with it. My sister used to anger her by calling to her from a distance: “Ya–niah!” – “Not me!” At Christmas, when we went to give her a Christmas present, she would change her tune completely with compliments and caresses. But an hour later she had forgotten everything and would chase us as if nothing had happened.

[Page 115]

As if to complete the image of a town as it was represented in our house, in front of us lived both the Cantor and the community's Rabbi who, at festival times generated an atmosphere of sanctity and happiness in the lives of the rest of the Jewish tenants At Succoth we ate our meals in the Succoth erected by the Cantor and after the meal my mother would bring a basket full of big plums from the stock we would sell at that time of the year. Our sustenance came from various sources. A few of the older children sold fruit in the streets of Miechów, my mother would travel to Bedzin taking milk products and chickens for sale and return bringing items of haberdashery for sale at home. My mother was known for her honesty and extreme righteousness to the extent that before she went to Argentina with a few of the family, she received clothes and frozen foods and commodities of various sorts because the shopkeepers knew and trusted her and were sure that she would send back to them the proceeds of her sales from Argentina.

School–time study was a happy period. I loved learning and did well in class especially handicrafts and mathematics.

My handicrafts also found a positive reaction from my teacher who was anti–Semitic, and she gave me her night–dress to embroider. To this day, I regret doing it.

Impressions of the Pogrom of 1920

by Moshe Burstein

Translated by Selwyn Rose

I was then at the dawn of my existence, a child, with the secrets of life still hidden from me when the frightening disturbance occurred that shook the very essence of my soul.

One Friday morning, a nice spring day, a rumor, like thunder from heaven, was heard: The Christians, and among them a mob of Poles, were attacking the Jews.

The center of the disturbance was in front of the gates to the synagogue, when the worshippers filled the place during the mid–morning hours of that Friday.

My father (Z"L), had managed to finish his prayers and returned home, but my brother, Raphael (Z"L), who had remained in the Study–House to finish studying a page of the Gemara, was one of the victims and received a serious head injury. Our brother was the most educated and esteemed of all the boys in our family, self–educated in secular subjects, specializing in Torah and languages: Polish, Hebrew and German; he was well–mannered with a personal charm, and loved by all who knew him.

My sisters Sheva and Tsiril were in Perchal the baker's, looking at the windows of the synagogue and before their eyes they saw the atrocity happen. They saw how the men, draped in their prayer shawls, were dragged out by the Polish mob, how they fell upon them with knives, iron bars and stones. The extreme brutality was carried out with sadistic pleasure and ended with acts of murder.

Our house bordered the synagogue building. To prevent the hooligans from breaking into it, we closed the corridor entrance door and hung an axe on a hook in the door jamb – it was the only defensive measure we took.

These violent disturbances continued until the evening of Friday. My mother (Z"L), was in shock and collapsed on the floor. As far as I recall and if I am not mistaken, at that time my brother Shai, Lazar, Leibel and myself – the youngest – were all at home. The injured, their heads covered in blood, managed with the last of their strength to get to Lewit's house, which also abutted the synagogue, and went down to the cellar of the house.

[Page 116]

When they had finished with beating up their victims, the bullies ransacked the synagogue itself, bringing out the sacred Scrolls from the Ark together with other holy books from the Study House, tearing and ripping everything to shreds and strewing the shreds all over the floor. When they had finished with this act, they pelted the beautiful stained–glass windows high up in the clerestory of the prayer hall, the windows I so much loved to gaze through their colored glass. Thus they continued until dark, the beginning of the Sabbath.

The Reception of the Sabbath my father performed at home. My mother spread the table–cloth, white as snow, on the table, lit the Sabbath candles and with great sorrow blessed the candles. My father put on his black silk caftan and in a soft voice we sang the "Lecha Dodi Likrat Kalah" Sabbath hymn, my father's face pale and the signs of his suffering clearly seen on his face.

All that same Shabbat we remained closed and secluded in our home with no one going out and no one coming in. We heard the Christian landlady chatting with the neighbors and saying that all the Jews needed to be slaughtered.

On Sunday morning, at dawn while dead silence still reigned outside, our mother sent the youngest of her children, Leibel and myself (for fear that maybe the disturbance will renew itself), through a window opening on to a lane alongside the post office, to our eldest sister Gittel (Z"L), who lived in the Karchova's house and there we stayed until Monday morning.

At night the heavens closed in and it began to rain heavily on the blood–soaked ground. Early in the morning, my brother and I returned home. The spring scent of flowers pervaded the air and the singing of the birds mingled with the smell of innocent blood that stuck to the walls of the synagogue and the adjacent houses.

The visible results of the dreadful events presented a spectacle before our eyes: the smashed windows, their shattered colored glass spread all over, the torn pages of our Holy Scrolls and books torn to shreds spread over the sidewalks and the road. A sight etched so deeply on my heart that never in my life will I forget it.

My hand will not stay from my obligation to add the following: At the time of the disturbances the district head, Kulesza, came into the Study House, spread his arms wide in front of the Holy Ark and said: "Don't touch this!"

Pogroms against the Jews of Miechów

by Ya'acov Spiegel

Translated by Selwyn Rose

We had in town an organization called "The Guard" whose function was to perform the Mitzvah of visiting the sick, helping and encouraging the needy. Ya'acov belonged to that association. In carrying out his duties, he went one day to visit Yosef Kornfeld, who had fallen sick with Typhus. On the way he met Berl Malinarski in Dzialoszyce street who said to him: "There's some news in town, the bookbinder Kowalski hit Berl on the head with a stick – and he wonders: Why and what for?" While they were talking David Mordecai Lejzorek joined them and told them that his landlord performed some act of villainy in town and as a result there was an atmosphere of extreme hostility among the Christians towards the Jews, pervading the town – without any cause or explanation...that happened on the Thursday, 1st May. As usual on that date the poor farmers would congregate in order to celebrate Labor Day. At the same time there was also a general mobilization of many men for the army taking place, following the advance of the Soviet Red Army towards Warsaw. In Miechów there was a gathering of young recruits from all the surrounding villages. This only added fuel to the fire. In the midst of rumpus, Ya'acov tried to run home but he was blocked by the inflamed farmers who already filled all the town's streets and lanes. Having no alternative he returned to Dzialoszyce street and climbed up to the roof of Ezriel Pulaski's house. From there he saw a harrowing sight: a beaten and stabbed Jewish man was being dragged along by the Christians. It was Ezriel's brother – Haim Pulaski, who died as a result of his injuries a few hours later.

[Page 117]

A rumor quickly spread that it was the intention of the rioters to set fire to Ezriel's house. The Jewish men began organizing themselves for self–protection and to repel the attack of the incensed hooligans. But the plan failed to materialize because the farmers from the entire area arrived in such great crowds and their numbers grew from hour to hour while the Jews were represented by only a small group. The town Governor was away in the county town of Kielce and the Municipal officials ordered army units from Wolbrom but they, instead of subduing the rioting farmers abetted them in committing further acts; alarm among the Jews increased from moment to moment.

They hid in their houses for all three days that the Poles rioted. The Jewish people that prayed in the synagogue took many casualties – some of them very serious – and only a very few managed somehow to escape their clutches.

In the meantime the Governor returned from Kielce and when he saw how serious the situation was and that there was a danger of even more murders – he mobilized army units from Kielce from General Haler's command and these opened fire on the inflamed rioters and even killed a few of them. That was enough to subdue the crowds and to suppress the Pogrom.

The old Miechów cemetery

[Page 118]

How the Jews of Miechów and Charsznica celebrated the opening of the Hebrew University on Mount Scopus

by Shimon Dov Yerushalmi

Translated by Selwyn Rose

In the darkness of Jewish life in the Diaspora there gleamed a large beacon of light.

The information that uplifted the spirit – the building of the Hebrew University in Jerusalem on the heights of Mount Scopus – awoke enormous excitement among the Jews of the Diaspora, among them, of course, the Jews of Miechów and Charsznica.

The rumor, that on 1st April 1925 our University was due to be consecrated in the presence of many notable guests from Palestine and Righteous Gentiles [1] from around the non–Jewish world and at their head Arthur, Lord James Balfour, added wings to it. In the hearts of our brethren throughout the Diaspora the hope grew that the days of fulfillment foreseen by our Prophets were indeed in the offing: "For the Torah will go forth from Zion and the word of the Lord from Jerusalem..."

And how much greater was the joy of our Jewish community when it was learned that our Chairman, Mr. Avraham Sercaz (May G–d avenge his blood), was scheduled to represent our community and go to Jerusalem in order to take part in those national ceremonies, the like of which had not been seen since the exile from our country and from our land.

The Committee that was created to celebrate the opening of the University included representatives of all the various Zionist and public institutions and was the body that decided to elect Mr. Avraham Sercaz as the Community's representative and in his hands a congratulatory epistle written on vellum and signed by the representatives of all the institutions and foundations.

The message was composed by one of the foremost Russian teachers and authors, Mr. Shmuel Nahum Kochanowski, whom fate had decreed that his latter years be spent functioning as teacher of religion in the primary school in Miechów.

The text of the epistle, composed by him and found to this day in the archives of the University on Mount Scopus, is as follows:

In the name of those of Zion

On this most excellent historic day, in the life of the Jewish People of today – in an era of its rebirth in its National Home, a day of the consecration of this Temple of Wisdom, The Hebrew University on Mount Scopus.

On this joyous, splendid and heartwarming day of peaceful victory, for the Jewish People, for its Hebrew Language and for the Land of Israel, we, our little community of Miechów, one of the many dispersed throughout the five continents, find ourselves hard–pressed to express our great happiness in fitting words and to convey our congratulations and our deep feelings of this event and with soaring spirit, intense gaiety, commit our thoughts to this parchment. To this Great House and those great ones of our people chosen to head the staff and pave our way forward, who have worked, are working and will continue to work for the benefit their People and its future and who are establishing this University.

We pray that it may it be the will of our Father in heaven to enable this establishment to project its wisdom on its environment with sense of security and confidence among its students such that they will not need to seek abroad in the Diaspora and its foundations for knowledge and wisdom and spiritual nourishment; that it should be open for all to study and learn without regard to religion, race, sex or creed; that it should radiate to the world the visions of Moses our Teacher and Law–giver (Deuteronomy 4, vi): "Keep, therefore and do them; for this is your wisdom and understanding in the sight of the Nations, which shall hear all these statutes, and say, Surely this great nation is a wise and understanding people." And the vision of Isaiah 2, iii: "And many people shall go and say Come ye, and let us go up to the mountain of the Lord, to the house of the God of Jacob; and he will teach us of his ways, and we will walk in his paths: For out of Zion shall go forth the law, and the Word of the Lord from Jerusalem".

May it be the will of our Father in heaven, that this House on Mount Scopus will shine forth as a Pillar of Fire that will illuminate the Universe with the light of Truth, Righteousness and Justice to open the eyes of the blind that they may find the way that leads to the happiness of Mankind and peace shall prevail throughout the world for a good and seemly life.

May it be the will of our Father in heaven that the founders of this House and their helpers will gather strength and courage to perform their sacred tasks for the sake of their people and that the memory of their toil shall not fade from the knowledge of Israel.

Amen!

The fourth day of the week, in the seventh month of the redemption, in the year one thousand eight hundred and fifty after the destruction of Jerusalem the Holy City 5685 (1925).

The Municipality of Miechów–Charsznica, Kielce County Poland.

[Page 119]

Signatories:

Community Rabbi: Hanoch Ha'anich Sheinfrucht, Rav Gaon, Our Teacher, May his Righteousness be remembered for a blessing in the world to come, Father of the Community Rabbinical Court, Miechów and Galilee.

Community Leadership: Avraham Sercaz, Shimson Dov Yerushalmi.

Miechów Zionists: Ephraim Blum.

Charsznica Zionists: Avraham Gertler, Shmuel Ya'acov Gleitt.

"Mizrahi": Shmuel Pagel(?), Ya'acov Tsvi Gitler.

"Young Mizrahi": Yitzhak Pri–Hadar.

"Hechalutz": Haim Itzkowitz.

"Hechalutz Ha–Mizrahi": Yesheyahu Burstein.

The Eretz Yisroel Office: Aharon Leib Adler.

The KKL: Moshe Koppelowitz.

The Foundation Fund: Ze'ev Dov Kaiser.

The Primary School: Shmuel Nahum Kochanowski.

The Mizrahi School: Shmuel Abramowitz, Yitzhak Tsvi Weiner - School Head–teacher.

"Ha–Zamir": Yerechmiel Isskowitz.

"Ha–Dror": Benyamin Elimelech Friedrich.

"Maccabi": Tsvi Lifsher(?).

"Kadima": Avraham Buchner.

"Book–Buyer": Yehuda Burstein.

The "Artists' Society": Yisroel Brumer.

The "Merchants' Society": Bezalel Weitzman.

The Small Traders: Ze'ev Weissfeld.

The Cooperative Bank: Yermiyahu Blum.

The City Council: David Isskowitz.

"Brotherly Help": Avraham Mordecai Stern.

Sick Visit Association: Haim Lewit.

The Synagogue: Shlomo Feigenboim.

The Burial Society: Avraham Goldberg.

The Committee for organizing the celebration of the opening of the college:

President: Shimshon Dov Rabbi Moshe Nahum Yerushalmi.

Secretary: Eliezer Lipa Yazkirowitz.

[Page 120]

Members – All Yisroel

I have put on paper the names of all the institutions and societies that signed the Epistle in order to emphasize the degree that the Jewish communities of Miechów and Charsznica felt involved in the enterprise and the extent of their wish to associate themselves with the other parties congratulating the University and to celebrate with joy its opening.

I think, and feel obliged, to note at the beginning, the behaviour of the heads of "Agudat Yisroel" in Miechów, that an order "from on high" forbad them to sign as themselves as affiliated to the movement, among the others and their names and signatures appear as follows: Chairman of the "Aguda": Mr. Avraham Mordecai Stern who signed as "Brotherly Help"; the member Mr. Ze'ev Weissfeld who signed as The "Small Traders Society"; Mr. Bezalel Weitzman who signed as The "Merchants' Society".

Those who attained the right to sign and also to see the country being built after immigrating:

The writer of these lines; Yehuda Burstein; Ya'acov-Tsvi Gitler; Mr. Eliezer Lavie. May they be blessed with good lives and long years!

The attitude of the Polish authorities to riots and disturbances

This is the language and instructions published by the County Governorship in Miechów from 28th March 1925 No. 5433/1 (Translated from the Polish):

"To the Jewish religious management in Miechów

To your request of the 26th March 1925, I hereby permit Miechów–Charsznica to organize celebrations connected to the opening of the Hebrew University in Jerusalem, according to the following program:

A meeting of the primary school children in the cinema hall "Uciecha" in which the teachers from the same school will deliver speeches suitable to the occasion.

1. Prayers in the local synagogue will be accompanied by suitable speeches.

2. Decorative illuminations in the windows of Jewish homes.
3. Parades in the city streets are strictly forbidden.

In addition, I permit emblems and stickers on the houses in accordance with the directives of the Ministry of Internal Affairs from 4th February 1921, as is shown in the attached copy. In respect of the income derived from the sale of emblems and stickers, etc., and the time and place of counting that income, you will inform the local Government police command who will send a representative to preside over the accounting.

The results will be forwarded to me no later than 5th April 1925.

Signed: in the name, and in place of, the governor Y. Lachowski.

The Festivities

And indeed, the opening of the Hebrew university was a great day for the Jews. From earliest light youths from the various Zionist youth groups moved from house to house and distributed the emblems ad stickers of "University Day". There, almost no single person was not displaying an emblem or failed to donate something. The spirit of the event raised the souls that showed on everyone's face as everyone and everyone wore festive clothes and every workshop and trading business was closed as if it was a religious Jewish holiday.

During the morning hours, Jewish children streamed to the cinema "Uciecha" – which means "Joy" – and indeed joy and happiness filled the hall that was full to overflowing.

[Page 121]

The children's festival opened with Zionist songs. Afterwards came the speeches of the school manager, teachers and public representatives, who explained to the pupils the value of the great day for the future of the Nation and its original culture. The enthusiasm of the youngsters is difficult to describe.

The central public celebration was attended by many people from all sectors of our society who hurried to the town synagogue which was illuminated and decorated with national flags.

Among the guests were present representatives of the authorities, the Mayor, elected Polish representatives of the city council, heads of the Polish Socialist Party and the Manager of the government Gymnasium Dr. Lech (who was associated with the extreme Polish Nationalist right–wing "Andak" party); and several other prominent Polish people in town.

Exactly at 4:00 in the afternoon, the writer of these lines opened the proceedings in the name of united committee for organizing celebrations on the opening of the Hebrew University of Jerusalem on Mount Scopus with these words: We are all, at this moment, in our hearts and thoughts, on Mount Scopus, Jerusalem where just a few hours ago were gathered together the elite of our people, our teachers, illuminators of the Nation and thousands of its guests who came together from near and far, to take part joyfully in the consecration of these Halls of wisdom and knowledge, in which our people will renew its youth and efforts to fulfill the vision of our prophets – "For the Torah shall go forth from Zion and the word of the Lord from Jerusalem."

Clearly the happiness of the Yishuv and of all our Brethren in all the places of their dispersion is also our happiness and in our hearts with appropriate enthusiasm in joining wholeheartedly in this historic moment.

We are happy to have been granted the privilege to be a part of it.

After the Chairman of the Organizing committee, our Rabbi, Hanoch Ha'anich Sheinfrucht, wrapped in his prayer shawl, took the stage and blessed the event as the entire audience stood and replied with a hearty "Amen". He continued with a tasteful sermon interspersed with comments and quotations from the Torah,, after which there was an appropriate prayer service.

Mr. Ya'acov Buchner made a speech in Polish, expressing publicly the thanks of the Jewish community of Miechów and Charsznica to the Polish guests for their participation in the festivities and their complimentary comments. The event came to a close with raised spirits and the singing of "Hatikvah" by the large congregation.

The Celebration in Charsznica

A large majority of the Jewish community in Charsznica, a community somewhat small in number in itself, took part in the gathering in the synagogue in Miechów, but it didn't stop there and they hurried to the congregation in the local Study House where prayers and the singing of suitable Psalms took place. Afterwards there were speeches on matters of the day by the writer of these few lines, Shmuel–Ya'acov Gleitt and Nahum Gertler.

Gala meal in honor of the event

The celebrations and festivities of 1st April 1925 ended but the spirit of the event and its impression lingered on. In every Jewish home, every workshop and shop and of course from every public institution and foundation and at its head the Jewish community, shone forth lights and candles from every window in candlesticks reserved for Shabbat and the Hannukiah from Hannuka all of which imparted a festive tone, sanctity and magnificence to a day of national, historic event.

In the evening the council gathered together from Miechów and Charsznica in one of best restaurants in town, and all enjoyed an excellent meal at a well–laid table.

[Page 122]

I closed the festivities with a blessing that we may yet attain the right to see the children of Miechów and Charsznica immigrate to Jerusalem as students of the Hebrew University of Jerusalem.

In the evening hours the "Ha–Zamir" library threw a party in the cinema hall.

The Children of Miechów and Charsznica as Students of the Hebrew University

Cruel fate determined that only a very few of those who were present at the celebrations survived to obtain the consolation of seeing Zion and the country being built; the rest were destroyed by the oppressive Tsarist regime.

Nevertheless we did have the satisfaction of seeing some of our communities sons – Miechów and Charsznica – counted among the students at the Hebrew University on Mount Scopus during its first years and they were:

The writer Yisroel Zerach Gertler (Z"L), who was also counted among the University Secretariat until his last day, and saved for a long and good life Mr. Shmuel Berger, Chairman of our committee and the originator of this "Memorial Book" and the living spirit of the fulfillment of the project, Ze'ev Dror (Friedrich), who served for some time at the head of the Students' Union of the University, my son, Lt. Col. Yesheyahu Yerushalmi, and Attorney Meir Fogel.

A Wish

It was a great privilege for me to be placed at the head of the committee organizing the celebrations for the opening of the Hebrew University on 1st April 1925 in Miechów and Charsznica and that I succeeded in uniting at that celebration both communities with all their respective parties.

As I give these compliments and praise to all, – may God bless them –I also give thanks that I was granted this privilege and that I lived to this day to write my memory of that day. I raise my eyes in Prayer to the Creator of the world, that I may yet see the buildings of the Hebrew University on Mount Scopus when they are free and given into the hands of the Independent State of Israel! Amen! May it be His will!

Translator's Footnote

1. Not in the present–day, post–Holocaust connotation – Trans.

The Foundation Fund for Israel – Miechów's Magnificent Operation

by Yehezkiel Dror (Friedrich)

Translated by Selwyn Rose

The involvement of Miechów in the operations of the Foundation Fund and the pleasure in its achievements there expressed the spiritual connection between the Miechów Jews and Zionism and everything connected with it.

Relatively speaking Miechów held fifth place in the listing of its donations among all the towns in Poland. The town was very proud of that attainment. Miechów was Zionist in spirit and not in order that once the admired Yitzhak Greenboim could state – without any hesitation – it would be possible hang a sign at the entrance to Miechów declaring “Zionist Federation – Miechów.”

The “Foundation Fund” boxes captured for itself a respected place in every house. It was integrated within the corpus of the family life, its events and its festivals: the lighting of the Shabbat candles, Bar Mitzvah parties, festival parties, family visits, squabbles between children, etc,

Family homes – especially with young people – competed among themselves as to who would be "number one" with their donations to the Foundation Fund.

[Page 123]

The organizing committee of the Foundation Fund bazaar

I recall how I used to examine test the weight of the box several times a month and gauge its contents by rattling the contents and I wasn't content if I didn't hear the sound of coins from within. Even the simple emptying of the box was performed with much preparation. Everyone of the collectors made efforts to increase the numbers of contributors and at the end of the year corticated were distributed to the collectors giving details of the showing the success of the donors' and collectors' activities.

When a delegate came to town the town's leaders immediately gathered together: they fixed quotas of donations and the project was conducted with religious punctiliousness and with the efficiency of men of affairs. Because of the success of Miechów's endeavors it was the top delegates who came:

Droyanov, Bistritzki and others. Bistritzki excited the whole town, he started dancing with the youth and was particularly well–liked by the businessmen. His visit left an impression that lasted for many days. Droyanov, of his own choice and volition added his own holiday to his workdays in Miechów and remained in town for eight days. When he left town people lined the streets on both sides and cheered him on his way. His jokes had the population rolling with laughter for a long time after he left.

Virtually the entire Jewish population of the town participated in the annual collection. Those youngsters who were unable to get their hands on the target sum as individuals joined together in twos and threes in order to achieve the requisite amount. The first promissory note I signed in my life as a young person was for the Foundation Fund when I was but 15 years old, together with my cousin Yona Blatt (Z"L).

During the years of riots in Palestine the contributions reached their highest, and that was in addition to the donations of gold, jewellery and other articles of value. The Jews of Miechów were deeply sensitive and who doesn't remember the weeping that broke out in the women's gallery when Lipa Yazkirowitz [1] shouted out: "Miechów women – weep!"

In 1927, the Foundation Fund organized bazaars throughout Poland. The Bazaar in Miechów became renowned in the area. Women decorated the town, embroidered, sewed, donated and got others to donate, lotteries, "selling kisses" – the whole town seethed with noise and activity. The "Israel" hut, which was decorated tastefully by our member, Dov, contained "Carmel" wines, Fruit from Palestine, candies wrapped in nice papers decorated and written in Hebrew, products manufactured by "Shemen", soap, "Bezalel" decorations, and Yemenite embroideries. We had never tasted such candies as those that we bought there.

The Bazaar lasted for eight days and attracted many people from the surrounding towns and villages: Działoszyce, Wolbrom, Dombrova, Olkusz and Charsznica.

[Page 124]

The synagogue, the Study Hall and the "Shtiebel" were used not only as a place of prayer and learning but also as a hostel for visiting Zionist delegates and everyone who was "Called to the Torah" during prayers, donated to the Foundation fund.

On festivals meetings took place of activists, lectures about Palestine, Flower days and on Lag B'Omer, when the local branch of the "Young Zionists" "captured" the town marching in their parade through the town, while in their uniforms, the operatives of the Foundation Fund were the mainstay of the project and the main speech was always made by a local representative of the Fund, or a delegate direct from the Fund to attend the event.

The Foundation Fund tried hard – and succeeded – to take part in all the festivals but the most conspicuous of them all was Purim in which the rebuilding of the National Home was merged with the fall of Haman and all persecutors of the Jews and the exultation and songs of prayers were many and great. The boys were accustomed to dress in the style of pioneers, according to the illustration in the Golden Book, mobilized rakes and shovels (the tool closest in appearance to the hoe), dressed up older men to look like A.D. Gordon, copied "Trumpledor" shirts and groups of these "pioneers" would roam the streets calling at the houses, producing pictures displaying the "Land of Israel" experience and reading excerpts from the ideals of D Szimonowicz, translated into Yiddish.

The Chairman of the Committee for the Foundation Fund of Israel in town, was Mr. Wolf Ber Kaiser (of blessed memory), and he was an indefatigable worker in its cause. He worked every single day, every hour with intense, efficient determination and understanding. He never looked for reward.

Everyone who saw Wolf Ber at work was caught up and infected with the same zeal, love and understanding that each cent that was collected for the Fund helped. His helpers of the Committee were: Elimelech Friedrich (Z"L), Tuvia Rosenboim (Z"L), Itzi Sheinfrucht (Z"L), David Burstein (Z"L) and Nathan Kornfeld (Z"L); saved for a long and good life were: Selah Sercaz, Yehuda Burstein and the writer of these lines.

Translator's Footnote

1. Today Eliezer Lavie, the secretary of the Religious Council in Israel

The "Miechów Group" in Israel

by S.D. Yerushalmi (Z"L)

Translated by Selwyn Rose

From the memoirs of Mr. Ya'acov Tsvi Gitler

Mr. Ya'acov Tsvi Gitler a luminary, grew up from his youth in the home of his uncle, Mr. Shimon Londner (Z"L), who later became one of its respected wealthy citizens.

His uncle deprived neither him, nor his brother Hanoch (Z"L), of anything yet for all that there awakened within him a yearning for Zion, his heart's desire and his ambition to "pitch his tent" on a plot of land acquired in the Land of Israel.

Already by 1912 a number of youngsters had decided to send one of their group to survey the country and examine the possibilities to immigrate and settle there. Y.D. Gitler, Avraham Goldberg, David Yehuda Marczyk, Shmuel Fogel and Ya'acov Zimmerman (Z"L), had saved together 100 Roubles and sent their colleague, Ze'ev Feureisen (Z"L), to Palestine. He remained in the country about three months, returned to Miechów and reported that each family of settlers would need about 6,000 Roubles, something that was well beyond their financial abilities.

In the meantime, the Great War broke out and all organizational activity of that nature ceased.

During the war years, when the economic situation improved somewhat for the Jews of Miechów, activity in that direction renewed and a few more people registered with the original group and among them Mr. Aharon Leib Adler (Z"L), and they began to collect together some funds, and deposited it in one of the banks. But a devastating devaluation struck their savings and a sum of 8,000 Roubles was lost...

[Page 125]

There is room to praise the fact that the determination to continue was not destroyed, neither did they despair of achieving their aims and began immediately to work towards their target of acquiring land in Palestine. This time, after having failed in their previous efforts, they decided to centralize their money in solid foreign currency and in the spring of 1925 Mordecai Greitzer and Haim Feureisen (Z"L), were sent to Palestine in the name of the Miechów group which now numbered 17 members. After they had criss–

crossed the country from north to south and east to west, they contacted the "Zionist Commonwealth of America" in Jerusalem and bought from them 1,000 Dunam (100,000 sq.m. – Trans.) of agricultural land and 10 lots as a commercial center in Afula.

Copy

To the Zionist Commonwealth of America

New York–Jerusalem

We, Mordecai Greitzer and Haim Feureisen, hold official Power of Attorney documents as delegated representatives of the "Miechów Group" affirm by this that the 1,000 Dunam that we purchased for our "Miechów Group" belong to the following registered members:–

Mr. Mordecai Greitzer	80 Dunam	Eighty
Mr. Haim Feureisen	80 Dunam	Eighty
Mr. Shmuel Fogel	80 Dunam	Eighty
Mr. Ya'acov Tsvi Gitler	80 Dunam	Eighty
Mr. Avraham Goldberg	80 Dunam	Eighty
Mr. Mordecai Rubin	80 Dunam	Eighty
Mr. Mendel Feigenblatt	60 Dunam	Sixty
Mr. Yudel Lishmann	60 Dunam	Sixty
Mr. Michael Wexler	60 Dunam	Sixty
Mr. Shmuel Burstein	50 Dunam	Fifty
Mr. Haim Kelewicz	50 Dunam	Fifty
Mr. Gershon Gimliekowicz(?)	40 Dunam	Forty
Mr. Haim Walberg	40 Dunam	Forty
Mr. Manish Yaskiel	40 Dunam	Forty
Mr. Yakel Salzburg	40 Dunam	Forty
Mr. Shlomo Yama	40 Dunam	Forty
Mr. Yesheyahu Greitzer	40 Dunam	Forty
Total	1,000 Dunam	One thousand

Within the city:	Registry of lots	
1). Mordecai Greitzer	1 Lot	One
2). Shmuel Fogel	1 Lot	One
3). Mandel Feigenblatt with Gershon Gimliekowicz	1 Lot	One
4). Yesheyahu Greitzer with Mordecai Ze'ev Flamenbaum	1 Lot	One

[Page 126]

In the commercial center:		
1). Ya'acov Tsvi Gitler	1 Lot	One
2). Avraham Goldberg	1 Lot	One
3). Haim Feureisen	1 Lot	One
4). Shlomo Feureisen	1 Lot	One
5). Yehuda Lishmann	1 Lot	One
6). Mordecai Rubin	1 Lot	One

At a general meeting of all the members it was decided to elect a group committee of three members to travel to Palestine as early as possible and they were: Shmuel Fogel, Ya'acov Tsvi Gitler and Yesheyahu Greitzer (who remained in Palestine).

These members were given the authority to accept into their hands the 1,000 Dunam and to allocate the lots among the members.

The rise in the value of the Lira and the fall in the value of the Polish Złoty caused a situation where the group members were unable to meet their financial obligations of payments on the agricultural land and the commercial lots they had purchased and according to a new contract that was negotiated between Mr. Mordecai Greitzer and the head of the "Zionist Commonwealth of America", Mr. Shimon Fishman (Z"L), when he visited Poland, the purchase was reduced by 50% – the Commonwealth waived its right to foreclose on the payment of the full amount due under the agreement.

Among the above members of the Miechów Group who are alive and dwell among us in Israel are: Ya'acov Tsvi Gitler, Ya'acov Saltsburg, Shlomo

Feureisen and Mordecai Rubin – may they be blessed with long and happy lives.

Mr. Gitler, who was the first to immigrate among the members in 1925, received Power of Attorney to arrange affairs for the group with the "Zionist Commonwealth" organization and the Afula Municipality and he performed that function to their complete satisfaction. The contract and agreement were kept by him in their original entirety and they are valuable survivors salvaged from the fires of destruction of our community.

Memories of My Birth-Town

by Henya Zingerman

Translated by Gloria Berkenstat Freund

My childhood years that were spent in my birth-town, Miechow, bind me closely to my Fajgenbaum family. My great grandfather, Bunes Fajgenbaum came to the shtetl [town] 100 years ago. I heard from my grandfather Dovid that when his father came to Miechow he was the tenth Jew and he completed the minyon [10 men required for prayer] in the city. My great grandfather had an iron business and his wife, Ruchle, bore him many children. Several among them remained in Miechow and my grandfather had a restaurant on Charsznicer Street. I, the oldest grandchild, from his son Moshe, actually was born there. I spent my early childhood years in my grandfather's restaurant. Merchants from the entire area would go there. My grandmother, Sura'le, also ran a guesthouse, a hotel, and there always were unfamiliar people there. If it ever appeared that a Jew did not have any money to pay, my grandmother did not drive the person out because she knew that if he did have money, he would pay with a thank you. The door was always open both for the rich and for the poor. Jews could eat well, sleep well and also simultaneously [hear] a chapter of Zionism.

[Page 127]

My grandmother was a fervid Zionist and when she would sit and read the newspaper people went on tiptoes and listened to the news from the wide world.

The Purim days are particularly etched in my memory. Jews from the entire shtetl came together at my grandmother's to hear my grandfather, Dovid Fajgenbaum, read the Megile [scroll of the Book of Esther]. My grandfather had a very beautiful voice and the sounds reached out far to the fields. After he read Megilus Ester [the Scroll of Esther], the Jews had a drink and had some cakes.

The housewives sent shalakh-manos [gifts of food] to each other during the day of Purim and they began to prepare the holiday dinner. The aromas of the food that she cooked for the Purim meal, baking fresh Challahs, roast goose, fish and so on filled the [rooms] at my grandmother's. We children waited impatiently for evening to come so that we could sit at the table.

My father had earlier ordered the music. The poor people and beggars from the surrounding towns waited for Purim the entire year to earn a few groshn. Whole groups went from house to house presenting scenes from Jewish history such as: the selling of Joseph, Haman and his 10 sons, Chana and her seven children, Bar Kokhba, Rabbi Akiva and so on.

One thing I remember is that they would make their first visit at my grandmother's because they received a good pastry there.

The pogrom that took place in the shtetl in 1920 still lies in my memory. I was a small child then, but it is engraved in my memory. After the pogrom our family began to think of going to Eretz-Yisroel. Miechow consisted of 10% Jews. Many of them were Zionists. A Mizrakhi [religious Zionist] organization and a Zionist movement were created that year. Ahron Leib Adler was the chairman of Mizrakhi and Avraham Sercacz was chairman of the Zionists. A Hakhshara [Zionist agricultural training farm] was created for Halutzim [pioneers] who prepared to emigrate to Eretz-Yisroel. My father also was one of them and he worked as a locksmith. His entire life he dreamed of going to Eretz-Yisroel, but, alas, his dream was not realized. My entire family perished at the hands of the Hitlerist murderers.

In 1921 three comrades immigrated to various countries. My Uncle Leibl Fajgenbaum to Eretz-Yisroel, Yekutial Grajcer to Mexico and Noakh Gruszka to Australia. All three were intelligent young men, full of life and a drive to learn. My Uncle Leibl studied with Gruszka the electrician. My grandmother once asked Gruszka what her son Leibl had learned.

[Page 128]

Gruszka answered her. He already knows the trade; he stands on a ladder and reads a book. The three comrades celebrated their last Purim in the shtetl before their departure and performed various humorous sketches. Two delegates traveled at the same time to buy land: Chaim Fajerajzn and Shmuel Fogel. My grandmother Sura gave them her entire [savings] to be invested in land. They searched for a long time for suitable land and they could not decide because Haifa was full of stones and Tel Aviv was pure sand. They finally decided to buy [land] in Afula because the soil there was good for agriculture and also for construction because it was flat as a table.

Meanwhile, my Uncle Leibl wrote from the country [Eretz-Yisroel]. He wrote that he was in the Jewish Brigade and was building the university in Jerusalem. Then he built a large synagogue in Tel Aviv. In 1925 my grandparents and four children went to Eretz-Yisroel. At first they suffered hunger here. They had no money to settle on the land in Afula and they settled in Haifa. My grandmother continued her tradition here in Haifa; the door was always open and everyone who was hungry went away satisfied. My father Moshe Fajgenbaum and his family remained in the old home. Times were difficult; there was an economic crisis in Poland. My father would go to a village to buy wheat from a peasant. Many Jews traded in the villages. They created a retailers' union. At the same time my father and Wolf Mandri, Brener and others created a bank kupiecki [merchant bank}. They discussed this for weeks. It cost them much effort, but they finally opened the bank. Earlier, my father had not looked for any income until he learned of the world political situation and about the situation in Eretz-Yisroel, in particular. He left for the market very early. Yosef Fridrich already was [reading]. He already had read the entire press and he was able to spread the news further.

At the same time, the young sons of the rich parents of Miechow were studying in Warsaw Tachkemoni [teacher training seminar], as for example, Yekezkial Fridrich, Zev Fridrich, Meir Fogel (now in Israel), Yona Blat, who died before the Holocaust and Yehuda Zelmanowicz, who died in Israel. The Miechowers in Warsaw were organized in Hashomer Haleumi [the National Guard] and when they went on vacation they recruited the young and founded an organization of Hashaomer Haleumi. The best young people from the shtetl were drawn to the organization. Elimelekh Fridrich, Moshe Finczowski and Yehezkiel Fridrich were the first leaders. They provided their great vigor to the organization. We learned much here. Both the poor and the rich children worked harmoniously in the organization. Courses were created.

In 1929 during the events in Eretz-Yisroel we were very worried. In Poland, anti-Semitism had increased and my father could no longer go the villages because the gentiles had begun to hate us. Earning an income became more difficult from day to day; the young people began to think of practical matters. We began to organize for emigration to Eretz-Yisroel. Yehezkiel Fridrich was the first member of our movement to go to Hakhshara. Some time passed and a large number of young people left for Hakhshara to be ready to emigrate to Eretz-Yisroel.

[Page 129]

But, alas, the English mandate government was in power then and only issued a small number of certificates. A few traveled with the Makabiade [Maccabiah games – international sports event for Jewish athletes], such as for example, Rywka Unger, Yona Zelmanowicz and Miriam Fajgenblat. Fridrich succeeded in emigrating very early.

Five years of the accursed war passed when the Nazis annihilated all Polish Jewry. My entire family perished as well except for my brother Benyamin who survived through a miracle and is with us in Israel.

Of Events in My City

by Ruwin Lewit

Translated by Gloria Berkenstat Freund

1919. I came home. It already was sinister in the street. The windowpanes already had been knocked out of our house. It was raining heavily in the street. This was lucky because the police could not control the situation. The military arrived from Kielce Friday at night. Wagons arrived from the villages on Shabbos [Sabbath] morning and the peasants gathered on Kielce Street. We called it the Kaiser Street near the church. Hercil Zalcberg [and] Ayzyk Zalcberg lived there. They had a business. They were rich men. The business was forced open, robbed. They beat the old Hercil so [badly] that he died immediately afterward. The military intervened; one of the robbers was shot. Rumors were spread among the pogromists that Jewish soldiers did the shooting. The mob became wilder. The situation began to become calmer when they began to arrest the leaders of the pogrom.

There was an inundation of water on a Shabbos in 1934-5. Houses were destroyed. People were dragged by water. Shaya Zelikowicz lived outside the city on Charsznicer Street near the bridge; the house was destroyed. They barely escaped with their lives. There was great damage not only in Miechow, but also in the surrounding cities and villages. It was a bad year for the wheat merchants and for other merchants as well, for whom there was too short a time for the wheat harvest because the fields had eroded. That year they depended on the peasants. And then the Hitler era arrived...

[Page 130]

A Monument for Miechow

by Shmuel Blum

Translated by Gloria Berkenstat Freund

Around the Synagogue

There are places and cities where people live and create for many generations and no one knows of their existence. Thanks to some event, these cities become known. The occasion arises pointing out a city where a historical personality was born, where a battle took place and so on.

Miechow, our *shtetele* [small town], had special documents in its book of lineage. Forgotten, yes. Maciej Miechowita, a Polish historian, lived here.

[It was] a shtetl [town] like thousands of other *shtetlekh* [plural of shtetl], where Jews lived together with non-Jews in good enough contact. Jewish middle-class [residents] and non-Jewish citizens were the municipal authorities. Jewish dozores [synagogue wardens] simultaneously were [city] council members and were concerned with the needs of the city. A memorial tablet has remained until today with the names of the councilmen who led the water management, and among them are many Jewish names.

[Miechow was] not necessarily a shtetl of merchants, but of a large number of artisans, cabinetmakers, blacksmiths, tinsmiths, wagon drivers, shoemakers and tailors. Despite the fact that the Jews were in the minority, it had its societies and institutions with an [organized] community and its own synagogue. Shabbos [Sabbath] was the day on which the Jews rested and it was silent and quiet in the city.

Exactly as in other Jewish *shtetlekh*, the more prosperous members of the middle class, the rabbi and the [members of the organized] community were influential.

The synagogue, a young one, was built at the start of our century [20th]. [It was] a tall building with two impressive windows decorated with stained glass, with galleries on three sides for the women's [section of the] synagogue.

It has no history to tell, except a small incident. During the pogrom in 1919, when an excited mob attacked the synagogue, the then starosta [village chief or governor] Kulesza went before the Torah ark with outspread arms, put his own life at risk, and made sure that the synagogue would not, God forbid, be set on fire.

The synagogue had a short, curious history described in these lines. In 1927, the synagogue was closed to the worshippers while the eastern wall and the ceiling were being painted. Boys from the nearby courtyard wanted to look in and to see what kind of paintings were being created inside. Their curiosity was not quieted until they knocked out a windowpane of a side window and crawled inside. I was just about to finish the symbols of the Zodiac.

Their eyes fell on Virgo, which was represented by the stylized, small body of a girl with closed eyes. This was enough for the group of boys to create turmoil in the city because naked women were being painted in the synagogue.

[Page 131]

It is easy to imagine how the news fractured the public, provincial fantasy. The thing ended equally well after the intervention of the city rabbi. However, the existing press in Poland already had sung and wrote about "a synagogue with naked women."

My father, Reb Yeremia Blum, of blessed memory, an esteemed member of the middle class in the city, a dozor [member of the Jewish community council] and councilman at the city hall, advised me against painting the synagogue, explaining that there would be no satisfaction from the kehile [organized Jewish committee]. It reached the point that at a vote taken at a meeting of the council, my father, Reb Yeremia, left the meeting because he was an interested party, since his son was doing the work.

The synagogue is the only thing that remains today, turned into a warehouse because there is no one to pray in it; the sidewalk near the synagogue is paved with headstones torn out of the Jewish cemetery. The feet of every decent person who steps on this place burn.

The Young

Unlike all of the poor shtetlekh that were called meylekh evyen giter [King Pauper estate – the nickname for an impoverished part of the Lublin area], because no railroad even came near them, our city was privileged because it was a district city and a Christian gymnazie [secondary school] existed here. The dozens of Jewish students at the gymnazie became a symbol of progress for the other young people; however those who did not have the material opportunity to study at the school, had a desire and willingness to leave a small place to study a trade and "become a person."

The parents, pious or not fanatical, looked askance at the doctrine of the young and were not happy that the young were distancing themselves from *Yidishkeit* [a Jewish way of life], but kept quiet.

The young men and girls who had good enough relationships with the Christian young people went to entertainments, sports competitions and spectaculars together. *Makkabi*, the Jewish sports club, won more and more in football [soccer matches] with the Christian sports club.

It is interesting to report on one of the amateur performances. It was our custom before opening the curtain [for a play] to play Hatikvah [The Hope – an anthem adopted by the Zionist movement and now the national anthem of the State of Israel] and everyone stood up. Among the spectators were Christian girls, invited by a Jewish friend. When the girls asked why [everyone] was standing at the playing of Hatikvah, a young man said that this was the Jewish Jeszcze Polska [Nie Zginęła – Poland Has Not Yet Perished] (Polish national hymn...).

Students brought from university cities helped to spread knowledge. Hazomir [a choral and dramatic society], with its own premises and library, was founded at the same time, a place where girls and young men exchanged books, discussed literature and actual problems.

The very young also remained daring. Based on the program of the the scout movement, Hazomir emerged with half-military discipline, with excursions and parades.

[Page 132]

There also was a desire to benefit from the creations of the personalities of the world. Hazomir would invite directors to lead the drama circle, brought the artist Zigmunt Turkow for a performance.

Gershon Sirota, the famous Warsaw khazan [cantor], was invited during the 1920s. He gave a concert of synagogue music and opera arias. Many non-Jewish music experts came to the concert. This concert was a financial success. The Jews left the hall with pride that Jews also could show that they had beautiful music.

Leib Bimka and Segalowicz would come with speeches. The writer, Maks Erik, lived in Miechow for a time. Who among us cannot remember his spirited lectures about the source of the Yiddish language? He had the makings of a celebrated man with his language, knowledge and fantasy. He was later professor at the Yidisher Visnshaftlekher Institut [YIVO – Jewish Scientific Institute] in Minsk. He perished under mysterious circumstances in 1934 in the Soviet Union.

The pulsating wave that held sway over the young also was partially connected to fear of assimilation. This fear enveloped the religious circles. As a counterweight, the pious Jews began to create schools, religious in the spirit of progressiveness. Their purpose was to draw the young into religion, but not to remain in a stagnant form. It actually was Zionism with a religious hue: Mizrakhi [religious Zionists].

Together, both, Zionism and Mizrakhi, had the greatest influence on planting the love of the national ideal in the young minds. The administrative bodies were the source of further events and of the hahalutz [pioneers] movement in the shtetl. They should really be thanked for the fact that so many Miechower survived in Israel because they understood the right time to leave Miechow before it was too late. This remnant of Miechower provided a hand in founding and building the Land of Israel.

Clothing, garments from [different] epochs, furniture, candlesticks, various objects that give evidence as a document of the past, are carefully preserved in various collections of folklore in museums. Of us, nothing, nothing remains of that golden time but our synagogue.

Miechow, the Polish shtetl, continues to exist. It continues to be a place where citizens remember their former Jewish neighbors when they eat challah [Sabbath egg bread], which is still baked today in Poland, or fish cooked in the Jewish manner, po żydowsku.

Thus did the small twig of Yidishkehit grow and develop in alien Polish soil. The Jews and the Poles lived together and created together over the course of generations, like husband and wife who live together in love and joy, interrupted from time to time by quarrels and squabbling.

[Page 135]

Personalities and Families

My Father's House

By Shmuel Berger

Translated by Selwyn Rose

It is now 34 years since I left my father's house and immigrated to Palestine. Until this day etched in my memory are the beautiful days I spent in my father's house, in the bosom of my family, surrounded by a homely atmosphere of warmth and care. Strong feelings of yearning remain within me for that small town of my birth in the county of Kielce, Miechów, in which, today, lives not one single Jew. Of the Jews of Miechów, who represented 40% of the population of the town, most were exterminated during the Second World War and only a very few managed to escape, some before the war and some afterwards. Most of the survivors are today in Israel and a few spread throughout the world, A few isolated Jews from Miechów remained in Poland – one can count them on the fingers of one hand – but in the town itself – not one.

Together with the Jews who perished were my mother, father and only brother.

My father's house was an excellent example of a Zionist home. From my earliest youth I was educated in the spirit of a love for the Homeland. My father, Aharon Berger, was among the first group to purchase the Zionist Shekel and until his last days never ceased to interest himself in the events of the country and the Zionist Party and his utmost ambition was to immigrate to Palestine. What bitter sadness, that on the threshold of achieving his dream he was murdered by Poles, and that only a month or two after the end of World War Two.

Our home was Traditional–Reform. My parents wanted with all their might to provide us with a good education, both a traditional and a general education at one and the same time, as far as was possible in those days and within the town. I always remember a sentence that my father often repeated to me: "We are not especially rich and we cannot leave you a large inheritance. But one thing we are determined to give our children is a good, broadly- based education. These are the foundations of your future and you will draw upon it all your lives." Today I see how right he was.

My father was very active in various public works in town. His own broad education, honesty and dedication to his fellow–man, paved the way to public activity in all the Jewish institutions in town. He was loved by all and wanted to help everyone to the best of his ability. The first days of the week were dedicated almost entirely to public activities and meetings. According to Polish law, businesses and workshops were closed on Sundays and thus Jewish people were able to devote their time to other activities especially public institutions. My father was a member of the local Zionist Council helping significantly in collecting money for the Foundation Fund of Israel and there was no Zionist institute in which he did not play some part, or motivated others to take part. He fought a stubborn battle against all the anti–Zionists and against any activity that obstructed the re–building of Palestine.

[Page 136]

Aharon Berger

Aharon Berger

To our good fortune, only a handful of residents refused to cooperate with the Zionists while the great majority of the town's Jews were significantly aware of Zionism.

In addition to his blessed work in that field he was active in almost all the social and cultural institutions in town among which one may mention:

1. A member of the Community Council for a number of years;
2. A founder–member of the Artisan's Society in town;
3. Chairman of the Cooperative Bank in town and was counted among the founders and managers throughout the years, from its birth until the destruction of the town. He dedicated much of his time and energies to its development and the prosperity of the bank and was considered its living spirit;
4. Chairman of the "Sick–visits" committee in town for many years;
5. Active member of the "Zamir" library and encouraged different cultural activities initiated by "Zamir".

Apart from his special activities in these institutions he assisted and acted in smaller foundations. With his activities in all these public institutions in town he still gave decisive preference to his involvement with his Zionist activities and on more than one occasion he cancelled meetings with another public or social group if it clashed with a Zionist meeting in which he needed to take part.

In spite of his dedication to public work the first of his concerns was always his family. He was a devoted father to his children and a good husband to his wife. The whole week he worried about providing for his family while Shabbat and the festivals were reserved for the family. On those occasions we would go out of town together for an excursion to the surrounding countryside, where beautiful forests encompassed the town, with small streams and productive farmlands (the soil in our county was among the most fertile in Poland). On these excursions we talked about our studies and education and our father would deepen our knowledge by explaining and completing the information we already had. We would read a popular book on science, converse on what was happening in Palestine and have lively arguments about it all. These excursions were special events for me and they are deeply etched in my memories.

My father was an educated man. He commanded several languages, a rare accomplishment in those days: Polish, Yiddish, Russian, German and a little Hebrew. Before his marriage he taught Russian in the town of Skala, near Miechów. He was very interested in general literature and we had a small library in our house that he had acquired with his limited means. In addition to the daily Yiddish newspaper we were also subscribed to various weeklies. After work our father would arrive home and read the papers and books until late at night. He was also competent in mathematics and helped me enormously with my school work. It was due to his persistence and guidance that I was able to gain entrance to the Polish government gymnasium, whose doors were not open to the Jews.

[Page 137]

With the completion of my studies at the gymnasium my father came up with the idea of sending me to Palestine to continue studying at the Hebrew University of Jerusalem. Even then it was clear that the numerus clausus was in operation in the Polish universities. My father insisted – almost physically – that I leave Poland and travel to Palestine and invested much effort in order to make it possible for me to study at the Hebrew University of Jerusalem. In his heart perhaps he sensed the Holocaust that was to befall Poland's Jews and wanted me to be the bridgehead for the rest of my family who perhaps will immigrate after me. To my sadness the Fates decided otherwise.

In 1935 I immigrated to Palestine and became a student at the Hebrew University, and the family thought that in due course I would be followed by my younger brother, Shlomo and afterwards my parents. For four years, until the outbreak of war, I was in close correspondence with my parents and I knew what was going on in town and at home. Heart and soul I was with them and I hoped that in time we would all be together again in Palestine. Before we had time to realize our dream World War Two broke out.

My father escaped from the Miechów ghetto a short time before its liquidation. According to what I was told by survivors and members of the family who survived, he hid for a long time in a bunker in very difficult conditions and constant danger at one of the farms in the surrounding villages. To my joy, he managed to survive the war and with the liberation of Poland and the fall of Hitler in 1945 he returned to Miechów together with a few other Jewish survivors. He lived in a room with the few other members of the family.

A number of letters arrived from him after the war but I don't know if he received my replies. The fact of his survival of the Holocaust I discovered in the press. Others told me that he was planning to leave Poland and join me in Palestine. On one of the Mondays in August 1945 he went to one of the surrounding villages to pick up some money due to him from one of the farmers, dating back to a business transaction from before the war. Towards evening, on his way back to town and just a few kilometers away from home, he was shot dead by a member of the Armia Krajowa, remainders of which were raiding in the area. He was buried in the Jewish cemetery of Miechów that had been totally destroyed and his was the first burial to take place in there after the Holocaust. Who knows if it still exists?

That was the bitter fate of my father, who had survived the "Seven Levels" of the Nazi hell, saw the liberation with his own eyes and was on the brink of immigrating and joining his only surviving son – his dream since childhood – and it was denied him.

May these few lines be taken as a memorial to a life rich in deeds and Zionist and blessed public activities. May his memory be blessed.

In a few words I will memorialize the rest of my family.

My mother, Simcha (Sala), née Wroblewski, was the daughter of an exemplary religious family. She completed elementary school and learned how to sew women's clothes at a vocational school in Warsaw, becoming a very competent seamstress. For many years she contributed significantly to the economic stability of the household through her work. My mother was a significant factor – if not a deciding one – in our education, to which she devoted the best of her efforts. She worked industriously from early morning until evening and all her efforts were directed to the welfare of her husband and children. She was also active in public affairs, Zionism and assisted in a number of enterprises for the redemption of the Homeland.

[Page 138]

She had exquisitely good taste for beauty and made sure she gave her children a good social education so that when the time came they would be prepared to integrate with the world and its mores. She especially made sure to instill in us the foundations of good behaviour in public, courtesy and the love of one's neighbor.

Shlomo (Zelek) Berger (Z"L) *and* *Simcha (Sala) Berger (Z"L)*

The fate of our mother was as with the fate of the other Jews of the town. With the liquidation of the ghetto she was sent to an extermination camp and there she returned her soul to her Maker.

May her memory be blessed.

My young brother Shlomo (Zelek), was younger than I by six years, handsome and excellent in his studies at school both primary and elementary. He completed gymnasium in Miechów two months before the outbreak of war, in June 1939. At that time I commenced the procedure to bring him to Palestine as a student at the Hebrew University. The riots at the time obstructed my plans. He was liked by his friends and loved life and was aware of events around him. He had great energy and was quick to make decisions. He was interested in the Jewish youth movements in town even though he was not a subscribed member to any one of them officially because the constitution of the school forbad its pupils to belong to any youth organization not approved of by the school. At the time of the war, he fled the ghetto and joined the Polish partisans. Since he knew Polish very well he integrated well in the group and was involved with his friends from school, he had no difficulty in being accepted by them. Thus he wanted to avenge his mother's blood and that of all the other Jews who had been sent to the extermination camps. In one of his operations he was injured and he found his way to our father in his bunker. Our father in great danger managed to get some medicine for him from Krakow that saved him and removed him from danger. But he couldn't stay with our father in the hideout. His strong desire to punish the Nazi enemy forced him back to the partisans and the forest.

Again he was injured in one of the operations and returned to the hideout. But this time our father was unable to help him. My father was unable to do anything and he died in my father's arms. He buried him with his own hands at midnight. His last words were: "Father, save me; I want to live!" I can imagine my father's feelings at that time, as his son breathed his last in front of him and he could do nothing to save him. His burial place is not known. May his memory be for a blessing.

That was the tragic fate of my dear family. May G–d avenge their blood.

[Page 139]

From the "Visionary of Lublin" to the "Grandfather" of Miechów
(The family tree of Mr. Ya'acov–Yitzhak Blatt (Z"L)

by Dov Yerushalmi

Translated by Selwyn Rose

Rabbi Avraham Eliezer Ha–Levi Horowitz (ZT'L)[1] sired the Holy Rabbi Ya'acov Yitzhak the "Visionary of Lublin" (ZT'L) and a daughter, Mrs. Esther, who married Rabbi Berekhya Blatt.

A. Rabbi Berekhya Blatt sired Elimelech–Shmuel and settled in Izbica. Berekhya Blatt died and his wife, the widow Esther, sent her son, Eliezer–Shmuel to her brother, the Holy Rabbi Ya'acov Yitzhak (ZT'L) and he was educated there,

B. Elimelech–Shmuel married Yokhed née Richter, the daughter of Berish Harif of Zarnovitza. The Rabbi Reuven from Zarnovitza, the author of " Duda'im B'Sadeh" on the Torah was the uncle of Yokhed. Elimelech–

Shmuel and his wife, Yokhed Richter in Zarnovitza had the following children: Berish, Avraham–Eliezer, Esther, Rivka, Perl, Hava, Berekhya and the youngest, Rabbi Ya'acov–Yitzhak.

C. Ya'acov–Yitzhak married Krayndle the daughter of Yona and Golda Porecki. Yona was the son of Rabbi Yitzhak and his wife Freydl. Rabbi Ya'acov Yitzhak and his wife Krayndle had the following children: 1. Avraham–Moshe, 2. Berekhya, 3. Esther–Hanna, 4. Freydl, 5. Yona, 6. Yosef–David.

1. Avraham–Moshe married Zlota–Perl the daughter of Rabbi Berol Yurister(?) of Zarnovitza, and settled in Działoszyce and later in Łódź. They had: A. Rivka. B. Yokhed, C. Aharon, D. Zainvel, E. Yona, F. Elimelech, G. Yosef, H. Golda, I. Baruch, J. Meir, K. Eliezer. With the outbreak of war they moved to Slomniki. Perl became ill and died on the journey in 1940; Avraham–Moshe was evacuated from the town on 9th June 1942 to Chodów, between Miechów and Charsznica, where he was shot and died a martyr's death.

1. Rivka married Fajwel Rozenek the son of Rabbi Avraham. Their children were: Elimelech, Yisroel, Hinda, Micha'el, Yona, Krayndle and Miriam. Krayndle and Miriam perished in the Holocaust it is not known where; their son, Yisroel immigrated to Palestine in1940; from Łódź their daughter Hinda immigrated to Argentina during the 30's and married Teitelboim; their children, Micha'el and Yona remained alive and immigrated to Argentina.

2. Yokhed married Meir the son of Rabbi Shimon Kaufman from Chielmnik. They had: Hinda, Yosef, Bella, Krayndle (Kielce). Yokhed died suddenly; Meir perished in the Holocaust, it is not known where; their son Yosef drowned in Warsaw when he was 20; their daughter, Hinda married Simcha Heller. They survived and moved to California with their son Yosef; the daughters, Bella and Krayndle also survived and live in Warsaw.

3. Aharon married Doba the daughter of Haim–Yosef Zeitzbend(?); they perished in the Holocaust and no one knows where.

[Page 140]

A. Zainvel married Faygle née Schmidt in Krakow. They had a daughter and they lived in Krakow. On 9>sup>th June 1942 they were transported to Chodów where they perished.

B. Yona married Esther the daughter of Yisroel–Moshe from Biała Woda, Slomniki. They had the following children: Avigdor, Berish, Krayndle,

(Slomniki). Yona perished in Chodów on 18th December 1942; Avigdor (HY"D)[2] died in an unknown location and Krayndle perished in Warsaw. Esther and her son Berish survived and live in Tel-Aviv.

C. Elimelech married Rachel the daughter of Yosef Pinczowski from Chielmnik. They had a daughter Yokhed (Chielmnik). They immigrated to Palestine in 1935 and lived in Kiryat Motzkin. Rachel (Z"L) was killed in a road accident in 1956 and Elimelech (Z"L) died 9th September 1965.

D. Yosef married Tova the daughter of Rabbi Yeshaye Greitzer of Charsznica. They had children: Shalom-Yonatan and Dov. They immigrated to Palestine and lived in Afula. Yosef and his son Shalom died in Afula. Dov was born in Palestine in 1926 and lives today in Neve-Oz, near Petah Tikvah.

E. Golda married Avraham Shalom the son of Rabbi Shlomo Ha-Cohen, of Biała Bołądź. They had two daughters. Golda and the two girls perished in Chodów 9th September 1942. Rabbi Avraham-Shalom perished on an unknown date and in an unknown place.

F. Baruch married Hanna Gottesgenaden from Łódź. They both survived and live in Palestine.

G. Meir and his wife, Sala, née Goldkorn, lived in Łódź, their residence up until the Holocaust; they perished in Chodów 9th June 1942

1. Berekhya married Sarah the daughter of Tsvi Hirsch Ha-Cohen Zylbermann of Zvierzyniec. Their children were A. Sheyndil, B. Yona, C. Elimelech-Shmuel, D. Haim, E. Dina, F. Dov, G. Golda, H. Yokhed. They immigrated to Palestine in 1936 with their children, except Elimelech who is in France and Golda who perished in Poland. They both died in Haifa.

A. Elimelech-Shmuel married {blank in original text - Trans.} (Lille, France).

B. Haim married Sarah and they had a son, Elisha (Palestine).

C. Dina married Avraham Kupermintz, and they live in Haifa.

D. Dov married Reyle née Schwarzbaum and they had a son, Tsvi-Yehuda (Haifa).

E. Yokhed married Shimon Grynberg and was widowed. She lives in Haifa.

2. Esther-Hanna married Rabbi Mordecai, the son of Rabbi Alter-Yechiel Friedman. Their children were: A. Rivka-Rachel, B. Yona, C. Freydl-Etke, D. Yosef, E. Yisroel, F. Perl, G. Kalman. They lived in Krakow and perished in Chodów on 9th June 1942.

A. Rivka–Rachel married Yehezkiel the son of Rabbi Yosef–Baruch Ha-Cohen Kahan. They lived in Krakow. Their children were: Alter–Yechiel, Avraham. They all perished in the Holocaust.

B. Yona married Faygle née Walter in Warsaw and their children were: Ruth and Aharon–Yechiel (Warsaw). They all perished in the Holocaust.

C. Freydl–Etke married Yehoshua Dresner and they lived in Krakow. They had two children, Mala and Yosef. They all perished in the Holocaust.

D. Yosef

E. and Yisroel survived and live in the United States.

F. Perl perished in the Holocaust.

G. Kalman was saved and lives in Israel.

H. Freydl married Rabbi Leibush Bachmeir. Their children were A, Berish, B. Shmuel, C. Malka,

I. Golda. She later married again to Rabbi Mendel Bornstein and they had two daughters: Tamril and Krayndle.

J. Berish Bachmeir and his wife, Leah, the daughter of Mendel Feigenblatt in Miechów, they had Zelda. All perished in the Holocaust.

K. Shmuel and his wife, Hava, the daughter of Yosef Rosenberg of Sosnowica, they had David, Krayndle and Raizel. All were lost in the Holocaust.

L. Malka married Eliezer Mintz from Szymkowicz and they lived in Sosnowica. They had two children Shlomo and Krayndle. All perished in the Holocaust.

1. Yona and his wife Dwashe the daughter of Avraham Rozenek from Działoszyce, lived in Krakow. They had the following children: Golda, Moshe, Micha'el and Miriam. Dwashe died towards the end of the 20's in Krakow. Yona immigrated to Palestine in 1935 and died in 1965. Miriam married Tsvi Horowitz and lives in Tel–Aviv.

2. Yosef–David and his wife Brayndl, the daughter of Yisroel–David Spiegel and Tamril, who is the daughter of Yona Poretski. Their children were: Golda, Yokhed, Yona, Benyamin and Elimelech–Shmuel. Of those only Yokhed remained alive; she married Avraham Rosenblatt and lives in Haifa.

* * *

The Holy Rabbi Ya'acov–Yitzhak (ZT"L), the "Visionary of Lublin" sired Rabbi Yosef and Rabbi Hirsch; Rabbi Yosef sired Rabbi Eliezer,

Rabbi Eliezer married Rachel the daughter of Rabbi Yosef–Baruch Ha–Levi nicknamed "The Good Jew of Nowe–Miasto", the son the Rabbi Kalonymus the author of "Or ve–Semesh" – also his nickname – on the Torah. Their children were: the Holy Rabbi Haim–Shmuel and Rabbi of Khentshin (ZT"L).

Rabbi Haim–Shmuel had two sons: the Holy Rabbi Herschel and Rabbi Eliezer.

Translator's Footnotes

1. "May the memory of the righteous be for a blessing"
2. Hashem Yinkom Damo = "G–d will avenge his blood"

[Page 142]

The Wealthy of the Town

by Hannia Feigenbaum–Zyngerman

Translated by Selwyn Rose

The Feigenbaum Family History

There is a house on Charsznica Street with many apartments but part of it is separated from the main block. It has a large glass sliding door. There is nothing special about it apart from its sparkling cleanliness. It is the Hotel–Restaurant of my grandfather David (Z"L).

The pedestrian, the wagon–master, the peddler, the businessman – all who pass by are attracted to it.

From the point of view of Jewish settlement my town is considered "young" – about a hundred years. I know from rumors that my great–grandfather, Bunim Feigenbaum was the richest man in town. Where did he come from? Who was he? So very little is known about him. I never thought the day would come when I should want to know so much about him. All that I know about him is that he completed the ten men necessary for the first prayer quorum in town and because of that they nicknamed him "Lord of the Quorum". He had five sons and four daughters, seven of them – David, Shlomo, Ya'acov, Haim-Leib, Miriam, Rivka and Hanna – lived in Miechów until the outbreak of World War Two and until the Holocaust came upon them.

His first-born, David, had four sons and one daughter. That hotel and restaurant was the commercial life of the town. The wagon-masters, businessmen, marriage-brokers, traders from the weekly market – all gathered there as if it was their own home. One of my father's (Z"L) occupations for a time was as a wagon-master and my uncle Ovshei, was the town's marriage broker – a sort of Hershel the clown of Ostropole because of the many stories told about his practical jokes and pranks that he delighted in staging.

My grandfather David was very precise and particular about "the small print" and something of an entertainer. While he was a soldier during the "Phoney War" of 1905 with Japan, he played in the military band. On the festival of Purim he would read the Scroll of Esther and many would come to hear him.

The meals and their popular dishes were famous. The celebrations that took place to honor the Rabbi of the Hassidim attracted the entire town; Yudele Koval, David Herschel. Shia, the whole family Weill – everyone who was anyone; they all came.

The noble-faced grandmother Sarah'leh used to sit reading the newspaper "Heint" or "Moment" and when someone dared – Heaven forbid – raise his voice, Moshe-Leib the "keeper of the peace" would fix his stare on him and the man's voice would die in the throat of the offender. There were those who would say: "We know he has great affection for her"; there were others who would say: "Grandma's fattened goose."

In 1920 Shmuel Fogel, Avrahamele Goldberg, Haim Feureisen, Yankl Zalcberg and Gitler and saved for a long life, the people from "Mizrahi", met there and there it was decided to buy some dunams[1] of land in the "Holy Land". In 1925 Grandfather and family immigrated to Palestine.

Grandfather's first-born, Moshe – my father (Z"L) – married Miriam Sosnowski from Kielce, and her brothers Moshe and Leibe Sosnowski, lived in our house. Our close family members were so many that we, the youngsters, found it hard to determine who was who and from which family.

Our mother's house (our father was almost never at home) was a sort of "underground" for the younger members of "Young Zionists". Here Meir G. Tova Z. clandestinely brought their belongings before going off to training camp for leaders of the "Young Zionists". Here they brought their torn trousers for repairs after an excursion of the movement, in order to be able to return home as if nothing had happened. My mother always helped with a secret smile to herself.

[Page 143]

My father held every position. He was also "in training": when someone was immigrating to Palestine my father would return from the railway station depressed and irritated murmuring sadly: "All of them, all of them – only me not! only me, not!"...In all his jobs it was "only temporary", until we, too, immigrate, therefore – "Much toil and only a little blessing."

In 1913 on the eve of the war, he was working as an iron–welder in Skala and constructing balconies in iron. Once he returned home for a weekly visit and never went back to work there because in the meantime war broke out and his salary and work tools remained there in Skala. The "Mond Rice" were produce dealers introduced him to that field. He visited the various farms and villages, buying and selling geese, field crops and whatever came to and in exchange for his success we ate and sustained ourselves.

When our grandfather emigrated from Poland we lost his help – and hardship descended upon our house. The torments and sufferings of finding a living were hard. In 1929 anti–Semitism began to grow, the farmers attempted to avoid payment of their debts and once, in the village of Komarów my father was almost murdered, and only his physical condition and resourcefulness saw him through.

Again unemployed, he wandered the streets, standing near "The Statue", idle conversations, jokes and a new job – "Transportation Company", but in that enterprise fortune again failed to smile on him. The partners, Tchaikovsky, Lansberg, Pinczowski and my father managed to get out from the business with great difficulty. Following that things began to improve with father "holding the whip" with horses and a wagon hauling flour to Silesia. They would go in convoy because of the danger on the roads from the villagers of Działoszyce, Slomniki, Wolbrom and others. The house was again noisy with joyfulness and a little ease. The new way of life was created that of a wagon–driver, I heard my father making jokes about how intelligent his horses were:

"They eat newspapers." The "wagon–master" also turned out to be just another "in the meantime".

My father never got to immigrate to Palestine; only I did, followed by my brother.

Regarding my brother's fate, between 1933 and 1939 some messages of "regards" arrived, reports from friends who immigrated, but the information was always mixed with bitterness and sadness about the fate of a youth and his sufferings, about journeys down endless roads, in the cold, rain and snow, a youth losing his youth.

In 1939, he joined the Polish army and was sent to the front. When the army retreated to Romania he was the driver for an army Major. In Sulina, a small port in Romania was the "Skaria" a "Beitar" organized ship and the last immigrant ship to leave Romania and my brother's soul yearned to sail with her but she was well–overloaded. My brother managed to steal aboard as stowaway along with 2,500 other people. Nevertheless, the "illegal" among the "Illegals" was discovered. But the ship had already set sail. She was caught eventually by the British blockade and here passengers transferred to Atlit.

After about six months my brother was released so he could enlist in the British army. He fought in Africa, Tripoli, and Italy – five and a half years he was in the war. In 1946 the end of hostilities saw the end of his wanderings and he settled in Palestine.

Translator's Footnote

1. One dunam = 1000 Sq. Meters

[Page 144]

A Tombstone for my Family – Like a Thousand Others

by Meir Goldberg

Translated by Selwyn Rose

Somewhere or another there must be some remnant of clothing after that horrifying storm, some isolated twigs and branches from a tree of such magnificence.

And in the isolation of that loneliness it shouts. The taste for living has gone: but in the sad loneliness of an orphan there is yet a desire for some sort of day–to–day life and the worrying concern of future life, perhaps the hope for the future, a vision of the family that was, so multi–branched. It proffers a taste for life and overcomes sleepless nights, drenched in perspiration of fright and panic. Nights in which one cries...

We "belonged" to the point of blurred borders between "uniqueness" and privacy. We were so many and to each one a name and family tradition. Perhaps the "uniqueness" found expression in the internal life of each of us, in the weaving of future dreams. But in tradition, family respect and glory, we were an example of a multi–faceted unit.

There were families woven into the mosaic fabric of our town with their sons spread over the country and beyond. But the root, the source, the belonging was in the town itself. Few were the number of "small" or "tragic" families, such as Unger (Z"L) that slowly became reduced in number until no one was left. There was the Kornfeld family upon whose last remaining member the horror of the Holocaust fell with the oppressor's (Y.S.[1]) axe and left behind small orphaned families, like spread fingers stretched towards heaven, terrible and like us, orphans.

I am trying to erect a tombstone to one name to one family among thousands like it – the Fogel family. I was connected to it in a close–distant way, distant and close.

There was only one brother in the family, Shmuel and seven daughters. The daughters married "other" names. But the "Fogel" prevailed. You could say: "Goldberg of the Fogels."...

Every one of the sisters, on marrying, called the first–born son by the father's name; there were: Meir Schwitzer, Meir Nirberg, Meir Lescha, Meir

Fogel and Meir Goldberg. Two of the daughters were sterile and one gave birth only to daughters.

Miriam married Ya'acov Lescha and gave birth to sons: Hershel and Meir and a daughter Hinda; Leah married Fayvl Chenczinski and had two daughters, Rivka and Bluma had no sons. Perl, the wife of Nahum from Olkusz, was sterile. Baltshe married the owner of an estate in the vicinity of Działoszyce; she too had no children. Rivka, the wife of Yitzhak Schwitzer from Będzin, had Meir, a son and Sarah, a daughter. My mother married Avraham Goldberg of Będzin. They had Haya Baltshe, Malka and me and my little sister Sarah'leh. The brother Shmuel was the first–born. Everyone esteemed him. Shmuel stood head and shoulders above us all and was among the first of the "Lovers of Zion" in our town and the activists in "Mizrahi". It was natural that the delegates from the "Foundation Fund for Israel" would stay in our house. It seems that it was their influence that drew my father to join the ranks of the "Mizrahi". When I bring to mind the extermination of uncle Shmuel in the time of the Nazis (Y.D.), I cannot imagine him among those who "went as lambs to the slaughter" and I want to see him with an aura of heroism surrounding him. They said of him that on the days of one of the pogroms, he blocked the door of the house and stopped the mob from getting in.

[Page 145]

Shmuel married Rachel and they had two sons: Meir and Moshe. The "Sejm" a gathering of the womenfolk of the family, met every evening in Miriam's spotless and shining house. The husbands were accustomed to it and surrendered to the wishes of "togetherness" of the sisters. There were pivotal evenings when family decisions were made; there were meetings for festivals full of warmth and open–heartedness. In those meetings many topics were discussed like, help for the needy, discussions on politics and so on. They also discussed the luminaries of the Talmud. I especially remember the "warnings" that were issued to everyone whenever the aunts Baltshe or Perl were expected in town; I remember the discussions between the sisters: "When an aunt comes to visit, aunt Sheyndil will take the baggage to her house and the others take the guests."...

My father came from Będzin to Miechów as a young "green" Yeshiva student; a few ups and downs ensued but eventually his funds increased. It appears that together with Mordecai Reuven he bought part of Kornfeld's house where he opened a wine business together with uncle Shmuel and they were partners in the trust run by Maltinski of Charsznica, for cognac and other distilled liquors. He slowly became involved in the life of the town, he was the sexton of the main synagogue and a member of the Burial Society, a member of the board of "Charity for the Needy" and active in "Mizrahi", he was a regular in the synagogue Friday evenings and known for his modern rendering of "Lecha Dodi". His education was in German and Polish and it made a name for him but it didn't prevent him from making connections with the municipal heads in town – in the police, city hall or provincial government. If a Jewish resident required a favour from the authorities, my father was the "address" to go to. My mother Hanna came from the Russian school. We loved to hear her declaim from Pushkin even though we understood almost nothing. She was a housewife to her very soul. We loved to see her face light up when she welcomed guests. It seemed to us that there was no sorrow or worry that her light would fail to lessen the sadness of. My sister, Chaitshe stayed home; Baltshe was always with her friends; Malka studied in Będzin. I was in the youth movements and always up to some kind of mischief; a member of a group of "reptiles" and our nickname was "Antak". My sister Sarah'leh was little when I left home. And what remains from all the family? A child could count them on the fingers of one hand.

I heard from the Red Cross that my father died from illness in 1941, in the ghetto; my mother, a real "Yiddishe Momma", and her two daughters, little Sarah and Baltshe, who married Zukerman from Sosnowica and gave birth to a daughter, perished in Chodów, as did most of the Jews of the town. Shmuel Fogel and his wife Rachel, a wonderful woman – a little strange to us because of her beauty and habits, the habits of an urbanite – and their son Moshe, perished, apparently, together with my mother and my sisters and only the lawyer, Meir remained. All the rest of the family were cut down and left no trace behind them.

I have tried to create here, a tombstone for one name, one family I am certain that many of my town's residents or from other towns will bow their heads in silence and will say to themselves: "Was it not thus also with me? With my family?"

Yes! We remained extensions and shreds of cloth after that terrible storm, solitary and sad branches and in our hearts the echo of memories of a many–branched and glorious tree.

Translator's Footnote

1. Yimakh Shemo = "May his name and memory be obliterated"

[Page 146]

The writer Israel Zarchi (1909–1947)

by S. D. Yerushalmi

Translated by Selwyn Rose

Israel Zarchi

Israel Zerach Gertler (Z"L), known by his pen–name, "Israel Zarchi", who in his short life managed to enrich the new Hebrew literature with 13 of his original books and two exemplary books from world literature that he translated into Hebrew, was born in Jędrzejów to one of the respected families.

He was born on 6th October 1909 at the end of the festival of Succoth to his father, Rabbi Shimon Gertler and his wife, Hinda the daughter of Rabbi Zalman Sternfeld, the owner of the Skroniów estate, near Jędrzejów. His mother died a short time after his birth and the orphans – his sisters,

Shprintzer(?) and Rosa and he – the youngest – were brought up by their paternal grandmother, Esther Gertler of Miechów–Charsznica. From there he went for training to Grochów, a suburb of Warsaw and from there immigrated to Palestine. In his letter, that he sent to his friend Haim Toren on 7th May 1946, (about a year before his death), in reply to one sent to him concerning Volume three of "Our Beautiful Literature from Bialik Until Today", are found some interesting insights into his life. This is what he wrote:

> "I received a free and liberal education in Polish (until I learned Yiddish from my friends, I was already a young man). At first I studied at a Polish National school and afterwards at the Jewish Gymnasium in Kielce where the teaching language was Polish. In that Gymnasium there was also the possibility of studying in Hebrew but – because I had excellent grades in all my subjects (except Hebrew) – I was exempted from taking part in lessons on Judaism and for many years I knew nothing of our language. When I was 15 or 16, I spent some time in northern Italy (in the Tyrol), in the home of an Ashkenazi family from Vienna, and while there I learned German. I returned from the Tyrol to Poland and there I became awakened to the study of Hebrew, I even went to a village of pioneers – Grochów – near Warsaw that was a Palestinian kibbutz in all essentials, and stayed there for more than a year.
>
> In 1929 I immigrated to Palestine as a pioneer: in the beginning I lived in the huts of the pioneers in Petah Tikvah on public land and worked making the new road from Petah Tikva to Kfar Saba. For personal reasons, I transferred to Kibbutz Givat Hashlosha and stayed there for more than a year working mainly in the citrus groves and the cow–sheds and prepared ground for planting citrus saplings for the artist Reuven and his brother. One day I was told that we would have a special planting ceremony in the grove – and the first sapling would be planted by Bialik. I wasn't present at the beginning of the planting – who was I – a young pioneer walking after the cows. Only the following day when I came to work did I find out and I was filled with anger.
>
> When I left Givat Hashlosha I was a "day–worker" in the citrus groves of Kfar Saba; but because at that time the trees didn't bear fruit, in the winter I moved between Petah Tikvah in winter picking oranges and thus I was, for a couple of years a seasonal worker in the citrus groves: in summer in

Kfar Saba working in the citrus groves and in the summer picking oranges in Petah Tikva.

At the end of that period I wrote my first story "Youth" and the manuscript wandered around together with me from place to place. Then I moved to Tel–Aviv working on a building in Yehuda Halevi Street and all the horrors that I endured still make my heart flutter to this day. In 1932 I entered – on the recommendation of Bialik – the Hebrew University and my time there is certainly well–known to you. I completed my studies there with my degree in the Humanities in 1938, although it had never been my intention from the start to study just to obtain a certificate, but as my studies progressed there awoke within me the urge to compete and I passed the entrance exams; from that came the impulse to acquire Hebrew.

In 1934 I went to Iraq, losing my way in the desert and forsaken places several times in the near east and as a result of that I wrote "The Oil Flows to the Mediterranean Sea". In 1938, with the completion of my studies at the University, I was in Europe – Italy, France and Belgium but mostly in England. I studied at London University at a special course for foreign academics. Of those travels I wrote "Traveling Light". The list of my journeys would be incomplete without mentioning what may appear to be a minor point but its influence on me was no less than that of my larger ones. In the summer of 1941 I wanted to stay a couple of weeks in the Old City. I moved to an apartment under some pressure to get closer to my Jewish roots and the Land of Israel (during the days of great despair when the hand of the Nazis threatened also Palestine) influenced me significantly, and here is not the place to dwell on its nature. After my stay within the Old City walls I wrote "Adornments of Jerusalem. I think that these are the visible impressions; the hidden ones – this is not the place.

My first work, a little worthy of the name is my book "Youth" published by "Mitzpeh" Tel–Aviv 1933. Here I must mention Ya'acov Fichman, who was its first reader and he it was who recommended it in writing to the publishers. The second is Asher Barash. I took part in the editing "A Jerusalem anthology of Literature", (published by Achiasaf in Jerusalem 1942, edited by Israel Zarchi, Ezra Menahem and Haim Toren).

My book "The Oil Flows to the Mediterranean Sea" we will translate into Polish and my book "Micha'eli's Big Day" to Yiddish and Polish (two separate translations); sections of the book "Adornments of Jerusalem" to

English; "Shimson the Perfume Marketer" – to Hebrew; more I don't know. I translated Heinrich von Kleists "Michael Kohlhaas" (from the German) and the stories of Josef Konrad and W. Somerset

–Maugham from the English."

Thus far his epistle.

[Page 148]

Already in his younger years Israel Zarchi suffered with serious problems from his lungs and was sent to Miran. His health improved and they hoped that he was out of a danger that had caused concern for his life. He married and had two daughters: Nurit and Michal, and he devoted himself completely with all his being to his blessed talent for writing. These are the books that were published: 1. "Youth", a novel, published by "Mitzpeh, Tel–Aviv 1933; 2. "Barefoot Days", a novel, published by "Mitzpeh" 1935; 3. "The Oil Flows to the Mediterranean Sea", published by "Palestine Book Publishers", Jerusalem, 1937, second edition, above, 1939; 4. "Journey without Baggage", (pages from a travelogue), published by "Palestine Book Publishers" , Jerusalem, 1939; 5. "Mount Scopus", four years from the life of Daniel Geffen, a novel, published by "Achiasaf", Jerusalem, 1940; 6. "Grandmother's Destroyed House", a story, published at first by "Achiasaf", Jerusalem, 1941, (later by "Omer" – the evening newspaper of "Davar"); 7. "Adornments of Jerusalem", paths in the Old City, , published by "Adi", Tel–Aviv, 1933; 8. "Blazing Archive", a cycle of stories, published by "Achiasaf", Jerusalem, 1933 (these stories were first published in different literary collections); 9. "The Evil Days", two stories (A. Death of the Doctor; B. The Preacher), published by "Ofer", Jerusalem, 1948; 10. "An Unsown Land", a novel, published by "Am Oved", ("Lador" library) Tel–Aviv, 1946; 11. "The Fathers' Inheritance", a story, published by Reuven Maas, Jerusalem, 1946; 12. "For What", a story, published by "Sifriat Hashaot", Tel–Aviv, 1946; 13. "Kfar Shiloah", a novel, published by "Am Oved", ("Lador" library), Tel–Aviv, 1948. Translations: "The Hour of Strength"[1], W. Somerset–Maugham, 1945 (from the English) and "Stories From the Grapevine", Joseph Konrad, 1945.

In addition to stories and monographs not included in anthologies of his works, manuscripts, "Records of Meetings and Conversations" which are of the nature of a literary journal, "Machanim" an historical story the first chapter of which was published in "Kama" – the annual of the Foundation Fund of Israel for the year 1948 edited by Natan Bistritzky, and “Michael Kohlhaas” by Heinrich von Kleist, that was translated from the German.

While he was at the peak of success with his literary career, he fell ill with a malignant disease that put an end to his fruitful life. In his monograph, “A Character Portrayal” the literary critic and his best friend Haim Toren, wrote:

“...and fate decided that his life and productivity, which was running parallel to his constant difficult and bitter struggles should end just when all the winds of the world were blowing in his favor and his ship of life plowed towards its target with strength and security. How proud our hearts were when we saw him, four months before his death, crowned with the “Jerusalem Prize” named for David Yellin – we were partners in his joy, his achievements and victories but who could think or expect that such an achievement would be the last station in the chapter of his life? Who could imagine that his beautiful words, heartfelt and considered, coming from his heart – of a man that he gave voice to, and gave witness to his maturity of thought and understanding, were his last utterances, coming from the heart of a man fatally ill and in his last days?

About one hundred and twenty days he struggled with a bitter death. On the morning of Friday 8th of July, 1947 he was released from his agony and taken from us before telling us all that was in his heart...and while his heart was overflowing with sweet dreams of life and his creativity, his pen slipped from his hand in the prime of his success, his flowering, his striving onwards and upwards, cut down one of the pleasant, refreshing stately oaks in the in our literary grove...”

With the end of the thirty–days mourning period, a memorial service was held under the auspices of the Hebrew Writers Society in Jerusalem at which his teacher and mentor Professor Joseph Klausner (Z”L), gave the principle address in memory of the departed. Among other things he said:

[Page 149]

“Israel Zarchi was plucked from our midst at the pinnacle of his flowering, at the moment that his talents gave the final touch to his maturity. During nearly fifteen years (1933 – 1947), he managed to have published in his life, ten major books, apart from many short stories, and apart from a large number that we will publish posthumously. Each book was a rung in the ladder of development, that the book which followed was one step higher on the ladder than its predecessor in its perfection and outlook, speculation and design.

He was my student, a talented and dear student and they are very few who will mourn his untimely passing more than I.

He was one of the first graduates of the University. His thesis was, if I am not mistaken, on "The Hebrew novel during the period of the "Haskala'"; the work made an impression on me and I recommended that it was worthy of publication. It is most certainly to be found as manuscript among Zarchi's papers or the University archives and it is seemly to find it and publish it"

He concluded by saying:

His creations signify new avenues of writing our native Hebrew. Let us collect all his writings in two or three volumes and put them into the hands of our sons and daughters. Thus the soul of our dear Israel Zarchi – as a writer and as a man – will be woven together with his eternal people in its eternal language."

In 1949 – about two years after the passing of Zarchi, "A Literary Anthology in Memory of Israel Zarchi" published as "Decorations", edited by his friend Haim Toren, in which acknowledged writers and poets took part, dedicating a work in his memory, appeared. Also published in that volume were a few chapters from Zarchi's diary, a biography of his life, a bibliography of his books and editorial comments published about them and some of his letters.

Translator's Footnote

1. No direct reference was found for this title, nor any title that could be a reasonable English rendering or paraphrase; possibly one of an anthology by W. Somerset–Maugham – Trans.

Shmuel Nahum Chanowsky

by Moshe Spiegel

Translated by Selwyn Rose

Few among us can remember the unique character in our town, of the teacher of religion in the elementary school and later the "Mizrahi" school, Shmuel Nahum Chanowsky.

When he arrived in Miechów he was already old. According to him he was a friend of Nahum Sokolow, the Mendel publishers, Frishman, Krinski, Linzki and others. Because he was single, there was a certain strangeness about his habits and many thought he might be a little unstable. I had the great privilege of being counted among his students and it is my wish to write a sketch of his character of my teacher and mentor.

We were four students who learnt privately with him in my parents' home, and they were Ya'acov and Elimelech Friedrich, my brother Yona Spiegel, and I. We learned Torah, especially the book of Daniel and Aramaic grammar. Hebrew we learned through reading books that he had written: Hebrew reader, Treasury of the Hebrew Language. A special book of his was – examples of special expressions that had great significance as quotations from the Torah and the Talmud. Chanowsky had an incredible memory. He knew by heart every chapter and page in the Bible and Talmud and in spite of his great age never made a mistake. There were very few people who learned Torah from him but the teachers in town knew of him and his extensive, many–branched knowledge and from time to time would come to him to hear his opinion on different matters.

[Page 150]

For two years he provided us with knowledge of the language and its treasures, and we praise him here as an outstanding pedagogue and an example to his pupils.

Chanowsky belonged to the school of "Maskilim" from the seventies of the previous century and it was a wonder to us that instead of seeking a post in one of the great cultural Jewish centers of Poland he came at the end of his days to our little town.

Eventually he fell ill, took to his bed and struggled with the Angel of Death but in vain. Lonely he walked among us and loneliness filled his soul. We, his pupils, sat at his bedside until his soul left him...

After his death the whole town – man, woman and child, Jew and Gentile, accompanied him to his last resting place; it was clear to everyone that one of our great scholars and rare scientists had left us and few like him were among us.

It was a great privilege that he came to us; in the local cemetery was the grave of a dear man whose name will never be erased from our memory.

Berish Frankel (Z"L)

by Tsvi Frankel

Translated by Selwyn Rose

"Berishel Glazer" they called him, my father (Z"L), his affectionate nickname; and not for nothing did they nickname him thus, for he loved everyone and everyone loved him and with everyone he found a common language; with scholars – and he was one of them, with young students from the "Steibl"[1] because he amused them and with simple artisans because he was a glazier. He prayed every Sabbath in the synagogue of the Righteous of Gur community although his place in the "Steibl" was among the moderate orthodox. Nevertheless, he made sure that he gave a Torah–based education to his children, especially to his youngest. All week he was concerned with the sustenance of his family, he would circulate among the villages in the area fitting or replacing windows. For all that he allotted times for the Torah and I can still hear the musical sound of his voice ringing in my ears each morning when I awoke in our small house, blessed with many children. Shabbat was devoted in its entirety to study with his sons, in order to comply with the commandment: "...and thou shall teach them diligently unto thy children..." He would fulfill the Talmudic teaching: "He who cares about the eve of the Sabbath will eat well on the Sabbath day." Therefore on Sabbath eve he involved himself with various activities and prepared for the Sabbath meal meticulously. When we returned from the "Steibl" and Friday eve prayers, the Sabbath candles were lit and the table arranged for us and we, the children and our mother (Z"L), sat around it. Father would commence with "Woman of value who will find..." and he didn't cease chanting between courses, when we all sang in chorus with him. Great joy ruled the atmosphere among us and we felt as if an additional soul had permeated the room. This aura persisted until the end of the Sabbath.

[Page 151]

Sabbath began with a walk to the ritual bath – in winter and summer – and afterwards Torah study eight o'clock in the Study Hall and a walk in company with the other Hassidim to the home of Rabbi Herschel in Wolbrom Street; there we drank coffee from the stove's hot–plate and tasted the tcholent also prepared the previous day and allowed to stew overnight because then it really had the taste and smell of tcholent...then again to the "Steibl" for prayers and the meal served with good dishes and seasoned with Torah and hymns as required.

After a light sleep my father would take me to the Study Hall. In winter, when the stove is hot and it's cold outside and there's snow and frost, a group of youngsters – us – sat and my father would prepare a number of questions from the weekly portion – question and answer. Between two questions he would say something humorous and using the joke would teach me something from the "Gemara", until the elders came for the recital of Psalms. They would crowd round him and insist: "Berishel – tell us something about the deeds of the great "righteous ones". My father was an excellent raconteur and his stories came easily and swiftly.

In education my father was notable for being somewhat heavy–handed, believing in the dictum: "Spare the rod and spoil the child." He always said: "I will not allow you to grow up ignorant and boorish." He exploited every spare moment to teach Torah. I remember an interesting event one winter evening when we were all sitting in our warm room, my mother was knitting and my father was teaching me from the Talmud's sixth "order" on the topic of "divorce" – "He who brings a 'get' from abroad...". My sister was also sitting and sewing and listening to the discussion while working. Suddenly she broke in, unable to contain herself: "Look! He hasn't yet married and already you are teaching him how to arrange a divorce!"

As a natural tendency my father tended towards socialism, perhaps from the fact that he wasn't wealthy and had many boys and girls...I was witness to many arguments he had with the young men of the town who tended towards communism. The "idea" was good he would say to them if it was accompanied with a little religion according to the spirit of our prophets it would be even better.

Once, in the "Steibl", my father was sitting with Rabbi Yehoshua Koplewicz (Z"L) and they were chatting on this and that. Rabbi Yehoshua was complaining that he was getting fat and must go to Karlsbad for a cure but this year was impossible for him. My father listened to him and said: "Yehoshua – I have some good advice for you – take over my job for a month, come to sleep in place of me on my straw mattress, we'll put two of my boys to sleep beside you, during the day eat a little "yushka" and watery coffee and in addition carry a few panes of glass on your back to the village and I promise you that if you do this you'll be healthy very quickly and you won't need to go to go to any expense and journeys.

He was also accepted by the Christians and when he arrived among them to do some work he would debate with them on religion. I recall that he always had arguments with Pan Kozlowski, the coffin maker at his shop on Krakowa Street. Kozlowski hated the Jews and accused them of crucifying Jesus. My father occasionally tried to reason with him and prove to him he was in error and show him that our religion was a forgiving one and had broader horizons. When Kozlowski saw he couldn't win with my father he said: "I have decided to send my son to the Seminary to become a priest; when he comes to visit our town – he will have the strength to argue with you." And indeed, after some time the priest came home and my father invited him to debate; without fear my father defended his stand and outlook. For that the Christians showed him much respect.

As a "Lover of Zion" and esteem for our ancient language my father sent me to study Hebrew, and always enjoyed hearing me when I spoke Hebrew. After my brother Arieh's marriage he received a certificate for him and he immigrated to Palestine with his wife.

My father also tried to help my other brother, Yehezkiel and our sister to immigrate although that didn't succeed: with the destruction of the Jews of Poland our town was also destroyed and together with it all the Jews and my father's family.

Translator's Footnote

1. The "court" of a renowned rabbi and his disciples

[Page 152]

Esther Etil Burnstein
wife of Rabbi Natan Ha–Levi Burnstein

by M. Sukenik

Translated by Selwyn Rose

Grandmother Esther was from the Lachs family, among the first settlers in Miechów. She received a Torah education at home just the same as the male members of the family. She knew the Torah and kept the laws of Kashrut as only the most punctilious know them.

There were two charcoal–burning stoves at home: a large one for meat preparations and a smaller one (that stood in another corner of the kitchen), for milk preparations. Also in matters of general cleanliness she was most careful. On occasion she would pour water on the hands of the kitchen maid to ensure she didn't contaminate the food.

For every question that arose, large or small, they would send me to the Rabbi; when Passover arrived they would purify the house thoroughly as commanded. The cupboard that was used for bread throughout the year they would scrub and scour well and take it outside the house with its doors towards the wall. The preparations for Passover were extensive and exhausting.

Grandmother had the habit of saying "without vows and promises" and took care never to promise something that she couldn't deliver on. She never let an oath pass her lips. I remember a typical event: she needed to attend court to give evidence. I accompanied her to the court and of course the judge asked her to give evidence under oath. But she apologized to the Judge that she had never sworn an oath in her life and therefore had no intention of doing so now. The Judge spoke to her seriously and explained that it was merely a formality that she needed to comply with because otherwise her evidence could not be accepted and the man being judged may be falsely convicted of an offence because of her refusal. His pleadings were in vain and she remained adamant. The Judge gave up and the accused man walked free. On her holiness and purity an event after her passing will bear witness. Grandmother Esther passed away in Krakow during her last visit to our house. Her only son, Yekutiel Burnstein was immediately called from

Katowice. He decided that the funeral should take place in Miechów; the authorities objected but eventually agreed to transfer the body to Miechów but only in a tin coffin and without permitting the ritual cleaning and preparation of the body before the interment. The vehicle with the body inside arrived directly at the cemetery accompanied by a policeman who was there to assure that the coffin wasn't opened before burial. The whole town turned out to accompany the holy lady. A miracle occurred! The policeman had a heart attack and died on the spot. Until a replacement arrived, there was time to open the coffin, purify and prepare the body and replace the body in the coffin.

Rabbi Natan Ha-Levi Burnstein (Z"L)

[Page 153]

May her memory be for a blessing forever.

Haim Tennenwurcel

by Raphael Mlinarski

Translated by Selwyn Rose

Haim Tennenwurcel, the son of Itcha (Yitzhak) and grandson of Yermiyahu Blum, was born in 1919. He completed commercial school in Krakow and was the only Jewish representative on the board of the "Society of Artisans". He was a respected Jew in our town, educated and genteel and knew the most excellent Hebrew.

In 1940 Haim Tennenwurcel began to organize our youth. Belonging to the organization were Abba Vanchadlovski, Shlomo Stein, Yitzhak Lieber, Natan Kleiner, Laybl Woznica (Z"L), while saved for a long life were: Abba Firer, Shlomo Plotnik, Brantshe Frucht, Raphael Mlinarski, Manya Zayid, Olshewski, Leyzerek Greitzer, Salzburg (Z"L). In great secrecy we met in the cellar of one of the members (Shlomo Stein, the son of Ya'acov Shia), who had used it earlier as a factory for making candles. He led debates and conversations with us on pioneering and gave us information on what was happening in the world.

The conqueror demanded that everyone should be engaged in productive labor. Most of our younger people were put to road–work and some of them in garages. Edelist Berl, Abram'tchyk Ephraim, Elimelech Fajgenbaum and I were sent to work with the German police, cleaning rooms, repairing boots, clothes, etc. Once, one of the German policemen sent me to repair his radio. With the help of Haim Pinczhowski, a graduate of the Miechów Gymnasium, whose hobby was amateur radio, we received broadcasts from abroad, and I managed to hear the radio station in England broadcasting in Polish. I met Haim T. and told him what I had heard, and he passed it on to others.

So things continued on until1941. That year the Germans began to send the Jews to labor camps. That's when the fates took Haim T. together with 50 or 60 youngsters. They were sent to Bonarka, near Krakow to work in a brick–making factory. Haim T. and Meir Grunewald were responsible for the work. Everyone loved him; he always came to help others, interested himself in everyone; he kept dreaming of how to escape to the underground.

[Page 154]

In 1943 he escaped to Sosnowiec and made contact with the Jewish underground. He operated with friends from the "Young Zionists": Yushek

Kozuk, Buluk Kozuk, whom he had known from before the war. Concerning him, Fredka Mazie wrote in her book "Evil in the Storm":

"...Winter 1943. One evening we met at Lulke and Szymek's, we were surprised at the sight of two fellows sitting there that we didn't know. They were Haim Tennenwurcel and Lulak Rozencweig who had come from Krakow; they had been in Krakow for the last two months. Neither of them were residents of Krakow. Haim's home town was Miechów. Lulak was from Częstochowa. He met Haim who was then one of the responsible Jews in Bonarka (a suburb of Krakow). They both integrated in the Jewish underground operations that were active there.

Stunned, we listened to their stories. They told us about the fighting organization that two leaders of "Akiva", Szymek Draenger and Dolek Liebeskind created, about the newspaper "The Fighting Pioneer" of the attacks against the Germans, acquisition of small–arms, the attack on the coffee–house "Cyganeria". Without any help from outside, without the support of Poles, by their own resolve and sacrifice these few fought not only for their lives but "For three lines in history." Haim told us about the tortures, about the harsh conditions during their arrest in the large Montelupich prison house. Haim's stories encourage us and added to our courage and energy. We felt we were not alone.

They brought with them a Yiddish song that excited all of us, a song by Mordecai Gebirtig "Es Brent" – "It's burning". Haim and Lulak settled among us and integrated with us, partners in all we did. We provided them with all their needs and learned from their experiences. Our family grew with two more good devoted friends. (Page 118).

Also mentioned in her book:

"...— the bunker. Haim T. was the "owner" of the bunker. He came to us last winter from Krakow and in a very short time became one of us, as if he had always been with us. Because he was "illegally" in the ghetto and didn't work for the Germans, and also had no family or home of his own, he devoted all his energies and strength to the structure. He never left the bunker from dawn until dusk." (Page 144).

"...— It was decided to send Haim T. to a village in the Carpathians and discover what the possibilities of hiding out there were. Haim accepted the mission, was given some food for the journey and a gift parcel of excellent woven wool; it was a very valuable weave and almost impossible to acquire. The present was intended for the village head who agreed to give Haim a genuine Christian birth certificate registered in the village's archives. Haim returned to us with the document and told us he had managed to make contact with smugglers to Slovakia. They smuggle vodka and tobacco but after a little negotiating they agreed to smuggle people as well." (Page146).

"...— again they succeeded in making contact with the smugglers willing to get people across the border into Slovakia and from there to Hungary and thence to Palestine. Again the two wandered from place to place, Haim and Kowa. They managed to get them accepted and organized among some farmers. They kitted them out as best as they could, with documentation, money and clothes but what happened across the border is a puzzle and unknown. Concerning Haim and Olek Guttman (now a Lieutenant–General in the Israel Defense Forces), they were required to cross over among the first group and carry explicit information.

[Page 155]

After a short while, Haim returned in a happy mood and told us he had been welcomed pleasantly by the Slovakian Jews. He told us about their constant resistance to his return and the struggle with Olek who also wanted to return. In the extensive argument that followed who will return and who remain, each came with their reasons for claiming precedence. Olek said that he was younger and relied on that and Haim T. indicated that it was precisely his greater age and experience that gave him the right. They finally decided to allow blind fate to decide and cast lots to decide who between them would return. Haim won. In spite of the warnings and pleadings from the local people Haim returned to Zwardoń and from there to Sosnowiec.

Haim was now free, he could move around without fear, he returned from a sense of responsibility for the fate of friends who wouldn't allow him to remain there. After Bolek Koz'uk's imprisonment we decided that Haim must return again to Slovakia and coordinate the whole group. He agreed and he had to go together with Ruth, her family, and with Lucia. At the Katowice the police came up to us. I showed them my documents and they were satisfied with them. Everyone else was held. Haim tried to escape but they chased after him. He pulled out his pistol but with bad luck it mis–

fired and he was taken. I kept a distance and followed after to see what was happening. They took him to the Gestapo and I followed at a distance. Near the "Astoria" café I met two German policemen; they knew me and tried to arrest me again but I ran for it. Under the bridge I shot at them – I had better luck and my gun worked correctly. Haim and Bulok were imprisoned together until about 10th November, the eve of Polish Independence Day, when they were both hanged as Polish Partisans in the village of Jabłonka, in order that 'they will hear and see'" (Page 266- *page number refers to the page number in the original Yizkor book*).

[Page 155]

Yehuda Zelmanowicz (Z"L)

By Ze'ev Dror

Translated by Selwyn Rose

It is difficult to eulogize you because above all things you disliked weeping and lamentation. Even under the most difficult of circumstances you knew how to practice restraint, you knew to smile, to smile even from within pain – and certainly not allow a groan to escape from between your lips, or from others.

You loved people, you loved to be in their company, to live their problems and understand their weaknesses, you were sparing with words but one comment from you was enough to convince to what degree you had penetrated deeply to the heart of the topic, pass over the incidental and expose the good in a man. You knew to be a friend in good times and bad.

You were honest with yourself and in your life. You detested empty talk where there was no substance in practical terms or from personal example. You were responsible at work and progressed by virtue of knowledge and organization. You were polite and courteous, a possessor of deep knowledge that you had acquired through reading, thought and conversation – you had good taste in literature, in theater and music.

In your awareness of your health you restrained yourself from building a home for yourself – although you loved family life. You interested yourself deeply in your friends' family life, in the lives of their children, you hared their joy at their achievements and you were pained with their hurt at their failures!

You were wise, proud and independent, a good friend and a good man – and as such we will always remember you.

[Page 156]

In Memory of Yehuda Zelmanowicz

by Yitzhak Pulaski

Translated by Selwyn Rose

Yehuda Zelmanowicz

I only know very little of him from his childhood. We were not at "Heder" and neither did we share the same class at school. As we matured I knew him only very superficially. He was a student at the "Mizrahi" school and afterwards at the "Takhmoni" school in Warsaw, while I was a student at the "Aguda[1]" school and afterwards the "Yeshiva[2]". I knew that he was always among the top excellent students; constantly persevering in his reading, and striving to be inconspicuous. When he was a teacher of history in secondary school we met each other very rarely. Already at these early encounters I was impressed by his manners and courtesy, and especially by his carefully considered speech and its significant content. During the period when I was affiliated to the Betar Movement we occasionally met, although I was unable to determine clearly where he was heading, I knew he was a serious Zionist.

Our relationship as friends became more evident and strengthened with the outbreak of World War Two. We especially became closer when the ghetto was liquidated and we were transferred to labor camps. There I was able to appreciate much more clearly his attributes. I was with him from the start until a very short time before the liberation. During that terrible period when the life of everyone depended on a crust of bread, Yehuda Zelmanowicz (Z"L) proved time and time again how far away he was from any form of egoism and how great were his good deeds,

In September 1942 we were transferred to the labor camp at Prokocim. A group of people stayed behind in Miechów (some with and some without the Germans' knowledge) his concern was for our welfare and our needs and he transferred – in all sorts of ways – quantities of bread to the camp. The people from Miechów in the camp were grouped together and worked in one place. When the first delivery arrived one of them tried to impose himself upon us as a "policeman" showing discrimination in the distribution of the bread; Yehuda Zelmanowicz resisted fiercely to the discrimination and succeeded in preventing it. In the camp's Compound 1, Yehuda Zelmanowicz was nominated as group head. In contrast to others who exploited that position for their own good – even to the detriment of other people, Yehuda (Z"L) was the complete opposite; he exploited the position to ease and improve the condition of each and every one of us. More than once he put himself in grave danger by leaving his place of work, entering into shops close–by to buy something. Had he been caught the outcome would have been quite clear: an arbitrary shooting on the spot. He always asked if someone had special needs and he would bring if, sometimes with his own money. He preached morals when he saw something unfair. He would help and demand that everyone helps each other but always in his quiet friendly voice. In the camp he never sought to make things easier for himself or looked for favors while holding his position. At the end of 1943 we were transferred to Skarżysko–Kamienna. The camp was divided into three sections A, B and C. Our group was taken to Section C. It was the worst section of all three. I and my two brothers by good fortune were transferred to Section A which was the best of them. After a few weeks, on a Sunday a group from Section C came to Section A to the shower room; there wasn't one in Section C. A few of the group, among them Yehuda (Z"L), looked for us to pay a visit and found us in our work place. They were completely broken and exhausted, hungry and thirsty; their hands and faces were green; their clothes torn and tattered. They told us of the bitterness of the fate of everyone in the camp. We saw ourselves as kings compared to them.

[Page 157]

It happened to be exactly at the time of the mid–day distribution of our food. We worked in the carpentry shop and we were about forty together working there. I and my two brothers asked the rest of our group to donate a small portion of their food which they did without hesitation. When we saw the manner in which they ate the food we all burst out crying. Afterwards I felt that Yehuda (Z"L) left a small portion on his plate. I asked him why and he said: "There is someone else hungry as I was and now I've had enough." From the remains we refilled their plates and Yehuda (Z"L) took the responsibility of delivering the food to those who had remained in the other camp. The following week the second group appeared and from them we heard from them how Yehuda (Z"L) had distributed the food fairly.

After the war, I met him in Miechów. We were happy to see each other. After a while I told him I was leaving Poland with the intention of going to Israel. He asked me to let him know after I arrived how I was getting on. When I arrived in Germany, I wrote him in full detail about my journey. When he got to Germany we met again frequently. When I arrived in Israel we met in Tel–Aviv. When he worked in Haifa he stayed with me for a while.

I learned of his death from the newspaper the day after his funeral. I was shocked and shaken to have learned about it in such a way. I had thought that in spite of everything he had survived the war as a victor but I was wrong, he was beaten. The sufferings and agonies that were his lot during the war years had destroyed the body of that man of such pure attributes and it could no longer continue. With his passing he left a void in his family and the remainder of the survivors of Germany's destructive mills.

Translator's Footnotes

1. Interwar network of religious schools affiliated to Agudas Yisroel political movement
2. Religious seminary

Rabbi Yankele Rottenberg

by Moshe Spiegel

Translated by Selwyn Rose

The Rabbi Yankele Rottenberg (TZ"L), the son of the Adm"or[1] of Czestochowa and the son–in–law of Adm"or from Kielce, arrived in Miechów in his youth with his wife, two sons, Berele and Motele and their only daughter Goldele.

Fate allowed me to find myself in his company for three years and hear Torah from his lips, as one destined to receive ordination to the Rabbinate. The topics of my studies were Talmud, Shulchan Aruch, Yoreh De'ah, and Yad Hazaka – the Mishneh of the Rambam, etc.

I remember the argument that broke at home out between my father, Avraham (Z"L) and my mother Sarale (Z"L). All his life my father had been a political activist supporting "Mizrahi" and also orthodox observant customs. My mother was even more so and tended strongly towards "Agudas Yisroel" and "Beit Ya'acov" following in her own father's footsteps, my grandfather, Rabbi Mendel Gutenstein from Wolbrom, one of the Righteous of Gur and close to the Court of the Rabbi. The argument broke out when the "Mizrahi" school was established in Miechów, the first schools to include general education in its curriculum. My father played a significant part in the establishment of the school and wanted his children to be among its first pupils. My mother, on the other hand, wanted to give her son a traditional Torah–oriented education, to make of the Torah "an axe to grind" and become attached to the dynasty of respected Rabbis of Israel. My mother was extremely proud of her cousin, the Rabbi of Kurzelów, Rabbi Arieh Leib Frommer who, in time became the Head of Yeshiva "Hochmei Lublin". The argument continued for a few weeks becoming quite fierce. In the end my mother won and the following was decided: My older brother Elimelech (Z"L), will go to Zawiercie to study Torah from our relative, the distinguished Rabbi from Kurzelów, and they would send me to learn Torah from Rabbi Yankele the Adm"or of Miechów, and my younger brother Yona (Z"L) will remain with Rabbi Yisroel–Eli Krymalowski, until he became a little older and increased his knowledge a little.

[Page 158]

The first time I entered the Rabbi's room I was most impressed with his noble countenance, his modesty and his soft caressing voice. His personality captivated me on first sight, every word that came out of his mouth was imbued with the fear of G–d and immeasurable warmth. And so my first lesson was as if entering a grove[2]. And indeed I entered the grove and the Temple of the Torah, pure and refined – to glimpse and not to be stricken; but my poor strength wasn't great enough to resist – I entered, glimpsed and was stricken...

We were three pupils with Rabbi Yankele: Berele – the eldest boy, Motele – the second boy and the writer of these few lines. We were three pupils and each one had a different personality, attention–span and behavior. Obviously their ability to succeed in their studies was also different.

Berele was a quiet boy, disciplined and with a great determination to learn Torah but his comprehension was slow. Motele was an imp, insolent with his head full of escapades and practical jokes and several times his father was obliged to lecture him about concentrating his attention on learning Torah. I, in comparison, absorbed the teachings of the Rabbi quickly to the extent that I was used as the Urim and Thummim to my two friends from the rabbinical dynasty.

Because I became so at home in the Rabbi's house I was treated very much like one of their own children and they made efforts to draw me close to them. The Rabbi's wife related towards me as if to one of her own and took pleasure in the success of my studies. The daughter, Goldele made a great impression on me from the first meeting and was, in my eyes the very symbol of purity. She had golden hair, and a fair skin like the face of an angel. I sensed she was following me with her eyes, listening to the sound of my footsteps in the room, always listening to my chanting. I too longed to meet her and all the time I sat with the Rabbi I struggled between the craving to see her and be with her and the reality that there could not be a closer relationship between us because of her status as the Rabbi's daughter. In the end the struggle resolved itself because quite suddenly I decided to leave my studies and travel to Warsaw to work more productively in the spirit of a Zionist education.

From the moment that I began to study as an adult with Rabbi Yankele – my eyes were opened; my faith and adherence to the faith of Israel weakened from day–to–day. I began to read secular books, books by Avraham Mapu, Samuel David Luzatto, Shlomo Yehuda Rapoport, Leon Pinsker and others. That – and more: The Zionist Torah that I absorbed from the dawn of my childhood cut me off from the Study–House of my mother and tied me in with the movement that had engraved on its standard the emblem of the national and socialist liberation of our people.

The house of Rabbi Yankele Rottenberg and his household shone a great light among those who gathered in his shadow and illuminated dark, forsaken corners of our world. Today, 40 years on, I still see images of him as if alive, before me.

I do not know the fate of Rabbi Yankele and his family when the Holocaust struck the Jews of Poland.

Translator's Footnotes

1. An acronym for “Our Master, our Teacher and our Rabbi”
2. A reference to the Kabbala from the Hebrew letters PRDS – Paradise.

[Page 159]

In Memory of My Parents

by Yehuda Burstein

Translated by Selwyn Rose

My Father (Z"L)

The commandment to honor one's father and mother is one of the things for which there is no measure and hence I am not sure that I have fulfilled it as required and if not I have besmirched their honor, especially when speaking of parents whose whole lives were holy and good in the eyes of G–d and man.

Here I will try in awe and reverence to raise up from the depths of oblivion a few of the memories of their activities and by doing so honor and esteem them.

My father (Z"L), Yisroel David Burstein, ritual slaughter and inspector in our town functioned all his days in that holy work. A modest man, good–hearted like no one else, most of his time he dedicated to the Torah and his work.

To the work of slaughtering and inspection, every detail of which is precise and which is performed according to canon, allowing for no deviation, right or left, he demonstrated a nobility of soul and kind–heartedness.

When, as happened from time to time, a question of "kosher or treiff" rose up concerning a beast or a fowl, my father toiled, greatly worried and agonized, sought and probed, running around hither and thither, disappearing for hours from home, alerting the Rabbi and an authorized arbiter until late at night, all to save the money of some poor Jew and deem fit to eat the animal that he had bought at great expense.

Courteous and pleasant to everyone throughout the year but as the Days of Awe approached and while standing before his Maker, in the central synagogue pouring out his prayers as a delegate of the congregation, his face shone and his whole being soft and gentle. His deep and pleasant voice and pure prayers softened the hardest of hearts.

He was a "Lover of Zion". I will not exaggerate if I say the first to awaken to a yearning for the redemption and the Zionist idea was my father (Z"L), who, in his own way, planted in my heart these feelings.

I remember when we sat together over a page of the Gemara on long winter nights, when we got to a place that spoke in praise of the Promised Land, he stopped teaching, sighed aloud and the strong longings that seized him were evident. A thick cloud of smoke came out of the cigarette he held in his mouth and covered his face as if he wanted to lessen the sorrow of sitting in exile.

A never–to–be–forgotten experience was when a delegate from Palestine came to visit, a friend of my father these many years, Rabbi Itcha Bonem. He explained the wonders of our land, its citrus groves, and avenues, towns and settlements, Rabbis and people. We sat and listened as in a dream.

My father ached to come but tragically his dream didn't materialize.

From the mouths of survivors who were with him up until his last moment, we heard that during the Nazi conquest he was a teacher and a comforter for the Jews of our town, gathering them, teaching them and breathing into them the spirit of hope and comfort. And thus in sanctification and purity his spirit rose upwards.

May his memory be blessed!

[Page 160]

My Mother (Z"L)

My mother (Z"L), Haya Leah Burstein née Elbaum, was one of the righteous women, who tried to know and understand the needs of the town and the town's "needy ones". In spite of her daily concerns in her holy work of raising her many children and their education, she didn't forget for one instant her fellowman, her generous support and anonymous donations to the needy. I remember on more than one occasion being sent on errands of good deeds – taking food–parcels etc., the homes of the poor at my mother's behest.

Her great knowledge of religious law and judgments handed down throughout the generations, astounded even my father (Z"L); that she had acquired by hearing and absorbing what she had heard of the Torah and studies in her father's house, the ritual slaughterer and inspector, Rabbi Shalom Elbaum (Z"L). Hence she would say: "A woman's honor should be guarded internally as befits a king's daughter"[1].

After a long illness, she passed away in her prime in 1931. May her memory be blessed.

Translator's Footnote

1. A somewhat curled reference to Psalm 45; 14

Avraham Yama and His Son Shlomo

by Haim Ze'ev Yama

Translated by Selwyn Rose

"Jews bring money! Charity saves from death!" – With these and similar words the little Jew, Rabbi Avraham Yama (Z"L), always spurred on the Jewish community of Miechów. He was among the important house–holders in town. A man with a gentle and pure soul, good–hearted, he was always the first to donate to charities. At all the festivities in town, circumcisions, weddings and – G–d forbid – funerals, his noble image was prominent. Rabbi Avraham Yama was especially present at any festival or mourning of the poorer members of Miechów's Jewish community and was always ready to congratulate the bride and groom or comfort the mourner. He returned his pure soul to his Maker on a Sabbath morning.

He was accompanied on his last journey by all the residents of the town, Jew and Gentile alike. All business–houses and workshops were closed on the day of his funeral and the entire town bitterly lamented the great loss of his passing. His first–born, Rabbi Shlomo Yama, inherited his father's high attributes. In his love of his fellow man, fear of heaven and the excellence of his knowledge of the Talmud and the rest of the Holy works, he became an example to all the residents of Miechów. He was the first, perhaps only of Miechów's orthodox residents to embrace the ideology of the "Lovers of Zion", and that stirred many people to oppose him in town and even within the bosom of his own family; he preached the doctrine "The Land of Israel, the People of Israel and the religion of Israel are one and the same." On that principle he educated his children and prepared them for immigration to Palestine.

He taught his children handicrafts. All his days he dreamed of settling in Palestine with his family. In 1925 he acquired together with a group of Jews from Miechów, a plot of land in Afula, in the Jezreel Valley. To his great sorrow he didn't realize his dreams.

At the beginning of the thirties, when Rabbi Yama with unbounded excitement accompanied his three daughters on their way to Palestine, people whispered on the state of his mind and his lack of love and consideration and love towards his daughters: time proved the correctness of his decision.

Rabbi Shlomo Yama was in the concentration camp of Prokocim–Płaszów together with the rest of the Jewish community of Miechów. No survivor of that camp will ever forget the manner in which that dear Jew prepared the Sabbath eve under indescribable circumstances.

[Page 161]

On Friday evenings virtually the entire population of the camp gathered in the bunk–house of Rabbi Shlomo next to two small Shabbat candles in order to draw spiritual encouragement for the following week. With tears in his eyes, he sang the Sabbath evening prayer : "Lecha dodi, likrat calah" and Rabbi Shlomo reminded the Jews – the forced labor workers of the concentration camp – in their imagination to the world of yesterday.

During working days he tried as far as was possible to help others who were suffering more than he. Through his deeds he became one of "The Hidden Ones" or "one of the 36 righteous ones" as they nicknamed him in the camp.

He perished together with his martyred brethren in the extermination camp of Auschwitz.

"It is a tragic loss when a great person dies and there is no one to replace him."[1]

Translator's Footnote

1. The Talmud: Tractate Sanhedrin, page 111a.

Personalities from among "The Hidden Ones"

by Y. Pulaski, Y. Grynwald, Y. Goldberg

Translated by Selwyn Rose

There were a number of people in town who made a deep impression although they made every attempt to remain obscure and inconspicuous. Among them were the rich, the middle–class and the poor, the educated, the partially educated and some who couldn't read or write. In spite of these differences there was a general feeling that all of us together constituted one large family. The unity, the dedication, the concern and mutual assistance were felt all the time in every place.

The slow solid gait, the noble features and courteous speech of Rabbi Moshe Sukenik (Z"L); the silver–knobbed walking stick of the shrewd Abramowitz (Z"L); the small beard on the elegant–faced Rabbi Hanich Cesar (Z"L); the hat and walking–stick of Aharon Leib Adler (Z"L); the bright intelligent eyes of Yermiyahu Blum (Z"L); the tall, erect regal elegance of Shmuel Fogel (Z"L); the yellow beard and curly hair of Avraham Goldberg (Z"L); the Kaiser–like expressions of Avraham Friedrich (Z"L); the soaring voice of the ritual slaughterer and inspector, Rabbi Yisroel David Burstein (Z"L); the dignified appearance of the secular Avraham Sercaz (Z"L); the reverberating laugh of Ovshe Zelkowicz (Z"L) – and many others.

And others, whose outward impression wasn't significant, they too belong to the group no less than the above. Such as Abele Melamed: He is short and under his rod passed rabbis, scholars, academics and successful Jews, Zionists and Mitnagdim, religious and secular. All of them, without exception passed like sheep under his hand. He would sit at the head of the table, with his long beard, his long tangled bushy eyebrows and a snuff–box alongside his hand. From time–to–time he would fill his nostrils with the snuff. With every sneeze we would all bless him in chorus with a loud "Gezundt!", and he would answer with pleasure "Scheine Dank!" There were three long tables in the room arranged in the shape of an open–ended rectangle. One table was for the children aged three who were learning the "Aleph–Bet", the second for the children who could already read and the third for the older children who would soon leave him and he is preparing them for higher learning with a festive meal. It was very exciting when the announcement was made in the "Heder". The Rabbi led the procession followed by his son Reuven (spared for a long good life). At home everyone was waiting. A short prayer, congratulations of "Mazal Tov!" and everyone got a little bag containing a variety of candies. Back in the "Heder" noise and confusion reign; everyone opened the bag and tried to prove that theirs had got more than anyone else. Outside it was already dark and on the way home we used a flash–light or a candle in a tin.

[Page 162]

Abele Melamed (Z"L), loved to be joyful; at every party, festival or just Kiddush on Erev Shabbat he was among the guests in our house. There was a special incident etched in my memory. At the festival of Simchat Torah; my father was keen to buy the honor of Hatan–Torah together with Kiddush. All those who came to the "Steibl" came to our house including Abele Melamed. After a few drinks of cognac he climbed up onto the table in his boots and began to dance and sing a festival song waving the bottle in his hand. He stopped for a moment and asked for a pinch of snuff. All those present proffered a box and he, with everyone laughing took out his own and began to refill it from all those offered him.

He passed away at a good old age. May he be remembered for a blessing.

One of the respected families in town, well–known and with many relatives was the Zukerman family. The head of the family, Abele Zukerman the son–in–law of Shimon Spiegel, owner of an elegant small beard, loved by the residents of town because of his good heartedness, and great honesty. He was from the orthodox Righteous of Gur sect and was especially loved by all those who came to pray in the "Steibl" when Abele prayed before the Ark on Sabbath and the Days of Awe. His immaculate, pure prayers captivated everyone's heart, while himself seemed on fire, as it is written: "...and all my bones shall say..."[1]. His sons and daughter managed his grocery shop and small hosiery workshop and for all that he was hard–pressed to make a livelihood. His health was fragile and he suffered much but his sufferings he accepted with love and never complained.

May his memory be for a blessing!

Mendel Goldberg (Z"L), the son–in–law of Haim Poslushny was publicly active in the Burial Society in town and also in the Ramban Fund as well as being among the first donors and fundraisers for many charities.

He was one of the important members of the Righteous of Gur sect and every annual commemoration dinner for the passing of "S'fat Emet"[2] was held in his house, a sign of his enduring respect and admiration of that righteous one. He had two sons and a daughter – the flower of the family –

each one active in a different field of public activity: the eldest, Leah – founded “Beit Ya'acov” in our town, where many girls were educated in traditional Judaism. Yehoshua – one of the activators of the young “Agudas Yisroel”, he persevered in the organizing of the young orthodox boys into the ranks of the youngsters. The mother, Miriam – a righteous woman, whose whole life was devoted to organizing charities for the children of poor families and for a Torah education her children and the children of the poor of no means. May their memories be for a blessing.

David Isser Eisenberg (Z”L) was a very unique character with not many equals. Seemingly a very simple Jew, but on lifting the edge of the veil one gets a glimpse of his many virtues and pleasant attributes. A measure of his modesty and activities in charities, open and hidden, became common knowledge only after his death (before the Holocaust), when the story of his deeds was told by those whom he helped almost every single day. More than that – his children behaved in the same fashion and their behavior adds to his honor. The son, Haim, was active in the “Revisionist Movement” and the “Zamir” library, intellectual and few resembled him; Shmaryahu and his brother Lazer–Yosef – persevered with their studies in the “Yeshiva” on the Mishneh and learned decisions at every opportunity and at the same time never neglected the delicatessen store – the family's main source of sustenance. The righteous and modest daughters sat at home and cared for the domestic scene following the death of the mother at an early age. Indeed an exemplary home, wide open to all who hungered and needed a favor. We cry over her loss.

David Unger – the son–in–law of Shmuel the Cantor, a modest Jew loved by all. He was never heard to raise his voice and his gait was light as if walking on tip–toe. He had five sons and one daughter – all of them tall and straight like a cedar tree and a magnificent example of the Jewish youth of that time. On them fell the fire and the fury and the flames consumed them.

May their souls rest in Paradise.

Translator's Footnote

1. Psalm 35:10
2. Rabbi Yehuda Arieh Leib Alter

[Page 163]

The Mlinarski Family

by Dov Mlinarski

Translated by Selwyn Rose

Until I left Poland in 1937 I believed that the Mlinarski family was "immortal": I didn't recall a single incident of death in our many-branched family until that day.

At prayer times in the synagogue it was a rare vision to see how the whole Mlinarski "tribe" left their seats during the Yizkor memorial prayer and fill the corridor while waiting for the prayer to come to an end. Inside there remained only the "tribal chief" – Menahem (Mania) Mlinarski.

Until this day I have been unable to come to terms with the fact none of them exist anymore.

My father was the second son of my grandfather Menahem and after he married he left Miechów and went to live in Jędrzejów, about 40 Km away, the home of my mother's parents, Josef and Malka Piatek

My family arrived in Miechów in 1924.

I stayed there about six years.

My Grandparents' Home

It was the house most distant from the center of town, at the end of Ratzlewiczke Street – next to the "Military Garden" and opposite the local hospital. It was the last Jewish house on the street, single storied; The central block that was brick-built faced the street and was leased to the bank manager; in another wing lived my grandparents, Menahem and Kyla; the third wing was the horses' stable which at a time of celebrations was, (after the "permanent residents" had been re-housed and appropriate cleaning and preparations had taken place), turned into a temporary hotel, for the guests and their children congregating from the surrounding towns, in order to take part in the festivities, like weddings, circumcisions and so on.

A broad yard spread between the three wings. On market days, which took place every Tuesday, it was the only private yard in Miechów that absorbed the tens of carts and wagons, with hitched horses (and sometimes bulls).

Grandfather's house was the first on the way into town of the visiting farmer who came to sell his produce in town. The villagers from the area called the whole family Mlinarski, "Barki". "Barak" was the name of grandfather's first–born, who between 1917 and 1925 managed a large business with local nobles, estate owners and others. Apart from him, my grandfather had another four sons: Feytl, Zalman, Baruch and Ya'acov Pinchas. Grandfather's pride was his two daughters Etil and Bluma, and indeed he married them to two scholars.

One immigrated to Palestine with her husband Eliezer Lavie and her family in 1933 and the second lives in Brazil with her husband, Mendel Sherman.

Eliezer Lavie – Jaskrowicz, was active in many fields in his public life and a brilliant orator. He was the secretary of three communities at one and the same time – Miechów, Slomniki and Charsznica. He was extremely talented with outstanding capabilities in organization and in community activities. In the beginning in Miechów, he taught Talmud in the "Agudas Yisroel" school. Later he transferred to the "Mizrahi" school and was conspicuous in his spiritual management of the "Mizrahi" movement.

[Page 164]

In addition to these activities he was also a teacher of Jewish religion in the Polish national school system and gained the respect of his Polish colleagues even the anti–Semitic ones among them. In 1933 he immigrated to Palestine with all his family.

In Palestine also he quickly climbed the ladder of seniority and introduced order into religious council in Tel–Aviv especially in the department of slaughtering which was virtually a no–man's land of "Might is Right".

With the establishment of the State of Israel he was installed as Comptroller of the Ministry of Religion and published several books, "A Treasury of Quotations" and his pen is still active.

Today he is the President of the Organization of Miechów Immigrants.

Mendel Sherman was grandfather's second son–in–law a scholar and bibliophile, intelligent, a violinist and political activist in the Miechów "Agudas Yisroel". He was an "Aguda–ist" in the style of members of the "Agudas Yisroel" in England.

From Friday afternoon until the late hours after the end of Shabbat grandfather's house resembled a bee–hive, the sons and grandchildren came in by turns for snacks of brown fava beans and before Shabbat and "Kabbalat Malkat Shabbat" – and yellow lentils, tea cake and candies, Saturday afternoon. The refreshments continued on through "the third meal" and "accompanying the Queen".

With my grandmother there was the tradition of a full–arranged table especially on Shabbat with a snow–white table cloth, two silver candle–sticks, grandfather's large "all–in" prayer–book with its Psalm pages yellowed from his snuff (before he proceeds to the portion for the week he reads the Book of Psalms from beginning to end), all of which gives a festive aura of sanctity and holiness and feeling of sanctification of the Sabbath.

Not all of grandmother's sons were lucky; especially not her son Feytl, a Righteous of Kromołów adherent, who travelled among the farmers and villages of Poland, buying anything that came to hand. He rarely made any profit, most of the time he sold at a loss.

Feytl and his family were grandmother's major concern. She often "smelled" his situation before he opened his mouth. She packed food parcels for him to take home and filled his pockets even in the most difficult times. On more than one occasion she sold items from the house and passed the proceeds to her son.

When the Jackboots of Hitler (Y.S.), trod on Polish soil, grandmother escaped to her future world from a natural death and laid to rest. Grandfather was murdered by the Nazis.

Remembered for eternity.

My Father's House

Yitzhak and Hendl–Leah Mlinarski (HY"D)

When I was seven years old, my father, together with a few friends from Jędrzejów, began making plans to immigrate to Palestine. Many articles from the home were sold in order to finance the journey and our first steps in Palestine.

One evening a wagon stopped outside our house at 23 Pinczhowski Street (my mother's parents lived in the same house – Piatek) and with many blessings mixed with tears, my father climbed aboard where two other immigrants were already sitting with their small belongings, all on their way to the railroad station in Jędrzejów, whence the train took them to Warsaw. On the way to the station the fourth immigrant joined us. My father's plan was to settle in Palestine and afterwards send the necessary documents for all the family and to bring them over. Fate intervened and disappointed the group and another group that arrived in Vienna from Warsaw. They were told that immigration to Palestine had been halted by the British Mandatory – because of all the disturbances that arose following the Tel–Hai attack in 1920.

[Page 165]

They were informed by the Jewish immigration organization that there was no possibility of immigrating and that they would have to wait for a few weeks and even perhaps a few months. The single men who were in the group stayed in Vienna. Husbands who had left wives and families in Poland returned disappointed. Father returned after having burnt all his bridges behind him in Jędrzejów. The situation at home was difficult. Yisroel Rosenberg, a rich forestry trader, came to our assistance. He was the owner of a large forest area of Pysznica near the River San between Rózwadów and Nisko. From the saw–mills there, the timber was sent to all corners of the state and the countries of Western Europe. Rosenberg offered father a job transporting the timber. In the beginning father was not all that enchanted by the work because of the great distance involved (about 300 kms) from home and also because of the minimal salary, but accepted for lack of options. After about a year the family moved to Pysznica.

With time my father became a specialist in forestry and its different off–shoots. However, at the end of three years the hewing of trees and their exportation ceased and he was again without the means of sustenance.

Eventually he found a position as an inspector of forestry – a forest scribe – with Itzkowitz and Friedrich, who had bought plots in Czapla 15 kms from Miechów. More than once when a forestry engineer came on an inspection, he was stunned by my father's knowledge of forestry. Even before the inspector had prepared his calculations of the cubic meters of a pile of logs and firewood, that a tree would produce, my father had measured it with his eyes and in a few moments gave an estimate which proved to be the same as the inspector's more sophisticated calculation.

We moved to Miechów. My father managed the hewing and selling of the trees and on Fridays arrived home for Shabbat.

In his leisure hours my father busied himself with book–binding, wood–carving of all sorts of items and miniature furniture decorated with carved bouquets and small Hebrew letters that merged harmoniously with the flowers and decorations in the bouquets. He used the most primitive of tools like a pocket–knife or small chisel and a small saw. He never at any time carved the figure of a man or living creature in compliance with the commandment "Thou shalt not make any image of any living thing..." Since even his present salary was not enough to sustain us, this work also contributed a little extra to the home.

He once built a six–sided Succah from the branches of a young fir tree that was in the shape of the Star of David on the inside. It was possible to erect and dismantle the Succah with ease, when needed – a Succah forever. Outside there was a bouquet in stylish letters and above it was written "For seven days thou shalt sit in booths". It was a real artistic creation made with much toil and care and good taste. It was bought by one of the rich men in town.

My father was an accepted "reader" when the weekly portion was read in the synagogue. He rose early on Saturday morning to prepare himself going over the portion from beginning to end to make quite sure he knew the incantation correctly and indeed he knew it all perfectly.

The main worry for our parents was the fees for the education of their children. Those payments preceded even the running of the house – food and clothing.

In spite of the economic situation at home, that was far from satisfactory, my father managed to secure an overdraft that enabled him to start trading in farm produce when the tree–felling operations with Itzkowitz and Friedrich ceased, leaving him without a job.

[Page 166]

The trade in farm produce demands large investments in cash. It is necessary to finance the farmers on "futures" – before harvesting – when the produce is still in the ground. In the last years before the outbreak of war, when anti–Semitism was on the rise in Poland, several of the farmers refused in a preconceived act to pay their debts as a result of the propaganda being put out by the Andek party and the anti–Semitic youth movement and became serious enough to prevent the traders venturing into the surrounding area in search of their money.

In 1931 my father became ill with appendicitis. After the operation in the St Lazarus hospital in Krakow, a complication arose and the healing of the operation dragged on for a year. The doctors in the hospital were fearful for his life. My father, throughout the crisis, was fully conscious and felt everything and insisted with our mother to take him out of the hospital because he wanted to die at home on his own bed. We rented an autobus because it was impossible to put him in a taxi – and we took him home. When the dressers in the hospital brought his stretcher out I heard one of them clearly say: "This patient will die before he gets to Slomniki." (25 km from Krakow). To the intense surprise of the doctors and professors in the hospital my father made a complete recovery. He was invited a couple of times to lectures during his recovery where he was presented before doctors from the Jagiellonian University as an interesting case history the first case of "Zatoka" – that the patient recovered and returned to us.

My father was murdered in Warsaw by the Germans thirteen years later – in 1944 – close to the liberation of the town by the Russians, when someone from Miechów who knew him exposed him to the Germans.

My older brother, now living in Poland finished a course in agriculture while a member of "Poalei–Zion" in Krakow. He left the training group with about half of the rest of the group after the Mandatory Authority closed the gates to immigration in 1930 and began the system of "scheduled immigration" that was far from solving the problem of pioneering immigration after tens of thousands had completed their group training.

The communist activity was illegal and the activists were persecuted and ostracised; the Jewish Communists were particularly hated. Nevertheless they found for themselves many different avenues for activity that disguised their actions, one way or another. They read and argued over the works of Marx and Engels during meetings in private homes, while spread on the table was the black and white chess–board or dominos as camouflage; they distributed illegal propaganda pamphlets on the approaches to town there were red flags with short slogans on them like – "Out with the Government Dictators", "Long live the revolution of the working classes!" They also scrawled slogans on the walls. The police immediately destroyed the flags and slogans and from time–to–time make searches in the homes of suspects to the disappointment of all the parents. A search of our house caused deep sorrow to my mother and father and concern for the fate of their eldest son, Zalman. It especially hurt my mother whose face paled like white–wash. Even after the police left she was unable to calm down for some hours.

One day in 1931 my brother Zalman Wolf Lansberg, Heskel Rosen – the son of the newspaper seller, Fromet Gludna(?) – the daughter of Leibele Poy and Dinah Kaminski – the daughter of the shoe–maker Wolf Kaminski, were all arrested.

The group was put on trial in Kielce. The parents paid a lot of money and secured an attorney for them – the daughter of Hershel Buchner. A sentence of two years imprisonment was imposed on all of them.

[Page 167]

During the time my brother was behind bars, my mother visited him a few times in Kielce. Every one of those visits caused my mother unimaginable suffering our father had not yet fully recovered his health and our financial resources were virtually non–existent. While there, she prepared soup, grits and other cereal dishes, the meat and three times a week (the times she was allowed to bring food in) she walked several kilometres on foot to the prison with the prepared food.

After the incarceration of the five Jewish communists the Andeks increased their anti–Semitic propaganda in town and from time–to–time attacked Jewish passers–by. We lived on Ratzlewiczke Street – on the ground floor – in the area of the gymnasium. All the windows faced the street. When the pupils left the gymnasium in a bunch catcalls occasionally followed them like: “Beat the Jew–Communists!” and smashed the windows of the house.

The parents refrained from lodging a complaint with the school manager, Tadeusz Lech who was the local leader of the Andek Party in the county and the delegate to the Polish Sejm. We preferred to notify the police of the incident. The police treated the complaint with disdain and failed to act.

The anti–Semitic incitement ceased for about two years and then flared up again with renewed cruelty when the Nazi monster began to run wild in Germany. When the Spanish civil war broke out in 1936, a wild anti–Semitic movement called Falanga – after Franco's Spanish Fascists – was established, and at their head were the photographer Spiechowicz and the young Nyschidlowski(?) (Incidentally – we lived in the same house as his mother).

From then until the outbreak of World War Two, we stationed “pickets” next to Jewish shops and we didn't let Christians enter.

The incitement directly affected our father's business which was connected with the farmers in trading their produce.

An unforgettable sight that caused deep emotion was when our mother, with tear–filled eyes said to our father: "The time has come to bless the children." It was the evening of the Day of Atonement after the second meal when the house was scrubbed clean, the candlesticks and the prayer–books laid on the gleaming white table–cloth and a sense of holiness pervaded the atmosphere. Our mother with her white scarf over her head lighted the candles and buried her face in her hands and poured out her prayers before the Creator of the world.

In spite of fact that blessing the children is a regular procedure, our father waited to get "permission" from her to continue. He was wrapped in his white caftan with a black girdle.

We, the children crowded together under the open prayer book that our father held while he blessed us with the special melody that "G–d will make thee as Ephraim and Manasseh." At the same time tears streamed down our mother's face. The big prayer book covered all four of our heads and it seemed to me that the Angel Michael spreads his wings above us. When the blessing finished we blessed our parents for a good year with warm kisses and an internal promise to be faithful children. Afterwards our mother stood and opened her own prayer book, covered her face again and prayed that the year ending will see the end of all evil illness and disturbances and that we should all be blessed with a healthy year, and that redemption of Israel will come speedily in our days – Amen.

Much has been said and written about the Jewish mother. In my opinion nothing has been written of the creativity that expresses her heroism, her sacrifices and her glorious soul.

[Page 168]

Kalman Mlinarski (HY"D)

The youngest son, the third in our family, was born in 1915. In his childhood he was dreamy and sensitive. He would sometimes disappear from his lessons in the "Mizrahi" school and when he was eleven our parents began to think about his future and sought a trade or profession that might suit him but without much success.

He liked to play around with screws, old clocks, and different wheels. He built small machines that made ear–piercing squeaking noises. Our mother especially suffered horribly from the noise of these "musical instruments". Suffered, but said nothing.

When the wagon-drivers of Miechów became bus-drivers and the first garage for repairs was opened facing Itzik the baker's shop, his whole world opened up. On the way home from school for lunch he began to stop by the garage or on the way back to school after lunch.

In the beginning he would just stand outside and watch but very slowly he began to approach closer and enter inside. He would get grease on his hands, face and clothes helping to lift heavy pieces of machinery or cleaning them.

For our parents it was disgusting: first of all, it was not a profession for a Jewish boy – a "garage worker" in their eyes was a forbidden act, another reason in their consideration was that the work of a motor mechanic was physically hard and not suitable for a young lad whose health was in any case somewhat fragile – he would occasionally faint and suffer severe headaches. But his stubbornness overcame all obstacles. At work the Christians bothered the Jewish youngster in different ways and couldn't accept that a Jewish boy wanted to be an auto-mechanic (in spite of the fact that their employers were Jewish) and at home he had to fight an unending war. Kalman refused to give up his intention of being a motor-mechanic, he refused to bow to "common sense" and after a long struggle he won and was accepted for work in the garage as an energetic and talented worker.

Kalman didn't read many books but every publication that came out in Polish on the subject of auto-mechanics, books in German on the subject he also bought and dug into them in his spare time.

Within a few months he made rapid advances; his arms became muscular and his whole body developed athletically. In the garage the kicks and punches he received stopped because he began to pay back double or more what he received, he settled the account on the spot and even gave "advance payments".

In short, Kalman achieved a high professional standing in auto-engineering – people in Miechów told me that his proficiency was so great that seeing a vehicle from a distance of ten meters he knew exactly which "screw was missing" by the movement and sound of the car. Another story among the residents of Miechów who served with him in the Polish army was that in one of the Polish army camps, he created a "graveyard" of old military vehicles, where they were left as wrecks. After visiting the "graveyard" he presented the command structure with a program for repairing the vehicles. Within a short time he had those vehicles on the road running like clockwork, to the astonishment of the Polish army engineers.

Hand–in–hand with his growth as an auto–mechanic was his physical development. The attacks on Jews in the town angered him and he found no rest until he paid the aggressors out in full. He only needed to hear a rumor that somewhere in town anti–Semitic hooligans were beating up Jews and he left work and ran there. The thugs would see him and immediately disperse taking with them bruises and broken ribs. Kalman instilled within them such fear that they refused to come face–to–face with him.

[Page 169]

When he was younger he belonged to the "Beitar" movement and after finishing his Polish army service his influence on it was significant and he was inducted into the "Jewish Legion" as an "Exemplary soldier". Physically very strong he knew no fear and demonstrated the finest qualities of a proud Jew of great uninhibited courage, drive and diligence, friendly to those around him and ready to assist those in need.

Hitler's Jackboots strode onto Polish soil. Kalman, who before the war was employed in a transport company – saw a vista of terror, killing and destruction in towns and villages. Kalman decided to help his brethren, the Jews, to save what was possible in a strange and unconventional way.

As a first step he left the town and made his way to Krakow and was accepted – as a Christian – into the Polish Underground, the "Armia Krajowa". Because that Underground was infected with anti–Semitism under the influence of the Andek Party and the NARA, it was essential that he monitor their actions on the Jewish people in the area. He grew a mustache and made sure that his exterior appearance did nothing to suggest he was a Jew and indeed he looked as Christian as any other Christian.

After a short while "his" Underground decided to "plant" Karol – Kalman's new name – as a Volksdeutsche, because he understood and spoke a little German. In time Kalman received a gun from the Germans and was seen in the streets of Krakow carrying a pistol in its holster on his belt.

Who knows if his activities of saving Jews would ever be discovered in time, that he was a planted spy of the "Armia Krajowa", in the "Germans' service". The little that was told me about him when I visited Poland in 1949 – four years after the liberation of Poland – only nurtures the stories of his deeds.

Even the Jewish survivors from around Krakow, Miechów and Slomniki don't know that it was Kalman who informed them anonymously by devious means that the Germans were about to execute an "Aktsia" and that they should leave their hiding places.

Kalman succeeded in getting his parents and our sister Hanna–Rachel out of Miechów and took them to a safe place in Warsaw. He guarded them for about two years until a Christian from Miechów who recognized him in Warsaw followed him and reported him to the Germans. My parents and Hanna–Rachel were murdered by the Germans about two months before the Russians entered the capital of Poland.

As a Volksdeutsche, who "cooperated with the Germans" Kalman was equipped with documents that allowed him free passage all over Poland and the owner of a free pass for unrestricted rail travel. He exploited it all for many important operations, among them transferring information between Warsaw and Krakow to Jews who were hiding outside the ghetto.

The following incident was described to me when I visited Poland (in 1949): when they were taking the Jews of the ghetto in Krakow from the camp at Płaszów, that had originally been a Jewish cemetery, to work at night or bringing them back from work in the evening, under armed German guards, Kalman would appear and begin to curse the "Leprous Jews" and throw stones at them. Those stones were, in fact loaves of bread or potatoes or other essential nutritious items and the marchers caught them blessed the "good Christian".

Because of an informer who hunted Jewish Poles in hiding, who knew Kalman, he was arrested by the Germans and taken to Miechów for execution together with about ten other Jews who were the remnants of those who remained there.

The Germans organized the murder as an exhibition in the "Rink" of Miechów. The "Rink was full of Christians who had come to watch the victims brought to the scaffold. The last of the orphans dressed in prison garb, standing in a row, a few of them murmuring their last prayers. The final moments dragged on, as heavy as lead, for the departure of the pure souls.

[Page 170]

The SS officer stood next to the machine–gun with the platoon of German murderers and showered his victims with abuse. The Christians stood around enjoying the spectacle, drunk with their "victory"; at last "Samson the hero" of the Miechów Jews had been caught, Kalman Mlinarski who they had been unable to defeat will immediately meet his end together with the rest of the town's Jews.

Kalman heard their sneering laughter and looked into the eyes of the blood–thirsty mob. In that hour of darkness and oppressive limbo Kalman gathered together his impregnable strength and tore the nightmare–web entangling him.

Like a flash of lightning he flew across the front of the mob. They couldn't believe their eyes! Kalman broke away from the row of victims, drawing a knife from his boot as he went and stabbing the German officer in the stomach. The Germans hurried to the aid of the officer wallowing in his own blood while Kalman succeeds in withdrawing his knife from the body and cutting down a second German who came to the officer's aid.

A shocked panic broke out. Shouts came from every corner of the square, together with a babble of admiration and esteem. Another moment and bullets from the machine–gun tore through the heart of the only Jew who had the audacity to rise up against his murderers and with him perished the last group of martyrs. Their blood washed the paving stones of the "Rink".

Thus fell Kalman Mlinarski – "great–grandchild" and "grandchild" of Bar–Kochba and Eliezer Ben Ya'ir – on foreign land, in exile, in Miechów, Poland.

My Sister Hanna–Rachel Mlinarski (HY"D)

Hanna–Rachel excelled in artistic handicrafts, embroidery, and knitting. Apparently abilities she inherited from our father while political party activity came from my influence and she belonged, like me, to the "Young Zionists", the youth section of the General Zionists from the "On Guard" wing of the movement at whose head stood at the time, Yitzhak Gruenbaum. As a dedicated activist of the movement she went on a leadership course and prepared herself for immigration to Palestine via "Aliyah Bet".

Her immigration date was fixed together with a group of immigrants of young Zionists, for the week of Succoth 1939 – about three weeks after the Nazi boots trod on Polish land. She was not to fulfil her dream; she fell victim about two months before the liberation of Poland.

Other Members of the Mlinarski Family in Miechów

Yosef and Etil Mlinarski (HY"D)

Uncle Yossel was a simple Jew; he was as particular about cleanliness, as he was about his daily prayers. He was clean about his clothes, his shining shoes, his neatly trimmed and cared–for beard and his casual strolling gait. Everything about him spoke of wealth and nobility, a man who had no concerns about his sustenance. But the truth of the matter is that he had to work hard and fought hard to manage his finances and he was unable to marry his two daughters because he lacked a dowry for them.

His wife, Etil was a righteous woman and known throughout the town for her observance. Her adherence to Kashrut was as strict as possible. She spent most of her time in prayer and collecting money for the needy who refrained from begging.

Yosef was the brother of grandfather Menahem – from my father's side; his wife, Etil was the sister of the grandfather Yossel Piatek from Jędrzejów – from my mother's side.

The whole Family Mlinarski his house was known as "the house of uncle Yossel".

[Page 171]

Yossel died from Typhus and his wife with their daughters was murdered by the Germans. There remained – after surviving the "Seven Layers of Hell" – just the two sons Hirsch and Mendele Mlinarski, today living in America.

Zalman Mlinarski (HY"D)

(The following lines were sent to me by Raphael Mlinarski, the son of my uncle Zalman).

At the end of August 1942 about 500 Jews from Miechów were taken for extermination to Slomniki – the center for transportation – and among them grandfather Menahem.

Rumors were many, that there was a German – one of the commanders at the above center – who for a sum of money would release Jews from the center.

One of the sons, Ya'acov Pinchas (the youngest) and Raphael, the grandchild, and the son of Zalman – preserved for a long life – travelled to

Slomniki to bribe this German and release grandfather. To their great sadness they didn't find this German anywhere.

That same evening Ya'acov Pinchas came back home and Raphael couldn't find his uncle, Ya'acov Pinchas, in order to take him back to Miechów so he stayed there over–night in Slomniki with an acquaintance. The following morning Ya'acov Pinchas and his brother Zalman tried again to find the German and went to Slomniki. But as they entered the town they were accosted by a group of Germans accompanied by some Polish youngsters and they began to beat them up with murderous blows. Ya'acov Pinchas fled covered in blood, Zalman fought back with his fists. The thugs picked up some hoes from some Jews – who were working on the road there under guard of the Germans – and beat him to death. His son Raphael was told of the incident by one of the survivors of the road workers.

Zalman Mlinarski pure soul left him there in September 1942

May he be remembered forever.

Members of the Mlinarski Family in Miechów who were killed:

Grandfather's sons:

Berl, the first–born (murdered by Poles while asking for shelter), his wife Hanna, their children, Laybl, Ziskind, Raizel, Rivka and Sheyndil and their families. Sarah Bezchinsky – living in Sharona, near Yavne'el, with her family; Meir and Yechiel and Moshe David live abroad.

Faytl, his wife Mindl (died before the war), their children: Yechiel, Haim David, Haya and Hannia. This family left no survivors.

Zalman (murdered as described above), his wife Bat–Sheva, and their children: Haim and Rikl. Haim Raphael Mlinarski survived and lives in Tel–Aviv.

Baruch (murdered by Poles while asking for shelter among them), his wife Zisl, their children: Simcha, and a daughter, of unknown name – this family left no survivors.

Ya'acov–Pinchas (murdered by the Poles while seeking refuge among them), his wife, Hanna and their children Bonem, and a daughter of unknown name. This family left no survivors.

Grandfather's close relatives:

His brother, Mordecai Mlinarski and his wife Zisl. Their children Mendel, Hannia and Etil. Survivors: Malka (her husband Warshawski) in the USA and Raphael with his daughter in Canada.

Etil and her husband Pinchas Moszkowski and their children Simcha and Leah. A son survived – Haim Moszkowski – in Petah Tikvah.

[Page 172]

The Vanchadlovski Family

by Tsvi Vanchadlovski–Vardi

Translated by Selwyn Rose

On 23rd November 1936 I arrived in Palestine with my family. It was without doubt one of the most important dates in the history of the family. It is thanks to that that we were saved from the extermination and destruction that Hitler brought upon the Jews of all Europe and on Poland in particular.

My family was comprised of six souls: Father – Dov Vanchadlovski (the son of Yehuda)

Mother – Rivka Vanchadlovski (née Berger)

Grandfather – my mother's father, Yechiel Berger

Me – Tsvi Vanchadlovski (now Vardi)

My sister – (Krayndle) Atara Vanchadlovski

My brother – Kalman Vanchadlovski.

Our grandfather joined us after much hesitation. I still remember his prayers before and during the journey and especially the crossing of the sea. He lived for a few years in Palestine and lived to enjoy its luster. He died at a good old age.

Before our immigration there was a pioneer in the family and he immigrated in order to continue his education at the Hebrew University in Jerusalem.

When I dive into the days of my childhood I remember our house which was in the center of town on the corner of Krakowske Street. It was large house mostly inhabited by Jews, apart from two Christian families. The cantor and ritual slaughterer and also the town Rabbi lived in the house. Their homes served as places of study and prayer and were the spiritual center for the Jews of the town.

The family of my mother (Z"L) and father was extensive and only part of it lived in the same house. My father's house served as a natural center for the family. During the day my parents' shop was a meeting place for the family most of whom were in business as traders with the local farmers; while during the evening hours and festivals, our large apartment, which was attached to the shop was a meeting place for the family.

Another element in the economic life of the family of the family, was the large flour mill (in Charsznica Street), which burnt down. I still remember how my mother (Z"L) cried that night at a loss that supported so many families.

My parents' livelihood came from their hardware shop where they dealt in iron tools and building materials. But I recall that my father also dealt in the timber trade. Because of that he was known to the land–owners and nobles of the district and he would ride on horse–back armed with a licensed pistol that protected him. That business was dangerous (although I remember lovely days when father organized picnic trips to the forest for the family) and on more than one occasion I caught a snatch of conversation between my parents on that topic. Eventually my father stopped with that trade and concentrated his energies on the shop.

I attended two schools at one and the same time; during the morning the Polish school and in the afternoon the Hebrew school. The Polish school was the first place where I encountered hatred of the Jews because the teachers in the school were not known for their love of the Jewish people. The Hebrew school, by contrast, gave us a feeling of security. Together with the members of my class I joined the Zionist youth movement in town; I was then twelve–years old.

[Page 173]

The activities of the Zionist youth movement, those that took place in the branch office on week days as well as the social activities on Friday evenings – had a common framework. It was the same idea with the trips that we organized out of town to meet with groups from other towns. The youth movement formed us to meet the future.

I remember an original idea that we created in the branch, in order to collect donations from the Jews in town for the "Foundation Fund of Israel".

With that as a target, we organized a number of groups and each group carried wooden–framed cartons that we placed over our heads and covered half our body so that we could move. On the front of the carton were different scenic views of Palestine which were already being worked with Jewish hands, like the Jezreel Valley, the Zebulon Valley and so on. At the head of each group were older boys, dressed–up as old men. Every group was assigned a different section of town. I remember that people contributed generously. In one of the streets we were set upon by a gang of young Christians who hit us and smashed our cartons. It didn't deter us; after we repaired the damage we continued with our task accompanied by a few older boys from the branch. The incident deepened within us the sense that our place was in the Land of Israel and not dispersed among the nations of the world.

Collecting donations for the Foundation Fund of Israel

The expressions of anti–Semitism became conspicuous when events in town occurred where both Jews and Poles assembled together, such as the town's football matches. There was an organized football team in town – called "The Strength" as far as I can recall, and the team sometimes played against the Polish team from town. We knew from experience that if our side won we would be attacked by the Poles so we would leave a few minutes before the end of the match to avoid the problem. Another example is during the winter when we would go to the public Wojskowy Park to ice–skate and they would throw stones at us or even prevent us from going on the ice if we appeared in a small group. With the rise of Hitler as Chancellor anti–Semitism increased significantly and began to be felt economically.

[Page 174]

Here is an example: there were three shops in town trading in ironware tools, general building materials and hardware, all of them owned by Jews. Suddenly there appeared a Polish Christian, M. Tott who opened a similar shop in the center of town. At first he wasn't particularly successful but when he sensed a new anti–Semitic atmosphere he began a program of incitement, especially on market days that took place once a week on Tuesday. He posted men outside the Jewish shops. As far as I can recall, he had them distribute hand–bills with anti–Semitic slogans.

The Jews began to face up to the problem of anti–Semitism in all its gravity. I remember evenings at home when our father debated the topic over and over again. My father, who had been a farmer before settling in Miechów, began to weave together a plan to leave Poland and immigrate to Palestine. When he first brought up the idea with the family of immigrating there was considerable opposition and doubts but generally the family understood the situation and father's ideas.

In 1935 my father had the opportunity to realize his vision. That same year a delegate arrived from Palestine looking for farmers of modest means who were interested in immigrating as farmers to Palestine. My father travelled to Warsaw and met with Tsvi Lieberman, a representative of Moshav Nahalal, and registered himself as a candidate. To this day I remember the repercussions that arose as a result when he brought to topic up with the family because only a few Jews had immigrated to Palestine from Miechów.

It is worth telling here an event that occurred that almost led to a pogrom here in town: On one of the days of the week I was in the shop with my mother. A Christian woman came in and bought something. Immediately afterwards a young Christian man came in and asked to see a knife. The man began to look at the selection and suddenly opened his shirt and stabbed himself in the chest a number of times and fell down smothered in his own blood. In a very short time a crowd gathered, Jews and Christians. These last began to fabricate all sorts of explanations as to what happened. To our good fortune the Christian woman gave a true account as eye witness. Tempers cooled but for some time there was a feeling of fear and insecurity following the incident.

At that time, together with the rest of my class, I joined the youth movement to go for training. Not a few of my friends were jealous of me knowing I had good chances of immigrating to Palestine. We waited many days for the approval to arrive because we were included among the immigrants and when it was received the joy was immeasurable. Feverishly my parents began to prepare for the journey. Many difficulties piled up during the preparation; starting with the sale of all our property up to obtaining all the necessary documents. The time between receiving the approval and the actual journey was the hardest part for us, we had to leave the home we had lived in and move to a small apartment in a distant neighbourhood, and there we waited doing nothing for the date of our travel. Only thanks to our determination to go and the courage of our parents – we managed to overcome the crisis. The long–awaited day arrived: we gathered together our few parcels and packages and loaded them on the sleigh, it was mid–winter now and in the company of the family and friends we went to the railroad station. After an emotional farewell we got on the train taking us in the direction of our heart's desire.

For the first few days in Palestine, we lodged in Haifa with the Feureisen family. From Haifa we went to Nahalal and there, we lodged with Lieberman who provided us with a chicken–house as living quarters. We stayed in Nahalal only a short time because father had bought a farm in Kfar Baruch. There my parents remained to the end of their days. The first days of our settlement in Palestine were very hard because of the very limited means we had to establish firmly the farm we had bought and the lack of knowledge we had of the agricultural conditions in the country. Here I must mention that a very large part of the progress we made is thanks to the labour and activity my late mother played in the advances we made. She organized the meagre cabin and encouraged all of us to toil hard and long in order to succeed. Only after some years did we manage to turn our plot into a prosperous and productive farm.

[Page 175]

During the war we lost contact with the family and only afterwards did we learn that only a few of them remained alive. One of them, my mother's brother, Aharon Berger, was shot by Polish thugs while on his way to one of the villages.

My parents and their children fulfilled their obligations defending and guarding during difficult days. My parents lived to marry their children to children of the Moshav but a short while after my own marriage my father (Z"L) died in 1950, after a short illness. The yoke of responsibility fell upon my mother's shoulders, which, thanks to her fortitude she managed for another 10 years. But the hard work subdued even her and after a long illness she died in Afula hospital and was brought to her resting place in the cemetery of Kfar Baruch.

[Page 175]

A Friend's Wife Who is no More

(In memory of the modest woman Mrs. Etil Lavie, may her soul rest in Paradise)

by Shimshon–Dov Yerushalmi

Translated by Selwyn Rose

We were happy, my wife – May she live long – and I, when we received the information that our long–standing friend Rabbi Eliezer Lavie, may he live long, and his wife, are planning to spend Passover in Tel–Aviv.

We had it in mind to host them in our home on one of the intervening days of the festival and to exploit the opportunity for a friendly chat on days gone by that are no more, and on mutual activities that we had shared and – especially – to fulfil the commandment: "...be joyful in your festivals".

The Eve of Passover arrived and I try to make telephone contact with my friends in order to bid them welcome and a happy Passover and confirm a day and hour for our meeting in our house. To my great surprise I heard the telephone ringing and no one answered...it was difficult to comprehend...I tried again and again and still no reply; I tried throughout the day with no success! As soon as the festival ended the following evening, I began calling again a few times and again early the following morning; it was as if the whole world was silent – no reply from the house of my friend's son–in–law Simcha Schaffrier(?)! In my heart worries began to arise...

I wrote to my friend and asked what the reason was and he hurried to explain that his wife's sudden illness had caused their plans to be cancelled. His son and his daughters and members of the family had all gone up to Jerusalem on Passover Eve to spend the Seder there, out of concern for her condition because she had been taken to hospital. He told me that according to the doctors her condition didn't give rise to concern but for all that he asked me to pray for her well–being – which I did with all my heart and soul. On Sunday, the last of the intermediate days of Passover, I spoke on the telephone with their son Alexander and what I heard from him that the patient had been transferred –not by their request but on the instructions of the doctor – to intensive care. My heart filled with worry and fear because I felt that her life was in danger. I kept my feelings to myself and prayed again for her full recovery.

Only the following day with the end of the prohibitions of the festival, I was informed that on the seventh night of Passover, the thread of her life was broken and she was brought to her rest when the festival ended (as is the custom in Jerusalem).

Our sorrow at her passing and our loss was great and the desolation of the Lavie family and our pain was that much greater that we were prevented from accompanying her and granting her our last respects at her interment!

[Page 176]

I see a holy obligation before me to bring forth from the treasury of my memories the way of life of this modest woman and to place them on record in "The Memorial Book of the Jews of Miechów", the town in which she was born and lived until her immigration to Palestine.

First Acquaintance

Although I had constant contact for many years with my friend Rabbi Eliezer Lavie in public matters (until I left Charsznica and settled in Warsaw in 1925 and also until I immigrated to Palestine from Warsaw in 1935), I knew his family – his late wife (may she rest in Paradise), and their children (may they be spared for a long life), only from just before their immigration to Palestine (the day after Yom Kippur 1934).

We see before us a most modest woman, a woman from the generation before Hitler (Y.S), from the towns of Jewish Poland, a continuation of the generations of true Jewish life, built on the foundations of the Torah and tradition from those who absorbed within themselves the excellent attributes that blessed the daughters of Israel from generation to generation whose natural slogan was the laws of the Torah defined by their mothers and their mothers' mothers. In addition there was Jewish grace on her face and with her, her three daughters and her only son – all of them in infant school. Conspicuous among the daughters was the eldest one – Zahava (Z"L) – in her intelligent glowing eyes shone great courage and the will to perform good deeds.

When I looked upon the wife of my friend and their infant children who are now leaving their home and their family and walking "...on a land not sown" (for they had no established livelihood waiting for them), I said in my heart: "Behold a fit and good woman who does the bidding of her husband" I am reminded of the words of Jeremiah the Prophet that my friend Lipa felt obliged he had to say to the wife of his youth: “I remember thee, the kindness of thy youth, the love of thine espousals, when thou wentest after me in the wilderness, in a land that was not sown.”[1] From the depths of our hearts we blessed them for a “successful voyage” and “a prosperous life”

Their first steps in Palestine

The “agonies” of immigrant absorption, the difficulties of very new immigrant were sevenfold for them. To our wonderment and the sadness of our heart, the history of his decades of public service and Zionist activity, the whole of his life's service of political activism were as if they had never been, as if they fell into the sea on the journey to Palestine and no memory remained of all his deeds and actions from his life in Poland. These activists are nourished with “promises” of delegates with their conventional cries “Come quickly!” and thus were fed my friends with different promises until he found for himself a source of sustenance – in his eyes disgusting and uncouth – and opened a restaurant “Hapo'el Ha–Mizrachi” in Ramat–Gan, for the workers who were working on construction sites in the neighbourhood.

In December 1933 my friend opened the restaurant in Ramat–Gan and his wife with her young daughters put their “shoulders to the wheel” in helping with the work – and work was not lacking...and there were plenty of needy people came to eat but unfortunately among them were many unemployed and with no money to pay. Mrs Jaskirewicz (Z”L) could not come to terms with the idea of not giving food to the hungry. She recalled the behaviour of her mother whose house was open to all the needy. She also recalled the saying: “It is a greater blessing to welcome guests than to receive the Divine Presence Himself”. Therefore she followed her mother's path and with a generous heart fed the hungry without payment. Clearly the debts began to grow and before Passover the restaurant was liquidated and they went to live in the Florentin area of Jaffa.

[Page 177]

The Measure of Her Hospitality

More than thirty years have passed and I still cannot free myself from the emotions she created in me that rise up when I think of her wonderful behaviour and the measure of her welcome and hospitality, the late, noble–spirited woman, and I have a heart–felt obligation to talk about it at length. When I immigrated in the spring of 1935 I had no idea where I would find a living. I lived for more than two months in Magdiel. Because Tel–Aviv was even then the center of the main institutions and the people that could help me with my arrangements were there, I would visit there a couple of times a week and sometimes sleep over. My friend Lipa (may he live long), would not let me go to any other place but insisted that I stay there with him, in his home.

I will never forget how I was received in that house or the warm welcome I received from her (may her soul rest in Paradise). How she insisted on knowing what are the dishes most tasteful to my palate and how sad she was if – heaven forbid – I should leave some of the food on my plate from the enormous quantities she piled on it: and on the days that I remained overnight in their home she provided me with the best of her daughters' beds and checked "seven times" the pillows and covers. And when I got up in the morning, she made sure that I had a cup of tea before the prayers and when I had finished the prayer everything was prepared for breakfast and thus also for the rest of the meals. More than once I thought to myself that if by chance there was a woman like her whoever it was who said: "Her eyes were not for her guests", would most certainly change his opinion about women!..

The Tragic Days

I saw the grieving parents, miserable in their mourning after the loss of the "apple of their eye", Zahava Shen–Scheinbaum (HY"D) on the premature, bitter day of 27th July 1955 when a murderous hand struck at an EL–AL aircraft and killed 58 Israeli souls from Israel and among them the excellent Daughter of Zion, Zahava, the golden–hearted, crowned with good–deeds.

The grief of these parents, whose world suddenly and cruelly became dark for them, was unlike the grief of parents. They didn't see their great tragedy as a private tragedy, a tragedy of parents who lost their first–born daughter in an air accident but they felt instinctively that on that same bitter and premature day a fit and good Daughter of Israel was sacrificed on an altar and fell victim to the hatred of Israel.

Everyone who looked at them felt what was in their heart. And thus I also saw them at the funeral and burial in Kiryat Shaul.

The mother of the deceased, may she rest in Paradise, carries in her heart in grief and sorrow the feeling that "My Zahava is one of the sacrificial martyrs of the People of Israel from before its redemption."

Donation to the "Book of Remembrance"

We all know how she cared for the health and well–being of her husband, the 'champion' of her girlhood years, may he live long, but for all that not only could she not prevent him from working on this "Memorial Book" of the communities of Miechów Charsznica and Kshoynzh, but she encouraged him to work faster and assisted him in recalling events that occurred in his home town.

The dear modest woman, Mrs. Etil daughter of Kaila (née Mlinarski) Lavie was taken from us in an untimely fashion and very suddenly. She didn't live to see the publication of the book on which she toiled.

May these few lines serve as a memorial light to her memory, as words of encouragement and support for her husband, her son and daughters and their daughters and a source of information and knowledge to her friends esteem for her modest life and many deeds.

Translator's Footnote

1. Jeremiah 2:ii

[Page 178]

Zahava Shen (HY"D)

by Dov Mokri

Translated by Selwyn Rose

I saw you Goldele Jaskirewicz

I saw you, Goldele, three years old, amusing your grandfather Menahem while sitting on his knees and clapping your little hands while singing together the song: "Patsh'n, Patsh'n, Kichelach."[1]

When you were only four it was already impossible to cheat with you on your knowledge of the "Aleph–Bet". I remember how it amused him – grandfather – from unfettered love for his beloved granddaughter – to "try it on" by pointing at the large letter 'M': on the cover of his big prayer book and saying to you: "Here is the letter 'B':, Goldele and his pleasure was doubled and his happiness complete when you said in contradiction: "That's the letter 'M': grandpa, because that's what daddy taught me!" and...Grandfather surrendered...

I saw you, Goldele with your school report at the end of each year. Even 'good': wasn't seen – only 'very good': or 'excellent': all the way down the page – from top to bottom. Always the most loved and the first in class.

I saw you, Zahava Jaskirewicz

I saw you, Zahava, as an excellent pupil in the gymnasium in Tel–Aviv; as an honor counsellor in "B'nei Akiva" and as an active member of the "Hagana", a person of responsibility and obligation.

I saw you at your dedicated work for new immigrants as an exemplary worker in the Jewish Agency. I saw you, Zahava, arranging medical documentation for new immigrants needing special treatments. You received them while still at sea and had not yet put their feet on the Homeland. I saw you listen hard to new immigrants who knocked on your office door – each one with his own story and each story a world unto itself. With love for man and fit for the task, you assisted these needy people.

I saw you, Zahava Shen

I saw you, Zahava Shen, in 1949 in the arrivals lounge in New York Harbor while you waited for a couple of hours for me to arrive until it was my turn to walk off the ship. How happy you were to receive the personal greetings I brought from your parents (my uncle) from the Homeland.

I saw you in America for a few years, in the Jewish Agency. In the beginning in a modest junior position but you quickly rose up to the post of General Secretary of the Histadrut Ha–Clalit in the United States.

Your house in New York was a meeting place for writers, poets, publishers, artists and public officials for whom Hebrew was the desire of their hearts and a place to meet Israelis who were visiting the United States.

Like your father, may he be spared for a long and good life – so for you, your work hours were long and your organizing skills exceptional.

With your appearance, the Histadrut in the United States won a person whom they didn't expect, during many years, with a personality to turn the wheels of a many–branched machine.

I saw you at your daily work in your office, dealing with issues of importance and lesser importance. Nothing was left without a solution, you were realistic, and you didn't beat about the bush with those who came to you. If by chance you came up against a difficult and complicated problem, you spoke to specialists on the topic by telephone – who were registered in your phone book – and made an appointment to discuss and arrange a solution.

[Page 179]

You introduced order into all the branches and departments, you cleared all the dust–laden desks, both figuratively and literally and the Movement – like a machine – began to work.

All those who surrounded you took pleasure in your native "Tsabarit" Hebrew. In your company they felt as if they were actually in the State of Israel. Your personal grace, elegant and modest dress, your quiet appearance, intelligence and attentiveness charmed them all and saw you as a polished crystal shining in all directions.

I saw you in your Zionist meetings, in presentations by Israeli artists, at different congresses supporting Israel that were sometimes held in luxurious halls, in different large towns of the United State, sometimes as the organizer of the event or project; you even worried about the little pit–falls, like how many chairs on the stage and who sits where, the back–drop, flowers, the readers and musicians, the violinists and...whoever; the old veteran Zionist, who has to be brought personally and seated on the stage and so on...In your organization nothing was forgotten, everything had to work without break–downs or hitches according to the plan you had prepared – from beginning to end.

Zahava Shen (Jaskirewicz)

With initiative and much toil with the quivering of a saint you programmed the second "World Jewish Congress" in Jerusalem and on your flight there – in the skies above Bulgaria – they deprived you of your life and you left behind you a gaping empty void.

On the 27th July 1955 – in the skies above Bulgaria – a Socialist State, the terrible slaughter took place on an El–Al aircraft killing fifty–eight people, among them Zahava Shen, who wove for herself a wonderful life.

With the death of Zahava, adorned with a halo on her head, the crown fell from the afflicted Lavie family (Jaskirewicz).

Translator's Footnote

1. A children's Yiddish song : "Clap hands, Clap hands, making cookies"

[Page 180]

In Memory of my Parents

by Eta Sherman (Née Horowitz)

Translated by Selwyn Rose

After the terror of the Holocaust, I returned to the square in our town Miechów. The tree still stood, the bench was also there. I sat there, looking round me and I saw that Nature stayed the same as it was. But our people, the Jews, were not there. If only nature could speak there is no doubt she would have much to tell. I flew in my memories to the time before the Second World War. I recalled my parents' house and all the family members who had perished.

My parents' house was a warm home. My father, Baynish Horowitz and my mother, Sarah Malka, cared much for the education of their children and their future. But at the same time they didn't forget the rest of humanity. Our home was an open house for guests and the needy, on Shabbatot and festivals, and students from the Seminary found food and shelter there. My father found his livelihood in the labor of his hands. He had a factory for knitting sweaters. In his little factory he gave help to all who needed it. Many young men learnt the work in his factory and afterwards became proficient and began to work independently. It could be said of my father that he gave help to many "An axe to grind" – a trade that gave an honest and respectable livelihood.

We were a united family. Close to each other and also we were witness to the respect and understanding between our parents.

My grandfather was also a resident of Miechów. My grandfather (my mother's father), Fishl Koplewicz, was a wealthy man trading in textiles. His house was double–storied with two yards. He was loved and respected by all who knew him. I discovered that on the day of his death, I was only small but I remember because at the time of the funeral all the Jewish factories and workshops were closed, children stopped their lessons and took part in the funeral.

Before the war my family left Miechów and moved to Łódź but with the outbreak of the Holocaust where everyone sought shelter, the family returned to Miechów. From there, together with all their friends and families, they went along that terrible road from which they didn't return.

May their memories be for a blessing.

The Names of the Family Members:

Father of the family, Baynish Horowitz; the mother, Sarah Malka; the children: Kayla, Baler Hinda, Yitzhak (living in New York), Sheyndil, Eta (Sherman, Ramat–Gan), Esther, Anszel.

Yona Friedrich (Z"L)

Thirty days after his death

by Moshe Spiegel

Translated by Selwyn Rose

Yona (Z"L) came from a special breed, whose mission in life is to help the weak, who cannot find the strength within themselves the basis on which to build their future.

He displayed a blessed initiative and resourcefulness of helping the needy. He encouraged them, showed them ways of how to get out of their difficult situations, and worried endlessly without reward to raise them up, both spiritually and materially.

[Page 181]

Yona (Z"L) didn't worry about the money that he had amassed during the years from his excellent and healthy business sense – even in the worst years – in order to help the needy. In that, he walked in the way of his father, Abramke (Z"L) who was known for the generosity of his donations.

Yona (Z"L) was conspicuously known and famous during the Hitler days when he was seen as the savior of the Miechów Jews in the Second World War, in the labor and concentration camps through which he passed and acted. Płaszów, Auschwitz and Mauthausen were the stations where his name was mentioned in awed respect by those who received help, support and sustenance from him in different ways; he dedicated all his time to helping humanity over a broad range of activities and in doing so, endangered his own life more than once.

On a few occasions he was sentenced to death by the S.S. and commandants of the German camps and only by a miracle did he manage to evade falling into the Arms of Death. But all his strength and connections couldn't help him when at a defining moment he was unable to save his own distinguished parents and sister Mania from the clutches of death and they were sent to the extermination camp of Bełżec where they perished.

It remains to us to declare in respectful and decisive awe on this thirtieth day of his death: Here is buried an important branch from the ancient trunk of the Friedrich–Spiegel family that understood that the aim of Man's life is the traditional Jewish precept: “Thou shalt love thy neighbour as thyself.”

May he rest in peace.

Moshe Sabotka (Z”L)

by Arieh Sheintal

Translated by Selwyn Rose

My first encounter with Moshe Sabotka (Z”L) was when I was still a youth. It was in his home town of Nasiechowice, near Miechów, where my father (Z”L) worked for a while as a forestry scribe in the area where the forests were rented out by my grandfather (Z”L).

On one of the mornings of the Succoth festival – a beautiful end of summer morning – my big brother and I accompanied our father to a near–by village for a public prayer service. The fruit orchards around us were ripening and the dark forests filled our hearts, city youths that we were, with limitless joy, and while we were still walking on the paths through the ripening wheat and on fields of stubble, I picked up the sound of festival prayers coming on the air. To my amazement my father smiled broadly and told us to hurry up and we immediately saw in front of us a group of singers – Shlomo–Yosef Sabotka and his sons – sitting and waiting for us at the side of the path. Apparently Shlomo–Yosef who acted as prayer–reader in the village prayer quorum, used the time while waiting for us to practice his prayer–rendering and his children accompanied him full–voice...that meeting is etched firmly in my memory because of the powerful impression the “choir” made on us. The father was a dignified–featured man, his white beard flowing down to his chest, but the general effect of his face, his sparkling eyes like the eyes of a young boy and his sons – three tall youths – amazed us with their happiness and their glowing faces.

Later it became clear to us that Shlomo–Yosef, whose livelihood came from a small village shop, was head and shoulders above the rest of the Jews in the surrounding villages in his knowledge of the Talmud and Torah, and more than once we were amazed how a Jew like him became rooted in such a small out–of–the–way village. Our hearts – the hearts of youths – trained by the education within the gloomy walls of the "Heder", took to Shlomo–Yosef with his good nature and especially his proverbs and legendary stories and homilies that come out of his mouth. And indeed a man of homilies he really was and when, later, I came up against the writings of H.N. Bialik and his "Enlightenment" and "Legends" the image of Shlomo–Yosef as a symbol of the illuminating side of the Talmud appeared before me.

[Page 182]

Moshe Sabotka

His bright face and pleasant temperament he bequeathed to his eldest son – to Moshe. Moshe was then a young man of about 19, shy in older company but open and free among his contemporaries and those younger than himself, he displayed friendship, spread over us his patronage and protected us from the ruffians of the village who used to stick out their tongue at us.

We didn't remain in the village for a long time, but all the time we were with Moshe and his brother. These two, for whom the ways of nature and her secrets were clear, wanted with all their might to introduce us to her secrets. With the urgent desire they spread her secrets before us, on the number of species, and their treasures as if they were their creation. Knee injuries, clothes torn we walked after them for long days in fields and forests. We waded through cold pools and streams, ran after rabbits, climbed trees looking for birds' nests and went down valleys to the dens of wolves and foxes. We gorged ourselves on fruit from gardens and forest and slaked our thirst to the full – the thirst of city boys caged all the year round – from drinking the nature that appeared before us to such an unexpected degree.

It was no wonder that we quickly became attached to Moshe with all our heart – the heart of a youth yearning for love – not only because his extensive knowledge of the treasures of garden and forest and not because of his good temperament but essentially because his fortitude and courage in confronting the ruffians of the village. They feared him but mostly liked him and befriended him and us, although we weren't used to it we were surprised at the display of friendship from the side of Christians from the village towards him. Wherever we went we were received in friendship because of his gaiety which overflowed, In spite of our youthful wonderment, it was not difficult for us to discern in the longing looks the girls in the village threw in the direction of the tall Jewish youth.

[Page 183]

About two or three weeks after Succoth we returned home to town and that short period remained engraved in my memory as one of the nicest times in my life and not only because of the pleasures I had but because of the wonderful friendship I had with Moshe which captured my heart in such an illuminating fashion – and not only me: when I visited my elder brother a few years ago in one of the south American countries he told me he frequently thinks of those same wonderful weeks in Nasiechowice and reminds himself of Moshe with much affection as a hero of his youth.

My second meeting with Moshe Sabotka (Z"L) was about 20 years later. One Shabbat he appeared at my apartment in Hadar Ha–Carmel in Haifa with his wife and two sons. The years and the woes of life had taken their toll – he was no longer the shy young man running after rabbits. Before me stood a man at the peak of his power, his face furrowed, the gaiety of his youth dimmed but still evident in him was his good humor and bright face and we quickly reestablished the friendship that lasted until the day of his death.

His adaptation to the conditions in Palestine was astonishing in spite of the difficulties that faced him. These were the 'Thirties':, the years of bloody disturbances and work was not easy to find. He made do with little and his physical strength stood him in good stead in the first years of his absorption during which he earned a bare living digging drainage ditches and foundations for buildings. Compressors were not yet seen in the country and the diggers were forced to pierce the rock–laden earth and stand bent over in the ditches for long hot hours. He worked for quite a long period at that arduous toil without a hint of bitterness or anger. To his wife, who was a worry for him, he answered with a laugh and assured her that he was happy with his lot and he accepted with love all the hardships he had to endure to integrate into the Homeland.

Later he left the digging work; he managed to acquire a horse and cart and transported various loads through "the ups and downs" of Haifa. That work was not easy either. The blood–riots concentrated in those times in the lanes and alleys of Haifa where he lived, but Moshe was happy with his lot, he never disclosed his fear and did his work throughout the bombings and shootings that went on around him.

With the improvement of the economic situation in the country he was able to free himself of the work and acquired a truck, at first with a partner, afterwards alone and became a road–haulage contractor for which there was a plentitude of work opportunities.

It was now that the full extent of his kindness and good–heartedness found its full expression. He answered every request, whether for charity or to lend assistance with a loan and was a guarantor for many. To the shy and hesitant to ask, he would encourage by saying: "You, the new immigrants, they won't give loans because they don't know you, but me, they know." His home was open to everyone and many came and found shelter until they found something and even though his own apartment was modest – just two rooms, a family of three souls stayed with him for about a year until they found something. With the increase in immigration, that also brought some of his own family, he would supply them with kitchen and cooking utensils and with his simplistic goodness of heart would say: "First of all a man must employ his wife in cooking so that there will be something for him to eat; when he eats, happiness will spread round him in his home; the Holy radiance will not shine on a man when sadness rules him."

These were the nature of the man and his deeds and everything in modesty and a happy face.

During this entire period I met with him and knew that his good temperament was now hidden behind the experiences and wisdom taught by life that the expressions were moderate and patient and characteristic and because of which he was loved by all who knew him or dealt with him through his work.

[Page 184]

His pride was his two sons – tall youths, like him – who turned out to be fine intelligent scholars and, as it seemed to me, improved for him his lot in life.

He said once – at the beginning of his driving career – on his lack of driving experience on the roads: If I were alone on the roads I wouldn't worry – the problem is that I'm not alone there are others on the road as well, it's getting hit by them that bothers me. And in saying that, he was prophesying without knowing it – being hit by "one of the others". At the end of 1947, disaster struck him with all its force. His young son, Elimelech, a youth nearing 17 years of age, fell victim to a traitorous murderer at the Haifa oil refinery.

From that day, when his beloved son died, the man began to decline. Although he didn't lose his good temperament and in time his cheerful spirits revived but his soul within him wept secretly. On passing the cemetery on the way in to Haifa he would leave the driver's cab and unite with the grave of his son. It was not difficult to notice this was not the same bright, Moshe.

Thus passed seven years in which he succeeded materially. He also left the transport industry and opened an ice–making factory with a partner but his heart wasn't in it, until his illness struck him down and within a few days he left us distraught.

Moshe Sabotka (Z"L) was a gentle person, having natural nobility and transcendental simplicity. His good nature, street–sense and moderation blended together in his personality and made him an exemplary friend.

He passed away when only fifty–five years old.

Elimelech Sabotka (HY"D)

by Arieh Sheintal

Translated by Selwyn Rose

Moshe and Hadassah's son (May she be spared for a long and good life), Elimelech, was born in October 1931. After finishing school at "Netzach Yisrael" he continued to complete his education at the Haifa Technion.

He was a member of the Scout Movement for many years and a leader in it. A few months before his death he became an apprentice in the Haifa Oil Refineries and in spite of his young age fulfilled competently his functions there in security issues.

He perished in the terrible slaughter that took place there, perpetrated by Arab workers on 30th December 1947. He was among those who valiantly stood their ground at the cost of their lives.

I knew him, I saw his growth.

I saw the child, the character of the young lad, how it changed and flowered in all its glorious youthful grace. I recall the steadfast erect growth, his sunburned face illuminated by his blue eyes. I followed his spiritual development and knew the hope growing in his parents' heart for their eldest son.

While he was still a young lad one could sense the excellent qualities – energy, discipline, responsibility and especially – love: of his parents, the Homeland for his people and for all mankind.

He paid with his body and soul, life enchanted him and his spirit longed for the future and on the threshold of it all, it was curtailed by villains.

[Page 185]

Childhood Memories

by Reuven Getzel (Levitt)

Translated by Selwyn Rose

I grew up in a traditional religious but not strictly Haredi home. My mother was orthodox and strictly guarded all the laws of Kashrut and festivals in her management of the home – in all their precise details. She fasted on all the fast–days without exception but was liberal and tolerant in her attitude towards others. She often quoted her favorite maxim: "It is not my world, and therefore I am obliged to ensure that order triumphs." In that she excelled in her attitude towards her children. "I must try to give them instruction and teach them the correct way in which to walk, but they are also individuals in their own right and have the right to decide for themselves how to behave." Each of us tried not, Heaven forbid, to hurt our mother. If we did something that was against her world view, we tried to ensure she was not made aware of it. Not out of fear but only to save her pain and disappointment. Father was the opposite; he demanded from us complete submission and to the laws and customs. He reacted severely and with a heavy hand and not with ears like our mother. He sometimes demanded and sometimes shouted and our mother cried and defended us. With the passage of time may father was also influenced by my mother and her ways and became more tolerant.

When my brother and I grew and matured our home became something of a club–house for the best of the town's youth: Manik Katzengold, Simcha Zibenburg, Wolf Blady, Itzik Scheinfrucht, and all the Bursteins took part in it. There were stormy arguments on all the problems facing the world. Every new book that appeared in the world, every new movement, every interesting phenomenon, social or cultural, from every corner of the world – earned a reaction from us.

For a short period I studied under Abele Malamud. Later on I transferred to the "Heder" of Yesheyahu–Shmuel Hirschenhorn who in spite of his orthodoxy excelled in his broad horizons and peeked also in books on Haskala and learning. His attitude to the Hebrew language was also positive. From his class I moved to the "Heder" of Yechiel, a righteous man but orthodox and conformist.

After I had spent a short time studying Gemara and Parshanut[1] I began to dream about a general education. I was joined by two others of about my age: Mordecai Rafaelowicz and Itcha Kornfeld, and we began studying. We received full value for our money from the teachers of the Government Gymnasium for the lessons we had in all the subjects. They prepared all three of us for examination to the sixth grade of the gymnasium. The nights turned into days: we studied between 20–22 hours a day. From the three of us I was the only one to pass and I was accepted by the gymnasium. I remember my father's great pleasure when he heard that I had passed the examinations, His face beamed with happiness and pride. An interesting and typical fact: all my life I dressed in the traditional clothing; a caftan, and kippa. When I attended the examinations I made an agreement with the building's guard: I went in dressed in my usual clothes and left them with him in the cellar changing into a normal jacket and went upstairs for the examinations. When I was finished, I went downstairs and changed my clothes and went home dressed as Jew.

After the gymnasium I registered with the High School for Commercial Studies in Krakow on Szpitalna Street but I think I stopped almost as soon as I started owing to the death of my mother.

[Page 186]

In 1947 I immigrated to Palestine from Italy. I had received an immigration certificate from my brother, Yantshe, in Italy, under a fictitious name.

My father took an active part in the social life of the town. He was a member of the Municipal Council, and I think also for a time a "Labnik". He belonged to the advisory council of a Polish bank and later was a member of the management of a Jewish bank, served for many years as a member on the board of the Jewish Community and for several years was the chairman of it.

My mother, although she took no part in the social life of the town, was very welcome at all their activities because of her pleasant personality and easy friendly greeting to everyone she met. She supported everyone in need to the utmost of her ability. I recall that at her funeral there were many local Christians. It was a very rare phenomenon. From an economic point of view my parents were considered to be "middle–class" and sometimes even "upper–class". There were ups and downs which were fairly drastic. More than once father felt the vise closing in on him but managed somehow to hang on. But throughout all the crises that hit them their spirits never fell and they always behaved and acted honorably.

From the days after the First World War several events are etched in my memory: The end of hostilities and the Polish army groups that took over the Government, The appearance of the Sztrelcy[2] and snipers who arrived from Krakow under the leadership of Józef Piłsudski, riding a small horse and in the middle of "The Rink" delivering his speech calling to the youth to join the "Sokolim" and fight shoulder to shoulder for the liberation of Poland; the laying down of arms by the Polish military organizations at the end of the war against the soldiers and officers of the Austrian army and their Allies their hasty retreat.

An important event is deeply etched on my memory and my heart from that period – the riots against the Jews that took place from the 1st–3rd May, 1919 (see the monograph in this book commencing at p. 115).

When the terrible days had passed a feeling that we had not earlier expected took hold, grew and became strengthened. We did not at that time feel any immediate and real threat to our lives, but that dark acute feeling, and the pain in the heart! Why? Why are we condemned to live like dogs? And why can't we and why don't we want to change our lives, that they should be more human? Will we be forever beaten and humiliated and grateful to those who hold the whip–hand but don't use it on our backs? Will we never wake up, rise up and build our Homeland and not be abandoned by every evil wind that blows? Is this really us? And by what right do we protest that we are "The Chosen People"? Insulted, burnt, sinning for which there is no discernable atonement.

The following day we began to leave our hiding places. We kept close to the walls of the houses like beaten dogs, daring to escape the whips of their masters, with shame and ignominy in our hearts. When we met our Christian neighbors we dropped our gaze as if it were we who were guilty while they faced us with a derisive smirk on their lips and mockery in their eyes.

Master of the Universe, Until when?

But that was just a foretaste of the Holocaust itself; a forewarning of the great pogrom to come that was perpetrated during World War Two in which my family perished.

And these are the members of my family who perished and died the death of Holy Martyrs:

1. My sister Faygle Goldsobel of Lublin: Her husband was a member of the Judenrat. He was known as being guiltless and innocent with a G–d–fearing heart. The Gestapo at first demanded from him 400 listed Jews for labor at the beginning of his membership. He gave them what they demanded. After a week they came to him again with the same demand. He asked them: "Where are the 400 Jews I gave you last week?" the reply: "That's none of your business." To which he replied: "I will not give you any more people until the first group is returned." As a reply to that "Chutzpah", he was taken out the following morning into the town center and shot by a firing

squad. My sister was unable to overcome the tremendous shock and lost her reason. She died in her madness on the streets of Lublin.

2. My brother, Ephraim–Yosef from Kielce didn't want to go for resettlement and was shot in his house together with his wife who joined him. The children a son and daughter, were taken to one of the camps where they perished.
3. My sister, Bluma–Rachel from Bialystok together with her husband Avraham Grossfeld was taken to the camps with their young son, Haim, and there they all perished. Their son, Yosef, jumped from the cattle–truck on the way to the camp and was shot and killed by one of the German guards. Their third son died the death of a hero during the Bialystok ghetto uprising.
4. My wife, Tsila with my daughter, Miriam–Hadassah, was taken to Auschwitz together with many Jews from Bialystok. There, the Germans wanted to take the children from the mothers on the pretext that they were creating a kindergarten for the children. The mothers refused with all their might because they knew what awaited them, so the Germans took the 700 mothers and the children straight to the crematoria where, fully conscious they were all consigned to the flames.
5. My brother, Moshe was taken to a labor camp. There he became a "Musselman", was transferred to an extermination camp in Upper Silesia, Ustzyca, where he died a short while before the liberation.
6. My brothers, Yechiel and Avraham, hid in a bunker on the land of a Christian in Działoszyce. When their money ran out the Christian stopped providing them with food. When the hunger began to trouble them too much, the younger one, Avraham, decided to go out looking for something. He was seen by a "sheygetz" who followed him stealthily until he returned to the hiding–place and then. informed the Nazi authorities. They came and fell upon the fugitives, taking them both for execution before a cheering mob witnessing the event in Działoszyce.

Translator's Footnotes

1. Holy writ interpretations
2. Riflemen

Shimshon Dov Yerushalmi

by Shmuel Berger [1]

Translated by Selwyn Rose

On 18th July 1967 our dear president, Mr. Shimshon Dov Yerushalmi (Z"L) died quite suddenly. We lost at that moment a very dear man, a man, who for 23 years from the day of the founding of the association, dedicated his whole being and energies to, and for the sake of, his friends. He left us suddenly in the midst of the very days he was deeply involved in preparing this memorial book for publication to which he devoted his last days and the best of his strength and energy. Not only did he work on the material himself but he hastened all of us along as well: "It's a pity for each lost day without advancing. We have to get it finished. We can't take our time. Who knows what is waiting for us?" We didn't know, although we well knew that he was ill and prayed for his wellbeing constantly and hoped that he would yet live many days and continue in his blessed work for years. But Fate decided otherwise.

Shimshon Dov Yerushalmi was born in Kaminka, Ukraine (Kiev County) in 1882 to his father, Moshe Nahum Yerushalmi (Father of the Beit–Din) Dakmona Osstrolonka and Kielce and his mother Rivka the daughter of Yona Rosenblum Makrilow (Volhyn County). He received his general education from excellent teachers well–versed in Hebrew and traditional Judaism, from his father who was a genius in his knowledge of Judaism and Torah. His house was a meeting place for the intelligentsia.

In 1913 he married Tovar the daughter of Mordecai Ha–Levi Greitzer from Miechów–Charsznica, a family well–known to us all. Even at that early date, he was interested in what was happening in Palestine and in 1925 he acquired, in the name of "The Miechów Group" a plot of land of 500 dunams in Afula from the "American Zionist Community". In 1910 he accompanied his father on a journey to a rabbinical Council in St. Petersburg in which the greatest of the Rabbis of the era took part. At that Council, and at the age of only 18 years, he was given the post of secretary to the Polish Rabbinical faction. At that council too, he took his very first steps in public activity. He was a member of the Jewish Community Council in Miechów. Later he became one of the Board of Trustees of the Hebrew School in Warsaw. He was a member of the Zionist Organization, a member of the editorial board of the Zionistische Blätter, founded by Yitzhak Gruenbaum, the representative of the Foundation Fund in Poland, in the central Palestine Office, a member of the Central Election Committee for the Zionist Congresses, and manager of the information department of the Foundation Fund. He immigrated in 1935. He took part in the foundation of the Association of Zionist Activists, "Brit Harishonim", and elected as honorary member of its internal court. He acted as manager of the "Society of ex–Students" of the Hebrew University and managed its social activities until the end of 1948. He was a member of the Cultural Committee of the General Zionist Organization and a member of its Civilian Guard from its founding; He also worked in the State Comptroller's Office. When he retired he busied himself writing on the different branches public service until the day of his death. To all these activities, in which he took part, whether private, public or cultural he dedicated his entire being, strength and energies.

[Page 188]

Shimshon Dov Yerushalmi (Z"L)

He was meticulous by nature and everything he did he performed faithfully. If he accepted any mission or task it would be carried through meticulously with amazing perfection.

[Page 189]

I knew the man for about 5–6 years, from active work in the Association. Every single meeting and encounter with the departed – and they were not many – was for me an experience in itself. From the moment I crossed the threshold of his home, I felt homely warmth that I hadn't felt in the days of my youth. With the opening of the door I was received with heart–warming sincerity by my host and his wife Tova, May she be spared for a long and good life, and you are immediately asked about your welfare and your family members. They always sympathized with you and gave good advice. That welcome and the personal interest in everything concerning you, is most touching; at those moments I stood my own home – the home of my parents. The furniture of their home reminded me of the furniture of a typical Jewish home that has gone and exists no more. From this point onwards you enter into a conversation of event of today – and that meant the topic of the Memorial Book committee. On reading the material I was astounded at his analytical ability and his healthy reasoning, his to–the–point observations (in spite of the fact that I not always agreed with them). But above all he showed himself to be a noble person, warm–hearted and glad to be of help to everyone. He was, in effect, the "father of the organization", the father of his comrades – the Holocaust–survivors. Whoever turned to him received good advice and he, himself, helped his fellow citizens by way of his many connections with the military and government personalities. For every problem that arose in the organization, he it was that decided and to him we turned with every argument. All the correspondence in the organization was, in practice, under his supervision and in the composition of letters he had no competitors. In the early years of the work he wondered a bit and had a little doubt as to whether we would really succeed in publishing the book. But with time, when the project began to gather flesh on the skeleton and the material for the book began to flow – articles, memoirs, photographs and documents – and especially that same day when the contract was signed between us and Yad Va–Shem, Mr. Yerushalmi became harnessed to the project and during the last period of his life he worked on the preparation of the book indefatigably and we had many conversations on all the problems connected with it. More than once I withstood significant criticism and a lively argument developed – sometimes he accepted my view and admitted I was right. Since I knew his expertise in the material was excellent and the experience he had acquired in editing many books of a similar nature, I insisted with him that he write a few of the main articles for the book, among them on Charsznica, on the activities of the council and others.

As I indicated above, Mr. Yerushalmi never did things by halves and if he became attached to a project he followed through with every part of his being and invested all his energies. He read all the articles and monographs and corrected their style. Made observations and comments, and returned several time to specific articles, such as that of Eliezer Lavie to which he added a number of details which he had himself researched the sources. It was not easy for him and several times he was forced to stop his work through weakness. In the middle of the article on the activities of the Council, a topic on which he had amassed considerable material from official minutes and the exchange of letters, he was taken from us.

From his public work one can see a characteristically clear line that was special to him and was his guiding principle: he always connected his public work with his cultural activities. That line, in his activities for the Hebrew University of Jerusalem is clearly conspicuous for on that same day in 1925 he was appointed President of the Committee organizing the official dedication ceremony in Miechów for the opening of the University. During the following years his connections with the Hebrew college never ceased. He well knew the value of Hebrew culture and wanted with all his might to forward the development of the University and its growth. As mentioned, the Jews of Miechów celebrated the consecration and opening of the Hebrew University in the town's synagogue in April 1925. That same day all work ceased in town and all the Jews in Miechów and Charsznica and representatives of the Polish authorities gathered together in the synagogue. There was a moment during that ceremony that I will never forget – the late Mr. Yerushalmi, President of the Committee for Organizing the Ceremony for the opening of the University took the dais in front of the Ark held his gold watch in his hand announced in a raised and emotional voice: "Gentlemen, the time is now twelve noon and they are declaring open The Hebrew University of Jerusalem at this time on Mount Scopus, Jerusalem. Long live the Hebrew University and let it be to the glory and splendor of our people for all the generations." To his credit we must also record the presence, in Jerusalem of a delegation from Miechów, bearing in their hands a vellum parchment signed by all the representatives of the town and when the time comes to write the Memorial Book we will remember the late gentleman in the scroll and turn to the archivists of the University in

Jerusalem and request a photograph of the document as a symbol of perpetuating his memory in the Memorial Book.

[Page 190]

He had the privilege to see his son Yesheyahu study at the university and with him a number of other students from Miechów who graduated with academic degrees.

On 24th July 1970 a gala festival was held celebrating the 50th year since the laying of the foundation stone of the University in the presence of the President, members of the Knesset, professors and Mr. Arthur Goldberg who received an honorary Doctor of Philosophy. While sitting in the amphitheater on Mount Scopus together with my wife, I was reminded of the multitudinous activities on behalf of the university by the departed. At that moment, standing before me, I saw the image of the man who did not live to take part in this commemoration of the University to which he had contributed the best years of his life.

In Israel he functioned for an extended period as manager of the Society of the Hebrew University Alumni in Tel-Aviv and as I indicated he combined the collection of funds for its development with cultural work among the citizens of the town. Similarly he arranged for University lessons in the national University. This was only one example of his public work that is known to me and we all know the extent of all his other activities. There was no project or institution in the context of rebuilding the Homeland in which he did not play some active role. Similarly he had a hand in all fields of activity in the World Zionist Organization. His connections with the leaders of Polish Jewry – Yitzhak Gruenbaum and other leaders, were firm and deep up until his last moments.

With the death of Mr. Yerushalmi a distinguished leader of our organization has been taken from us, a spiritual and practical leader, noble-spirited, loved by all of us and loving every man, happy to help wherever and whenever he could with unflagging vigor, pleasant to talk with, good-hearted, his home open to all. He sought after justice all his life and was uncompromising. Intelligent and infused with the Jewish spirit, broadly educated, a writer and journalist, he published many articles and monographs and conducted serious research into the history of the Holocaust and wrote much on the topic.

Lost to us is a man head and shoulders above his fellows. We will never forget him. His extensive, diverse blessed activities, endless infinite deeds, within and without our organization he illuminated our path as an exemplary symbol to every one of us and will be an example to us and to our children for all generations.

May his memory be blessed.

Translator's Footnote

1. Eulogy delivered on the annual anniversary of the Association 15th Elul 5728

Miechów Types

By Shmuel Khazan

Translated by Gloria Berkenstat Freund

Even though he never had a good voice, he was unique as a preacher. His way of reciting the prayers was easy, as he simply talked with God. In his later years he prayed with such ecstasy that even the non–pious eagerly listened to him. With his ecstatic praying during the Days of Awe, reciting Kol Nidre [opening Yom Kippur prayer] and especially Neilah [closing Yom Kippur prayer] when everyone already was tired from fasting the entire day, when few people really understood the exact sense of the prayers, he so heartily conversed with the loving God that by stretching the point he wanted to give the ruffians an understanding of the prayer.

[Page 191]

Shmuel Khazan [cantor] was the first Khazan in the only synagogue located in the shtetl [town]; the second Khazan was the new shoykhet [ritual slaughterer]. By the way, he was called "the new shoykhet" when he already had been the shoykhet for many years. The name remained until, alas, he perished at the hands of the German murderers.

The new shoykhet always prayed Shakhres [morning prayers] and Shmuel Khazan the musofim [supplemental prayers on the Sabbath and holidays]. All his life, Shmuel Khazan had a poor, small shop on Krakower Street. He also was an extremely poor man for his entire life, but despite this he always was satisfied because according to him this was the will of the dear God. His naïveté was so great that when someone entered his store and asked for an article that he actually did not have – the store was almost always empty – he told a customer, "Wait a little, I will run to Działoszyce and I will bring it to you." Działoszyce was 20 kilometers from Miechów.

Shmuel Pravda

He was really named Shmuel Fridenberg. He was a grain merchant, one of the largest in the shtetl. After the First World War, he and his son–in–law and partner, Shmuel Almer, bought Shmelke Kacengold's house where he built his own large warehouse in the courtyard in which he also had machines to clean the grains and seeds. At the time this was great progress.

His nickname Pravda came from this: when he had travelled to Działoszyce every Sunday to the fair to buy grains and seeds, he would arrive there very early when everyone must look for a [bathroom] and earlier there was only one such institution for the entire shtetl in Działoszyce. It was near the synagogue and when Shmuel Pravda emptied himself there, the first minyon [10 men required for prayer] already was reciting a loud Shemoneh Esrei [central prayer recited three times a day] and, when it was time to say "amen," each time he said a loud "Pravda" which is vor, truth, in the Polish language. He was such a naïve man that in his understanding one had to say "amen" and one must not use the holy language in such an unclean place, so he used the word in Polish. The people who were also there then heard this and from this he remained with the nickname Pravda for his entire life. Few people in the shtetl know that his real name was Fridenberg.

Chaim Lewit

There were two men in Miechów who by chance were named Chaim Lewit. The two Lewits were not from the same family. Chaim Lewit from Działoszice Street was known as Chaim Shel Osher [Chaim of Wealth] and the second Chaim Lewit from Shul Street was named Chaim Shel Khovod [Chaim of Honor].

The two names were based on the fact that one of them was well–to–do, but a boor, and the other one was more educated and raised very genteel, successful and intelligent children.

[Page 192]

Chaim Shel Osher would always ask me: "How can the Polish newspaper Kurier Codzienny na Jutro [Daily Courier for Tomorrow] know what will happen tomorrow to print today? The Polish words "na Jutro," mean "for tomorrow" and after all my explanations, he did not under this.

Alter Warszawki

He was the richest man in the shtetl, but a miser who was not beloved. He owned the large mechanized mill in partnership with Avraham Sercacz and Henech Kajzer. It was called "Marimont." Alter Warszawski's mentality was such that when he was satisfied with an official he would always rebuke him saying that he was a bad official, untrustworthy and that he would like to be rid of him. He did this especially so that the official would not feel important. And on the contrary, when he had a bad official, he always praised him, saying that he is a very successful and reliable person so that he would be rid of him quickly.

The Lazar Family

by Rafael Mlinarski

Translated by Gloria Berkenstat Freund

a. The Father

The Jewish community perished along with their doctor, Moshe (Maurici) Lazar. He was born in 1895; graduated from his studies in 1926. He practiced as an internist and gynecologist in Charsznica and Miechów; he committed suicide in Kielce in 1942.

b. The Son

Friday, September 4, 1942. Total deportation of our town. We gather near the synagogue and march to the train station. I will not forget the joy of the Poles while we were led to the train station by the Nazis; and I will not forget the Poles who found an 8-year-old boy in the town and brought him to the train station too. This boy was the son of the physician Dr. Lazar who, together with his wife, had committed suicide on the deportation day. Women, children, old people—sent to who-knows-where...

[Page 195]

The Holocaust

The Destruction and the Holocaust

by Yehuda Greenbel

Translated by Selwyn Rose

Summer 1939. It seemed like all the summers that had preceded it but the atmosphere seemed more stifling than usual and a strange feeling of oppression descended upon the world and especially on the town. From day to day the atmosphere became more electrified and the situation more dissociated from reality. The various newspapers are publishing varying opinions and information and it is impossible to discern where events will lead. Will Nazi Germany really attack Poland? Didn't the allies of this anti–Semitic Poland declare that they will come to her aid? How is it possible that the Nazi beasts were not deterred by such a declaration? And didn't Poland herself – so proud of her "courageous heart" and her corrupt government, right from the beginning, guarantee that she would never capitulate; that not one inch of her territory would be ceded to Germany and that blood would be shed if they made any attempt to do so by force of arms? Indeed, a real confusion of the senses and meantime, in spite of the internal woes, the Andak party continues to add its Satanic propaganda against the Jews in the form of stationing "sentries" outside Jewish shops lest Poles who choose to shop there should try to enter. There were also many anti–Semitic slogans to be seen and heard recently like: "Jews, go to Palestine," and "Jews! Hitler is coming after you!" All the absurdity of the last comment failed to awaken in those Poles who voiced it the awareness that it was likely to continue and include them also. The Jews in the town were more perturbed and were it not for their concern for their families and businesses would have picked themselves up and gone to other places. But where? And thus, day followed day and there was no escape from the tangled situation. It was already mid–August. The wheat in the field was ripe and the fruit on the trees juicy and ready for picking but who had a head clear of worries and nerves of steel to wander abroad in the fields and orchards in these darkening days?

The first signs of Polish mobilization began to appear in town and established themselves all over, even in the club–house of the "Hashomer Ha–Dati" in the "Community Council" offices who brought out mattresses for them. Lines of communication were established and the overtones of war were felt. The L.O.P.P. [1] and the Strzelec [2] and other similar organizations woke up and began to act and spur–on the townspeople to take steps to defend themselves. Defensive trenches were dug around the town and bunkers for cover in the event of aerial attacks; The Jewish population voluntarily took part in all this work and proved their loyalty to the State by doing so and perhaps also calmed themselves that they had done everything they could to save themselves. The mobilization of volunteer began in earnest. Notices were stuck on the walls of houses and the residents clustered round to read them and tried to absorb their implication. They said "The Reserves" are called to report for duty – but where, when and how remained a puzzle for everyone. It simply increased and multiplied the confusion and bewilderment of everyone which in any case spread throughout the country. It contributed to the wandering of the population throughout Silesia.

[Page 196]

The towns close to the German border began to empty of its residents and that was in answer to the influence upon them by German spies whose sole purpose was to empty the areas of its Polish and Jewish populations ahead of its annexation into the "Greater German Reich". And indeed they achieved almost complete success by inducing panic among the masses and caused everyone who cared for their own and their dear ones' safety to flee from the clutches of the German forces.

The Jewish people among the refugees found shelter among acquaintances and some among their Jewish brethren. The Poles, in contrast, found little succour among their countrymen who turned them away and slammed the doors in their faces. The town was full of people. Families with small children on their last legs, baggage on their shoulders, managed to proceed "eastwards" only with great difficulty. There were some lucky ones who managed to acquire a horse and cart but even so their journey were slow because of poor roads and the many people forced to go on foot. In the evenings the town became shrouded in darkness and only here and there a faint light twinkled only to be quickly extinguished. Groups of people congregated together in the town square – "The Rink" and discuss the events of the day and when the time came for the news they crowded round the few available radios owned by the wealthier of the people – the Polish residents, still optimistic and certain that victory would be theirs – but not for long.

1st September 1939 towards morning. A German bomber, black like a crow, with swastikas on its wings flies over the rooftops; he circles in the air without interference as if enjoying himself and without any sense of being in enemy skies. Indeed it is a sign that the war has begun and there is no longer room for self–delusion.

Erev Shabbat. The town is humming with refugees and more are arriving together with the first of the retreating Polish Army falling back under pressure from the German forces. Machine–guns have been hauled up and installed on the roof–tops of "The Rink" to scare off the German aircraft that have begun to reconnoitre the area at will in order to track the movements of the Polish army. The Municipality has no advice to give and in order to make some impression publish a few lines of instructions and orders totally devoid of significance. The Jews – apparently resigned to the situation make preparations for whatever comes next. They share their food with their brethren among the refugees but their supplies are small because no attempt has been made to stock up earlier in anticipation of hard times. The prayers in the synagogue and the Steibls are hurried because everyone is anxious to be at home together with his family.

Sunday 3rd September. The radio broadcasts warnings repeating and repeating and also reports on the retreat of the army. That can be clearly seen by the stream of defeated soldiers passing through the town in flight. The last of the municipality representatives who have held firm until now have joined the flight and for those who are left there is nothing to be done other than to form some kind of local militia whose only purpose is to hunt down German spies who have infiltrated among the incoming refugees – and liquidate them.

Complete chaos reigns throughout and rumours about the approach of the Germans are rife and increasing and there can be no doubt left when the last remaining Polish soldiers leave the town and, indeed, that same day the first of the German soldiers appeared in Miechów

Quite quickly two German soldiers entered our house with rifles and fixed bayonets, ordered us to raise our arms and searched the whole house looking for Polish soldiers who may be hiding there.

Later, we came to know that most of the houses had been searched and that several hostages had been taken, Poles and Jews, who were held for a couple of days in the church and there was some concern for their lives. Apart from a few shots that were fired to frighten us when the Germans entered town, the day passed in relative quiet. The people closed themselves in their homes and rarely ventured out. The German garrison wasted no time and set about its work; the Communications Platoon climbed the telephone poles – the exchange building was next to our house – and repaired the disconnected lines while the military command published various emergency orders while fighting was still going on outside the city limits. The accursed Fascism already began to give signs of its presence in town, first of all in the figure of Polish "Patriotism" – well–known to us for a long time – non–other than Dr. Lech, the head–teacher of the town's gymnasium.

[Page 197]

Already during the days of reform he was known as an "Andak" man and now, with the fleeing of the legal Mayor, Marczewski, – he claimed for himself the chair of the Mayor and among his first acts was to oblige all Jewish shops to display a large, visible "Star of David" in the shop–front window with the word "Jew" written underneath. His days in power were brief, however and with the return of the legal Mayor a short while later, the posters were removed. Essential foodstuffs in the shops were sold quickly for as long as supplies lasted and everyone tried to stock–up with as much as possible. White flour was confiscated by the Germans and the bakers were forced to use a lower grade that turned the bread into something poor–tasting and glutinous. In addition, the bread was sold only on production of vouchers and it was necessary to get up at dawn and stand in line at the baker in order to get the inadequate ration.

Other foodstuffs were in any case virtually unobtainable and were available only on the "black market" and the prices rose alarmingly from day to day. In the beginning the Germans did not noticeably interfere in daily life because they were mainly engaged in clearing the conquered territory and with their siege on Warsaw. We saw their destructive armor passing through Miechów en route to Kraków and Warsaw for that purpose. Terrifying fear struck us at the sight.

On the second day of Rosh Hashanah an armored column pulled up and stopped in "The Rink" and a hunt immediately began for bearded Jews. When caught they were forced to clean the German tanks and trucks just for the sake of abusing them. That same afternoon a number of SS men stopped in front of the locked synagogue door and began striking it with their rifle–butts trying unsuccessfully to break in. Unable to give up with nothing achieved, they smashed some of the windows in the basement and threw in some incendiaries not leaving until they were certain that the place was burning. Our house quickly filled with thick smoke since it was right next door and we were concerned for our lives.

In the meantime the soldiers left and the town's fire–brigade chief Czeczinski(?), whose house was also threatened, arrived and managed to put out the blaze before it did any real damage. The fire encouraged us to leave our home immediately and we moved to Rabbi Shmuel Fogel's house. That transfer would come back to haunt us later when the ghetto was established.

With the entry into town of the German forces the elected officials of the Jewish Community who had ceased their routine public activities now began to function again albeit somewhat hesitantly. They were concerned that the control of the community would pass to the hands of a refugee by the name of Applebaum who had settled in Miechów and even in the first days of the conquest had displayed considerable initiative in keeping close to the rulers. His ambitions were quickly realized and he was nominated Mayor, while the legitimate members of the council were "second fiddles" and their activities now curtailed to executing the orders of the Germans. Their first one was that all Jews of fifteen and over must wear a white arm–band with a "Star of David" on it. The order went into effect in December 1939 and the "Council" had to provide for sale the necessary cloth for the Jewish residents. It was the first sign of discrimination and the white arm–bands on the sleeves coincided with the snow that fell at the same time.

[Page 198]

It is worth mentioning that there was still an air of optimism among the people at the time, in spite of the fact that the conquest of Poland and its division between Russia in the east and Germany in the west, was already an established fact; there was great hope of an early counter–attack by the great powers of France and Great Britain. It was that hope that breathed the spirit of life and faith into the people that the miracle would shortly come to pass.

Because of the confiscation of radios and the prohibition of receiving information from abroad the population was fed with information from the Germans and that was obviously one–sided although it was, in general accurate. The sources gave food to the thought that the information being passed by word of mouth was just a rumor that someone was thinking up. Nevertheless it found a strong echo among the people and had a great influence on them A few of the residents, Jew and non–Jew alike, who had fled eastward to Russia at the outbreak of war, returned with greetings from friends and acquaintances they had met on the Russian side of the border and who had decided to remain there until they could safely return home to a liberated Poland. There were divided opinions about the fundamental nature of Russia's regime in the eastern region and her attitude towards the Jews in particular was unclear. A little comfort was taken by the optimists from the fact that Jews were serving in the Red Army and even achieving high officer–rank, and "there" at least, people were not bothered simply for being Jews. Hearing these stories and others, a number of people stole across the River San – the border – to the "Paradise" of the other side.

To this day we have no idea how many succeeded in making it safely. It is worth pointing out that until 1941 for as long as the 1939 German/Russian Pact remained valid, the postal services between the two states operated normally between the residents of both sides and even within our own family we sent and received regular letters from an uncle who had immigrated to Siberia and from my sister who had got stuck in the town of Stolin not far from Baranovich.

Winter 1939/1940 passed without serious disturbances apart from those instances of the "kidnapped Jews" for urgent forced labor such as snow–clearing and so on. At 8 o'clock in the evening, the curfew began and no Jew was to be found on the street.

With the thaw and the coming of spring a German company named "Klei–Jäger" arrived in town and made preparations to pave the highway between Kraków and Warsaw (which crossed the town) to facilitate the movement of German military transport. Obviously in order to execute a project of such a scale the company would require a large, cheap work–force and that was to be found in the "Jew" who could be forced into labor without even paying him. The German "Labor Department", to which the Company turned, ordered the Jüdenrat to supply as many workers as possible and as quickly as possible. The wealthy, who had never in their lives done any physical labor, anticipated being beaten severely by the German overseers and in their place paid poorer men to work for them; this was seen as something of a "life–saver", as a way of earning some extra rations at a high cost. There were also incidents of "privilege" which caused anger among those who saw themselves as perpetual "victims" for all hard work. It is worth remembering that the Jewish population in town was not large and the number of young men was correspondingly low. For every German demand to supply a work–force the Jüdenrat would mobilize virtually the same men who were forced to present themselves for work and if they failed to show they could expect some form of unknown punishment...

At this same time the local government recalled that it needed to control the river flowing at the edge of town, a project that was now made possible because of the availability of the supply of Jewish labor – an inexhaustible supply. Even the municipal road–works department didn't hesitate to make its demands of the Jüdenrat to supply laborers, in short, anyone who wanted to could impose upon the Jew bitterness and abuse as much as he wished.

[Page 199]

I still need to mention the heavy and arduous work we were forced to do by the Luftwaffe, in loading ammunition onto railroad trucks in the Chodówka Forest, accompanied by crippling beatings with sticks to keep up the pace for 24 hours.

At the end of the summer of 1941 The Jews were ordered to congregate in the area designated to be the ghetto that included Mickiewicza Street, Słowczikiego(?) Street and Joselewicza Street. The small number of Christians living in those streets were required to evacuate their homes and move to the now–vacated Jewish homes scattered throughout the town. The above streets, which even before this were densely populated, were now forced to absorb the whole Jewish population of the town; overcrowding reached epic proportions.

Immediately after the move the streets were closed and brick–built walls erected with narrow, locked gates in each wall guarded by the Jüdischer Ordnungsdienst [3]. From now on we were as if in a narrow cage and the German hunters' search was made significantly easier. Indeed the soldiers would come about every two weeks. In the beginning – sending younger men for forced labor camps and later – total extermination.

At the end of June 1942 they locked us in from all directions and the "kidnappings" began. About 50 young men, among them my brother (Z"L) and I, were taken to the Great Synagogue and held there for a night and a day without knowing what would happen to us and where we were going. The parents of these young men ran around and turned to the heads of the Jüdenrat and pleaded for their children's lives but in vain. The following morning we were transported to the Kraków suburb of Bonarka and there we were put to work in a brick–making factory (that had belonged to a Jew and confiscated by the Germans who put a Volksdeutsche from Silesia in his place). In spite of the grueling labor and meagre rations, we managed to keep our spirits up. Our consolation came from the knowledge that we still had a "home" in Miechów and from time to time, especially on Sunday, it was even possible – but dangerous – to get home to see the family if only for a couple of hours. That consolation didn't last long.

While passing through the streets of the ghetto I was struck by the feeling of suffocation and that a ghost of some sort was chasing me. Stares of despair looked out from the eyes of the passersby I saw and it was difficult to talk to them. Even at home, in the bosom of my family the tension was evident and that was in spite of the fact that no one knew what awaited them in the next few days. Early Monday morning, when it was time for me to return to Bonarka to work, my mother (Z"L), accompanied me to the gate of the ghetto where the truck was waiting to take us to work. Before I climbed aboard my mother fell upon me crying bitterly. When I recall that moment my heart aches remembering that last separation in which a mother's heart sensed a bitter and tragic end. Indeed, no more than a few days passed and the terrible news arrived in Kraków that hundreds of Jews from town – among them my grandfather and parents (Z"L) – had been transported to some marshy dunghill in Słomniki where the murderers collected together Jews from the surrounding towns and from there transported them by train to extermination centers.

Operations of this nature were undertaken in most of the towns, mostly on the Sabbath.

From witnesses who were present and saw and heard, we learned that on that black Sabbath day, my grandfather (Z"L), Rabbi Yisroel David – ritual slaughterer and inspector –who was loved by everyone in town, wrapped himself in his prayer–shawl and after finishing his Sabbath prayers, went out with his stick, knocked on the doors of the synagogue and called out to the Master of the Universe: "Master of the Universe! All my life I have served Thee with love and perfect faith and never transgressed Your commandments and now that sentence of death has been decreed why have You forced me desecrate Thy Holy Sabbath by riding on a wagon? Why has my soul been deprived of its purity?" All who heard him stood crying bitterly but there was no salvation...in the words of Jeremiah: "...behold, and see if there be any sorrow like unto my sorrow, which is done unto me..." [4] The decree has fallen upon the Jewish people of the town and we among them are the orphans and the mourners. Everyone who was directly touched by that "Aktsia", wrapped himself up in the corner, crying and uniting with the memory with his loved ones who only days before they saw them. Who could imagine to themselves that the end was so close?

[Page 200]

Less than a week later the ghetto was again surrounded by the special platoons of the SS, the Gendarmes and others. All the remaining Jews in the ghetto, women and children, were gathered together in "The Rink" and immediately separated into two groups: one – men in the full vigor of their strength, and the second – the elderly, the women and the children.

They were all taken to the railroad station and there crammed into cattle–wagons closed and crowded. The men selected as a work–force were loaded separately and were transported not far and arrived at Prokoczym camp, remembered in infamy by all who were there. But not so the others; the appalling conditions in the wagons meant that many died on the journey before even arriving at the crematoria. Only one sole surviving woman lived to tell the story of that transport of death who managed by a miracle to jump from the train and survive to hide among farmers who took pity on her – K. Pawlowicz, living today in Canada.

The ghetto remained empty and forlorn and around it wandered the Nazi beasts as if seeking prey. When we heard at work the news that some of the people from Miechów were in Prokoczym only some few kilometers from us, we took the risk and went there to try to glean some information from them concerning the fate of our families and indeed, their own situation and any help that we perhaps can give them. Even though our own conditions at work were far from good, we bribed some of the overseers there and managed to secrete a number of people and bring them back to be among us. For those, it was a real life–saver for them after tasting just a few days of the hell of Prokoczym. It seemed that now the terrible tragedy that fell upon the Jews of Miechów and its surroundings had come to an end but fate continued to add to its cruel treatment of Miechów's Jews. A few weeks after the liquidation of the ghetto a number of escapes took place from the various work– and concentration–camps in the area of Kraków and the ghetto of Miechów began to show signs of life again with some of its earlier residents and also with Jews from other towns in the area. The homes that had been empty now absorbed the few who had returned to them thinking that life was again in tranquil waters.

The Germans thought otherwise. When they saw the movement of the Jews who dared to return to the destroyed ghetto they burned with anger. They seemed to accept the fact that the ghetto was again “crawling with Jews” and full of life but at the same time they tightened the encirclement lest this time the “birds escape”. It was not long before “the hunt” began. The town's residents beyond the ghetto's walls even took pleasure in helping the Germans as much as they could. The victims were taken to the Chodówka Forest where they were shot and thrown into a mass grave that had been dug by the farmers and their sons.

Those who succeeded in hiding during the hunt later came out of their hiding–places thinking that the Germans' anger had subsided and that they were safe. They had failed to learn that their fate had been sealed earlier and continued to live in the closed “cage” just like before.

On 18th January 1943, during the morning hours, the Germans burst into the ghetto while an increased guard surrounded it on the outside, and commenced slaughtering on the streets the remaining Jews that had escaped the earlier round–up. Only a very few isolated individuals managed to escape this time while the majority fell into the hands of the cruel murderers and died. The corpses were collected by Poles and brought for burial in a large common grave in the Jewish cemetery which today has disappeared and left no sign because the tombstones were removed and the ground plowed over.

Our town was gone – destroyed – and with it our world and there is no mourner to cry over our immense tragedy.

Translator's Footnotes

1. State Air Defence League
2. Snipers
3. The ghettos' Jewish police service
4. The Lamentations of Jeremiah 1:xii

[Page 201]

The Struggle for Life

by Pesach Bezerdki

Translated by Selwyn Rose

In the Warsaw Ghetto

I walk homewards to my wife and children with my brain gnawing the whole time on the question – What next? And for how long will I be able to hang on in this struggle for life that has no chance of success?

On the way I hear the rumor spreading like lightning that war had broken out this morning against Russia. From minute to minute the confusion increases, the price of bread rose from 18 złoty to 30 złoty, potatoes – from 5 to 10 złoty a kilo and are difficult to obtain for money even so. People run, alarmed and frightened, hither and thither. There in front of my eyes I see a shocking sight: A Jew is walking along the street eating a slice of bread. Suddenly another Jew comes along and tries forcibly to take it from him. An argument breaks out between them and in the midst of grappling they both end up eating the bread together; and here are two children rolling on the ground searching for the crumbs and swallowing them. Depressed by the sight I arrive home and spoke to my wife about what I had seen. She comforts me and says: "We'll find a way out of our rickety situation, try to find a better job."

How can I find a better job – I ask her – at the same time that the Germans don't let us go outside the ghetto? And while I am talking I have a sudden idea and I say to her in a decisive tone: "Tuvia, We'll take the children and go to your sister in Miechów!" Hearing that she looks at me angrily and says with finality: "Have you gone crazy Pesach? You seem to have forgotten – Jews that are found outside the ghetto are shot on sight!"

When I saw couldn't persuade her I told her resolutely that if she refuses to go I'll go alone, with the children. Then she began to insist: "Pesach! Think of what you're doing to us; they'll kill us like dogs." – "In any case death awaits us from all sides," I said to her – "and we have to take a chance in order to survive." I added that I would prefer to die from a bullet rather than a slow death from starvation, and in the end she agreed to come.

I had a cousin in Warsaw – Melach Rosenberg – who, like me, also worked in the printing trade, who managed to join a smuggling ring. They had casualties every day but he had developed a special sense to perceive danger before it arrived and survived every situation unscathed until he became known as "the 'King' of Smugglers". I asked him to arrange our escape to Miechów for me, my wife and children, with his Aryan friends.

He tried to dissuade me from what was indeed a perilous undertaking and also very expensive in bribes demanded by the smugglers. When he saw that I wasn't deterred we agreed that we would all meet at a certain place the following day at five o'clock ready for the journey but entirely without baggage. We were scheduled to travel by train at 6 o'clock, travelling in complete darkness to avoid attacks from the air.

I went home and sent for my brother–in–law, Yossel Groman to hear his opinion. We decided that he and my sister–in–law, Hanna, will take our apartment and their son, Meir would come with us to Miechów.

We didn't sleep a wink all night; I lay awake in bed and watched as my wife went from room to room, touching and fondling all the articles, talking to them as if they were living beings that she was seeing for the last time, beloved treasures that we had used all our lives. Thus she parted from our furniture and clothes, bed linen and kitchen–utensils. In the morning we parted from our friends and acquaintances. When I parted from my good friend Motel Bornstein he said: "Pesach! I am amazed at your courage and convinced that you will all arrive safely."

[Page 202]

At exactly 5 o'clock we arrived at the meeting–place where my cousin Melach was already waiting. At a quarter to six the signal came from the Aryan side and we began to cross over. At first they took us through a bombed–out house on Sienna Street, from there we arrived at a hidden tunnel where we were met by 4 scary–looking but strong Christian men who led us through a cellar and out on to the Aryan side in Złota Street.

We continued on the street in the direction of the railroad station with two of the men in front of us and two behind, hearing from passers–by whispers of: "Jews walking." But no one harmed us or interfered with us because of our escorts. At the entrance to the main rail station another of the gang's men came to us and gave us five rail tickets with four platform tickets for our escorts – and disappeared.

The moment we entered the railroad–car – we began to move and we were on our way. During the ride none of us spoke a word. We prayed anxiously that it would get dark quickly so that no one – G–d forbid – could identify us. Very slowly it began to get dark and when we arrived in Radom we were wrapped in complete darkness. We travelled the whole night and with dawn arrived at Miechów.

Miechów

We get off the train and I glance round the station and can see that it is small and being cautious we walk along the path at the side rather than along the platform until we reach the road.

Around us an eerie silence, no one to see only the tweeting of birds can be heard and the fresh scented air stops the breath; my impression is as if we have been confronted with another world; a world without locked gates and corpses lying in the streets. We continue along the street and the town appearing in front of us, until we reach the home of my sister–in–law at Number One, Ratzlewiczke Street. As we crossed the threshold of the house joy and happiness burst forth; everyone jumped from their beds and came downstairs and began to clean, cook and bake for Shabbat as if there were no war going on in the world.

My daughter, Malka, asked me: "Daddy! Are they getting ready for a wedding here?" My sister–in–law didn't join in the laughter together with everyone and I wasn't at all certain she was entirely happy about us coming. (Later she complained about their extreme poverty and I reassured her and promised her that our stay with her would be at no cost to her and entirely at my expense).

After that pleasant greeting I went out for a stroll to get to know the place. I stood somewhat stunned with wonderment at the scene before my eyes. Jews are busy buying and selling and bartering with the farmers. Buying butter, cheese, eggs chickens and even fish for Shabbat as if the Germans didn't exist in the world.

From the market square I walk to the Jüdenrat, to my nephew Shlomo, who works there as a clerk in the Labor Department and ask him to find me a job as a replacement for someone who doesn't want to work. He tries to dissuade me but sees that I am determined and gives me a replacement authorization for someone called Posluszny – in the City Park, where Jews were working preparing for a swimming pool for the Germans using forced labor. After a long search I found the park and next to the entrance was a large notice: “Jews and dogs not allowed.” I am impressed by the beauty of the park, by its lakes and the deer enclosures. From a distance I can see our brethren the Children of Israel working. As I draw closer I hear them whispering: “Hey, Yehudi! It's good here.” A swarthy–skinned man comes striding towards me and introduces himself as the group–leader, Tscharwonogoda(?). I present him with my work–pass from Poslushny and he assigns me to my place among the rest of the Jews. In the blink of an eye I am surrounded by Jews sticking out their hands to shake mine and welcome me asking: “Where are you from?” “I'm from Warsaw; I'm Yossel Bornstein's brother–in–law,” I reply. They treat me as if we were all of one family and ask me to tell them about myself. I describe at length the terrible destruction of Jewish life taking place in Warsaw. They listen silently in sadness but were unable to believe me and considered it an exaggeration.

[Page 203]

I walk to lunch accompanied by the team–leader, the swarthy seminary student. He tries to urge me not to return to work in the afternoon but to rest from the fatigue of travelling. Back at home my sister–in–law begins to prepare lunch. She lays the table and places a plate of soup with pasta in front of me that awakens my appetite while I push it to one side and state: “I don't want to be a burden to you.”

My sister–in–law begins to cry and says “In this gloomy war we have lost the image of humanity and the fear of hunger overshadows our opinion and be sure – if you don't eat it I'll kill myself! I sat down and ate the meal and afterwards lay down to rest and immediately fell asleep.

In my sleep I had a dream: I am in a cemetery digging graves. All around me are piles of dead bodies for burial I am the only one here and I can't do all the work. I feel that I am using the last of my strength while there are still a lot of corpses. Suddenly I stop and throw away the shovel and start to walk round the cemetery wall looking for a way of escape. But I can't find one. While I am still standing there disappointed an idea blossoms in my mind. I start to pull out the tombstones, drag them along and build steps with them up the wall until I get to the top, jump down to the other side and fall...and fall...until I wake up covered in perspiration.

The dream had a great influence on my future life even at moments of crisis, and was a source of encouragement.

As payment for my work as a replacement I received 10 złotys a day. After my bitter experience in Warsaw I began to feel out and investigate whether Jews are sent for labor and paid in foodstuffs and I discovered that in Miechów there was a cooperative run by agriculturalists that was supplying to the Germans in the county various foodstuffs at a fixed quota – items such as cereal, wheat, barley, oats, potatoes, eggs and even honey. In return, the farmers received from the Germans sugar and hard liquor. Imagine to yourselves my amazement when I heard that the Jewish men didn't want to work there. A Jew who received a work–authorization to work in the cooperative – saw only a black world in front of him. According to his perception the work there was too hard – carrying heavy sacks with no opportunity to rest and chat during work. From Jews like that I demanded double pay. I soon became known the king–pin, that it was possible to rely on me to complete the work efficiently. I exploited the opportunity and brought to my sister–in–law's home sacks of potatoes, coal, flour and even liquors.

Thus I wrote to my sister–in–law in Warsaw:

"To my dear Sister–in–law, Hanna!

Forgive me for waiting so long to write to you. I knew you would be anxious and curious but I wanted to wait a while here in order to tell you everything.

[Page 204]

First of all, know that Miechów is a virtual Paradise! Even better than that for a Jew that only recently came from the nearby Warsaw ghetto. Food! While hundreds and thousands die of starvation food here is all over the place; A kilogram of bread can be bought for three Złotys and a sack of potatoes for 40 Złotys.

I am sending you two small parcels to two different addresses; otherwise the post–office will refuse to accept them. As soon as I hear from you that they have arrived – I'll continue to send them every week. In addition I need to tell you that Malk'eleh is learning together with the neighbor's daughters and can already read and write a bit. Avigdor is also growing, learned to smoke cigarettes and plays cards with his friends."

She replied:

"Dear Brother–in–law,

I have received your letter and thank you for the food parcels that arrived safely. You have no idea how valuable they are for us; without them we would die of hunger together with my child so I wish that you live forever. For now, my dear brother–in–law I have to describe the destruction of my family. My brother–in–law, Hanoch with his wife and children all died of hunger, the whole house is destroyed, Yutke's Avigdor also died. My husband and brother–in–law, Yossel were sent for forced labor to Treblinka and I know news about them. The only comfort and consolation I have is that you at least are alive and are not suffering from hunger. When I read Malk'eleh's handwriting tears of happiness came to my eyes..."

In the Miechów community my "fame" grew. When there was a need for a hard worker in one of the store–houses, the store men would come to the community and look for the "Warsaw–man". And look what happened: on one occasion the Works Department manager, Shmuel Kleiner, appeared at my house and asked for my help. "The work in Warshawski's flour–mill is very hard," he said, "and every day the workers run away. As a result I received a warning from the County Governorship that if there should be another incident he would send half the town to Płaszów camp. I urge you to organize a group of six strong men to work as a team for as long as is necessary to supply the necessary products and for this the Jüdenrat will pay you well."

That same evening I scoured the town and found five good workers for the team: 3 wagon–masters, two horse–thieves and I was the sixth. I convinced them it was good deal: 1) we will get good money from the Jüdenrat. 2) Every day we can smuggle a little produce and if the store–man catches us we'll include him as a partner – and that's how it was. We began working energetically and by noon we had managed to sack, weigh and dispatch to the railroad wagons 40 tons of wheat. The store–man was satisfied with our work and said: "You certainly are well–suited to this work."

That same day we also managed to smuggle out part of the produce but the store–man caught us. We tried to convince him that we didn't earn a fair wage for the hard work we perform and that heavy workers need to eat. He replied: "I will try to get the management to give you the same pay as the Christians – 4 złotys and a loaf of bread each day." "Do you think we can survive on those wages doing this hard work," we asked. "It's hard for me on my wages as well, but I manage," he replied.

[Page 205]

In the end he became convinced and agreed to my suggestion – to sell for him the extra produce he put aside from the farmers' produce.

Immediately on the following day, when we transferred the wheat to the railroad, we transferred a wagon with 18 tons of wheat from Ruszecki's flour–mill and sold it for hard cash. Thus I became a businessman in Miechów, although that operation ended badly because of an informer. The Police knew of the smuggling and from time–to–time confiscated the goods and distribute them among their colleagues for money.

Not long after a flood of edicts descended upon the Jews of Miechów, one after the other: Jews are forbidden to live outside the ghetto, whoever wants to go to the Aryan side of the town must possess a special pass and anyone found without the document would be shot on the spot.

The local police were removed and in their place a new police force was brought in all of them wickedly evil and bad. One of them demonstrated unprecedented sadistic cruelty. Not a day passed without victims falling prey to his brutality. He was a butcher by trade and boasted that it was easier to hang a Jew than to slaughter a pig.

On hearing that the "Pig–butcher" was in the ghetto the Jews hid themselves away in panic. Even I was caught up in the situation: the house in which I lived with my sister–in–law in Ratzlewiczke Street was outside the ghetto. After much trouble and influence my sister–in–law managed somehow to get an apartment inside the ghetto and we all moved there.

After all the Jews had crowded themselves into the already small confined area of the ghetto the authorities suddenly became aware that there were too many Jews in Miechów. Then the troubles really began. The Germans, with the help of the Jüdenrat began organizing transports: the younger people to the Płaszów concentration camp, the old and the children to Działoszyce. Thus the Jewish population of Miechów was reduced by half.

Winter passed and spring arrived and with it the festival of the Exodus from Egypt – Passover. But how feeble the sufferings of those days seem compared with the horrors caused us by today's "Pharaoh" – Hitler.

In spite of that every Jew in Miechów prepared himself for the festival: matzos, fish, meat and even raisin–wine for the four glasses. In that respect I was a little remiss – I was so busy on the Eve of Passover that I forgot to bring home some meat. On the other hand I remembered to take two parcels of food to the mail to send to my sister–in–law Hanna in Warsaw but to my real sorrow I was forced to take them home with me because they told me that according to a new regulation it was forbidden to send parcels. I arrived home broken–hearted and sent a letter to Hanna.

> Dear Sister–in–law,
>
> My only consolation is that I left you my apartment with all its contents and I grant you the right to sell them. Do you hear me, Hanna? Don't have any regrets about anything; if we survive and come through this alive we'll buy everything we need – and if not, then we won't need anything.
>
> We hope you are well and send you and your child kisses –
>
> All the family in Miechów.
>
> Dear Brother–in–law,
>
> Don't apologize about the parcels of food; I still have plenty in reserve that in any case I will not be using. You should know, the Warsaw ghetto is being liquidated step–by–step and these are the last days of my life. They are already eliminating Nowolipie Street and every minute I expect to be sent to Treblinka. Perhaps it is better this way rather than the torture of helplessness – have done with it! Do you hear me Pesach? This is my last letter to you! Be healthy and live forever.
>
> Yours,
>
> Hanna.

[Page 206]

With the reading of that letter, we became very melancholy, crying in sadness and torment.

That same day towards evening I received from Warsaw one more letter – from an acquaintance, my friend Motel Bornstein: "My beloved friend Pesach! The beginning of the end of the destruction we expected is here; we are now face–to–face with the reality. The Warsaw ghetto is being liquidated. The Jews of Warsaw have at last rid themselves of all the illusions they cherished concerning their fate whose only aim is the destruction of Judaism. That awareness has caused a certain solidarity among some of the remaining Jewish refugees to formulate a definite plan and who are determined to go down fighting and die as martyrs: in other words a rebellion against the Nazi beasts; if we are to die then let it be with honor.

With that in view a fighting organization has been formed in which are quite a few people from our "Union of Printing-house Workers" with Lazar Sklar as Chairman. I advise you all in Miechów to do the same. It is possible that at the moment you can't because the Jews there have not yet reached the same stage of awareness. Other news is that Czerniaków lost his mind.

One fine day we received the information from a contact outside the ghetto what the German murderers were planning to do to the Jews of Warsaw. We decided to sabotage their plans. When Czerniaków returned from the Gestapo to the Jüdenrat offices three of us, armed with pistols walked into his office. We locked the door and drew our pistols and told him: "We know you have just returned from the Gestapo and that you received orders to send ten-thousand Jews to the Umschlagplatz [1] every day for extermination in Treblinka.

We are here to tell you and warn you: either you refuse to carry out their orders or we will shoot you ourselves, here and now. After thinking for a few moments he asked for time until tomorrow to think about it. His answer was clear!!! The following day the information was relayed to us that he had committed suicide. In connection with the death of Czerniaków certain elements wanted to turn him into a national hero but we know that Czerniaków and heroism are two diametrically opposed concepts. Yes, he was a hero compared to those Jews who went like sheep to the slaughter but he was a collaborator and faithful servant of the Germans.

It is possible that in his last moments he became aware of his bitter mistake and perhaps understood, although too late, that after fulfilling the orders his fate would be the same as that of his fellow-Jews."

We received news in Miechów that the town of Słomniki was being liquidated. The rumor hit us like a thunder-clap on a clear day. In the wink of an eye the information flashed across the Jews in the ghetto and a state of mourning descended on every house because nearly everyone had family there. All of a sudden a panic-ridden Jew who had escaped from there by a miracle came running with more news: They want to evacuate three-quarters of the Słomniki Jews leaving just a quarter of them there temporarily. All those destined for removal have been closed inside the synagogue and they have already been shut up there for two days with no food. Today they are being evacuated. While I am still standing there listening, Kleiner from the Jüdenrat came and asked me to help him unload some furniture. We went to the warehouse and immediately began working. We unloaded from the truck good furniture belonging to a rich family from Słomniki. Among the items that we unloaded was a bag of phylacteries with the name of an honoured resident of the town embroidered on the bag.

My heart ached carrying the belongings of the victims, as if I carried a double weight, a weight drenched in the blood and tears of the murdered Jewish people! When I returned home after this sad work I see that I am in the ghetto surrounded by Jews and one of them is talking: "A girl came to me today, the daughter of a relative in Kraków. She managed to escape from the camp at Belzhetz and she told me that there is a gigantic oven there and they are burning alive all the Jews who are brought there; every day trains are arriving full of Jews and the same day they are incinerated."

On hearing this story the crowd got angry and began shouting at the speaker: "What are you coming with these fabrications? You believe them? You rely on the stories of this stupid girl? It's true that the Germans are cruel – but that they would never do, they would just simply send the Jews to Russia. Go home and stop telling 'fairy stories' – scare–monger!"

[Page 207]

I stood there stunned beyond belief at the reaction of the Jews and their insistence on ignoring the sad reality. My friends take me aside and ask my opinion. I explain to them that to my sorrow the story is true and instead of deceiving ourselves we must arm ourselves as best we can and at the appropriate moment resist and not walk like sheep to the slaughter.

A few friends hurriedly left as soon as I finished talking and those who remained said: "Pesach – it's 'healthier' not to talk like that – the Jüdenrat has spies everywhere. If these ideas get to the Gestapo – we're finished, liquidated." "Aren't we done for in any case?" I asked. There was no reply.

The Jews have already been evacuated from all the surrounding counties around Miechów. Now it was the turn of Miechów. A mood and atmosphere of depression spreads throughout the ghetto. The impression arises that everyone wants to escape but doesn't know how.

Broken–hearted and depressed I leave town in order to clear my mind and try find a life–saving plan for myself. I am careless of the death awaiting me on every side and stroll through the fields. On either side of my path, in the glaring sun stand the sheaves of golden wheat. There is a good harvest this year! But we, the Jews, have no right to live. Suddenly I stop in the middle of the field with a heavy aching heart, my eyes streaming tears down my face and I raise my voice: I shout! To the sheaves of wheat, to the fields, the earth, heavens to all creation! Why??? Why is the world silent? – As if nothing is happening, I sit tired, weary on the log of a hewn tree and try to find a way out of the tangle web for me, my wife and child. I am unable to find a solution. All the routes are blocked and enemies ambush us everywhere.

No way is open to me other than to hide in the attic in the house on Ratzlewiczke Street where we lived before the ghetto was forced on us. I knew it was no solution but when a man is drowning he will grasp at any straw in order to save himself.

(Translated from the Yiddish by Moshe Spiegel).

Translator's Footnote

1. The central square from whence "Transports" to the various extermination centers departed.

Our Family in Miechów

by Eliezer Dresner

Translated by Selwyn Rose

During the summer months of 1939, the citizens of Poland lived under the mistaken illusion that in the end war will be prevented. The development of events in Europe from the entry of Hitler into the Saar region until the Munich Agreement only strengthened the illusion. No one could imagine that Hitler would dare to challenge the Western Powers who had signed a defense treaty with Poland, but above all – that Poland's fate would be sealed within a matter of days.

The rapid collapse of the State stunned and depressed everyone. Before we had a chance to recover from the confusion there came the information of the invasion of eastern Poland by the Soviet Army. A short period later and we, the Jewish population of Miechów felt the full force of suffering and torture throughout our entire beings – body and soul. Our family was a typical Jewish family in Miechów. My father, Pinchas Ben Eliezer Dresner, was a G–d–fearing Jew and businessman of respect and standing in the town. He had been a fervent Zionist for many years, to which he remained faithful both in his relationships with the town and also in his dealings in larger cities.

[Page 208]

Our family tree included extensive branches and was well– and deeply–rooted in the life of the town. I remember my grandfather, Elimelech and the four brothers of my father (Z"L) – Herschel, Mordecai, Meir and Bezalel and his two sisters – Hanna and Baltshe.

My father's main businesses, from which he basically subsisted, were a storehouse for the sale of coal and various wood–products and from this he supported his family honorably. The measure of his loyalty to Zionist ideals can be measured by the fact that already in 1936 he travelled to Palestine to discover first–hand what was going on there. Already at that time – without knowing what awaited him in the future – he began planning the immigration of his family to Palestine but the Second World War put an end to all his plans.

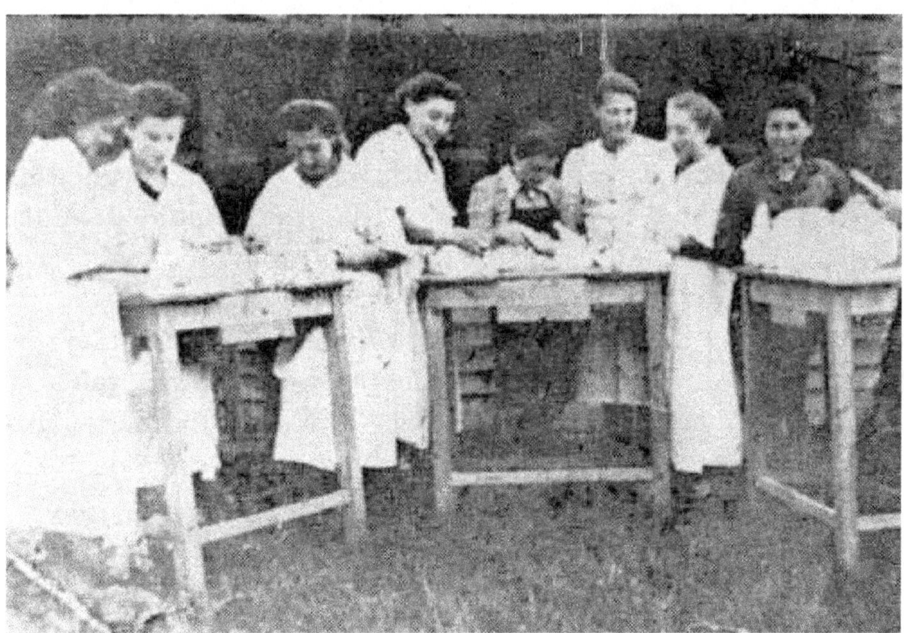

Płaszów camp

My sister, Sela (Z"L) and I were my parents' only children. I learned Hebrew, Torah and Judaism at the "Yavneh" school. They were beautiful days full of a child's dreams and when I recall them hot tears well–up in my eyes.

With the outbreak of World War Two Our situation was no different from others. When the first "Selektsia" was carried out we were included. My parents went to the local "Jüdenrat" and asked not to be separated. But to our sorrow their request was not granted and the first attempt to separate us ended with us escaping and hiding with Christians in the nearby villages.

Day followed day. The "chosen" among the Jews of Miechów were already gathered together waiting for the "transport" but were still held in town. When the time arranged for their evacuation passed, we returned to Miechów and continued to live in a difficult atmosphere of fear of the future.

We later travelled to Kraków where a large group of Miechów Jews were living and working. We were interested in intermingling with them. Our thought was quite simply that whatever happens to those Jews will happen to us as well. That – and more: it was very likely that as long as they kept working under forced–labor their chances were that much better than the others.

[Page 209]

After a short while we were separated: my father and I remained in town while my mother and sister were transferred to the vicinity of the local airfield. After some time we were all together in Jarosławska, near BłaÅ¼owa. It was a large work–camp, created after the liquidation of the Kraków ghetto. We were one of the very few families in that camp that had remained united. In the midst of the days of fear and terror the fact of us remaining together was some sort of consolation and we thought – for no good reason – that we would remain together in the future. But here also the cruel hand of fate reached out and separated us without mercy and pity. My sister was taken from our mother and sent somewhere, my mother also was sent to another place while my father and I remained together. For us the hardest days of the Holocaust began in earnest. Our fate included being transferred from place to place endlessly, staying at fifteen different concentration and labor camps and to experience all the tortures and horrors until I arrived, together with my father at Bergen–Belsen, that same death–camp where thousands of our people were tortured and exterminated and among them the last of our own flesh and blood. Words have not been invented to describe the dreadful scenes that were played out before my eyes in that awful place.

I stayed in the camp with my father (Z"L) for a long time; again, we had no doubts that our fate was sealed and that we would perish during one or other of the "Aktsias". We were sure of it because virtually every evening we saw the skies would turn red with the reflection of the fires from the chimneys of the crematoria.

Everyone who could possibly hold on with what little strength he still had would do so, but in my father's case it was not to be. My personal tragedy attained a new dimension when just 5 days before the liberation of the camp my father returned his soul to his Creator. On the horizon we actually saw the parachutes of the first British forces landing in the vicinity. My father, who was even then utterly exhausted, asked me to fetch him a drink of water. I ran to the "Blockältester" [1] and asked him if I could get some water to save my father and his rough answer was: "He's already dead and in another hour it will be your turn."

When I returned to my father in our own hut I found him without any sign of life. He was taken to a huge pile of human skeleton–like bodies and thrown together with them like an empty vessel having no value. Thus my father's life came to an end – 5 days before the camp of Bergen–Belsen was liberated.

My sister Sela, who was then a young 14–year old girl, breathed her last one month before the end of the war in a concentration camp near Leipzig.

From my entire family I was the only one who survived together with my mother Yocheved – May she be spared for a long life – who was sent to different camps the last of which was Theresienstadt. In that camp she underwent indescribable horrors and there she stayed until the liberation.

The images of these dear ones stand before my eyes to this day and through the fog of the Holocaust period project sharply before my eyes the town of Miechów, the town of my childhood. Each and every one of its streets, every character whom I knew is etched on my memory and deep in my heart and was a part of me. And my pain is increased seven–fold when I recall that all that what was – is no more.

Translator's Footnote

1. Barracks "overseer"

[Page 210]

The Transport

by Natan Rosenkrantz

Translated by Selwyn Rose

In 1942, two weeks before Rosh Hashanah, the men of the SS surrounded our ghetto Friday morning. The order was given to go outside and form into ranks of five. It was 9 o'clock. Everything that had been prepared for Shabbat was left behind us. It all seemed like a nightmare that would disappear when we awoke. We arranged ourselves as ordered and were made to march holding hands. We were dumfounded and didn't know how to cope or react. We arrived at the railroad station. We waited throughout the whole day until evening. It was an extremely hot day – as if cruel fate had decreed it so to trouble us. They forbad us to move from the place and of course there was no food or water to be had.

The previous day the Jews from Działoszyce had been held there and we had supplied them with food and water. We had not dreamed to ourselves that the following day it would be our turn. In the evening there was a "Selektsia". The younger ones – to one train and the older ones to a second, the last with my family among them were sent to Majdanek from whence they never returned.

I, my brother–in–law and nephew Moshe were taken by the work–train to Prokoczyn. I was the only one who survived.

The Jarosławska Camp 1942

Two young women were hanged; I couldn't stand any more. I waited for the opportunity to escape and in 1943 I kept fleeing from camp to camp until I found myself in Grünberg Camp in Germany. From there I was transferred to Kittlitztreben, (near Berlin) and from there I escaped to the forests. I learned to understand that during the years that I was pursued and that I must escape – always escape, escape. To where, I knew not. The aim was to stay alive. And that seemed to me to be the only way to stay alive – and so it was.

Miechów 1939–1943

by Yitzhak Weinreb

Translated by Selwyn Rose

Already on the first day of the Nazi conquest of Miechów we felt the presence of the of the oppressor's arm. They assembled all the male Jews in town, in a church. Fear and tension spread through the town but after a few days all were released.

Not long after the Nazis created the "Jüdenrat" which was responsible for supplying labourers for different types of forced arduous labor such as snow–clearing in winter, caring for the German toilets, road–works and so on. Young men were also sent to work in other counties like Dębica.

During that same period there was an outbreak of Typhus that felled many of the Jewish population of town. In 1941, after the outbreak of hostilities against Russia the Jews were dispossessed of their homes and ordered to confine themselves to the ghetto under awful conditions of overcrowding. A wall was built surrounding the ghetto and the Jews were forbidden to cross it. The situation worsened more and more and the enclosed Jews had great difficulties in obtaining adequate supplies of food.

[Page 211]

That same winter the first Jewish victim fell – a tailor who was senselessly charged of a crime devoid of all reason: hiding a fur in his home after the Nazis had issued an edict ordering all furs to be surrendered to the authorities.

The bitter day arrived. It was the day in which all the elderly of the ghetto were ordered to pack their few belongings and report for evacuation from the town of Miechów and from all the local area. I remember my grandfather Michael Skowron who shouted out with courage while being led from the ghetto: "Down with Hitler!" All the Jews of Miechów were taken to Słomniki where they were cruelly exterminated.

A few days later the ghetto came to an end. The ghetto of Miechów was surrounded by the Nazis and their aides. All the Jews were ordered out of their homes onto the street and were marched to a field near to the railroad station…

This was the so–called "Aussiedlung" [1] and here I want to mention Shlomo Bornstein, among the finest young men of the town who tried to resist the evacuation with all his strength and refused to go. He was shot to death in his home.

When the Jews arrived at the railroad station they found they were not alone. There were many Jews concentrated there from all over the local area. (Only the previous day the residents of Miechów did all they could to supply food and water to those who had been brought there from the surroundings!).

Men who were fit for work were separated from their women and children, bitter cries and wailing split the air. But even in that tragic moment the Jews of Miechów had no idea and could not for a moment imagine just what was to befall them. They fed them on stories about evacuation to the east and promises of life and work.

About fifty Jewish men were left behind, by the Nazis, in Miechów, for various tasks and also as a trap for those Jews who had somehow managed to hide and evade the evacuation, among them my uncle Haim Cziner Laki and his family. Indeed in a very short while about two hundred Jews who had been in hiding close by emerged and joined them and all of them were taken to the Chodów forest near Charsznica and murdered. Here, too, there was an example of valor: during the liquidation one of the Jews (it was said afterwards he was the brother of Yosef Stern from Miechów), attacked one of the Germans and seriously injured him.

A few weeks later, about fifty Jews – women and small children – were murdered in the Jewish cemetery and buried there in a common mass grave by the residual permanent residents of the ghetto.

On 15th January 1943 the ghetto of Miechów was finally liquidated. The Germans, together with their Ukrainian collaborators burst into the ghetto slaughtering everyone they found. About twenty Jews managed to hide and most of them survived. The gentle, noble–souled Ya'acov Kornfeld, a teacher in Miechów, managed to hide for a couple of days but was soon exposed by the Poles to the Germans, who shot him.

It was on the 16th January 1945 and a few days before we had heard the sound of explosions and learned that the Russians had launched a massive attack against the German army. My father, Yehezkiel Weinrib, my uncle Skowron and myself lived in a hideout with a Polish farmer for two years. That night we heard voices, the echo of marching feet, a motor–vehicle, the barking of dogs and a general commotion. We had no idea what was happening. Fear and trembling took hold of us. Perhaps the Germans were again taking vengeance on the village as they had done so often before?

We were tense. Suddenly we heard voices speaking in Russian and it was as if we were dreaming. Had the long–awaited moment arrived? Were we again free? Had the end come to our suffering? We couldn't believe it. My father could no longer wait and wanted to go outside but we restrained him forcibly. Only after the farmer came and told us that it was indeed the Russians who had arrived we left our hiding place for the unknown.

Translator's Footnote

1. "Relocation"

[Page 212]

The War Years 1939-1945

by Arya (Leib) Sosnowski

Translated by Gloria Berkenstat Freund

In September 1939 a panic began in the city with the outcry that the Germans were coming. We began to run without purpose. There was great confusion. No one told another where he was going because they were afraid that the other one would run ahead on the road. I ran with the Fintshe Zalcberg's family, Harsh (Hirsh) Leib Brener, Ahron Brener. Alas, Ahron Brener fell in Zaklikow as a result of the bombs. We went by horse and wagon, but we had not put anything in the wagons. We sent a wounded Harsh Leib back to Miechow and we traveled further. Arriving in Sandomierz, we met Wolf Ber Warszowski and we were happy as it were and we took him into our group. Before Sandomierz we noticed a small light in a house and we left for it, hungry, thirsty and tired. We had money with us, but there was nothing to buy. We asked the old gentile woman if she would give us a glass of tea, to pay for it. Leaving, we met a large caravan of wagons traveling in the opposite direction; a nobleman stood on one of them, shone a reflector into our eyes and asked where we were traveling. We were afraid to speak with him, but we spoke a little bit with him. He advised us not to go further because the bridge to Sandomierz was burning. Therefore, he advised us to go back, avoiding the city and to travel to Zawiszów. The nobleman showed us a map and we traveled back according to it [the map], turning with various back roads and arriving in Zawiszów. On the way we had to buy another horse because the road became more difficult.

A rumor again spread in Zawiszów that the Germans were coming from another direction. It was eight days before Rosh Hashanah. Suddenly, all of the roads were blocked by the German military. We became confused, not knowing where to go. We arrived in Lublin after wandering for a long time.

In Lublin we began to look for a place to lay our tired heads. You can imagine how tired and beaten up we were. We were taken to a certain Szreibman, who owned a brickyard and was also a relative of Avraham Cercaz and as Wolf Ber Warszawski, also a relative of Cercaz, was with us, he took us in.

Arriving in the brickyard we found about 100 people who also had looked for a place of refuge in which to lay their bones. We did not receive any food, nor any water to drink. When we felt faint from not eating, we dug out a few potatoes in the field and from these we nourished ourselves.

[Page 213]

The great rich man, Wolf Ber, received nothing for his money and delighted himself with us with a bit of raw potatoes with a little water.

We sat in this place until erev [the eve of] Rosh Hashanah in the evening in such inhuman conditions. Suddenly we saw that Lublin was on fire from the German bombardments. We again began to run, not knowing where.

I saw that the German ran faster than us because he was motorized.

We ran toward Luboml. The Vistula [River] flows near the shtetl and the gentiles took 1,000 zlotes from us for taking us across by horse and wagon on a raft. We went to a Jew who stood ready to escape on the other side of the river. He gave us something to eat and joined us in our wandering.

At night we finally arrived in Luboml. There we found a wall of Jews because Jews left all of the shtetlekh and villages with the purpose of reaching the Russians.

A heavy rain fell, actually a flood and it was impossible to move from the spot. I asked a small boy to show us a place where we could place the horses. The young boy led us to a shop that was locked and told us that the owners of the shop had escaped. Therefore, "Tear off the lock and take the shop." We arranged the horses in the courtyard and we entered the shop. We lay down on the floor, wet and tired, in our clothing and fell asleep immediately.

Waking up in the morning, we went out into the street and sniffed out what was happening. We noticed a sea of people and all were looking for a way to escape.

We spent several days in Luboml not knowing what awaited us.

On a clear day, we heard that the Germans were entering Luboml; the question arose for everyone, what should we do?

People arrived from Lemberg [Lviv] and told us the sad news from there, that they were dying of hunger and thirst there.

We learned that there was a great rabbi present in the city. We decided to visit him and ask his advice.

We gathered several Jews and went to the rabbi; we found a room full of Jews. We barely reached the rabbi. We said to him that we were not from there and we did not know what to do; should we go to Lemberg or not?

The rabbi answered us with great sorrow and tears in his eyes – the Name be Blessed [God] would help and we would survive the enemy, but he did not directly say where we should go. "The only few words I can tell you – that the city of Luboml has a great privilege and all the Jews located in this shtetl will come through everything in peace." It was night and all of a sudden we heard the bombardment of the nearby area.

[Page 214]

It did not take long for the Germans to enter the city. We lay on the floor until it grew quiet. We immediately heard the noise of the tanks. It became quiet all around. No people were seen in the street. We were afraid to stick our heads outside. An order was given immediately. "Alle raus! Juden raus! [Everyone out! Jews out!] Open the shops! Everyone out to marketplace!" Military vehicles arrived and threw packs of food at us for the hungry masses.

They erected a tall tower and a German climbed it and he gave the following speech:

"Jews! Do not be afraid. We are not murderers. The Russians are coming here in about three days and whoever wants to can go home and everyone can move freely and do what he wants. Whoever wants to remain can do so." There was enough food and there was an uproar. We did not know what to decide. The next day we noticed that preparations were being made to welcome the

Russians. The Germans gave us complete freedom and the ordinary people did not know what to think.

We finally decided to return home. We arrived in Miechow motzei Simkhas Torah [at the conclusion of Simkhas Torah – the holiday commemorating the completion of the yearly reading of the Torah and the start of the reading for the new year] after traveling for a long time and we found everything in better order. We found the wives and children, the entire family at home. Everyone was in his place and they lacked for nothing.

Several days passed and an order arrived that all men should gather in one place. There were two rows of German murderers and we passed through the middle. They asked everyone about their occupation. I said I was a grain trader. He said: "Yes, yes, we need such people." Everyone was sent into the church. We spent the night there. We were freed early the next morning. A Jewish community council with Hirshl Edelist at the head and a few more Jews from Sosnowiec, such as Minc, Aplbaum, and so on, was created a few days later. At the same time, a Jewish militia to help the Judenrat [Jewish council] was created. They began to rule over the few Jews in the city. They looked for new edicts with which to serve the German rulers.

The Germans immediately placed two Jewish haircutters, Feibl Danciger and Adolf Rozenbaum-Tarnowski, in jail under the pretense that they were communists. They were held for several days and then they [the Germans] informed the Judenrat that two dead bodies were in the jail and they should remove them and bury them.

At that moment we felt that a black cloud was moving over Polish Jewry.

They provided new orders every day, that jewelry, furs, bed linens should be brought to the commandant for the German soldiers. In short: our houses began to be emptied slowly and they became very empty.

[Page 215]

On a beautifully clear day, a German named Kozak appeared – a murderer. He entered the house of the blind Sura's son, a tailor, Dovid Chmielowski, and found that he had a small piece of fur. He [Kosak] shot him [Dovid] on the spot. They began to take us to forced labor. The young people were sent to the lotsniska [airfield] to Krakow. We remained in the city at various public works.

With others I was taken by horse and wagon to remove the snow from the train station. When I stood with the whip in my hand – a German approached me and called out: "Why are you standing? You accursed Jew." He slapped me twice and went further. Then I understood plainly and clearly that our lives no longer had any value.

I sold the horse and wagon and thought that I would do nothing from now on and I would be a man equal to everyone.

I was taken to work on the Krakow-Kielce highway, paving the highway outside Slomniki.

The Germans supervised us and the work ended quickly.

I worked for a certain time until the ghetto was created. We left our apartments and we all were squeezed into the narrow ghetto.

We were in the ghetto from 1940 to 1942 in need, hunger, poverty and persecutions.

With an embittered heart and with blood, I write these lines about my bitter fate, which I went through with my dear family – father, mother, sisters, brothers, wife and children. Alas, all died kiddish haShem [in sanctification of God's name – as martyrs]; annihilated and burned in the gas ovens. In 1942 a small number of Jews were living in the city, along with our Rabbi, Reb Henokh Szajnfrucht, may his memory be blessed. It was the only time we came together with him for Minkhah-Maariv [afternoon and evening prayers]. We always heard good promises from him, that God would help, would not forget us. This was a Monday night, when all of the Jews were brought from Ksiaz, and early Tuesday the Jews from Dzialoszyce. Everyone was at the Ridzewski field. The sun burned during the day and at night they froze from the cold. Dear Jews! As much as was possible, we helped them; we brought them food and drinks. This lasted until Thursday. Thursday at night, we were sitting with the rabbi after praying. We were talking about our calamity. It was late, the community dispersed to go home and I remained alone with the rabbi. Suddenly, I heard the rabbi say to me: "Arya, hide me with you because I am not confident that my mind is working well!" I stood amazed: the holy tzadek [righteous man] remained silent and did not say anything more. I noticed a great sadness in his eyes. Suddenly he raised his head and said to me: "I will go with all of the Jews, Arya! You will remain with me in my house." I said "good night" to the rabbi and went home.

[Page 216]

These were his last words. The next day, early Friday at six, the ghetto was surrounded by S.S. men. Everyone had to leave their house; everyone in great haste dragged a small pack not knowing for what. The Jews from Ksiaz,

Dzialoszyce, and Miechow marched with the Rabbi, Reb Henokh, may his memory be a blessing, at the head. The Germans arranged women and children on one side and men on the other side. The picture was cruel and heart-rending. We felt as if everyone was going to a certain death.

Reflections of a Miechow Concentration Camp Survivor during the Commemoration of the Dead during the Days of Awe

Translated by Gloria Berkenstat Freund

It seems absurd that everyone remembers for themselves their closest perished martyrs, such as parents, brothers, sisters, the innocent children. Almost every family all over the world had mourned dozens of their family who perished and were murdered in an inhuman manner by German killers. We need to remember six million souls who perished. It is easy to say six million martyrs, but when we consider the true number, it is almost beyond comprehension. A number larger than we now have residents in the country [possibly Israel].

During the commemoration of the dead, I first see the hundreds of thousands of perished children; the small souls fill the prayer house, then the hundreds of thousands of souls of the young Jews who perished and, finally, the millions of other souls. Despite the fact that they are only souls, they cannot enter the prayer house because of the great crush [of their numbers]. The walls collapse because of the great crush and only an empty spot with six million souls – martyrs – and in my heart remains an emptiness, which it so difficult to bear.

[Page 217]

In the Ghetto and Camps

by Doba Lewin-Abramowicz[1]

Translated by Gloria Berkenstat Freund

The ghetto in Miechow was created in 1940; the ghetto took in the Synagogue Alley from the post office to Krakower Street and all of the side alleys. The crowdedness was great because several families lived in one room! A Jewish militia was created and the German regime organs began to force us, the young and even the old people, to work.

The ghetto existed until 1942. But I left for a brick factory in Podgórze near Krakow. I worked there for half a year. Then I escaped and returned to the Miechow ghetto. The first deportation took place at the beginning of 1942. The Germans sent away 600 Jews to the Bełżec annihilation camp. With the help of a Polish police commissar, our family succeeded in hiding in the old building of the church, where the commissar lived. We, my father, my sister, Genya, and I were there for six to seven days. When we left, Miechow was Juden-rein [cleared of Jews]. Only the Judenrat [German-created Jewish council] and the Jewish militia remained. All of the Jews had been sent to Bełżec.

We were afraid to move around the ghetto. My three sisters and I left the city and went to the Camp Lotniska [airfield location] in Krakow. We worked there under the supervision of the Wehrmacht [unified German forces] and we only had to be obedient. We were there for four to five months. Then the Gestapo removed us from the camp and sent us to Plaszow. This was a more severe forced labor camp. In 1944 the camp was transformed into a katset, concentration camp. My father, Yehiel Shmuel Abramowicz, later came here and worked here until the selection, when the Jews were sent to Auschwitz.

And my sister Rayzl and I later arrived at Auschwitz-Birkenau. We were there approximately nine months and tried to work despite all of the difficulties and illnesses. At the beginning of 1945, we went along with the evacuation and after wandering for a long time, we arrived in Bergen-Belsen, a camp in Germany, where around 50,000 concentration camp inmates were tormented until the English soldiers liberated us on the 15th of April 1945.

Translator's Footnote

1. The name of the author of this article is given as "Doba Lewin-Abramowicz" in Yiddish. In English, it would be "Doba Abramowicz-Lewin."

[Page 218]

Episodes from the Time of War

by Yonah Fridrich, may his memory be blessed

Translated by Gloria Berkenstat Freund

Mrs. Rafalowicz

[She was] a widow for many years, who always lived with her children. Her youngest daughter married Zelik Mulsztajn. Mrs. Rafalowicz was one of the older people who were chosen for deportation by the Juden–Rat [Jewish council] during the first resettlement. Saying goodbye with Zelik Mulsztajn and with her daughter, going down the steps in the first house in the ghetto on the first floor where she lived, I heard her words:

"My dear children. I know that I am going to my death and my only prayer to God is that I will be a redemption for you."

I cried very hard. We did not, in general, know then what the fate of the deported people would be. It was said that a Jewish refuge was being created in the Lublin area, where the Jews would be able to live among only themselves. However, it appeared that Mrs. Rafalowicz was a truly clever woman and foresaw why the Jews were being resettled.

At this opportunity, it is worthwhile to remember something that happened to Zelik Mulsztajn at the Auschwitz camp. God forbid, this should not be taken as a good word for the German murderers, but a fact remains a fact. Zelik Mulsztajn worked with the "transport commando" at Auschwitz and once when unloading a large crate, the crate fell on his jaw and the [bones in the] entire area were broken. The murderers took him to a dentist and he [the dentist] repaired the jaw and placed braces and everything healed after a few months. During the time when the braces were in place, he could not open his mouth, he could not speak and he had to take his nourishment from clear liquids. His closest comrades` created liquid for him.

Zelik Mulsztajn now lives in Australia.

Liba Lawcze

Liba née Lawcze lived with her husband and children in the cellar of the synagogue with many other Jewish families because of the great crowdedness in the ghetto. As revenge because Liba did not want to devote herself to the Jewish ghetto commissar, he [the commissar] came with two German murderers. One of them was known in the shtetl [town] because when a Jew needed to be shot, he did it. He was called "Cossack." All three stood opposite the synagogue and one could observe the Jewish commissar whispering something in the ear of the German murderer and Liba and her husband were immediately led out of the cellar and the murderous Cossack shot them on the spot. Those shot had to remain lying in the middle of the street until evening and all of the Jews in the ghetto had to march past and look at them.

[Page 219]

The Testament of Avraham Sercasz

Avraham Sercasz was one of the founders of the Zionist party in the shtetl and was a true Zionist, a very smart and intelligent man of the older generation. When he was hidden with a Christian with his family in a village, simply in a hole near the latrine, he wrote his testament on toilet paper because he had no other kind; he wrote it and placed the testament in a bottle and sealed it well and threw the bottle into the latrine. In such conditions, Avraham Sercasz did not forget to record a part of his worth to be given to the *Keren Kayemet L'Yisroel* [Jewish National Fund].

After the war, the Christian, with whom the Sercaszes were hidden, found the bottle with the testament when he was cleaning the latrine and gave it to Mrs. Sala Sercasz who now lives in the land [Israel].

Avraham Sercasz perished in a tragic manner. During an experiment in a concentration camp by the German murderers of how long a person could last without food and drink and without light, several hundred Jews were confined in an isolated barracks. They all perished in a frightful death. One wanted to devour another out of hunger and thirst. The screams from the barracks were inhuman and I am sure that in cleaning the barracks after a month's time, an image was seen of what the human imagination cannot conceive.

[Page 223]

Charsznica and Ksiaz

A. Charsznica

(Charsznica, Poland)

50°25' / 19°26'

The Town of Charsznica

by Yisrael Rogovski

Translated by Selwyn Rose

The Railroad Station

Before Charsznica became a place of Jewish settlement, it was a neglected agricultural area with no discernable produce; just a hilly area whose surroundings provided pasture to the farmers for their cattle and sheep.

Transportation was by horse and two–wheeled carriages in the summer and sleighs in the winter. The farmers had no means of transporting their herds' and flocks' produce to commercial centers which were located in coal–mining districts close to the German–Russian border.

The development of industry in the towns of Zaglambia and their surroundings created a demand for agricultural produce in ever increasing amounts and the consequent need for rapid transportation became urgent. The Russian treasury agreed to finance the construction of a railroad between the centers of food–production and the consumers in the south west of the valley.

On a flat plateau in the valley a structure was erected that was to serve as the railroad station and on both sides of it, at a distance of some hundreds of meters, at the lowest areas in the valley, two high stone bridges were built to protect the tracks from the flood waters that flowed down the valley from the mountains in winter. Two tall levees of earth were built on either side of the station and these joined the two bridges together.

The earthworks and construction of the levees on such a scale required the employment of a large labor–force together with the workers and professionals brought in from the larger towns. All this together with the local day–workers constituted a large work–camp needing significant food supplies and clothing. The Jewish traders and peddlers, always on the look–out for new sources of income in the surrounding farms and villages, found in the new railroad station an additional source of income. In time they transferred their homes from the surrounding villages and settled in the areas close to the station.

The railroad station was destined to become the area of settlement and commerce for both the Jewish and Christian villagers from round and about. The Jews became agents and intermediaries as traders in food and agricultural produce and a few of them opened shops there. As time went on personal and friendly relationships developed between the new settlers and the local Polish population from the villages and farms and when work finished on the station a few of the traders made the "town" their permanent home.

[Page 224]

The nearest town was Miechów, about eight kilometers south of Charsznica. In the west and north were Wolbrom and Żarnowica and to the east Kielce – the county seat with the small towns and villages teeming with Jews.

The first permanent settlers round "the station" (also known as "Miechów station" or Miechów–Charsznica), were: Mr. Khamil Wadowice, Mr. Simcha Sztych, Mr. Alter Chudwar(?), Mr. Reuven Chudwar and others. (As was usual among the Jews at that time, in addition to their first name they often added the town they came from).

Charsznica was a small Christian village with few residents; they found their living in the small surrounding farms or as porters and in services. They were daily workers and their homes were dilapidated wooden shacks, their food poor and their water they drew from the wells that they dug with their own hands. The "station" was their gateway to the outside world.

Even the larger traders who, because the nearness of the Austrian border somewhat restricted their activities, began to operate via the "station" at Charsznica. The railroad carried them to industrial areas and factories and the coal– and salt–mines. Goods–trains laden with solid and liquid fuels and industrial materials unloaded there and then loaded–up with agricultural produce. Warehouses and storerooms were built, vast unloading and vast storage areas for coal, salt, farm produce, fuels and timber. Some of the facilities were financed by the authorities and some by private merchants and entrepreneurs – Jewish and Christian. The wholesale trade in fuel and food was undertaken by a few Jews and the rest of the Jews mainly lived from small trading and peddling in the surrounding villages. They would travel by horse–drawn wagon or on foot and their wares consisted of eggs, cheese, butter, chickens, goose–feathers, waxes, hare– and rabbit–skins – all of which they carried in wicker–work baskets. Those among them who were able to acquire a horse and wagon also spread to the local villages and traded in waste metal, wrecked machinery, old clothes and rags and also decorative colored glass items and general haberdashery, to catch the eye of the farmers' wives and daughters. They rose early in the morning, before dawn saying the morning prayers for travelers, sometimes combining the morning and evening "Amidah" prayers together before eating their one hot daily meal prepared by the wives and mothers and waiting for them on their return.

Social life

The "Station" acquired the character of a country village. Additional homes were built, the area was leveled and any furrows or deep crevasses filled. The value of the land increased and several families purchased lots, building homes both of timber and brick and they became house–holders.

On the Shabbos, they would meet for prayer in one of the prayer–houses, dressed in their "Shabbos finery", their children behind them carrying their bags containing their prayer–shawls. The women–folk read their prayer–books or the "Tze'ina Ve–Re'ina"[1], and on festival days they would sit in the "Women's gallery" reading prayers and supplications, dressed modestly, displaying their finest jewelry from their bridal days.

With the increasing economic stability of sections of the Jewish community came a certain but recognizable segregation between the "elite" and the simple folk. The status was determined according to appearances, manners, style of speech and behavior of each individual Jew. The simple folk centered themselves in the Study–House of Rabbi Reuven Ziegler (Z"L) while the "elite" in the Study House of Rabbi Micha'el Zukerman (Z"L). There were also a few established "Steibls": that of Rabbi Mordecai Greitzer, of Rabbi Reuven Kleiner and sometimes, when the pride of one of the "elite's" congregants was hurt, he and his supporters would congregate in his own house until "peace" was restored. Those who had reached the age of "common sense" and understanding claimed for themselves special attention.

[Page 225]

All the other "decent" people – community leaders and others, claimed for themselves the status of a scholar or noble.

The differences in status caused a stir in the community sometimes reaching serious proportions that required the intervention of the town Rabbi, Rabbi Hanoch Scheinfrucht and the ritual slaughterer Rabbi Yisrael Lazer, also a community preacher.

The town of Miechów, whose excellent location was marred because the railroad track by–passed the immediate vicinity, was compensated by the paving of a roadway which joined it to the "station" and later by a small–gauge railway that was routed via Charsznica, Miechów and Działoszyce. These two arteries constituted supply routes that eased the transportation of goods to the wholesalers, industrial workers and artisans from the "station" Miechów. The Miechów residents sold the goods to the retailers of Charsznica, Ksiaz, Działoszyce, Skalmierzyce and Słomniki which was located close to Kraków whose border with Austria was closed. These towns contained small communities of Jewish residents and vibrant Jewish life flourished there.

For many years the cultural influence of Charsznica prvaded the route of the railroad.

During the First World War

With the outbreak of the First World War a period of great economic and social change began. Many centers of Jewish settlement throughout Eastern Europe became killing–fields for the various armies of Nikolai II, Kaiser Wilhelm II of Germany and Franz–Joseph of the Austro–Hungarian Empire, whose targets were Warsaw and Moscow.

Fear and panic gripped the population of Poland. The industrial towns of Zaglambia remained cut off on the western side where, behind the front was Wolbrom where bloody battles were taking place. Trade and workshops came to a standstill, the warehouses emptied. It was impossible to obtain industrial materials and fuel – a great proportion of which was pilfered by residents who profited by the situation. Jewish war refugees began arriving in Charsznica seeking refuge and food.

All roads were full of an unceasing flow of military traffic of the Reserve Army carting injured from the front and the wounded were transferred to hospital via the railroad to the west, nonstop night and day.

The motto of the Russian Army of Defense was "Beat the Jews and Save the Homeland" – and it inspired a terror among the Jews of Charsznica that froze the blood in their veins. They beat, robbed and snatched whatever came to hand. When they had finished pillaging the shops to the last item of value the Cossacks turned their attention to the homes of the residents. They conducted searches in cupboards, drawers and beds, filling their pockets with watches, rings, religious items – everything that seemed of value that they could lay their hands on. And when they left they even stripped the door–jambs of the Mezzuzot. With the disappearance of the Cossack riding his horse, the people breathed a sigh of relief and thanked G–d on high that at least they had not been physically harmed. The Cossacks hurried to turn their booty in to cash. The Christian population grasped the "goodies" from the Cossacks and the Jews redeemed their property at double and triple the price lest the sacred and religious articles fall into the hands of the "uncircumcised" and become defiled.

The Jews of Charsznica shut themselves up in their homes and refused to take to the streets. When the situation of food supply within the home worsened only a few dared to take their lives in their hands and venture to a near–by village for essential supplies. Cossacks ambushed them taking everything they had sending them on their way after horse–whipping them on their backs.

[Page 226]

There were Jews who were caught and accused of treason and cooperating with the enemy and the evidence – telephone wires strung between the poles along the boundaries of their courtyards, after the wooden fences had been destroyed and the wood taken by the army to use as fuel for their field–kitchens.

During these days of madness the teaching of Torah to the little children did not stop. They were collected together in the small room of Rabbi Yitzhak Yoel the teacher who awoke envy in the hearts of the needy women because his work was done without danger to his life, even though he had not received any salary since the outbreak of the war – many weeks; they were appeased only because one night a rifle bullet came through the door into the laundry–tub while the Rabbi's wife was working there. After that terrifying night the children dispersed and the lessons stopped.

The Cossacks disappeared over the horizon but the Wolbrom Front continued to claim victims. The army continued to stream towards the front.

All the roads were clogged: the infantry and cavalry, artillery and horse–drawn wagons loaded down with military gear. The movement continued night and day. Suddenly, as if by a magic wand, the whole thing went into reverse, the army turned round and headed east. The sound of artillery ceased, only occasionally in the far distance the sound of explosions was heard. The reddened skies cleared and even the nights became less threatening to the residents' hearts. The roads and courtyards emptied of Russian soldiers who ran for their lives and silence reigned over all. The last train made its way eastwards with the few injured that had managed to find their way to the station; the others were abandoned to die of thirst and hunger, where they lay on the battle–fields, the corpses became food for the crows and other predators.

Since Friday morning a deathly silence spread over the town and the smell of gunpowder was in the air. The people who lived close to the railroad and those whose apartments were built of timber left their homes and sought shelter between stone walls. Mr. Teiwel the baker lived in the house of Mr. Pan Leiman, It is a two–storied, brick–built house with a cellar and the cellar was now packed with frightened mothers with their children. Suddenly an enormous explosion split the air...

The big stone bridge on the east of town had been blown skywards and all the bricks cascaded back down onto its foundations and made a hill of rubble.

With the Shabbos Eve Kiddush approaching the families sat around their dining–room tables over a loaf of dry bread, waiting for what will happen next; thus passed Shabbos with that question hanging on everyone's lips. Early Sunday morning the approaches to Charsznica became choked with the soldiers of the invading army. They greeted the people with a friendly "Good morning."

The battles moved eastwards and Congress Poland fell into the hands of the Austrian army. The Jewish population, Yiddish–speaking, understood the language of the German–speaking conquerors. Life became routine quite quickly. Industrious and enterprising women under financial stress turned their living–rooms into tea–salons. Soldiers, residents and army–employees paid well for the cakes and pastries and donuts supplied together with the tea and rum. The youngsters busied themselves on the streets selling cigarettes that they had made themselves and the men–folk sold farm produce that they had brought in from the surrounding farms and villages.

On the heels of the invading army came an unending stream of smugglers making their way to Charsznica from the hungry towns and villages of Zaglambia. They bought up all the available food supplies that they could get their hands on, out of sight of the Austrian police force. The Austrian Koruna became the trading conversion currency which the farmers gladly accepted and in which they had confidence. Silos for storage were erected and filled and food–trafficking flourished. The farmers' pockets bulged with Korunas which eventually found their way to the pockets of the traders in Charsznica.

[Page 227]

A rumor spread among the towns and villages of Zaglambia that "there were food supplies in Charsznica" and the local landscape began to fill with new faces and the town found itself hard–pressed accommodating the growing population.

During those days a family of four arrived: Rabbi Baruch, whose appearance alone inspired confidence, his wife and two sons. The children of Charsznica had remained without Torah instruction from a teacher. Rabbi Yitzhak Yoel, their teacher, since the crust of bread – so to speak – had been snatched from his mouth, opened a small tea–salon and supplemented his income with food–trafficking, which damaged in the minds of the fastidious – his reputation – and prevented him from retrieving his place as the teacher. The men also stopped holding public prayers during this period and the women–folk were no longer to be seen in the women's gallery, nor were the sounds of study and dissertation heard in the "Beit Ha–Midrash".

The "Staff of Office" of teacher passed to the hands of Rabbi Baruch; the women's gallery was used as a residence for the family and a classroom for tens of children at one and the same time. The large hall, in the past the study room of the men was given to his son, Moshe, a most pleasantly mannered man, well–experienced in the ways of life, who spread his spiritual personality over the older boys. In addition to Torah studies time was also set aside for "external" (secular) studies, Rabbi Baruch taught them to write in Yiddish using black clay tablets and red markers. When necessary the slate could easily be wiped clean and re–used. The youngsters, under the care of Moshe, achieved learning to write using a foreign alphabet. In time, the "Metukan" school staff added to its strength a new member – a German teacher: a young, religious Jewish woman from Zaglambia elegantly dressed and well–mannered. She quickly became well–liked by the parents who welcomed her into their homes inducing the children, too, to enjoy her lessons, learning assiduously the rules of German grammar: the nominative, genitive, dative and accusative cases... the parent's hearts warmed within them and without understanding the significance of the words were certain that without them their children would be held back from advancement.

The sounds of the war grew more and more distant. The military restrictions on trafficking of food supplies were loosened and transport was renewed. The levees were repaired and strengthened and trade broadened. Products of good quality from Austria and Germany appeared in the market and local farmers, who had never seen the like, envied them and paid well in products from their fields and hen–houses.

Passover was on the horizon. The Jewish people felt blessed in their hearts from what little rest they had and hoped that the Russian terror would never return – ever.

The Russian language, that had been the lingua franca of everyone, was discarded and people trained their tongues to speak German and correct Polish. On the night before Passover, when homes were cleansed of all remains of leavened and other forbidden foods, all reminders of anything from Tsarist Russian were consigned to the flames. Among the items destroyed were portraits of Tsar Nicholai the First, Tsar Nicholai the Second and Nicholai Nicholowicz, the failed commander of the great Imperial Army. On Passover night, when families sat at their festive tables to relate the Exodus from Egypt, they spoke too of the "exodus" of the Russians, their hatred of the Jews and the anti–Semitic deeds of their former leaders.

But their days of peace and quiet did not last long.

The Hallerczyks' Mistake[2]

It is 1918. The end of the war between the opposing armies is approaching. Rebel movements are organizing in all the Polish villages under the very noses of the Austrian army and removing their uniforms and hurrying to return to their homes in the over–crowded trains.

[Page 228]

The administration of the town fell into the hands of Polish patriots, who treated the local population as if they owned them and financed their expenses by extorting donations from the residents.

In the footsteps of the new administration came groups of youths not from the local population, who had come to Charsznica at the outbreak of war from larger towns and the surrounding villages. They were poor youngsters sent away to save their lives and survived mainly by stealing anthracite from the railroads and selling it to the residents. Because of this they were nicknamed “snatchers”. Since there was no way to obtain coal during the war their presence became tacitly “essential” and their name was known throughout the region. Even the police force was helped by them especially in spying.

With the cessation of hostilities the transportation eastward of coal by rail also stopped. The “street–gangs” who, in the meantime had grown and matured, found themselves without the means of sustenance; they turned to robbery and looting, spreading their terror among the population, particularly the Jews.

Another negative element operating in town in those days were the “Hallerczyks”. They were much admired and praised soldiers from the liberating Polish army, highly trained soldiers, taking their name from that of their Commander Józef Haller. These soldiers, the pride of the Polish people, found for themselves a unique form of amusement: catching the Jewish men and pulling their ear–locks and cutting off their beards. When they realized that the onlookers enjoyed the spectacle they widened their activity: no longer satisfied with simply pulling the beards – together with the flesh – they began throwing Jews from moving trains in full view of the population and the authorities.

Fear and terror returned to the Jewish street. Again the Jews were fearful of travelling on the roads and many were afraid to even leave their homes. About 80 people were harmed or injured, some seriously and there were those who died from their injuries.

Rabbi Leibush Mendel, who had a striking beard, had his beard tied up and wrapped in a large kerchief, maybe because of a tooth–ache, and didn't move from his doorway. His children kept watch alongside and when they heard the sound of heavy footsteps of the Hallerczyks approaching rushed to climb the ladder in the house leading up to the attic and hid there.

One Sunday morning, people who lived near the pharmacy were filled with anxiety on hearing blood–curdling screams outside in the street. The screams continued repeatedly accompanied by heart–rending groans. The few Jews who dared to peek outside through the cracks of shuttered screens, saw an atrocious scene: the figure of an old gray–haired man, half his beard hanging from his cheek and the other plucked; his jaw covered in blood, his eyes expressing terror and his lips seeming to tremble in prayer. Two “Hallerczyks” released their victim from their grip and, completely helpless, he collapsed on the sidewalk. The Jews rushed to help the injured man and as they approached heard him murmuring: "Jesus, Mary – save me!" and while they were dressing his wounds in the pharmacy where he had been taken, they discovered the cross, drenched in his blood, hanging round his neck. After they had attended to his needs and nursed him, they sent him on his way. He had simply been a passerby, a poor Christian who had the misfortune to grow a beard...

That same day the "Hallerczyks" disappeared from the streets of Charsznica. Rabbi Mendel and the rest of the Jewish people of the town began to walk freely again in the town, proudly displaying their bearded faces.

Searching for Ways Forward

The three years of war – the first two for the independence of Poland, opened the eyes of Polish youth, and allowed them to see clearly and their hearts filled with longing, and they began to weave for themselves dreams of a new life.

[Page 229]

The movement for the liberation of the whole of Poland began to achieve its targets and became responsible for the administration of state affairs. Economic and diplomatic connections were formed and there were many ignorant Poles who were inclined to see the Jews as interlopers snatching positions.

The official authorities adopted Grabinski's policies, impoverishing the Jews and excluding them from any commercial standing; anti–Semitism became open and reached a peak in a bloody pogrom on 3rd of May 1919.

The Jews of Charsznica began selling their goods and chattels. A few of them dreamed of going to America, and acquire wealth there; others had wider dreams, of expanding their knowledge, or a quiet corner somewhere, their own independence. Those who were still held by their forefathers' ways, married, had families, made flimsy homes and delayed the fulfillment of their dreams for some misty future.

The economic possibilities grow less and less and the stranglehold on Jewish life increased. Only a few succeed in uprooting themselves and fleeing the country that was rejecting them. The number of those needing some community assistance grew and the coffers always empty. The teacher and

Study–House beadle, and his family, suffered extreme hunger and the social aid services able to help by obtaining a franchise to sell yeast and raisin wine for Kiddush were unable to save him; for the majority of the Jews only coarse challot are available while raisin wine is no longer seen on the table even though it is being sold legally by the teacher.

The last of the first generation of settlers and the two following generations were deeply concerned. The maturing generation hung on to the faintest shadow of hope looking for a future with the "Bund", in communism, in assimilation. There were those who fell into the arms of their "Yiddish" origins and despair gnawed at their hearts; others still hoped for a miracle.

The Zionist activity in town increased. The number of houses accepting KKL collection boxes which are viewed with favor increased. They hang on the wall next to the collection box of Rabbi Meir Baal Ha–Ness, so favored and blessed by countless generations of mothers and grandmothers.

On Sabbath Eves, before lighting the Sabbath candles, they stand before the boxes hanging on the wall, their fingers tightly holding on to the few coins they managed to save and drop half of them into the box of Rabbi Meir Baal Ha–Ness and half into the KKL box. Then they turn to the lighted candles and their lips whisper a prayer moistened with their tears, asking for salvation.

At the end of the 'Twenties, the first two youths went to training kibbutzim; the first of them was the Israeli writer Israel Zarchi (Zerach Gertler).

Translator's Footnotes

1. A prayer book in Yiddish composed late in the 16th Century by Ya'acov ben Yitzhak Ashkenazi, mainly for women who were unable to read Hebrew and is based on The Song of Solomon Cap. 3 v. 11: "Go forth ye daughters of Zion..."
2. Named after their commander Józef Haller (see below).

A Family that Was Cut Down

by Israel Rogovski

Translated by Selwyn Rose

Mr. Reuven Rogovski (Chodów) was one of the first Jewish settlers in Charsznica. The beginning of the construction of the railroad station – the future Jewish Charsznica – found Mr. Reuven Rogovski who dwelt in the village of Chodów, a community of prosperous Christian farmers – just one kilometer from the station. From there he conducted his business with the rest of the villages in the area, and from that he made his living and supported his wife Malka (nÃŠe Matizansky), from Ksiaz.

[Page 230]

Before that, he had lived in Brogowa, a village close to Ksiaz. From there he moved to Chodów. He acquired a good name and reputation among the villagers because of his fair dealing and honesty and he was nicknamed "Truth Speaker".

Reuven was convinced that there was a good future for him if he moved to the "Station" so he took his wife with him for help and put down roots in the new place. He opened a shop, supplying haberdashery and textiles – Emil Woitowitz, his neighbor, living in the same house, was similarly engaged; the house was rented from one of the local dignitaries who had abandoned it because of the distance from the town.

At the start of the family's "integration" in their new home, their income from the shop was not sufficient to cover their household expenses and when their first son, Mendel was born, their expenses also grew. Then Mr. Reuven began his business as a tailor, a profession he learned as a soldier in the Tsarist army – it happened like this: One day standing on parade, the officer cast a glance along the row and saw to his surprise a thread of cotton hanging from a soldier's collar. He walked over and pulled at the thread and found at the end a shining sewing needle... the needle and thread had been put there by the soldier's mother on his departure so he would have the means of sewing on his shirt buttons so he shouldn't – G–d forbid – catch cold.

The following day, the soldier Reuven was designated as "tailor'...

Reuven served in the army for four years and was registered officially as "Tailor". The whole of his service was spent sewing on buttons – his hands never touched the sewing machine.

Now the idea of being a tailor caught Reuben's attention and he thought he could see a promising future and hoped to build on it. He bought a big sewing machine, a pair of tailor's shears and a thimble and his wife took on the job of managing his dealings with tradesmen and negotiations with buyers.

One day a villager came in with a request: “I want you to make me a sheep–skin coat for the winter!” The words “sheep–skin coat” fell upon his ears and filled him with fear. The thimble fell from his finger, the tape–measure round his neck seemed to choke him and his voice shook...when his wife Malka realized the degree of his “expertise” as a tailor, she didn't despair. She took courage and said: “A tailor of women's garments it shall be – and why? First of all the Christian women are very modest in their dress and the quality of work on undergarments need not be high since it will not be seen publicly and secondly – it will give a lot of work.”

At first, on hearing the words “women's undergarments” Reuben shouted: “What have I got to do with women's undergarments!? I'm a men's tailor!” But when he reminded himself of the man's serious requests he relented and surrendered to his wife's suggestion and thus he began to make long warm winter underwear for the Christian women. Malka his wife spoke with her regular women clients who came to the shop and convinced them to order their underwear from her husband Reuben and occasionally succeeded in increasing the turnover by selling extra material, suggesting to a young pregnant woman jokingly: “Perhaps they're twins?”

Their commercial activities were a success and Malka, in their new home brought them much business. Their shop prospered, their family and their apartment expanded and their reputation spread. They acquired a plot of land and a two–storied wooden house with a well and front yard – their first proper dwelling–place since they first came to Charsznica. After many days, his commercial contacts multiplied with wholesalers and his business expanded significantly, his work as a tailor ceased and the sewing machine fell into disuse.

Reuven was familiar with the Holy books and his studies drew much for his spiritual nourishment from the writings of our learned men throughout his life. While still in his middle–age, he fell ill with sugar diabetes and when he was only forty–nine he died from his sickness after the enlightened doctors of Vienna were unable to cure him. He was buried in Miechów because Charsznica had no cemetery of its own.

[Page 231]

He left behind him two sons and four daughters, he lived to see thirteen grandchildren and after his death were added a further twenty. His offspring survive to this day, a few in America and Argentina and seven in Israel.

Mr. Mendel Rogovski, the eldest son of Reuven and Malka, inherited from his father the same superior qualities and even exceeded them. His reputation preceded him in all the surrounding villages and was nicknamed "Mendel the Pleasant" and known to all by that soubriquet.

At the age of seventeen he married Rachel'eh Zonshain of Olkusz and together they brought into the world five sons and three daughters.

He made his living from the shop in which one could buy everything: needles, shoe–laces, marinated fish, pitch, oil, bridles and whips, violins and batons, women's stockings and men's socks, shoe–repair kits and wood–glue, sewing–machine needles, plows, food–stuffs and herbs, colored paper to make decorative flowers, horse–shoes, decorative colored glass balls for Christmas trees and many other things. Apart from all this, he bought eggs from the villagers, cheese and butter and sold them to the traders from Zaglambia in large quantities. In exchange for the produce of their farms the farmers' wives would take sugar, tea, coffee, salt and soap and also buttons, sewing needles and articles to decorate themselves and their homes.

Jewish customers would also come and purchase wares – some for cash and some on credit; they paid if they had the money or deferred payment until they had earned it. Mendel would also supply them knowing they hadn't the money to pay because he was good–hearted and understood their position.

All this broad–based and increased trade was not sufficient to support the large family and when his children grew Mendel opened another shop and that, too, was insufficient to cover their needs, even though Mendel, his wife and children worked to exhaustion from dawn to dusk.

Rachel's assistance in the shop was made possible by having an honest Christian woman, who served the family faithfully for many years, manage the home. The woman freed Rachel from many kitchen– and other household–chores, and over the years fulfilled the role of the house–wife; she fed and dressed the children, sent them to the "Heder", reminded the children to say their prayers at the appropriate times, put them to bed at night, etc. But one day the woman was caught with the stolen money on her person and

Rachel'eh was surprised and unbelieving: “Is it really possible that such a woman would steal?”

The children of Mendel were called “Rubenki” in the name of their grandfather.

On every Erev Shabbat the whole family would gather round the table with Mendel sitting at the head and by the light of the Shabbos candles would sing the Sabbath hymns. When they reached “The Sabbath Day is Holy” Mendel would raise his eyes and look at Rachel'eh, who had changed her dress in honor of the Sabbath, and sing the hymn to her and tranquility would enwrap the whole family.

Mendel continued to walk the same path as his father, Reuben; the doors of his home were open before all who came, among them non–Jews. Farmers among his acquaintances who chanced to come to Charsznica on cold winter days found a dish of tcholent and a blazing fire waiting for them. His home was especially welcoming to collectors from other villages and towns making the rounds and taking donations for the needy and poor. His good deeds were performed modestly, with others he dealt honestly, greeting all in peace. At the time of his first daughter's wedding all who entered his shop, without exception, were greeted with a glass of cognac.

[Page 232]

He raised his five sons and educated them in the spirit of achievement; he taught them trades so that in the future they could live by the toil of their hands, and be “dependent neither upon the gifts of mortal men nor upon their loans,”[1] with Racheleh's help at his side.

Charsznica the town that was his home, he never left; there he was born and there, at the hand of the Nazis (may their names be blotted out), he and his growing family and their bones dispersed together with the rest of the Jews of Charsznica and the place of their burial is unknown to this day.

May their memories be for a blessing.

Mendel and his wife left behind them one surviving daughter and three sons with their families, three of the parents with five grandchildren and six great–grandchildren – three boys and three girls (may they be fruitful and multiply), alive and growing in the Homeland.

Translator's Footnote

1. Paraphrased from the “Grace after meals” prayer

Charsznica

Translated by Gloria Berkenstat Freund

Jews first began to settle here [in Charsznica][1]) at the beginning of the 20th century and their numbers kept increasing until the outbreak of the First World War. A small Jewish kehile [organized Jewish community] was created here with a house of prayer in which to pray, a shoykhet [ritual slaughterer] and support for all of the Jewish institutions that a Jewish area in a small shtetl [town] had to have at that time.

After the rise of independent Poland, pogroms also arose here in 1919–1920 as in the entire Miechow Poviat [county]. Therefore, a large number of the resident Jews moved to the larger cities (Miechow and so on); others left Poland completely and emigrated abroad. Several who had the possibility (capital or were sought–after specialists and the like) emigrated to Eretz–Yisroel (Mordekhai Weklser).

In later years, the young – organized in youth organizations – worked as halutzim [pioneers] here, (studied) agriculture and dreamed about receiving a certificate [from the British mandate government necessary for emigration to Eretz–Yisroel]. The majority of them had not received a certificate ny the time of Hitler.

At that time in Poland, Charsznica was considered a village and was the only village in Miechow Poviat that, according to the census of December 1921, contained more than 100 Jews and here, out of a population of 1,568, 446 were Jews, 28.4%.

The Jews here worked at agriculture, "kept" orchards (leased from the owners and sold the fruit), some were artisans, others were merchants, had shops or went through the villages [selling goods]... There also were two melamdim [religious teachers]: Ruwin Beder and Shmuel the shamas [sexton].

[Page 233]

The iron foundry belonged to a Jew, Dov (Bernard) Goldkorn, and also employed Jews. A small, narrow–gauge railroad, waskotorowa [narrow gauge], went from Charsznica to Kacimierz, about 97 kilometers, through Miechow, Dzialoczyce to Kacimierz. In addition to the passengers, it mainly served the foundry.

The Jews here experienced the same fate of the Nazi–hell as the entire Miechow Poviat. Only a small number who had escaped to the Soviet Union or survived the German camps or – individuals – who hid with the Poles remained alive. No Jews remained in Charsznica after the terrible destruction. In 1948 the bodies of the Jews shot by the Germans and buried somewhere outside the city were dug up and brought to Krakow where they were given a Jewish burial on a Jewish cemetery.

Footnote

1. According to the information from the former secretary of the Miechow community before the war, Maior Piwowarski.

Jewish Life in Charsznica

by Yisroel Shlomo Wajcman

Translated by Gloria Berkenstat Freund

I moved to Charsznica during my 17th year of life. This was in 1918 at the time of the Austrian occupation. Jews traded and shipped various food products and it can be said that they more or less survived on this income. It was not so easy because the merchants competed among each other in order to win the trust of the peasants, the merchants who resold goods to residents. The trade lasted like this until the end of the war.

Then, when Poland finally received its independence, Jews again continued the trade in wheat and vegetables. In 1919 soldiers and officers from General Haller's Army came from France to help the newly arising Polish Republic in its struggle against the Bolsheviks. First, they went after the Jews – when they met a Jew, they beat him. Sometimes they even threw the victim through a window from a moving train. I remember they saw my father–in–law, Reb Hershl Rajnharc, of blessed memory, on the street and cut off half of his beard and knocked out two teeth.

At Passover time in 1919, the Jews from the surrounding shtetlekh again met a misfortune. A wheat merchant in Miechow was taking a wagon of wheat to Krakow, which was not permitted. A member of the militia, who did not permit him to go, ran into him. Then when the merchant did not carry out the wishes of the militiaman, they wrangled and wrestled for so long until the gentile fell severely wounded and several days later he died. Immediately, there was great turmoil. The Endekes [members of the anti–Semitic Polish National Party] organized pogroms against the Jews in all of the shtetlekh [towns] in the area. The pogrom took place here in Charsznica on the 1st of May 1919, a Shabbos [Sabbath]. Organized bands attacked the Jewish residents and beat them severely. They did not bother the women. The writer of these lines received several wounds in his head then and lay in bed for four weeks. Several weeks later an investigating commission headed by Deputy Hartglas came from Warsaw and the commission visited all of the Jews wounded in the pogrom and then they presented a report to the Polish Sejm [parliament]. Several hooligans were then arrested, but they were freed after three months.

[Page 234]

From year to year the situation for the Jewish masses in Poland became worse and catastrophic. Several families rescued themselves by emigrating to Eretz–Yisroel, Argentina and America. But the majority remained and struggled for their income and with the dangers, which hovered over Jews.

In 1918 I married my divine wife Bluma. She bore us three daughters. The oldest was named Frayda, the second Brukha and the third Yokheved (Yadzia). The entire family perished in Bełżec. My brother–in–law, Avraham Moshe Rajnherc of Bedzin, also perished there. My other brother–in–law fell in the Chodów Forest. His wife, Rayzl, and her daughter, Frayda, were deported to Bełżec, his son, Avrahaml to Auschwitz.

Eidl Rajnherc, of blessed memory, was murdered in Chodów and his wife, Ruchl, and their children were murdered in Bełżec. My sisters Chaya Rywka Sercaz, Ruchl Frenkl and a year–old child and Beyla perished in Bełżec; my brother, Moshe Wajcman, of blessed memory, in Auschwitz.

The Destruction of Charsznica

by Sura (née Grajcer) Rozenberg

Translated by Gloria Berkenstat Freund

Right after the outbreak of the Second World War, Charsznica was fired upon by Nazi airplanes, which destroyed the railroad station.

The first “welcome” for the Charsznica Jews was the murder of 31 people (including one Christian). Reb Moshe Szeniawiski, a grandson of an old Charsznica resident, only was wounded. They all hid in attics and warehouses. They were all brought to the courtyard of my God–fearing father, Reb Mordekhai Grajcer, and they were shot and buried on the spot. A few months later we took those shot from the mass gave and brought them to the Miechow Jewish cemetery.

This mitzvah [commandment, often interpreted as "good deed"] was carried out thanks to the great effort of Reb Shlomo Ranowski, may God avenge his blood, who later was murdered with all of the other Miechow Jews.

[Page 235]

We, like others who had means of transport, ran from place to place, seeking a refuge, alas, in Miechow, Działoszyce, Skalbmierz, Stęszew and other places, wherever one could.

We all returned two days later, convinced that there was no safer place than at home.

Jews no longer had any rest. They were forced to go to various work even on Shabbos [Sabbath]. Arrests and other persecutions and humiliations took place. Their furs were taken from the Jews. The Germans shot my cousin from Krakow, Hela Grajcer, during this "collection action."

Moshe Janowski and Sztajnberg, one of our neighbors, were also shot a few days later.

The "deportations" of the Jews began right after Rosh Hashanah 5700 [1939].

The first deportations took place in Charsznica on Shabbos. The Germans drove the Jews together, men, women and children, old and young to the Witowka [River] where "Polish wagons" awaited the Jews and they were loaded quickly and transported to Słomniki. The cruelty of the German murderers was so great that they forced the old and weak people to walk and many empty wagons were sent back...

All of those on foot were shot on the spot – during their "march" to Miechow.

Reb Shmuel Ragowski was "qualified" by the murderers as a "one on foot"... And his young son, Ruwin, received a spot on a women's wagon. His [Ruwin's] mother, Chavale, who also was in the transport, asked her son, "Ruwin! How do permit your father to go by foot?" Ruwin quickly jumped off the wagon and for this "sin" he was shot with his father!

Ragowski's two daughters were also in this wagon and they perished in Belzec with the entire transport.

Czarna (Simkha Zilberberg's wife) and Ruchla, the wife of Reb Mendl Ragowski, old residents of Charsznica, were murdered at the "performance" of the German "chaperon" of the transport, who shot at the transport.

The small number of remaining Jews were forced to accomplish all of the work for the Germans.

I was hidden with my entire family at [the house of] Malatinski, our Christian neighbor, during the second and last transport of the Charsznica Jews to their death (with the Miechow kehile [organized Jewish community).

Alas, we could not remain there for long and after eight days of living in fear, we reached the Lotnisko camp with great effort and had the privilege of suffering with all of the Jews gathered from the Miechow and Krakow region.

[Page 236]

We remained there for five months. We were taken from there to the Jerozolimski concentration camp[1]) where the Germans had driven the Jews from all over Poland and other nations, and at first they gave us work in groups and finally forced us to bury or burn the dead, or similar terrifying things.

I was there with my children, relatives and many acquaintances from Miechow, Charsznica and the surrounding cities and shtetlekh [towns].

All of the women at the Jerozolimski concentration camp were called together. They all had to get undressed, naked as when they were born. Doctors examined everyone. The weak and thin, as well as the small children, were concentrated on a side of the large square that was surrounded by the military. They said that the weak ones would receive better food... However, in truth, the victims of the "selection" and the children were sent to Auschwitz, to the gas ovens. Among the victims of this "selection" was my sister–in–law, Rucza Rozenberg (a daughter of Reb Feywl Chencinski of Miechow) and her daughter, Felia.

My God–fearing husband, Shlomo Rozenberg, may his blood be avenged, and his brothers, Yakov Kopel and Shmuel Zaynwel, may their blood be avenged, were sent to Mauthausen with many other men (where they were then murdered) and I and my two daughters as well my sister–in–law's daughter, Leah Anker, were sent to Auschwitz.

There, a new well of calamity and pain opened for us when we became "prisoners," and the inhuman, horrible attitude [toward us] began. We had to appear for a roll call at five in the morning in winter, in the greatest snow and frost, barefoot and naked, in wooden shoes and "uniforms," thin headscarves on shaved heads. After counting the number of victims, the German soldiers accompanied by four muzzled dogs drove us to work. There was varied work.

We built highways; some carried heavy stones here and the others did the same, back!... We unloaded wagons of bricks or loaded other freight. This was designated for unqualified people. Tradesmen were sent to workshops. There was no designated time of work; however much our oppressors wanted... There also were no predictable workplaces. Many times [they were] four kilometers and more away... A walk was necessary to bring the kettle of food and the same to carry it back.

We were in that terrible situation until the 18th of January 1945.

That day everyone received two blankets, enough bread and cans of meat and we marched in the accompaniment of soldiers, not knowing to where. We marched 30 kilometers a day. Those accompanying us were qualified bicyclists. We had to throw away the blankets because no one had the strength to drag them. Many people even threw away the bread.

[Page 237]

We rested during the night in cold sheds. They tried to load us into boxcars twice on the road (to Bergen–Belzen), but because of the heavy gunfire from the Russians at the train tracks, we had to be unloaded.

On the road, the Germans shot the weak "prisoners" who, because of their weakness, could not march 30 kilometers a day. Only some of us "dragged" ourselves in those conditions to Bergen–Belzen.

We no longer worked there, but the dirt and lice simply ate us up. When the English and the Russians neared Bergen–Belzen, the Germans turned off the water and we remained without a drop of water for 10 days...

One evening we heard heavy fire; we began to shout and the German guards demanded that we remain quiet, but we did not hear them...

In the morning, we found a white flag at the gate and all of the German murderers had escaped, like poisoned mice...

The British and the Americans entered a few hours later. Salvation had arrived! We became people again We saved the sick, buried the dead!

Recorded: Sh.D. Yerushalmi

Footnote

1. On Jerozolimski Street. Krakow–Plaszow.

[Page 238]

B. Ksiaz

(Książ Wielki, Poland)

50°26' / 20°08'

Yizkor[2]

Avraham Yakov Walbromski

Translated by Gloria Berkenstat Freund

God, ennoble the souls.
Of the murdered kehile [*organized Jewish community*];
Sanctify the martyrs,
And say a prayer for them.
God, take them under your wing,
Say Kaddish [memorial prayer for the dead] Yourself.
Revenge! Make them pure
From shame and derision and sin.
You are the accuser and the judge of the world;
[You] sent them into hell.
[You] created the slaughterer yourself,
Who slaughtered and suffocated,
The trees with firm roots;
Not answering the crying with mercy.
[You] weakened Your chosen people
God, erect a headstone on the ruins!
Fiery letters like once the Tablets;
So that the words call for revenge.
Give your people, Israel, back their honor,
That will be the Kaddish, the headstone and the revenge.

Translator's Footnote

2. Prayer recited in memory of the dead.

[Page 239]

Ksiaz Wielki

by N. B.

Yiddish translated by Gloria Berkenstat Freund

Hebrew translated by Selwyn Rose

In Jewish sources, the name is written in various ways: in the minutes of the Council of the Four Lands we have the name "Ksiadz," "Ksiaz"; in Polish, the name was often written variously as Xiąż, as Książ; and to differentiate the community from smaller ones (villages) that also carry the name, it was called Wielki [big or grand].

An older, large settlement with the name, mentioned by various Polish sources, existed in the 12th century and the Polish king would often spend time there. The name Książ comes from Ksiacz (Książe) furst [prince]. In the past, this was a princely seat.

Nothing remains of the former palaces. Only the Catholic Church remembers the old times. The zamek (castle) of the 17th century that was there was rebuilt many times and finally lost its earlier character as a fortress.

In the course of many years, in the 19th century the settlement became the property of the powerful Tenczynski magnate family. It was passed on to the family of Margrave Aleksander Wielopolski, the well-known Polish statesman and reformer in the time of the Polish Kingdom (popularly known as Kongreswovka – Congress Poland), which was created at the Vienna Congress (1815) after the defeat of Napoleon and after this part of Poland was occupied by Russia. At that time Książ belonged the Miechow powiat [district], Kielce gubernia [province].

There never was a ban on Jews settling in Ksiaz, so they came there and settled in a comparatively large number.

In the 16th century, the "Krakow-Sandomierz lands" (Tzouzmir [in Yiddish]) (Ziemia Krakowska-Sandomierska) were divided into six regions as a part of Jewish autonomous Poland: 1. Centrum-Krakow; 2. Opatow; 3. Szydlow; 4. Checiny; 5. Pińczów; 6. Wodzislaw.[1] Ksiaz, Czarnowiec, Dzialoszyn and so on belonged to the last district. That is, Ksiaz appeared as an independent kehile [organized Jewish community] (kahal), as all smaller Jewish settlements were organized that did not have their own rabbi, cemetery, etc., called przykahalek (kahal [Jewish community council of the kehile] in Polish. Two Jewish chief-kehilus, Pińczów and Wodzislaw, fought over Ksiaz as to which of them Ksiaz belonged and to which Ksiaz should pay its dues; this was the most important factor, in addition – it should be understood – to submitting to the religious court of the kehile and so on.

It was decided at the meetings of the Council of the Four Lands in the years1692 and 1712 that the nearby kehilus, in the villages or small shtetlekh [towns], which did not have their own synagogue (house of prayer) and which were located not more than two miles from a kehile, belong to that kehile from a financial standpoint. This law was approved in 1717 (the 21st of November) and clearly underlined that it also was part of the Krakow voivodeshaft [provincial government). In 1758 the distance between one kehile and another kehile was restricted to more than one mile (1.6 kilometers).

[Page 240]

Therefore it was decided at the session of 1717 that the treasury and books from Ksiaz needed to be taken to Pińczów, but the kehile in Wodzislaw laid claim to the kehile in Ksiaz, arguing before the commission (in 1759) in Radom that the Jews in Ksiaz did not come there from the Krakow area, but from Wodzislaw.

Ksiaz wanted to free itself from both cities that wanted to rule over it and strove to be independent. The kehile in Ksiaz bought a cemetery and in 1742 (the 10th of December) received from the Krakow Bishop Lipskin the right to bury its dead here without the permission of the Wodzislaw or other kehile. The Ksiaz kehile had to pay two stones [about 10 kilograms] of wax (for candles) annually to the kośció? [church] in the shtetl [town]. The bishop also permitted the Jews in the shtetl to elect their own kehile. However, the kehilus in Wodzislaw and Pińczów appeared against this. At first, Pińczów held that according to the decision of 1717, Ksiaz belonged to Pińczów. They argued that it lost 10,000 zlotes because Ksiaz belonged to Wodzislaw. The Radom commission turned to the Polish Finance Minister, (Podskarbi [treasurer]) Siedliecki, who again ruled in favor of Wodzislaw. The Pińczów kehile appealed and it was promised the right to Ksiaz. However, Wodzislaw still demanded of the Jews of Ksiaz that they pay [Wodzislaw] its taxes...

Then the kehile in Ksiaz finally decided to accept the hegemony of Pińczów and from 1765 paid it all of its taxes (as well as the state) through the kehile and from then on belonged to the Pińczów kehile (parafia [parish]).[2]

Such disputes would take place among the previous kehilus. As for Ksiaz, we learn from the conflict that it was a larger Jewish settlement and a rich one, paid high taxes (including also a head tax) and that it was worthwhile to rule over it. The Jews of Ksiaz wanted to free themselves from the rule of a strange kehile because they also wanted to be free of excessive expenses.

We further provide here the three eras of the Council of the Four Lands, as they were recorded in the Pinkes Va'ad Arba Aratzot [Book of Records of the Council of the Four Lands].[3]

[Translator's note: the following section, ending with the words "under threat of ostracism," was translated from the Hebrew by Selwyn Rose.]

On the 21st July, 1759 (26th Tammuz 5519), Poland's Minister of Finance in Constantinov(?) (at a meeting of the Council of Four Nations), handed down a judgment on the argument between the communities of Wodzisław (Vodislov) and Książ (Keshionzh) regions and "all the communities of the Greater and Lesser regions."

In 1760 (5520), the Council adjudicated in the conflict between the region of Lesser Poland and the Sokołów (Sokolov) community authority of the Książ community and conveyed its decision to the court of the Royal Treasury in Radom.

[Page 241]

(991)...[a] and with this we are not attempting to minimize but to authorize the jurisdiction of the leaders of the above Holy Community and also of Książ (Keshionzh) who agreed, after a certain period of time, to belong to the community of Pińczów; and we reinforce this, our decision with an embargo and proscription by the rabbis and we affirm that the leaders of the above Holy Community of Keshionzh will do the bidding of the community leaders of Pińczów who will have the superior authority, and will ask of them at all times on all matters whether they be questions of law or on all other matters, and in all matters will be subservient to the community leaders of Pińczów and to no other body. And as to the taxes of the community of Keshionzh, how much they will pay annually will be according to the evaluation fixed by the honorable leaders of the Warsaw community – may G-d preserve them – together with the famous great rabbi and leader, our Teacher and Rabbi Mordecai of Dukla, the leader of the committee – may G-d preserve him – and what they decide, that will be the sum. The same situation pertains and will apply in future years including those taxes due to the Royal House. Heaven

Forbid that these, our words, be changed or disregarded, except by order of the Governor, under threat of ostracism.

A Few Figures

According to the count of the Jews, which took place in old Poland, before its downfall in the years 1765-6, in order to establish the size of the head tax that they had to pay – the tax was paid by every Jew (even if female), older than one year – there were 36 Jews in Ksiaz, with nine heads of families. The rest were members of the families or servants who also were counted as members of the families. If we want to include the nursing children and the possibly uncounted Jews, [the number] would indicate that about 50 Jews were found in our city then.

They lived in five Jewish houses.

Two of the Jews were arendars [lessees or estate managers].[4]

The economic situation of the Jews in Ksiaz certainly was not completely good, but we find one young man from Ksiaz at that time as a servant in the Dolczic community, also in Krakow province. The population consisted of:

Year	Christians	Jews
1827	480	392
1856	460	487
1897	683	729
1921	858	852[5]

The number of Jews in 1921, according to "religion," according to the mother- tongue (Yiddish or Hebrew) was 169 people fewer in the shtetl, only 683 Jews, probably Jews were not well versed in the question and said "Polish" thinking that they were being asked their citizenship, which matches the growth in the number of Polish speakers – and the regime was interested in this – because [the number of] Poles according to the Roman Catholic religion in Ksiaz in 1921 (December) was 858. On the contrary, Polish as a mother-tongue was given as 1,030, 172 more people; that is, 169 Jews are included in this number. Ksiaz lost the status of city in independent Poland (1918-1939) and was transformed into an urban settlement (osada miejska).

[Page 242]

Ksiaz was a cultured shtetl; it numbered 89 brick houses and 15 wooden ones in the 19th century. The entire city was paved; it had a hospital, two churches; an elementary school and four guilds (of artisans). The Jews were employed in agriculture and artisanship.

Large fairs would take place here six times a year, when artisans would sell their products.

[The city] had a reputation among the Jews as a center of learning. Its yeshiva [religious secondary school] was well known in near and distant areas.

Various Jewish personalities boasted then that they had studied in this yeshiva and, particularly, that they received rabbinical ordination from the Ksiazer Rabbi, Mosiek Natan Kahana Shapira, father of the Beth-Din [religious court] of Ksiaz and the region.

This rabbi also was the author of writings from which one book was published; its name, Sefer Tehilim [Book of Psalms], Shemen L'Maor, with commentaries of Rashi and traditional Masoretic text and new added illumination, which was published in 1911 in Piotrkow. A second edition [was published] in Warsaw in 1913.

It is understood that in addition there were teachers, khederim [religious primary schools], where children learned before they entered the yeshiva. On the other hand, not all children entered the yeshiva; children from other cities would also attend the yeshiva, just as young men from Ksiaz studied in other well-known yeshivus in Poland.

Avraham Korngold, one of the city teachers, was the teacher of the youngest children, taught children from eight to 14 (led various classes). Gemara [Talmud] was studied with Moshe Ziberberg, until the arrival of Rabbi Szpira. These were capable and richer [students]. The remaining young people were forced to go to work, to help their parents earn a living and ended their studies by learning only how to pray and some a chapter of the Khumush [Five Books of Moses] with Rashi's interpretations.

And although Ksiaz was a smaller Jewish settlement, Jewish institutions and organizations of all kind existed there, as is known about other settlements with larger numbers of Jews.

There was both a bikor-kholem [help for the sick] and a khevra-kadisha [burial society], and a hakhnoses orkhim [hospitality for the poor guest on Shabbos and holidays], Hasidim and misnagdim [opponents of Hasidus], political parties with their youth organizations, etc. etc. There also was a gmiles khesed kase [interest free loan fund] here.

There also was a hakhshare [agricultural training to prepare for emigration to Eretz Yisroel] area in Ksiaz for halutzim [pioneers] from the area and other communities.

Young men from Ksiaz also attended a hakhshare area outside their home city.

A bad effect on the development of the community certainly was that it was located far from a train station (12 kilometers from Kozlow). Along with Miechow, the [main city in the] county was not far from Ksiaz Wielki; there lay the colony and farm Ksiaz Mali. The city and other communities (Jędrzejewo) were connected to it by autobus. And [also to] the historical place Raclowice, where [Tadeusz] Kościuszko won a victory over the Russian military in 1794.

[Page 243]

*

Many jokes, anecdotes about familiar personalities went around the city. Ksiaz was a joyful shtetl.

Yosl Szlamowicz, the shamas [assistant to the rabbi] and bookseller, was described thus, that when he was asked if he earns anything from the books, he would answer: "I would look nice if I looked out at Jewish customers."

When he once was asked if he beat his wife, he answered very naively that he had to go to ask her.

And in addition to this source of income – shamas, bookseller – on Friday mornings he also was a barber, going to the houses to shave the heads of the owners.

When the Germans entered Ksiaz, the Jews endured all of the terrorist acts as nearby Miechow. A Judenrat arose here, an aid committee that maintained the people's kitchen. The young tried to have access to work: first on the spot and then in the labor camps. Until the large deportation took place; the Jews were assembled in September 1942 and taken outside Slomnik and from there to the train station along with the local [Slomnik] Jews, from where the majority were sent to the Belzec death camp. A smaller number of the healthy young people were sent to camps at first in Plaszow, Bonarka, Prokocim and the nearby areas, later to Auschwitz and from there further to Germany.

Only a small number of this group could endure the hell and survive.

A small number of Jews, who were to gather together all of the possessions of the empty Jewish homes, were left in the ghetto.

This group of Jews was shot on the 15th of February 1943 and this ended the history of the Jews in the once well-known city of Ksiaz Wielki.

Original footnotes

1. Balaban: Historia Żydów w Krakowie [History of the Jews in Krakow], vol. 1, p. 351.
2. Page[s] 258/260, volume II, the above cited work, M. Balaban.
3. Pinkes Va'ad Arba Aratzot [Book of Records of the Council of the Four Lands], Jerusalem, 5605 [1945].
4. The number according to Dr. R. Mahler: table 12, part VI; p[ages] 68, 160.
5. The citation according to (see above) Bogdan Wasiutynski. According to Argelbrandt's Encyclopedia.

Hebrew Translator's footnote

a. 991 is an Aramaic letter-value. Its meaning is not known

[Page 244]

An Anthology of the Rabbis of Ksiaz

Collected by Mr. David Shapira (Z"L), the grandson of Rabbi Moshe Natan Kahana Shapira (Z"L), Shimshon Dov Yerushalmi (Z"L) and, May They be Spared for a Long Life, Eliezer Lipa Lavie, Avraham Wolbromsky and Yehoshua Ze'ev Abramczyk. Prepared for publication by Moshe Spiegel.

Translated by Selwyn Rose

The Community of Ksiaz was blessed with its spiritual leadership, a dynasty of Rabbis whose names preceded them from generation to generation as incomparable scholars, renowned for their knowledge of the Mishna and as Posekim[1] who knew to lead the Jewish flock on the correct road and who, themselves, studied the Torah day and night.

The greatest of the luminaries in our generation from among the rabbis of Ksiaz was the Gaon, our teacher the Rabbi Moshe Natan Netta Kahana Shapira (May his Righteousness be Remembered for a Blessing) who was unique in his generation, a wise scholar in the fullest sense of the word, excelling in the Mishna and Posekim, who preached and disseminated knowledge among many, an erudite scholar digging out the finest points and weighing this opinion against that in a ceaseless search of the sayings of our scholars and their writings and in addition to all that, published a book "Shemen la–Maor"[2] in which are found new and illuminating different explanations on the Book of Psalms.

His predecessors were:

The Rabbi Yosef Dover Ha–Cohen the son of the Gaon Rabbi Arieh Leib, author of the book "Ketzos Ha–Choshen" who's father ("Ha–Ketsos"), was the author of "Avnei Milu'im" a commentary on "Even Ha–Ezer" ("The Stone of Help")[3], (Chap. 51) and similarly in the last comment printed in that book.

Officiating after him as Rabbi of Ksiaz was the rabbi fromWodzislaw , Rabbi Moshe bar Ya'acov from Apatów, pupil and son–in–law of the author of "Maor Shemesh". He died and was interred in Kraków on Yom Kippur 1832.

He was followed by the rabbinical genius and righteous Rabbi Simcha the son of the superlatively spiritual Holy Arieh Naphtali, the author of "The Implications of 'He who causes damage'...." as discussed in the second chapter of Talmud on "Nezikin" - damages Bava Metzia (Warsaw - 1864); written in the Foreword is the following:

In this book, there are significant innovations on the tractate, "Bava Metzia"[4] that I composed, the least of my family[5] here sit I, among my people, in the town of Ksiaz (May G–d preserve it), Simcha, the son of my lord, father, teacher and Rabbi, the righteous, orthodox and keenly perceptive well–known thinker and teacher in our generation the spiritual Rabbi Ari Naphtali.

After him came Rabbi Ya'acov Yitzhak Frankel Teomim to officiate as town rabbi and his signature is to be found on a proclamation on the day following the festival of Shavuot, 1869 in the matter of a dispute between two rabbis, in the following words: "Ya'acov Yitzhak Frankel Teomim, Chairman of the Community Bet–Din, Ksiaz, Poland." The proclamation was signed in Tsanz (Nowy Sącz).

Rabbi Yeshiah Fisch (May his righteousness be for a blessing) was one of the distinguished rabbis of Ksiaz. He was the only son (he had five sisters), of his parents, Rabbi Yedidiah and his wife, Tsirle (May she rest in peace), well–known in their day. Rabbi Yeshiah's mother was full of wisdom, appreciated for her intelligence and earned the respect even among the estate owners in the surrounding districts of Ksiaz.

[Page 245]

Rabbi Yeshiah Fisch was a distinguished Gaon and officiated under the auspices of the Government; apparently Rabbi Moshe Natan Shapira (May his righteousness be remembered for a blessing), failed to pass the examinations in Russian and was not licensed to officiate as a registered government rabbi and therefore his official place was filled by Rabbi Yeshiah Fisch (May his righteousness be remembered for a blessing).

According to information from the court of the Rabbi of Gur, he and his wife were murdered Rosh Chodesh Iyar, 1898, by robbers who entered their house at night, while they slept.

The circumstances of his birth are outlined in the following popular legend:

The noble Hassid Rabbi Yedidiah from Ksiaz was always to be found among the throngs in the holy shadow of Rabbi Yosseleh Neustadter, known as "the Good Jew" author of "Ma'or Veshemesh" (May his righteousness be a blessing in the world to come). His wife would often travel to Lelów to the Holy Rabbi the Gaon, Moshe and would occasionally complain to him that she had no male child (she had five daughters), and ask the Rabbi to pray for her. Long periods passed with no signs of further pregnancies and even though the sainted Rabbi had assured her that he had no power to help her she refused to despair and maintained her faith and always sent her written "plea" to the Rabbi to pray for a male child. On one occasion on sending her plea the Rabbi turned to her and said: "I am determined in my heart and soul, to travel to our Holy Land of Israel, therefore – if you will give me enough money to cover all the expenses of my journey, I promise you that with G–d's help you will be remembered this very year with a male child but only on the condition that you return now to your home and get your husband's permission to all this. On hearing the Rabbi's words the wife was overjoyed, returned home and related everything to her husband who answered: "I won't do a thing about this until I have spoken with my teacher and Rabbi in Neustadt and asked him. I cannot decide without his opinion." He travelled immediately to the Rabbi – "The Good Jew" in Neustadt – and laid before him the suggestion from the Rabbi of Lelów. "The Good Jew" replied that that he agreed to the suggestion of the Rabbi of Lelów and that Rabbi Yedidiah can give his permission but first he must speak with the Rabbi of Lelów and stipulate that the child should be granted a long life. And so; the wife travelled to Lelów and put into the Rabbi's hand the required sum of money and a long life for the child. The Rabbi of Lelów replied: "Throughout the entire time I in am the Holy City – Jerusalem – every single day will be counted a year in the boy's life – a day for a year. The Rabbi from Lelów went to the town of Ksiaz and prayed there and during the prayer a wondrous event occurred: it is said that he prayed in such a loud voice they thought the very walls shook and after the prayer he called Rabbi Yedidiah and his wife and toasted them with cognac and cried out "Mazal–Tov" and added that it was hard work and that with G–d's blessing he succeeded. Rabbi Yedidiah immediately journeyed to "The Good Jew" and told him everything that had happened and the Holy Saint "The Good Jew" said "It is true that I know the Holy Rabbi of Lelów but I was not aware of his awesome holy power," and toasted him with cognac honey–cake and congratulated him with a "Mazal–Tov" and they had a son – the intensely sharp–witted genius Rabbi Yeshiah (Z"L).

And when Rabbi Moshe'leh of Lelów had been in our Holy Land 70 days and in the Holy City of Jerusalem fifty–five days, thus was it also with the Holy Sainted Rabbi Yeshiah Fisch (Z"L), who lived fifty–five years until the day he was murdered – a year for every day, as the Sainted Rabbi of Lelów had predicted (may he be protected).

(Extract from "The Merits of Abraham" by Rabbi Abraham of Parysów, Jerusalem, 1949).

[Page 246]

Rabbi Moshe Natan Kahana Shapira

The Rabbinic genius Moshe Natan Kahana Shapira was born to his father Rabbi Raphael Naphtali Hertz (Z"L) and mother Leah (Z"L). His date of birth is not known. He died at the age of 84 on 10th January 1937 and is buried in Ksiaz.

The family of Kahana Shapira is an ancient and important family going back many generations as far as Natan Shapira of Kraków, the author of "Megaleh Amukot", who lived 1585–1633, and beyond that to King David (Z"L). The family relationship to King David (Z"L) is one of the reasons to which our Rabbis have attributed his great talent and energy in interpreting the Book of Psalms with new, basic and original explanations.

Already in his youthful years, when he was about 12 or 13 years old he studied under the rare genius, Avraham Bornsztain, the author of “Agudat Azov” and the father of the great and genuine genius and ADMOR[6], the holiest of holy, author of “Eglei Tal”, Shmuel Bornsztain also known as the author of “She'eilos U'teshuvos”[7] and by his soubriquet “Avnei Netzer”. He was much liked by his Rabbi, the ADMOR and holy genius (May the righteous be remembered for a blessing) of Sochatchov. He was highly honoured as a master of pedagogy.

Our revered Rabbi (May he rest in peace), was widowed in the prime of life. His wife, his boyhood sweetheart Shprintsa Brandl (May she rest in peace), left behind two orphans: the Holy Rabbi and genius Mordecai Tsvi Kahana Shapira (May G–d avenge his blood) aged about eighteen months and a daughter, Gittel (May she rest in peace) about 3–years old. Later he remarried a widow of good family, Golda Szydlowski (May she rest in peace), of Miechów. She was a great and important woman and the owner of a haberdashery store.

[Page 248]

When he came to Miechów he immediately opened a Yeshiva and learned students began streaming there from all over and the pulse of the Torah began to beat in the town and the surrounding area. Quite quickly his good name and reputation spread far and wide. Sometime later the shop began to fail and he was compelled to take upon his shoulders, against his will, the office of the Rabbinate of Ksiaz. The union produced two daughters: the Rabbanit Hindle from Czeladź, (May G–d avenge her blood) and the Rabbanit Miril'e (May G–d avenge her blood) of Sochatchov.

In his old age after the death of his wife Golda (May she rest in peace), his son and daughters convinced him to marry a woman so that he should not be solitary and alone and he married the widow Mrs. Langfus of Bedzin and she gave birth to his last child Brandl Leah (May she rest in peace and may G–d avenge her blood).

His father–in–law, the great ADMOR of Sochatchov and also his son–in–law, the ADMOR author of “Shem from Shmuel”[8] both of whom admired his study “Shemen le–Maor” on the Psalms, also grumbled at him because he devoted himself entirely to Torah when in their opinion his future lay in the realm with the greatest and most important thinkers of his time because of his depth and clarity of thought. Every difficult, abstruse problem from far and near was brought to him because he was the one specialist to debate and clarify arguments and disagreements among the communities and their rabbis, according to our Holy Torah.

ספר

תהלים

עם פירוש רש"י ומסורה

ונוסף עליהם ביאור חדש בשם

שמן למאור

אשר יפרד לשלשה ראשים:

משה נתן כהנא שפירא אבד"ק קשונז והגליל.

פיעטרקוב

שנת תרע"א לפ"ק

ТЕГУЛИМЪ т. е. ПСАЛЬМЫ ДАВИДА

Shemen le–Maor Commentary on the Book of Psalms

Several communities, like Wolbrom, Olkusz and others, tried with all their might to persuade him to accept the post of Rabbi in their respective towns and always he found some good excuse to avoid accepting the honor and additional onus and imaginary "extra honors" and a larger income, and to dedicate his energies and time to Torah.

Once, the Haredi community of Łódź voted for two great extra rabbis in the hope that by their influence and their wisdom of the Torah, the honor of the Torah would return. One of the rabbis was our Rabbi (May his righteousness be remembered for a blessing), whose speciality was in the field of marriage and divorce; but he declined the offer in spite of the efforts and pressure from the Haredi community and the Hassidim of Sochatchov.

His dedication and perseverance were exceptional, both day and night. For forty years, during which he was engaged in composing "Shemen le–Maor" and the rest of his works that remained in manuscript form and were lost in the Holocaust, he never slept beyond midnight. He was known among a closed circle to be much interested in the Kabbala, to the knowledge and agreement of his Rabbi (May his righteousness be remembered for a blessing).

He was important to – and much respected even by the local nobles, non–Jews and large estate owners in the area. As a sign of their esteem for him they contributed generously for needy Jews in Ksiaz with gifts of timber, field crops and other produce from their lands during the winter months.

His only son, Rabbi Mordecai Tsvi Kahana Shapira the Holy genius (May his righteousness be remembered for a blessing and May G–d avenge his blood), was among the most important Rabbis of Kraków and was a member of the distinguished Great Rabbinical Court of Kraków. Before that he was the Father of the Rabbinical Court of Brzesko.

After the death of Rabbi Moshe Natan Kahana Shapira and after his son, the rabbinic genius Rabbi Mordecai Tsvi Kahana Shapira (May G–d avenge his blood), officiated on the council of Rabbis in Kraków and was unable to relinquish his seat in order to inherit the Chair of his father (May his righteousness be remembered for a blessing), their candidacy was put forward by two of the grandchildren of the late Rabbi (Z"L) and they were Rabbi Avraham Zinger (May G–d avenge his blood) and Rabbi Raphael (Z"L). Both of them appeared before our town's community and the first of them was preferred and much liked by the public and elected by about 90% of the residents.

Notwithstanding that he was much liked in town, his salary was very small and he was the head of a large family, while our town was not considered by any means to be among the wealthy and was not able to provide a generous salary to its Rabbis, our Rabbi accepted the situation and a life of hardship and near–poverty lay before him.

[Page 249]

Rabbi Mordecai Tsvi Kahana Shapira

Rabbanit Rivka Zinger wife of the young Rabbi Avraham Zinger

[Page 250]

I recall in a conversation I had with him, he said: "When the time comes to go to 'the next world' and they ask – How dared you officiate as Rabbi in such an important town as Ksiaz while you were still so young?" the community will testify that I made no attempt to seek the position so it seems that the Almighty decreed it so and I accepted the will of the community.

To our great sadness of heart he was not to officiate long in our town and the Holocaust that cast its shadow over the whole House of Israel touched him also and during the month of Elul (August/September) 1940 when his wife, the Rabbanit, with all her children were taken with the rest of the residents in the first group of exiles to the death camps.

Our Rabbi, (May G–d revenge his blood), stayed with the remainder of the refugees and accepted his torment with love and lived with the remnants of his community until the first day of the month of Kislev (December) 1943 when the rest of the Jewish residents of Ksiaz were liquidated together with their Rabbi and Teacher with extreme, unimaginable cruelty, unprecedented in the history of our people (May G–d avenge their blood).

We will mention one other beautiful flower in the House of Israel in Ksiaz and that is our ritual slaughterer and inspector Rabbi Haim Shraga Galster (May G–d avenge his blood) the son of the Rabbi of Chaba.

He was a dear man of many fine attributes, an excellent scholar and a faithful disciple of the ADMOR of Alexander. One might say of him that he was loved by all sections of the community who saw his contributions as a miracle. On him also fell the cup of poisonous bitterness – and with the second Transport on that same eve of the month of Kislev 1943 – he was sent for extermination. May G–d avenge his blood.

Translator's Footnotes

1. Particularly brilliant luminaries and scholars who hand down learned decisions covering all aspects of juridical Judaism.
2. A reference taken from Exodus 25: vi
3. Itself the basis for Rabbi Yosef Karo's later "Shulchan Aruch"
4. The second of the first three tractates of the Talmud dealing with "Nezikin" – damages
5. Taken from Judges Chap. 6: xv
6. An Acrostic for "Our Master, our Teacher. our Rabbi."
7. "Questions and responsa" – replies and decisions of learned rabbis.
8. A comprehensive scholarly work on the Bible, the Pentateuch, commentaries and cabala

High Holydays in Town

by Avraham Y. Walbromski

Translated by Selwyn Rose

During the month of Elul (August/September) with the approach of the High Holydays, a strong sense of awakening was apparent among the Jews of Ksiaz. With the ending of summer and the approach of fall everyone wondered in his heart and began to think of his place in the world to come and to repent of his ways. During the month all the people living out of town gathered together and came to visit the graves of their parents asking them to plead for them before the Holy One, Blessed be He, for them and for their families and to request forgiveness and pardon for their sins, "...for there is none who is perfect and sinneth not."

Throngs of people hurried to the cemetery, to the mausoleum of the distinguished Rabbi Yeshiah'le, to pour out their hearts in prayer, lighting many candles. They begged from the departed soul to be a true representative for them and the small congregation. The Cantor, Rabbi Avrame'le chanted the prayer "O, Lord Who art full of compassion" and everyone repeated it after him in their hearts for themselves and the whole House of Israel. The emotional situation sensitized the hearts of the Jewish people and all of them donated generously to charities for the poor. In addition, on hearing the sound of the Shofar coming from the Study–house, a feeling of dread gripped everyone realizing that the Day of Judgement was drawing near. Even trees in the forest – their canopies trembled from the threat of the judgement, as it is written: "Shall a trumpet be blown in a city, and the people not be afraid, and the Lord hath not done it?"[1]

"Forgiveness"

At the end of the last Shabbat before the New Year, during the late evening hours, as it gets colder and darkness spreads over the streets of Ksiaz, I remember the feeling and disposition of everyone as the time for the first prayer for "Forgiveness" in the town's Study House approaches. After midnight everyone rushed along the darkened streets, women and children with the prayer–book in their hands. From afar it looked like a great light spewed out of the Study–House and the light brought a sense of great warmth in everyone's heart. A few of the men–folk returned from the ritual bath–house found at the bottom near the stream in an isolated building. The owner of the bath–house,

Mr. Wolf who lived in a room next to the bath–house, made great efforts to prepare the water–boiler for them so that they could purify themselves before the prayer for "Forgiveness".

[Page 251]

The Study–House was full to bursting with people and the atmosphere was tense with the significance of the event. The peak arrived with the opening prayer: "Glorified and sanctified be G–d's great name throughout the world which he has created...." chanted by the Cantor, Rabbi Moshe Shlomo Abramczyk and when he reached the phrase "The soul is Thine and the body is Thine..." the entire congregation entered into an ecstasy of outpouring of their soul that sprang from fear of the Creator.

In the evenings, during the month preceding the Festivals, we could hear the Cantor's voice pealing out from his home, rehearsing the tuneful prayers in preparation for the services and the sweet melodies penetrated our hearts and from deep inside welled up a spiritual preparation for the coming days bringing with them redemption for all of us for the coming New Year.

On the Eve of Rosh Hashanah two residents from a local village, came especially to pray with us on the Holy Days. One of them was Wolf Herszkowicz (Z"L) nicknamed Wolf Gewaltower, who rented pasture for his milk herd from a local Polish Paritz[2]. He arrived with his son and settled in the town. The second one was Yitzhak Drevnowski from the village of Zarszyn, a farm worker who lived by the toil of his hands. He rented a room for the period of the High Holydays and prayed in the synagogue and was determined to purchase the "Maftir"[3] of the Torah reading. Both of them were villagers who lived in a non–Jewish environment and in spite of being far from town were zealous in keeping the commandments.

Most of the Jewish population gathered in the synagogue for the New Year prayers. The town Rabbi, Moshe Natan Shapira (May his righteousness be remembered for a blessing), usually prayed in the synagogue on Rosh Hashanah as was the custom in the community. For as long as I can remember he was the one who sounded the Shofar and as usual preached a sermon first, encouraging the congregation to repent.

The Ten Days of Penitence

The ten days between the New Year and the Day of Atonement constitute a natural follow–up towards the great anxiety surrounding the act of G–d signing and sealing His decrees of the fate awaiting us and culminating with the Day of Atonement, during the coming year and according to tradition it is the custom to offer a chicken or rooster as atonement which is then presented as a charitable gift to the poor and needy for food. Already in the first days after the New Year the crowing of roosters and the clucking of hens can be heard throughout the courtyards of the Jewish quarters because the families had hastened to secure the creatures according to the size of their families. Early in the morning of the Eve of Yom Kippur, I, together with my sister, took our hens to the slaughterer Rabbi Moshe Natan Silberberg. During the day we congregated round the heads of our families to be blessed with "A good signature."

After partaking of the last meal before the Fast the homes of the people emptied out: men, women and children hurried either to the synagogue or to the Study–House or to the Steibl to take part in the opening "Kol Nidrei" prayer. In front of the Ark in the synagogue stood Reb Avrame'le the Cantor and mouthing quietly together with him the yearning for forgiveness and absolution that each and every one of us hoped for from our Creator from our sins and iniquities. A large proportion of the congregation remained all night long in prayer.

Immediately, with the early morning, prayer continued with "Shahrit" – the morning prayers, the reading from the Torah, the memorial prayer for departed souls, "Musaf" – the additional service – and "Ne'ila" – the concluding service and I remember when the Cantor Reb Avrame'le, was already weary and hoarse, came the last appeal to heaven: "Open the gates for us at the time of the closing of the gates, for the day declineth." Each of us believes with complete faith that his prayer was acknowledged and that the Creator will forgive us for all our transgressions.

With the conclusion of the Day of Atonement, after we had all eaten to satisfaction after "The Great Fast" every house–holder inserted the first peg of the Succah in the ground for the up–coming Festival of Tabernacles.

Translator's Footnotes

1. Amos Chap 3:vi
2. Landowner
3. The concluding portion of the weekly reading

[Page 252]

Friends and Teachers from the Days of My Youth

by Avraham Y. Walbromski

Translated by Selwyn Rose

Oh, that my head were waters, And mine eyes a fountain of tears, That I might weep day and night for the slain of the daughters of my people! Jeremiah 9:1

Very often, when I am deep in thought, I recall from the recesses of the past memories of my youth, the surroundings where I grew up and where my personal identity was formed and nourished spiritually and morally for all the days of my life. Then I see before me the period 1926–1932 – the years of my youth.

Three major spiritual streams influenced us in those days:

A. The Zionist Movement in all its manifestations and multi–faceted activities, stamped its signature on Jewish life in every town and village in Poland. The fact that within the Movement there were opposing streams, Left and Right not only did nothing to reduce the intensiveness of the Zionist activity but even went to increase it.
Of special note was the Mizrahi Party that created training in Ksiaz during 1933–1934 for members of the Mizrahi workers who were preparing themselves for immigration to Palestine.
The initiative to organize the training crystallized after the disastrous fire that broke out in town at that time and brought down a major tragedy on the local Jewish community. A large proportion of the homes were burnt together with the only synagogue in town that represented the focus of Jewish life.
The members of Miechów and Ksiaz then decided to organize a training Kibbutz of the Labor and Torah Movement, that would bear the name of Rabbi Ya'acov Reines[1] (Z"L).
The initiators of the project were Yosef Horowitz (Z"L) from Ksiaz and Yehuda Bornstein (may he be spared for a long life) from Miechów, now living in Israel. Yosef Horowitz acted as works coordinator and organized operations at the farm of the Polish Paritz and at the local saw–mill. In addition the trainees also worked rebuilding homes and the synagogue. The activities of training left a deep impression

among the residents of the village and awoke in them a spirit of pioneering that had lain dormant until then. Next to that group was a Zionist Youth group "Working Youth" that was also drawn to the training activity and later - immigration.

B. The Hassidic Movement centered itself in our town round the two "Steibls": Gur and Alexander. The argument that raged between them was for the sake of G–d but neither of them forgot the Mitnagdim, and especially the Zionist factions. In the eyes of a number of Rabbis the Society was even flawed and invalid. All the religious streams concerned themselves with their own youth: "Yeshivot" taught Torah and didn't forget in the mean–time the Rabbis. The Society maintained a "Beit Ya'acov" school like the others around the world. The number of Jews in the village was small and their resources meager.

C. The Communist Party whose influence among the young grew from day–to–day, following the economic crisis that struck Poland, acquired "disciples" even from among the religious and affluent sectors. The Communist Party was, of course, illegal and its members liable to heavy penalties. A family, one of whose children was a communist saw it as a tragedy. The information that the son "fell into bad company" spread from mouth to mouth. The affected family prayed that he wouldn't fall into the hands of the police, something that had happened from time to time and caused a tempest throughout the village.

Following the struggle between these factions a special spiritual atmosphere was generated during which I spent the years of my youth. Among the teachers from whom I learned I will mention chronologically: Avraham Eizenoff, who was the first of my teachers; Moshe Mohar who taught us to read; David Birenboim, who taught Torah and Mishna – he knew excellent Hebrew as if born with it and spoke it in the Sephardic fashion.

After them came Shlomo ———(?), who taught Gemara.

When I finished "Heder" I found myself at a cross–roads. My parents (May they rest in peace), were G–d fearing and lovers of Israel and, concerned that I would stray from the straight and narrow path as they saw it, and that I would be "swept up in the storm" that parted children from their parents and the traditions of the forefathers, sent me to the Hassid Akiva Luft; he was considered a youth leader who centered around the Steibl of Alexander, founded the Yeshiva "Beit Yisroel" (named after Rabbi Alexander (Z"L), author of "Yisrael will Rejoice".)

The young men studied in the town's Study House with older students who were referred to as the "big boys". I also began to study under their care and scrutiny and I recall their names with some emotion and good memories and they were: Shaye Erhlich, Avraham Nerdan(?), Haim Friedberg, Yitzhak Leib Abramczyk. In addition, Akiva Luft taught us a page of Gemara every day and "Tosafot"[2]: Yerachmieyl Luft, Shabtai Silberberg, Altar Friedberg, and Yerachmieyl Weinberg). The "Steibl" of Alexander was situated in the home of Shlomo Zagnil(?), (a metal worker) who acquired from Hirsch Leib Gewirtzman work from the community; he was a G–d fearing man, a simple "tent–dweller". He owned a large shop dealing in skins that he presented to the "Steibl".

I perceive it as a Holy obligation to myself to mention my friends with whom I went to "Heder" and learned together with them in the Polish school and with whom we observed the Memorial days of our Rabbis, carried lanterns, took part in welcoming the Sabbath and bidding her farewell, with ritual meals and festivals.

With them, I spent my loveliest youthful years. With a few of them I went to study at "Yeshivot" outside Ksiaz: in Zduńska Wola, Bedzin and finally in Warsaw.

And these are their names: Yonatan Sultanik, Hirsch Leib Sultanik, Berish Friedberg, Leibush Mendel Winszman(?), Yerachmieyl Birenboim, Ya'acovVishlitzky, Matil Wajskol, Yerachmieyl Friedberg and Lazar Rozmaity. All these demonstrated friendship towards me; I learned much from them and I am grateful to them for many things. It is impossible to detail all the many good things about them. All of them perished, either in the German extermination camps or during the evacuation programs or by other means. They were for me a source of "water of life" from which I drank but my thirst was never satisfied... "My soul thirsteth for G–d, for the living G–d."[3]

Translator's Footnotes

1. The founder of the Mizrachi Religious Zionist Movement
2. Medieval commentaries on the Talmud as critical and explanatory glosses.
3. Psalm 42:iii

[Page 254]

Memories of Ksiaz

by Yitzhak Silberberg

Translated by Selwyn Rose

I was born in Ksiaz in the last years of the nineteenth Century to my father, Rabbi Moshe Ya'acov (Z"L) who was a G–d fearing distinguished scholar. I learned with a number of teachers in the "Heder" and later in the Study–House. Older Yeshiva students would teach the younger ones.

In 1924 I married the daughter of Rabbi Abba Shochet of Piotrokow and I moved there to live. As one of the disciples of Gur I frequented the Yeshiva and drank thirstily from every word that came out of his mouth. The ADMORIM of Gur were always against immigration to the Land of Israel. They commanded their followers to await the coming of the Messiah and not to force the issue against the will of G–d. Nevertheless during the thirties, with the growth of anti–Semitism and persecution in Poland the people of "Agudat Yisroel" with the Rabbi of Gur at their head, began to change their stubborn stand towards the Land of Israel and began to allow the Hassidim to immigrate to Palestine.

In 1935, together with my family, I immigrated to Palestine.

One of the spiritual leaders in our town was Rabbi Yeshiah Fisch (Z"L), the brother–in–law of Rabbi Yehuda Arieh Alter, the author of "S'fat Emess" the pre–eminent G–d–fearing Torah scholar who knew how to lead a community. Rabbi Yeshiah was the official appointed Rabbi and was supported by the Russian authorities. He rented land in the village of Zygmuntów that belonged to Graf Wielopolski.

Rabbi Yeshiah, together with his wife met a tragic death in 1903 (or 1905), when they were murdered while they slept when their home was invaded by two murderers, one Jewish from the town of Władysław, and one non–Jewish.

A mausoleum was erected to their memory over their graves by the community and every year on the memorial of their death people would come and pray for their souls. The mystery and motive of the deaths remain clouded and unknown until today.

The accepted Rabbi of Ksiaz was the esteemed Rabbi Moshe Natan Shapira (Z"L), the renowned scholar, a G–d–fearing Jew and the author of many well–known books among them "Shemen le–Maor". Rabbi Moshe Natan was the son–in–law of the ADMOR of Sochatchov and the leader of the esteemed long–lived dynasty of great Rabbis of the Torah.

His apartment was attached to the Study–House and he rarely left it during the six working days. Only Erev Shabbat he would go to the ritual baths to purify himself for the Sabbath. On his way he would hurry the other Jews to close their shops in order not to profane the Holy Sabbath.

Rabbi Moshe Natan was also the leader of a small Yeshiva in the Study–House for the young men who had finished their earlier studies and wished to continue on to higher levels.

Students from other small towns round and about and beyond came to his Yeshiva to study Torah at his feet because of his widespread reputation as a learned scholar and knowledge of the Talmud and relevance of his decisions.

Ritual Slaughterers in our Town

The first slaughterer in Ksiaz that I remember was Rabbi Yitzhak Mendzigursky (Z"L); He was injured by a horse when riding to the Rabbi of Gur and died from his injuries. He was buried in Warsaw in the month of Elul (September/October) 1936. His son Rabbi Mendel (Z"L) was appointed in his place in Ksiaz. He died before the war. After him came his uncle Rabbi Natan Silberberg (Z"L).

[Page 255]

Rabbi Natan, my uncle, was very shy, quiet diffident and modest and didn't have much contact with people. He was extremely accurate in all matters concerning the ritual slaughtering of animals and all the people in town saw him as one of the "36 Righteous Ones". He walked in the way of his fathers and strayed neither to the left nor the right. His wife, Nekha was well–known and recognized as being very righteous. She habitually spent the week–days going round to the houses of all the wealthy people collecting food and cast–off clothing later distributing it all to the poor and needy in town. She was tireless in her toil always ready to extend help to those in need. In the women's gallery in the synagogue she was highly respected and esteemed for her noble attributes.

My memories lead me to the period at the beginning of the month of Nissan, before the Passover. As is usual every year we would go down to the stream near the bridge and draw water in clean utensils for making the matzoth in the bakery of Mr. Nahman David Friedberg and his sons. Those who needed Matzo "Shemura"[1] would arrange a certain time for every family and someone from each of the families would come to the bakery at that hour and do all the necessary preparation of the dough including the prescribed waiting time, placing it in the oven with his own hands.

They tried to improve the taste of the matzoth. The stately ceremonial, the traditional meal of Passover spread a festive atmosphere on the whole family for all the days of Passover and the year.

Trade and Labor

Our town, Ksiaz was surrounded by many successful farms and the estates of Counts and other notables of Poland like Count Wielopolski, Count Taczortynsky(?) and others. Because of this, most of the traders and businessmen in town dealt in farm produce. The small traders would buy the produce from the farmers and sell it to larger traders who passed the cereal to mill–owners for milling and the rest of the crops – like broad beans, beans, grits and oats as animal feed to a grinding–mill.

The farmers would come on Wednesday - market day - with their small home–made products: chickens, geese, ducks, eggs and butter. After they had sold everything to the Jewish folk they went shopping for cloth, clothing and other products for their homes.

A small number of Jewish artisans in the town like tailors and shoe–makers also provided services.

Translator's Footnote

1. Exceptionally Kosher to the Nth degree

The Town Markets

by Haim Friedberg

Translated by Selwyn Rose

For many long years the townspeople were accustomed to hold the market every Wednesday, in the center of town and prepared themselves for that day; either in their shops, workshop or bakeries. The street–traders were especially active in their preparations in readiness for the day. They wandered round the market eyeing keenly the farmers who came from the nearby villages with their carts loaded down with goods for sale to the residents of town. The farmers brought chickens, butter, eggs, vegetables and all sorts of produce, items that the residents of the town were in need of, and at the same time they would purchase sugar, kerosene, salt and especially clothing and footwear.

The People of the Market

Already early in the morning there was a long convoy of wagons and carts on the horizon making its way into town. They were the people from Wodzisław coming to Ksiaz with their wares that included textiles, ready–to–wear clothing, shoes and haberdashery and so on.

[Page 256]

These were the main traders who managed the market; fair weather or foul, rain, burning sun or snow, nothing deterred them or stopped them from coming. They were the biggest specialists in trading in the area. They erected their stalls in the center of the square in their regular individual places. Occasionally a few would ask a chair from an acquaintance in town and with planks of wood they had brought with them erect their shelves and stalls and arrange the goods they had brought to sell. The local farmers from neighbouring villages would come with their families. They hitched their horses and wagons in the square next to the shop of “Mordecai the Tailor”. Apart from that “parking–place”, next to the synagogue was a water–well and they would tether their horses there next to a trough and water–pump, place a feeding–bag of oats over the horse's head and leave them to rest while they hurried off to the market to attend to their trading business with the Jewish traders.

But there were others who came on foot with their small quantities of, perhaps a fattened duck or a large earthenware pot of butter covered with large leaves. With these small–traders came their wives who would purchase this, that or the other that seemed to them to be a bargain item.

The Market in Full Swing

On market days there was noise, movement and throngs of people crushed together, compared to the peace and quiet of the other days of the week. It was difficult to walk along the street. From every side were heard the shouts of the vendors inviting purchasers or calling back one who stalled at paying the price for this or that; and when eventually a compromise was reached the sale was completed with a handshake. Apart from the traders there were also drunk or half–drunk villagers roaming around the market stalls causing minor disturbances.

There were interesting types there as well. One of them was Miriam Rochmes, an old poor woman with rosy cheeks, whom the traders nicknamed Old ————![1] because she kept repeating the expression over and over again. She sold broad beans summer and winter – sour apples and pickled cabbage. She roamed around the market among the stalls calling out "Heisseh Bubbes" ("Hot broad–beans"), and with a friendly smile offers her beans to the market people for a miniscule profit.

Before the summer sowing, after Passover, the Toplonski's appeared with their wares. They settled themselves in the market square next to the church and sat on the ground or large stones and offered different kinds of seeds and fresh vegetables just coming into season. When the Christian farmers bought from them they habitually gave a little more for the master of the farm to encourage a good yield and a little for the inevitable "thief" among them.

The Cattle Market

The cattle–market was outside of town on the road to Wodzisław, opposite the saw–mill. There, live–stock was bought, sold and even exchanged – cows, horses, goats, pigs, etc. Most of the larger middle–men were from Jewish towns and even Christians from all the surrounding towns and villages. The dealings weren't conducted in the best of good faith and management. It happened that the Christian or farmer who bought an apparently healthy beast arrived home with a corpse. By various tricks and chicanery they tried to sell their animals to the farmers and even succeeded in making a profit from both sides.

At the end of the day the traders, the middle–men and the buyers would go to "fat" Shboyntik's(?) banqueting rooms or Szeid. There they drank half a liter of vodka and dined to their hearts' content on sausage and white bread that is unavailable in their villages. On more than one occasion the evening ended up in loud arguments and disturbances from the drunks, to the point that the police were forced to arrest some of them until they sobered–up. Thus it was every week, every year until the coming of Hitler.

Translator's Footnote

1. A Polish curse

[Page 257]

Avraham Zelig Silberberg

by Avraham Zelig Silberberg

Translated by Selwyn Rose

In the middle of the month of Elul 1942 Erev Shabbat at 10 in the morning, my mother (Z"L), stood in the kitchen preparing the dough to make the Shabbos "Challot" and the "tcholent". Suddenly there was the sound of a commotion coming from outside in the town. The bad news immediately became known, that by order of the German authorities leaflets had been posted in town ordering all Jews to report Saturday morning in the town square for "resettlement".

It is difficult to describe the depression that spread amongst us that Friday evening. There were among us those who escaped from the Gestapo by a hairsbreadth and found shelter among us. Now the process of resettlement had reached them – and us – here. I will never forget all the days of my life our last night in our town, my mother crying while lighting the Shabbos candles, as if feeling that it was the last Shabbat of her life. That same night we heard shooting and we discovered that the Nazis had murdered the town's leaders. In the morning we were summoned to the market square and there we were transferred under heavy guard to nearby Słomniki.

From time to time, the SS men would take Jews from the wagons and shoot them. It is hard to describe the fear and terror that fell upon us.

For three days and nights we were held in an open field without food and water. During the day the sun was burning hot and at night we froze in the cold. After three days they separated the old people from the children and younger people. The old men wrapped themselves in shrouds and their prayer–shawls and put on their phylacteries in the knowledge that this was their last hour. At 12 noon the Gestapo came, drunk as lords took the old people and led them away to about a hundred meters distance, or so, and there they shot them. In front of our very eyes they killed the innocent old men from Ksiaz and the surrounding area.

I am not able to describe at length that horrifying scene; my hand shakes and my heart pounds as I recall those bitter moments and my lips mumble "Our Father, our King, for the sake of the martyrs of Thy Holy Name."

Later they took the men, women and children, loaded them onto rail–cars for their last journey to Bełżec. All the remaining younger people were eye–witnesses of the terrible journey. We saw how children in the cattle wagons choked for lack of air and from thirst. After that they took us to the Płaszów camp near Kraków. I stayed there for about a year. From there, in the autumn of 1943 we were taken to Camp '3' at Skarżysko (Werke 'C').

When we arrived it was night and dark in the town, the Gestapo fell upon us with their dogs and made us run to some distant place in the forest that appeared to be some kind of fortress fenced all around with barbed–wire and with armed Tatar guards (Russian soldiers who had betrayed their country), patrolling between the fences. They stood us in front of the SS commander who said: "Everyone who has articles of value – gold, silver or other valuables will hand them over now – if not, he will be killed." And in the blink of an eye, they took one of the men and shot him on the spot.

He was simply an example for the others. We shook from fear and cold; we gave the Gestapo everything we had but they didn't believe us and made body–searches until the morning. Eventually they sent us to empty barrack blocks.

[Page 258]

In the morning we exited the barrack to see and grasp the nature of the camp and its inmates. We saw people with yellow and green complexions dressed in torn and worn paper sacks that had contained crystalline Trotyl and Picric Acid (both chemicals used in the manufacture of explosives), and every one of them a bag of dry bones. We asked them where they were from and they answered "From Warsaw and the surrounding area. We took part in the uprising and they sent us to Majdanek and Treblinka."

After cruel tortures, they chose the youngest among them and sent them to Werke 3 where they lost all image of human beings.

When the "veteran" workers went to work, the Gestapo came with the German works manager and sorted out men for the different departments that were changed every few weeks. I was a carpenter by trade so they took me to work constructing barracks and the others they distributed to the various departments. The Managers of the Jewish camp – Isenberg and Markowitz, and the men of the "Ordnungsdienst" distributed everyone to the various barrack–blocks, according to their work department. I was considered very lucky since I had no night–work.

I could not adjust myself to the sight of the older prisoner–workers when I stood with them to get our food – yellow–faced bags of bones. It was enough to see how the starving men leapt at the food to understand what the Gestapo had done to our people. From that sight alone the scales fell from our eyes and our world fell apart for we understood then that we had fallen into the deepest part of Hell.

At three o'clock in the morning we suddenly heard the sound of a trumpet: "Every one out for night work!" I went out to see who and how many would go. And I heard: "Hall No. 53 form up here and Hall No. 58 Trotyl form up here." Men of the SS and the works' manager count the number of people and there is always someone missing. Men of the "Ordnungsdienst" with sticks in their hands roam around in the barracks and the toilets looking for people and when they can't find them they round up replacement victims from other departments and beat them until they get up and join those outside. Suddenly I see a horrifying sight – they catch a young man sobbing bitterly "I'm ill, I've got a fever and high temperature." He got beaten and was forced to go to work.

In the end they had the right numbers and after standing outside for an hour, they went to the factory. The factory was massive, in the center of town, surrounded by a few fences, tens of different workshops with sophisticated store–rooms and underground bunkers large arms store and rail–lines leading from and to all of them.

The camp spread over 10 kilometers. In that factory we manufactured mines, ammunition for rifles and artillery of all sizes and weights up to 50 kgs., all in noisy surroundings. Steam–locomotives were coming and going and teams of men pushed wagons from store–room to store–room with the overseers brandishing their sticks, and hurrying the workers along with shouts.

Who can imagine those working on the transports; at night they loaded the armaments on the wagons, each unit weighing 50 kgs., every wagon had 4 men working and the schedule called for loading 3 wagons during their shift – all to German specifications of perfection and accuracy. The verse: "The gates of tears are not closed"[1], did not apply to these men. They worked in pain, hunger sweat and blood. A man simply cannot carry that heavy burden of back–breaking work for more than a few weeks. So every once in a while new groups were brought in to replace those that died. I will never forget the following incident: they once took me on a Sunday for work; when we were on the way to the factory, we saw a dead man lying on the roadway. He had walked – and he died. No one looked at him. We passed by his corpse and continued on our way. It was not an isolated incident. Men weakened – and fell; walked – and died.

[Page 259]

After a few weeks they brought young women from Kraków and after two months a number of them died from exhaustion. To those who worked in Workshop 53 the Germans gave a liter of milk every day because the picric acid damages the lungs in a very short while, often before a new transport arrives with new workers. Every morning next to the wash–room stood a large wagon loaded with planks and every day the dead were brought out and put on the wagon. The number was never less than 16 or 17 a day.

Our town Ksiaz also provided two victims: Avraham Nordau and Moshe Silberberg, who perished there, may G–d avenge their blood.

To my good fortune I worked in the barracks. The work was lighter and I was able to get out of that hell alive. Once my section was employed in repair work; suddenly we saw at a distance a wagon loaded with material we were unable to identify from a distance. We were called to help thinking something required repairing. When we got closer we saw the wagon was loaded with corpses and limbs. On another occasion an explosion occurred in the ammunition workshop No.58 and destroyed the entire building killing many Jews and the workshop managers. We were called to bury the bodies. Many of the limbs had become detached from the bodies by the blast and it was difficult to arrange it all for burial. We took them to a large trench that had been prepared about four hundred yards away, 10 meters deep and 50 meters long. We took some of the Trotyl paper bags and covering the bodies laid them side by side, layer upon layer in a common grave. In that common grave were eventually buried thousands of dead – May G–d avenge their blood.

In the middle of the forest the SS arranged a large area and enclosed it with high "walls" made of bales of straw so that passers–by outside were unable to see what was being done. That was the place where the corpses were incinerated. Every day empty buses went out and returned full. Our own eyes did not actually see what was being done but every evening when we neared the fires of the "crematorium" our nostrils were filled with the smell of burning bodies.

One afternoon we heard a voice shouting in the compound: "Everyone out!" The SS men came to the factory. Fear and dread swept over us – who knew what awaited us? They got us all together – about 2000 people, and read out "The sentence": since one of us had taken a piece of rubber from one of the wagons to repair his shoes, he was guilty of sabotage. His sentence: hanging by the Jews. They searched among us for strong men to carry out the sentence on the unfortunate man and eventually the sentence was carried out.

There were also instances of thoughtfulness and care for the individual: I wish to mention Mrs. Markowitz, who saved Etta, the wife of Meshulem Friedberg, from hard work and who remained in the factory right to the end.

In the end they decided to take us westwards, in the general retreat of the German army; thus started a fresh round of atrocities against us. Every day the SS would come and select the weakest among us and take them away for execution. After a general selection they took part of the people and sent them to Częstochowa; from there we were taken to the notorious Buchenwald.

The camp is situated near the city of Weimar, in an extensive forested area. Near it was a large sign–post saying "Buchenwald" there was nothing to be seen in the way of buildings or infrastructure. We were not allowed out of the railroad wagons that had brought us until many of the SS had come with dogs and torches. They fell upon us and rushed us to the closed camp. As we arrived allied aircraft were heard overhead and sirens sounded. We were ordered to sit on the ground. Close to us we saw a large building and on top of it a tall chimney from which smoke was streaming. Then I understood that here was the site of "The Final Solution". After the "all–clear" we were led to the shower shed. They took all our clothing and gave us prisoners' garb with a number imprinted. We had no name – just a number. My personal number was 68468.

[Page 260]

From Buchenwald we were sent to Schlieben Camp. That camp was situated between Berlin and Leipzig. There was an armaments factory there manufacturing anti–tank artillery. We suffered much in that place both from the bombings by the Allies and from the Germans who, while retreating, mistreated the small number of remaining survivors of the various camps. Later we were transferred to Theresienstadt and there I was liberated by the Russians on 9th May 1945.

Translator's Footnote

1. From the Babylonian Talmud, Tractate Baba Metzia

The Evacuation from Ksiaz

by Avraham Ya'acov Walbromski

Translated by Selwyn Rose

The Last Friday

On Friday morning in the month of Elul, 5703, (4th September 1942), the information spread that the German authorities were demanding "contributions". We believed that the money would be used as a ransom for our lives and redemption from the evacuation orders.

Every house–holder brought the required sum to the Jüdenrat because that was how it had always been done on previous occasions when the Germans promulgated their decrees and they were rescinded through the Jüdenrat. In spite of that illusion, fear and despair descended on all of us. The anxiety increased from hour to hour. Tears choked our throats. A few families left town and went to the surrounding villages, to their Christian neighbors, in the belief that they could save themselves.

During the afternoon hours it was possible to discern a lot of movement among our Christian neighbors who came to acquire "bargains" when they realized the "Yids" were being banished from town. There were also those who came to help and offered their friends the Jews hiding places in the homes and farms and refused any form of payment or recompense that was offered them. Everyone acted for himself as he saw fit because there was no one to ask for advice. Many sold their jewelry for the most ridiculous prices in order to get their hands on cash in the belief it would help them get organized in their new place.

Erev Shabbat, with the setting of the sun, when the last of the Jews were hurrying homewards from the ritual bath to their homes in the little back–street lanes, the stunning news spread around that according to the “Landrat” all Jews must leave town tomorrow morning.

An atmosphere of grief fell upon the population; from every Jewish home bitter crying could be heard. At home my mother raised her arms to heaven to cast her woes upwards: “Master of the universe, tear up this decree for the sake of Thy holy Sabbath, for the sake of the righteous great ones of our faith, for the sake of the infant school and remove this shame on Thy people Israel.” Bitter sobbing filled our home. My three sisters, Shifra–Leah, Serka and Sarah–Ruhama suggested fleeing and hiding with a Christian family and even began preparations for doing so but almost immediately changed their mind. How could they leave their parents, to separate from their family and the entire town? The sound of shooting echoed from outside interrupted the continuation of thought. The first victim was the secretary of the Jüdenrat, Yossel Horowitz (Z”L) who had been shot by the Polish detective, Masseter, near Kachalsky's house. Terror descended on the town. Within minutes the streets emptied. It was the sign that the operation of banishment had entered the stage.

[Page 261]

My father Rabbi Aharon (Z”L) and I prayed silently and said Kiddush, we didn't want to cancel the last Sabbath evening meal. But the holiness of the day didn't prevent the murderers from continuing their actions. The Mayor of the town, Kraschynski, entered the house of Rabbi Nahman David Friedberg together with a group of Polish policemen and shot to death the Rabbi's eldest son, Haim Friedberg (Z”L).

Afterwards they came to the house Moshe Shalom Abramczyk and killed his son, Mordecai (Z”L), as well and from there they went to Yechiel Sultanik' house and shot both him and his eldest son, Hirsch–Leib (Z”L).

Footsteps approached our house and in a flash there were loud knockings on the door. My older sister Sarah'leh (Z”L) opened the door. Two Polish policemen came in and ordered us not to leave the house until morning. They ordered me to go with them.

The pleadings of my family were in vain. I went under the guard of one of the policemen while the second one stayed in our house and as I was told later, demanded ransom for my safe return. Everything that was available in the house of value – silver, jewelry and valuables were given to him to save my life. As I went out I saw a group of Polish policemen standing in the street not far from our house, in conversation with the wife of a policeman who lives in our house.

My guard told them that he had found me trying to run away. They began to beat me and shouting at me making fun of me, telling me that a 7 gram bullet would be enough for me. Luckily the policeman's wife recognized me and persuaded them to let me go. They told me to go home and as I started to hurry away they fired a shot after me to frighten me.

Returning home, I heard how they went to Laybl Teitelbaum's (Z"L) house and taken him to the same group of policemen. From there they took him though a narrow lane to Staskiewicz's carpentry shop and there they shot him to death. Until late at night the shouts and the disturbances and the abusive drunken language continued. The town synagogue sexton, Yossel and a few other householders were forced to bury that night's victims in the cemetery.

Shabbat Morning 5th September 1942

From all the lanes and passageways the families came loaded down with their packages. They come, plodding their way to the market where Polish and a few German police awaited them. This was the central meeting point. Within minutes the market place filled to over–flowing. Immediately the wagon owners appeared – farmers from the villages and their horses and carts who were ready to transport all the Jews of the town. Ordered by the Germans the police entered the homes and with shouts and bullying drove out those who had not yet completed their packing or thought that somehow they could evade being caught.

From a distance the Christian neighbors looked on and jeered at the banished Jews and waited for the moment when they had gone so that they could loot whatever got left behind in the rush. Many of the Jewish people were deeply depressed, broken in spirit and body and no longer believed in any hope of salvation. They wrapped themselves up in their cloaks and blankets and said their "confessions". Others exhibited revolt, convincing each other they were walking like sheep to the slaughter and the fires of vengeance burned in their eyes.

The pain was enormous, unbearable. Not because of the property and belongings left behind did the heart ache, but the desecration of the Shabbat that they were forced to perform and for the fact that we were forced to leave the town in which Jews had resided for tens of generations. With broken hearts and eyes downcast in shame before their Christian neighbors each one climbed aboard the wagon appointed to him. At a given signal from a German officer, the long convoy began to leave the market square towards Miechów.

[Page 262]

Tens of wagons and carts, loaded down with people, women and children, continued along the road. We were accompanied on both sides by Polish police, who were carefully guarding us made sure that no one got off the carts. In addition a German guard in control of everything rode alongside, back and forth, overseeing everyone. They removed Yossel Bornstein, Lazar's son, shot him to death and left him lying by the road–side.

The heart screamed out and cried for vengeance. It was an unheard cry, a cry from the heart.

We passed by Miechów. Not a single Jew was to be seen, the beloved town was deserted. We passed the market square and arrived at the suburb of Słomniki. Here, in flooded fields, was the central collection point of the villages of Ksiaz, Miechów and Charsznica, Działoszyce and Proszowice. We found there hundreds of families sitting on their bundles. Noise, bustle, crowding – in short: hell – nothing like anything I had seen in my life. It was hard for common sense to grasp what one saw going on here. Our new "lords and masters" hurried us along with shouts and shoves. The entire town like one immense family climbed down off the wagons and carts with the Germans speeding us up. With our bundles on our shoulders we plodded to the place appointed for us in the center of the soggy field. Everyone took out his good clothes and spread them out under him, otherwise we would simply have to sit or lie in the mud.

More than 8 thousand people, women, old men and toddlers were concentrated in that place. Guarding them were Yunaks[1], with shovels in their hands. Both the Polish police and a few German police kept order and ensured obedience to their commands. Men were picked out to dig trenches that were to be used as toilets for the thousands of people. The spiritual and physical degradation of our condition – that was the immediate target to which they were striving at the time.

Broken, depressed and exhausted, after such a terrible day of suffering and torture, without food and water, I wanted to burst through the barrier and fetch a little water from the barrels that were standing next to the Jüdenrat from Słomniki. A German soldier sensed my purpose and hit me over the head with the butt of his rifle. I managed to evade him and disappeared among the throng of people, drinking the blood pouring down my face. A Jewish doctor there gave me some first–aid treatment.

A cool breeze began to blow signalling the coming of evening. The sky was tinged red from the setting sun as if reflecting the blood that had been spilled that day. Like a flock of sheep the people huddled together and tried to sleep. Everyone waited for the night and hoped it would bring some rest and relaxation. But quite the opposite was the case. From all sides came calls for help. They were the cries of those who were robbed and beaten or had put up a fight against the thieves who came to rob them, or insult their Jewish dignity. Our guards fired their rifles above the heads of the crowds. Suddenly something passed over my head with a deafening whistle. Immediately after I heard a Jewish man give a heart–rending moan and he began to recite the death–bed "confession" with the last of his strength, asking to be given a proper Jewish burial. Suddenly everything became quiet until the break of day.

With morning, the night's victim was given a proper Jewish burial in the Słomniki gathering point, between two aged trees.

At mid–day, while all the citizens of Słomniki were strolling freely about town, the Jewish population of the surrounding villages was standing in the muddy fields in rows of ten. The "Selektsia" was conducted by the labor office of Kraków and its assistants. First of all the took out all the old people, sat them on carts that were standing ready and took them not too far away from us where they were murdered. I remember Shlomo Bardin sitting on the cart wrapped in a blanket, his prayer book in his hand reciting the "confession". Afterwards they took another 800 young men and stood them to one side. I was one of them. In front of our eyes we saw how they sent our fathers to the railroad station where stood tens of cattle–trucks ready to receive thousands of people.

[Page 263]

In the distance we could see how the dark gray cloud was billowing up. There were some of our families who had made their way to the cattle–cars and climbed aboard with their bundles urged on by the Germans.

The guards used their rifle butts to push everyone who slowed up the movement or broke file. We tried to get closer to the railroad station and could see that the cars were already crammed full of people.

They stripped off some of their clothes because the heat inside the cars was intolerable and the floors had been treated with a solution of chlorine. The cattle–cars were shut and the tiny windows barred. Through these windows we could see the pale faces and frightened eyes looking out. The people were begging in vain to the German guard for a little water to drink. Even the children had no water.

The sun had already set when the train started to move. We already knew that our families were being taken to Bełżec and we were wondering to ourselves what fate awaited us.

Indignant, despairing and depressed we were ordered to climb into the open cars guarded by the surveillance police of the train travelling in the direction of the Prokocim camp.

From a distance we saw some flood–lights. It was a sign that we were nearing the camp.

We were forced to enter the camp at the run urged on by our guards. We were welcomed with abuse and curses and shouts as a calculated means of stunning our senses as to what was happening to us. There were Jews in Prokocim camp who had arrived earlier but the Germans made sure that we were unable to communicate with them or be in any kind of contact with them. We were taken into a large hut and told that we must turn in all our possessions: gold, silver, watches, gold pens and any jewellery. We were allowed to keep only 25 Złoty and in order to instil fear they took one of us and shot him in front of our eyes; it worked. In the blink of an eye crates were filled with gold and other valuables. The procedure lasted until late at night.

The following morning we were released from work and we were able to talk with some of the Jews who had arrived before us. From them we learned we were to be sent to another camp. At nightfall we were marched to "Julag", or, as it was called, Kraków–Płaszów. I, personally, had already been in that labor–camp and escaped from there before the exile and when I learned we were being taken there I feared they would recognize me, because the

Commandant, Müller, punished escapers when caught with hanging. There was no way I could escape. I threw away all my documentation so they couldn't identify me and together with everyone else entered the camp so well known to me...

Płaszów

In Julag camp, under the command of Müller, hunger and infection ran riot. The sanitary arrangements were indescribable. Every day there were killings by shooting of totally innocent people for the slightest of offences. Thus, for example, a man was shot by the police for going to the toilet outside the permitted time. During the same period Simcha Mlinarski, the son of Itcha Fischer and his grandson of Sandor Yosef from Kraków were also murdered.

We rose at dawn for work. We worked for Siemens–Bau–Union who had built the Kraków–Warsaw railroad. The company employed thousands of workers and accumulated millions while the Jewish workers died by the bullets of the railroad police or lost their lives through starvation and torture. When I saw that my life was in danger I decided to escape a second time from the camp and with that in mind I chose a suitable day – the evening of Kol Nidrei.

In the morning, after going out to work, I managed to slip away in the direction of the Płaszów brick works intending to walk from there to my town where there were still a few Jewish families living after the first exile.

[Page 264]

When I got to my home sometime in the afternoon, I was gripped with fear. The floors were destroyed, everything was in turmoil. It was the work of our Christian neighbors who exploited the opportunity of the deserted house. I found a prayer–book from the Day of Atonement. I went into the Succah in Laybl Teitelbaum's garden and there I spent the whole night of Yom Kippur; I will never forget it. At the same time I took stock of myself and asked myself: Why does all this happen to the Jews?

That was on Tuesday morning 22nd September 1942. In town, there were still the Jüdenrat members of the Jewish police force and their families who had hidden during the "Aktsia" and returned home afterwards believing that they will be safe. When I went out into the street I saw they were taking the dead to the cemetery. There were twenty Jews who had been strangled to death in the Wielka Wieś prison together with tens of other Jews from the entire area who had hidden themselves at the time of the “Aktsia” and when the order came from the Germans to return home they came out of their hiding places only to be captured at the second “Aktsia” and liquidated.

A short time before the second “Aktsia” I left Ksiaz. When I heard that at the brick factory in a near–by town there were people from our town I decided to go there and try to find some work. It was a private factory owned by a man called Wencel. The German Commissars took it from him but left him there in charge and restyled him as Volksdeutsche.

We could move around freely and I noticed that at that time I was getting good food and also a salary of 30–40 Złoty a week. With that sort of money it was possible to buy two loaves of bread. The work in the factory was hard. My job had various components, like taking all the bricks out of the machine and transferring them to a trolley arranged in rows. The tempo of the work was so high that I hardly had time to spread sand on the floor of the trolleys every time I returned for a fresh load of bricks.

We also had to load the dry bricks into the furnace and remove them after being fired, when they became ready for use in construction work. Wencel also had a delivery service and we were used as assistants for loading. From time to time we also worked the field that belonged to the factory. When an order came to collect all the Jews for transfer to labor camps Wencel made efforts to keep us in the factory.

One day the Gestapo came and ordered all of us back to the Kraków ghetto.

The meeting place where we started out for Płaszów was no. 17 Krakusa Street.

One day in February 1943 a harsh winter's day, with threatening skies and streets covered in snow a group of Ukrainian guards came to the ghetto in Kraków and we were ordered by the German officer in charge to form up in fours and we were marched away in the direction of the labor camp in Jaruzalymski Street; there was a cemetery there.

The Ukrainians hurried us along with shouts of “Hurry–up” “in fours, in fours”. When we got there we found a group of Jewish workers and a few large barrack–rooms already waiting for us. The camp Commandant and the Jewish commander of the Ordnungsdienst, Goldberg, were waiting for us.

The barracks were cold and damp, without beds – just three tiers of bare planks. The cold was severe when we lay down on them. We didn't get undressed because we had nothing to cover ourselves with.

We were woken at dawn and formed pairs and were taken to work. The work was mainly constructing barracks and the uprooting of tombstones which we used to form a foundation for the floors.

[Page 265]

The work uprooting the tombstones was very hard indeed and consisted of hauling them up the slippery hill covered in snow.

We worked hard, accompanied with curses and blows from the SS until we had uprooted all the tombstones. We made a make–shift sledge from some planks and harnessed ourselves like horses, hauling the tombstones up the slope. The Germans made sure that they didn't get broken and that we got them safely to their new location. During that work there were many victims.

After all the tombstones were in place, tractors came and trundled over the area smoothing it out. Hundreds of buried bones were unearthed and mixed together with the earth and nothing remained to show that there had ever been a cemetery there. It should be said that after the area had been cleared mass graves were dug in the same place and tens of thousands of Jewish victims from the Kraków ghetto were buried there.

When the time came for Müller to transfer the camp to the second German murderer, Goetz, he made a “Selektsia” on the open area used for “appel”. In front of everyone he shot Goldberg with his own hands and a few workers. A group of women, babies and weak people were sent to the Kraków ghetto which was used at that time as a collection center for transportation onwards.

Goetz, the new Commandant of Płaszów camp, had tens of new barracks erected, organized a new Jewish Ordnungsdienst, liquidated the ghettos of Tarnów and Kraków; the fit he sent to work and artisans and professionals went to the camp.

Many Jews from Ksiaz who were at that time in the Kraków ghetto or surrounding labor camps were brought to Płaszów. The camp became redefined as a Concentration Camp and the number of victims who fell during Müller's time seemed as nothing compared with the “reign” of the Commandant Goetz. Day after day he would kill with his own hands 10 or 12 people when he walked through the camp with his big dog or rode by on his horse. He would set his dog on his victim for the slightest reason.

I will never forget the terrible sight at "appel" when he set his dog on Almer (Z"L) of Miechów. His screams reached to the heavens but they did nothing to soften the heart of the murderer. The dog tore his victim to shreds before our eyes and Almer's soul breathed its last there at "appel".

On another occasion Goetz ordered the hanging of a young man and a young woman in the presence of the whole population of the camp on the "appel" compound. On his orders entire groups of laborers were shot to death when they returned exhausted from a day's toil.

Among them were two youngsters from Ksiaz, Shabtai Silberberg (Z"L) and Baruch Mlinarski (Z"L), the son of Itcha Fischer.

He had his victims taken up to the top of the rise, which had turned into a Martyr's altar. Not a single day passed without corpses burned as martyrs.

Goetz particularly liked to be present when the punishment was 25 lashes with a whip. The sadist took pleasure in seeing the terror on the faces of the victims and their terrible shrieks of agony caused him maximum pleasure.

However much I paint the picture of life in the camp at Płaszów, it pales in contrast to the reality. Our lives turned to living hell with no possibility of hope.

Translator's Footnote

1. Youth Labor Brigade

[Page 266]

Ksiaz under the Nazis

by Yehoshua Wundersman

Translated by Selwyn Rose

After the Germans conquered Miechów they sent out patrols to survey the area, in the direction of Ksiaz. But they were intercepted unexpectedly by Polish soldiers who shot and killed them. As a result the German advance was held up for three days; The Germans supposed that a strong force of Poles was firmly entrenched there. On the fourth day a force of German troops in close order entered Ksiaz in order to neutralize the Polish defense post that the Germans thought was there. Immediately a German appeared and ordered all the residents – Jews and non–Jews, to assemble in the market square. There was panic everywhere because no one knew what the Germans were planning and what their intentions were. The Germans soldiers entered the homes in order to ensure that there were no hidden arms or Polish soldiers who were scattered everywhere.

Facing all the residents gathered in the square, the Germans placed a machine–gun intended to frighten and subdue the population. After a short while, a German cavalry officer appeared and asked: "Is everyone still alive?" and left everyone sighing.

Deep depression descended on everyone gathered there; one of them – Lazer _(?), suffered a heart attack and died. He was the first victim of Ksiaz. At last the order came to release us. From then on the Jewish population hid themselves away in their homes looking to the future with great concern.

The following day the German headquarters based itself in the new government school building of Ksiaz and issued "Order of the day" to the citizens to return to work, open the shops and for everything to return to its normal function.

Already in the first days of the German occupation the town began to feel the absence of many supplies such as: kerosene, candles, coal and bread because the bakeries did not have the facilities to supply such a large sudden influx of refugees from the surrounding towns and especially from Zaglambia.

The authorities nominated as mayor, Hibner, a refugee from Silesia, who had married a woman from one of the local Christian towns. From the first moment he cooperated with the German and acted as the major advisor on all activities in the area. The first action of the German command was to create a Jüdenrat that would organize the work–force that the German authorities were interested in. The main work was the paving of a road between Kraków and Warsaw, via Kielce. They also built a rest–camp for the military for soldiers returning from the front.

Now and again the Germans issued orders to the residents to provide articles such as coats, furs, jewellery and radios. The stranglehold on the Jews tightened progressively.

In 1942, during the month of April, a representative of the "Arbeitsamst" (works department), arrived from Kraków; all the young women, capable of work, were brought out and the representative himself chose twenty of them and sent them to the Lotnisko airfield, near Kraków. A few days later, he appeared again and collected all the fit young men, chose fifty of them and put them in the Wielka Wieś prison. He held them there all night and the next morning sent them to Płaszów under the command of the notorious Müller. The camp was encircled with a fence. We were kept there as prisoners under the guard of the "Schützbahn Polizei"[1]. We worked at various tasks such as road–making in the area for the Siemens–Bau–Union company. Müller behaved with unbelievable cruelty and many fell victim at his mercy.

Translator's Footnote

1. Railroad security police

[Page 267]

A Matzeyvah[1]

by A. Y. Walbromski

Translated by Gloria Berkenstat Freund

Dedicated to my father and mother:

Ahron and Tsirl;

Sisters: Shifra Leah, Tsorka and Sura-Rutma

There in Bełżec, far from Ksiaz,
Perished with the entire shtetl [town];
With graves spread through the fields
And I cannot find your grave.
From sadness and the cry of pain
I have written these words for you.
Father, mother, three sisters
Of all I remain alone.
There is no trace of your bones,
My tears pour out on your grave.
May this poem be a matzeyvah stone
To the memory of ash-burned limbs.
And I also will say Kaddish [memorial prayer] for you,
My head bent in sadness.
My heart will always mourn,
I will not rest, nor be silent.

Translator's Footnote

1. Headstone

[Page 268]

Reb Dovid Walbromski
– the House of Prayer gabbai

by A. Y. Walbromski
Translated by Gloria Berkenstat Freund

Reb Dovid Walbromski, of blessed memory – tall, broad shouldered, sturdily built, with a snow–white beard that enveloped his entire face, with his thick eyebrows, with his sharp glance – was well known in the shtetl [town] as a communal worker and gabbai [manager of synagogue affairs] of the house of prayer. We called him Dovid shnayder [tailor]; during the last years before the war, he sewed a cloth robe for a businessman and, very rarely, a Shabbos [Sabbath] coat or a kaftan for a well–to–do member of the petty bourgeoisie. But all of this was not enough for an income. Thanks to his sons, who left for America after the First World War and sent him dollars, Reb Dovid could be the gabbai for the house of prayer and the Khevra–Kadisha [burial society] and do other communal and charitable tasks. Every Monday and Thursday Reb Dovid shnayder and his constant partner, Reb Shlomo Glezer, went through the shtetl and collected money and other things such as Passover flour, heating material in the winter–time and would distribute them to those people who were in need of them. It was known that if Reb Dovid collected donations it was needed and they gave generously. There was no funeral or celebration in which Reb Dovid did not take part. He lived more for others than for himself. Thus he lived his years as a true, devoted communal worker. He was the gabbai at the house of prayer for as long as I knew him. He was the first one there in the morning and the last one at night. He made sure that there was light for the young men who sat at the long tables studying until late at night.

I often saw how he would prepare the lamps himself and simultaneously clean the small glasses, despite the fact that this was the work of the shamas [synagogue caretaker]. He made sure that the ceramic oven would be heated on winter nights and that there was water for washing the hands in the ritual washstand.

As Reb Dovid, his wife, Faygl, of blessed memory, also helped her husband and was the gabbita [wife of the gabbai] for the women and helped every one in need with what they needed.

Reb Dovid Leads the Creation of a *Sefer*

I remember how Reb Dovid went through the shtetl to collect money for the writing of a Sefer–Torah [Torah scroll]. Every week a list was hung in the house of prayer with how much everyone had donated. When Reb Dovid saw that this would take a long time, because large sums of money were not flowing in, he himself gave a larger sum of money and thus he made it possible to finish the scroll quickly. Who does not remember the joy in our shtetl when the Sefer–Torah was taken to the house of prayer? The entire shtetl was gathered at the synagogue square: men, women and children. There was joy in Reb Dovid's house. Every respected Jew wrote a letter and this was done with awe and love.

[Page 269]

The family of Reb Dovid Walbromski.

His wife Faygl, daughter Bluma, [her] husband Dovid Waczrinski and children

It should be understood that at such a celebration they drank whiskey, ate honey cake as a celebration of the completion of the new Torah scroll, they did a Hasidic dance in which everyone was intertwined. When they were to take the scroll into the house of prayer, Yehiel Lezarek, disguised on a horse, went into Reb Dovid's house and with a cheerful song from the entire group and the accompaniment of music, the scroll was taken in under a canopy, placed in the Torah ark of the house of prayer of which Reb Dovid the shnayder was the gabbai.

Reb Dovid – the Leader of the Hakhnoses Orkhim[1]

As was the custom in all Jewish shtetlekh [towns], it was the same in Ksiaz The orkhim [guests] found their first stop in the house of prayer and particularly the guests who remained for Shabbos [Sabbath]. Reb Dovid made sure that they would be taken care of with a festive meal as well as a place to sleep. No Shabbos passed on which there was not a guest at Reb Dovid's table. In addition to food, there also was a bed for several guests. His wife, Faygl, was particularly involved with this mitzvah [commandment; popularly translated as good deed]; she made sure that there would be a well–made bed on the straw mattresses as well as a warm meal with tea for the guests. She often lamented that a certain guest had taken an object of hers from the house, but this did not affect her in a bad way. On the contrary, she again continued with the mitzvah of Linas haTzedak[2] and the Hakhnoses Orkhim.

During the Time of War

During the time of the war, when the Germans were stationed in the shtetl and always grabbed people for forced labor, there was a fear of praying collectively in the house of prayer or in the synagogue; therefore, they adapted to praying with Reb Dovid in his house. Worshippers wearing talisim [prayer shawls] also were taken out from there and forced to work on Shabbos. Once, on a Shabbos winter afternoon, when the group was gathered at the house of Reb Dovid shnayder preparing for Minkhah [afternoon prayer] and for the third Shabbos meal, a German foreman, who was at that time leading the work on the highway on the Krakow–Warsaw line, suddenly entered and removed several Jews to work and as a punishment for so many Jews gathering in a house, raised his cane to Reb Dovid, beat him savagely and beat out one of his eyes. He [Reb Dovid] was half blind from then on.

[Page 270]

Reb Dovid and his wife, Faygl, and all of the Ksiaz Jews were deported during the deportation from the shtetl. In Slomnik I happened to stand in the same row – of 10 people wide – with him and my entire family. He and all of the thousand Jews from the area perished in Belzec. May God avenge their blood!

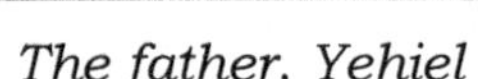

The father, Yehiel *The mother, Shprinca* *The daughter, Golda*

Walbromski Family, my God avenge their blood

Translator's Footnotes

1. Sabbath shelter for poor guests
2. Society for the homeless

[Page 271]

Yosl the Town *Shamas*

by A. Y. Walbromski

Translated by Gloria Berkenstat Freund

In every *kehile* [organized Jewish community] where there was a rabbi, there also was a shamas [synagogue attendant – sexton]. There was a shamas in our shtetl Ksiaz named Yosl Szlamowicz. Yosl was left an orphan[1] with his sick mother, Fraydl, who lived in a dark room in the courtyard of the good-hearted Christian, Alkusznial, who it is more than certain never asked her for rent money because she did not have any livelihood with which to raise her children, Yosl and his sisters Hinda and Rywka.

The kehile took pity and decided to make her son, Yosl, the town shamas, thus giving them the means to exist. He had his good qualities, which made him beloved at the kehile as well as with the city's shop owners; his honesty and naivety and his willingness to work gave him the ability to carry on a family life with a wife and three sons. His work as shamas consisted of bringing water for the house of prayer, heating the oven during the winter, sweeping the floor of the synagogue and house of prayer, going on assignments for the rabbi during a [session of the] religious court, reminding everyone of the time to light the candles on erev Shabbos [the eve of the Sabbath] as well as during the time of the High Holidays during the month of Elul [corresponding to September and October], being in attendance at the cemetery, waking [people] in the morning for the penitential prayers [shlikhos] with three knocks on the door, so that people almost jumped out of their skin in fear, shouting in his stuttering voice: "Jews, wake up for shlikhos, Jews wake up for shloysh esre mides [13 rules for interpreting the laws of Moses]."

In Ksiaz one was not allowed to carry things on Shabbos because there was no eruv [an area enclosed by a ritual wire, which permits the carrying of certain items on the Sabbath]. One could only carry things in the Shul Gas [Synagogue Street] up to the mikvah [ritual bathhouse], and when orkhim [guests or poor people] would arrive in the shtetl who would be invited to Shabbos meals, they would go through the shtetl and ask for food, not knowing that one must not carry things on Shabbos. Yosl the Shamas, seeing that they were committing such a great sin, would run after them and strongly reprimand then. He himself, reaching the tkhum-Shabbos, took off his chain and watch and lay it on Reb Shimkha Avramchik's threshold and ran after the orkhim who already were on the next street, protecting them from sin.[2]

Returning, he did not find his watch. He uttered a cry of lament, humming in an undertone: "No father, no mother, no watch."

His Shabbos was disturbed, and the jokesters at Minkhah [afternoon prayers] at the synagogue made jokes on his account. In addition to his income as shamas, he also was the haircutter for the Hasidic group, which did not want to come into contact with Kapecz, the anti-Semitic haircutter. Yosl the Shamas would come to every home and cut the hair of the group. He was a bookseller. During the war, Yosl the Shamas walked around the street, with a rope on his shoulders, a little like a Warsaw porter and was not afraid of the Germans who, in truth, did not bother him. Every day he would go to work for anyone who would pay him.

[Page 272]

At that time, they had to present themselves for work every day at the Judenrat [Jewish council], which had to provide 30-40 workers a day for the German Wehrmacht [armed forces].

And whoever did not want to go to work could hire a worker and pay the daily price of 12-15 zlotes. Thus, Yosl the Shamas went to work every day in order to earn a piece of bread for his family.

At the deportations, he and his family along with the people of the entire shtetl were sent by transport to Bełżec and perished there.

May the Lord avenge their blood.

Translator's Footnotes

1. In Yiddish the word *yosim* – orphan – can refer to a child who has lost one parent.
2. *tkhum-Shabbos* is the distance (2,000 cubits – about half a mile or 914 meters) a pious Jew may walk from where he is located on Shabbos. Yosl lay down his chain and watch because there was no eruv present and, therefore, he could not carry his watch.

My Family in the *Shtetl* Kzias

by Yitzhak Meir Wyerza

Translated by Gloria Berkenstat Freund

Many years have passed since the tragic annihilation of my *shtetl* [town] birthplace.

I am tormented by my feelings and I cannot free myself from what was deeply etched in my memory during the years of my childhood: the *shtetele* [small town] with its residents in general and my dear family in particular. Individuals from a number of families survived after the destruction, as it is written: ["I shall take you, even] one from a city and two from a family, [and I shall bring you to Zion." – Jeremiah 3:14]... Therefore, I feel a duty to contribute to the Yizkor Book within the framework of my abilities and describe the death of my family.

My grandparents, Yosef and Rayzl Lefkowicz, whom I remember, lived in Kzias for their entire lives, had a small food shop on Kozlower Road and lived and led a middleclass life, married off their sons, Henokh, Shimeon, Avraham and my mother, Rayzl, who lived through the seven levels of hell in the camps and perished there.

My father, Yosef Wyerza, born in Kzias, a tailor by trade, was occupied with communal problems in addition to his daily work. He was a *dozor* [member of the synagogue council], a councilman at the community council and helped to create the guild, the union in Kzias and was the secretary there for many years. This was the only organized worker union that bore no political character. He went through all of the deportationd during the war with all of the Kzias residents, was in various camps, such as Plaszow, Mauthausen, Melk and Ebensee, from which he was liberated by the Americans.

Broken, sick, without the courage to live – I found my father in such a state after the liberation. I, myself, also was in the camps and could not help him very much at that time. We decided to join our family, which had been living in America since before the war.

[Page 273]

But my father has suffered too much in the camps; he could not build a new life. My father died after a few years in America.

Thus did my family perish; I will never forget them.

The Families in the Bunkers

by Mordekhai Herszkowicz and Ahron Matuszinski

Translated by Gloria Berkenstat Freund

On the 24th of February 1938 I was in the Polish Army in Krakow. I served in the artillery. When the war broke out I fell into German captivity. I returned home to Ksiaz in1940, when the Germans were already torturing the Jews and were forcing them to work. They took my father, Wolf Herszkowicz, of blessed memory, from the house with his hands raised and he had to march through the streets and shout that the Jews themselves were responsible for the war.

At that time I was the only money earner in my family, so I risked my life and went to the surrounding villages to gather a little food.

In 1942, when the Germans began to send the Jews to labor camps near Płaszów, I did not appear. The Germans with the help of the Polish police took me to the middle of the market, severely beat me and placed me in the Ksiaz jail. Thus they forced me to work. I jumped out of the vehicle in the middle of the road on the way to work, escaped and hid in the villages.

[Page 274]

My father left during the deportation of all of the middle class from the city. On the contrary, my mother, Hinda, of blessed memory, my brothers, Yitzhak and Ahron Noakh, of blessed memory, my sister, Dwoyra Brayndl, of blessed memory, and Gutsha and my brother-in-law, Ahron Matuszinski and I left for the nearest village, Gebeltow, and hid in the ice house at the estate of the noble Drzanat. My father had been a pachciarz [tenant] of the noble for many years. At night we would sneak out and look for something to eat. We lived there for eight months, lived a bestial life, nourished with raw beets and whatever appeared.

Others were hidden by the Christian, Yozef Konieczny's family in a bunker under the stall. Hidden there were: Meir Matuszinski, of blessed memory, and his wife, Rywka, of blessed memory, Yisroel Leizarek's daughter and their four children, Chanala, of blessed memory, Yosela, of blessed memory, Malkala, of blessed memory, and Wolf, of blessed memory, and [Meir's] brother, Yekl Matuszinski. Yehiel Leizarek, of blessed memory, Henokh Leizarek and their youngest sister, Toyba, of blessed memory, also were [hidden] there. And it happened that when Yekl and Henokh went to look for food they came to us in the bunker. It was a miracle from heaven.

Until then, no one knew about the others; when they saw in what conditions we were living, they took us with them to their bunker at the Christian, Yozef Konieczny's [stall].

We experienced a difficult life there, but we were all together and lived on whatever was available.

There was even more fear and the situation grew worse from day to day. The Germans, using every means possible, began to search for all of the Jews who were hidden in the villages and in the fields. There was no lack of helpers.

In 1943 the situation became unbearable. We could not remain in one place. My brother-in-law, Ahron, and his wife, Gutsha, decided to move to Wladek Kukuryk, one of their Christian family acquaintances in the village of Szwienczica and they were there until the liberation on the 15th of January 1945.

We helped the Kukuryk family in their work in any way we could. They did not ask for any money. Every morning when the wife brought food for the cows, she simultaneously took care of Them.

There with the Christian family of pious and good gentile people, we lived through the difficult war years. We feel as a debt to mention the Kukuryk family for their humane attitude.

[Page 275]

I and the rest of my family who remained with the Konieczny family went through difficult times. Meir Matuszinski, who had left money and things of value with the Christian, Marjan Zeliczkewicz, before the deportation, risked his life and came to Ksiaz and asked him for food as well a part of the money, which he needed very badly. The Christian drove him off and told him that he should not dare come to him anymore. If he tried, he would turn him over to the Germans. This time he would allow him to live.

He returned to the bunker broken, without courage, full of fear and again suffered with his family but believed that maybe they would live through the war.

But fate wanted something else... On the 5th of May 1944 the A.K. [Armia Krajowa - Home Army - main Polish resistance group] group arrived at the village of Gelbultub and the [house of the] Konieczny family. It appears that they had received information from the collaborators that Jews were being hidden. The Polish partisans, who actually did fight against the Germans, also [fought] against the Jews. And as they could not fight enough of a war with the Germans, they let out all of their hatred and anger on the remaining Jewish survivors.

A division of 50 men and horses and machine guns arrived, surrounded the Konieczny's house and demanded that we leave and join the partisan group and take all of our things with us.

They took additional horses for this purpose. We sat on the wagons and traveled far from the village. A terrible scene took place there.

They asked us to get out of the wagons in the Adama Forest, tormented us to reveal other hidden Jews whom we knew. It should be understood that, God forbid, we did not reveal anything; we understood our situation, that they were going to shoot us all and, at the field near the Adama, the Polish partisan A.K. shot the Meir Matuszinksi family, his wife, Rywka, and their four children, the Herszkowicz family, Hinda, the two sons Yitzhak and Ahron-Noakh and the daughter Dwoyra-Brayndil [previously spelled Brayndl], Toyba, the youngest daughter in the Leizarek family. This took place on the 5th of May 1944, in the month of Iyar 5704.

At that moment, Yisroel Leizarek's daughter, Toyba, begged that she be the first one to be shot. We made use of that moment and began to escape. Yankl Matuszinski, of blessed memory, Yitzhak Herszkowicz, of blessed memory, Yehiel Leizarek, of blessed memory, Henokh Leizarak and I, Mordekhai Herszkowicz, each ran without a purpose. We just wanted to save our lives. I found a pit and I entered it. The A.K. members riding on horses chased me and did not notice me.

[Page 276]

Henokh Leizarek met a peasant plowing his field; he joined him and going along with the plow, he saved himself. The peasant then took him in and kept him for several days. He survived.

Yehiel Leizarek, of blessed memory, escaped to the village of Krzesiwka. He had many acquaintances there and believed that he would succeed in saving himself, but it was different. His acquaintances, the gentiles, turned him over to the Germans and some say that they themselves [the acquaintances] killed him. My brother, Yitzhak Herszkowicz, of blessed memory, was a stout man and it was difficult for him to run; he removed his boots and thought it would be easier to run, but the A.K. caught and shot him.

Yankl Matuszinski, of blessed memory, survived the war and when he went to the village of Maciejow to demand his money from the Christian, Kania Jendryk, he [Jendryk] did not only not want to give him his money, but murdered him on the spot with his own hands.

The A.K. shot the rest of the family; their grave is located in the Adama Forest.

All of the Christians who hid Jews were almost all murdered by members of the A.K. The Konieczny family, which hid the Ksiaz families, had a bitter end.

The house of the Christian Konieczny was set on fire. His wife and daughter were shot by the A.K. members. The father and the son, on the other hand, were in the field then. Hearing what was taking place, they never returned to the village, but wandered homeless, without a home, in the field, and without food for keeping alive.

How I Survived the Germans

by Ruchl Wilczkowski

Translated by Gloria Berkenstat Freund

I am Alta Ruchl, the oldest daughter of Sheva and Shmuel Zaynwl Wilczkowski, I am also the oldest grandchild of Perl and Shlomo Nalefka. My mother's parents had a bakery in Ksiaz. There were three brothers and a small sister in our house – one sister died when she was eight years old. She was a year younger than I was. She was named Rywka Rayzl.

I was 12 years old when the [Second World] war broke out; I had not yet graduated from the folks-shul [public school] because they no longer permitted Jews to attend. My parents sent me to private teachers and thus I studied a little bit. But this did not last long; they constantly tortured us in Ksiaz. The Germans had taken my father to be shot several times because they had found several white breads in our bakery. A short time later they took the bakery away from us. Everything we loved was taken from us. In the end we were still all together, but this did not last long.

[Page 277]

It was the month of September 1942 when the first deportation took place in Ksiaz. On a Friday afternoon we were informed that we were surrounded by the Germans and Polish police. We were told to stay in our houses and to appear on Shabbos [the Sabbath] morning for the transport. We heard heavy gunfire the entire night and we lived through a bitter night. When dawn arrived my entire family went down and hid in the cellar of a Christian neighbor, Baczek, and we were very quiet there so no one would hear us. My father wrapped himself in his talis [prayer shawl] and silently asked God for our escape from the Germans. We heard almost everything that was happening outside. At first there was noise and tumult in the street; then suddenly it became quiet.

Mrs. Baczek went down to the cellar for potatoes at night and almost fainted when she saw us. But the good woman did not say anything; she sent down her son, Zigmunt, and he helped us go to a room in which we hid for several weeks. Then we returned home to our apartment and remained there for approximately two months until the second deportation. This was on a Sunday, the 8th of November 1942. At night we again heard that we were surrounded. My father took the money and divided it among us: we gave the jewelry to our Grandmother Perl and we decided to hide.

I still remember as if it was today how my father took his Khumish [Five Books of the Torah] and cried so terribly. We felt as if this was the end...

We planned to go to Głogowiany. My parents had a Christian acquaintance there, but as the road was heavily guarded, my father and I went earlier to find a road. And my mother and grandmother and the children remained and waited. It lasted a half hour in total until we returned – my family was no longer there. I sobbed. We began to look for them in every corner, but alas, they had already been taken to the transport. My father believed that they might succeed in turning around or bribing the Germans with the money that my grandmother had with her. There being no other choice, we lay near a mountain and were there the whole night. And in the morning my father and I left for Głogowiany and sent the Christian to learn something about our mother and grandmother and their fate. However, she brought back bad news for us – she saw my entire family and the remaining Jews loaded into train wagons and they were taken away under heavy guard.

[Page 278]

My father and I still hoped; we thought that perhaps they would be taken to the Krakow ghetto and that they might succeed in smuggling themselves out of there. Alas, we do not even know where and when they perished.

We hid there for a week and then the Christian became afraid because of the threat of the death penalty for hiding Jews. The gentile took us through the forests at night to Wodzislaw. It was a little quieter there. A number of Jews had returned to the shtetl after the first deportation. In addition, the people were good to us; everyone wanted us to hide with them.

When the deportation took place in Wodzislaw, my parents in Ksiaz had taken into our house as many people as they could, in the attic, and everyone was well hidden. My father went to the Rabbi, Reb Yankele from Czenstochow, who was the rabbi in Wodzislaw, and I was with the Dembski family.

Several days later my father's brother from Jędrzejów learned about us; he sent a Christian for us and we traveled to Jędrzejów at night. My Uncle Layzer was one of the 200 Jews whom the Germans left to work.

We were hidden for several days with the Christian, an acquaintance of my uncle. And in the meantime, my uncle was successful in arranging work for us and for several women and girls who were also there.

Every day we thought we would be sent away to a camp; thus we lived in fear until the month of February 1943.

One morning we were surrounded and we were again taken to a transport; not more than 25 percent of us remained because the Germans finished off the rest of the sick immediately on the spot. We were chased into trucks and they drove us for many hours. We thought that this was our end and suddenly we were let down into a camp, HASAG [Hugo Schneider AG – a German metal goods manufacturer that ran a forced labor ammunitions factory] in Skarzysko in an ammunition factory. And from then on I no longer saw my father, nor my uncle.

I was allocated to Plant A and heard that my father worked in Plant B and my uncle in Plant C.

It was very bitter at that time. We worked very hard.

They took away the money we had with us. I had succeeded in sewing a few zlotes in my coat and they did not search me because I was a young girl.

[Page 279]

Things were bad for me several times at work; I fainted from hunger. Various illnesses rampaged where we were. Typhus literally tore [our bodies] and it was so bad that I thought I would not be able to bear it. At the roll call every morning, I would wait to be chosen to be shot. People convinced me that I had nothing to worry about because I looked like a Christian. They advised me to escape and, perhaps, I would be able to stay alive as a gentile girl. I had childish commonsense and I let myself be convinced. But I wanted to let my father know about this step [posing as a gentile girl]. With great difficulty, I sent a note with a man who had come from Plant B. In the note I wrote that I could no longer endure and I would try to sneak in among the Polish women who worked as supervisors. I also wrote with which Christian I would be in Jędrzejów. I completed my plan in two days.

At five o'clock I was back from work and I prepared myself and appeared for the shift at seven at night. I moved around a little bit until the seven o'clock shift would return again.

It was a week before Passover and between day and night, leaving the camp, I sneaked among the Christians. God protected me. I do not have the ability to describe how great the risk was, but I did not have anything to lose. I no longer had anyone. I went with them until I came among the houses. Then I knocked on a door of a small house and asked that I be allowed to spend the night. They took me in because they thought I was a lace maker. In the morning I paid them and I left for the Skarzysko train station. I sat on the train and traveled to Jędrzejów. When I went to the Christian acquaintance, she was afraid, but then she gave me food and closed me in a small room where no one entered. However, at the same time, she said that she could not hide me. I explained that I had written to my father that I would be with her because when we had been in Jędrzejów a Christian had told us that she had a bunker for several people and on that basis I had come to her now. She gave me a bread and said that I should voluntarily register for Germany because many Poles had done so.

I left again for the train station and bought a ticket back to Skarzysko. I traveled to Skarzysko and I registered there at the labor office for Germany. But as I did not have any documents, I said that my sakiewka (purse) had been stolen with my money and documents, that I had no one – my father was in Russia in captivity and my mother had died. They believed me and sent me to Germany. I had only one prayer that, God forbid, I not speak Yiddish in my sleep so the gentile girls would hear [me].

[Page 280]

I arrived in Loewenberg near Pomerania on the 4th of April 1943 and I worked there until the liberation by Russia on the 15th of March 1945.

I heard that my father had escaped from Skarżysko and that he was in Jędrzejów and then had left for Ksiaz. The gentiles in Ksiaz turned him over to the Germans. I heard this after the liberation.

Thus I remain the only survivor in my entire family.

The Last Friday

by A. Y. Walbromski

Translated by Gloria Berkenstat Freund

A long funeral train of living corpses
With frightened, half-closed eyes;
He was cursed, mocked, belittled,
Languished in the ghettos and camps.
The hundreds of train wagons sent to Bełż;ec,
The free world was silent at the time.
Millions suffocated in the gas ovens
Burned like a burnt offering in the crematoria.
The pain was unbearable;
The heart suffocated from unshed tears,
Murdered, chased from the shtetl,[1] driven off,
Not permitted any longer to return home.
The camp fence united us all:
All, young, old, poor and rich,
All were tortured;
All were equal in the murderer's eyes.
The sun washed the body with sweat,
The frost froze the marrow of our bones.
Barracks grew on the cemeteries
On the foundations of the headstones.

[Page 281]

Jewish blood flowed like water.
Was this the will of God?
Children held by their mothers were shot,
His people were treated with mockery and derision.
And the sun shone no more,
Birds no longer played for us.

There were no friends
To feel compassion for our suffering.
The day was so long
And the night was short.
Twenty-four hours with the sound of time
Always thinking of freedom.
Our will was strong, our spirit weak,
Without hope, without consolation.
Our strength weakened, without courage
Thirsty for revenge for the spilled blood.
May the words remain in our memory,
Sung at the last minute,
"Take revenge on all the murderers
Who have spilled Jewish blood."

[Page 285]

Miechów Survivors in Israel

Activities of the Miechów–Charsznica Association in Israel from its Inception until its Foundation

by Shmuel Berger

Translated by Selwyn Rose

A. Activities from 1945 until 1963

Even before the termination of the Second World War worrying rumors were infiltrating and spreading in Palestine concerning the situation of survivors of the Holocaust scattered in various places throughout Europe, utterly destitute and without any hopes whatsoever of a future. The British Mandatory Authority had securely closed the gates in the face of the homeless Jewish refugees and prevented their brethren, already there, from welcoming them with open arms.

In that difficult hour, a great awakening arose among those already in Palestine, whose origins were the towns and villages of Poland, and they were constrained to stretch out a helping hand to their unfortunate brethren. At their head stood the politically active Zionists of all the parties who were still acting in their towns in exile. As was their habit, they were the first to act. Among those from our town were Sh. D. Yerushalmi (Z"L), Michael Kaiser (Z"L), and spared for a long life – Eliezer Lavie (Lipa Yaskirowitz), and Yehezkiel Dror (Friedrich). All four of them met at first in Mr. Lavie's apartment in Tel Aviv in order to plan a course of action to found a national Association of survivors from Miechów–Charsznica in Palestine.

On 4th September 1945 the founding committee of the Association met in the Community Hall in Yavneh Street, Tel Aviv. About one hundred people from all parts of the country arrived to take part in the event. The meeting opened with an address by Mr. Alter Bruckner, one of the first refugees from our town, who shocked those present with his description of the magnitude of the destruction that had visited the town. Afterwards a committee for the Association was chosen and they were: Sh. D. Yerushalmi (Z"L), Michael Kaiser (Z"L), A. L. Lavie and M. Goldkorn – treasurer, YehezkielDror – organizing secretary. Following this, the meeting adopted the following resolusions:

The Committee will organize a one–time delivery of food–parcels to the survivors who are still to be found in Miechów–Charsznica.

From left to right: Honorary President Sh. D. Yerushalmi (Z"L); Chairman S. Berger (speaking); Yitzhak Pulaski, Mr. N. Blumenthal, A. Wolbromsky.

[Page 286]

Commemoration ceremony for the Martyrs of Miechów, 1966

The Presidium

From left to right: Moshe Savitsky, Treasurer; A. L. Lavie, President; Sh. D. Yerushalmi (Z"L), Honorary President; Yitzhak Pulaski, speaking; Shmuel Berger, Chairman; Mr. N. Blumenthal; Avraham Wolbromsky, Moshe Spiegel

Active workers

Sitting from left to right: Avraham Bryn, Meir Goldberg, Moshe Gerstenfeld, Yehuda Grynwal, Gershon Sarig, Shmuel Berger, Sarah Sukenik, Hannia Singerman, Hanah Zelikowitz, Sarah Rosenberg and Bella Weisbrod

Standing: Moshe Burstein, Avraham Goldkorn, Moshe Savitsky, Yitzhak Pulaski, Michael Sukenik, Benjamin Feigenbaum, Shlomo Weitzman, Yehezkiel Dror, Benjamin Zelikowitz, Moshe Spiegel, Avraham Wolbromsky

s

[Page 287]

Commemoration ceremony for the Martyrs of Miechów, 1966

Standing on the presidential platform

From left to right: Moshe Savitsky, Treasurer; A. L. Lavie, President; Cantor Silberstein; Shmuel Brenner, Chairman; Avraham Wolbromsky; M. Sukenik, Secretary; Meyer Goldberg

Active members

Sitting from left to right: Moshe Gerstenfeld, Julius Spokojny, Moshe Savitsky, A. L. Lavie, President; S. Berger, Chairman; A. Wolbromsky, M. Bornstein, A. Rogovski, Sarah Sukenik, Yehuda Grynwal

Standing: S. Weinrib, Moshe Koplewicz, Laybl Sosnowski, Frankel, A. Bryn. Shlomo Weitzman, Benjamin Feigenbaum, Sarah Rosenberg, Michael Sukenik, Paula Mahal, H. Grynbaum, Sarah Ilan, Ita Sherman, Meir Goldberg, Hendl Yaskirowitz, Yehezkiel Dror, Benjamin and Hanna Zelikowitz

[Page 288]

Every new member joining the Association will pay a monthly membership–fee to finance the activities of the Association.

Every effort will be made to locate and contact all survivors in Israel of our town and urge them to join the Association.

A Branch will be opened in Haifa to encompass all the area of the north and the Galilee.

One of the first projects of the new Committee was to arrange a Memorial Meeting to honor the fallen Martyrs from our town. The members of the Committee travelled to Haifa and met at the apartment of Mrs. Yocheved Blatt Rosenblatt) with most of the survivors of our town living in

Haifa and the north. At that same meeting a committee for the Haifa branch was elected independent of the central committee and its members were: L. Feigenbaum, Hannia Feigenbaum, (Singerman), Paula Feureisen (Mahal) and as secretary – Uri Lacki, the son of Gershon Lacki (Z"L). At the same meeting it was decided to arrange a similar memorial service in Haifa which will take place the day prior to the one in Tel–Aviv, with the participation of the distinguished members Michael Kaiser, Moshe Bryn and Yehezkiel Dror.

The Memorial Meeting in Haifa took place in the "Beit Halutziot", and the attendees donated significant sums for financing their activities.

During the years 1945–1955 the committees functioned routinely. Throughout the period tens of Jewish survivors of our town came from their various places of exile and the Committee decided to organize the annual Memorial Day to take place on the known date of the final destruction of the Miechów ghetto, the "Aussiedlung" – the "resettlement". Thus the activities of the Association entered a fixed agenda and the Memorials, in addition to the annual meetings of the Association, functioned as a vehicle for veteran survivors of the towns of Miechów and Charsznica to get together with the newly arrived immigrants.

In 1956 Mr. Lavie resigned his position on the Committee for reasons accepted by the members. In 1958 Mr. Yehezkiel Dror was forced to resign his position as Secretary as the result of a road accident and in his place Mr. Avraham Bryn was elected.

B. Activities from 1963–1970

From 1962 a special committee, whose specific purpose was to bring to fruition the publication of a Memorial Book to the martyrs of our community, began to operate alongside the main committee. In 1963 a National committee was chosen and took upon itself the mission of publishing the Memorial Book and the earlier Committee was disbanded. The members of the National Committee were: Shmuel Berger – Chairman, Moshe Savitsky – Treasurer, Yehuda Grynwald – Secretary, Avraham Wolbromsky, and the Haifa delegates were Yitzhak Pulaski and Benjamin Feigenbaum. In time the secretary was changed and Michael Sukenik was elected to the post and an additional member co–opted – Moshe Spiegel.

Essentially, the burden of the work of bringing the Memorial Book forward for publication fell upon the shoulders of the respected Berger, Savitsky, Sukenik, Wolbromsky and Spiegel. The remainder of the members helped as best as they could and the members of the Association took part in special activities organized by the Committee and occasionally called for a plenary session of the whole Council to debate necessary elements requiring a broader–based action.

At the same time the Association continued to hold the annual Memorial Ceremonies and tried to improve their meaningfulness and content. They were no longer held in the open air, a suitable venue was rented – the "B'nei–Brit" building that spread a atmosphere of greater respect over the participants. Speakers were invited who were involved in various topics relating to the communities of our towns, and for special mention is Rabbi Yedidiah Frenkel, who made an impressive speech on the Holocaust in general and on his recent visit to Poland.

[Page 289]

As well as all those activities, the Committee started organizing Hanukah parties at which our members were happy to have the opportunity to meet each other in a less formal and freer context of a festive party. Throughout these years there were three such parties and the one which took place in 1968 will be particularly well remembered when the broadcaster, Hanna Rosen, and the Sosnowski couple from among our members, who appeared in a couple of humorous skits.

More modest gatherings also achieved notable success in a smaller venue over a cup of tea; at one of the parties Mr. Lavie gave a talk and at another the broadcaster Shamai Rosenblum who excited his audience with excerpts of readings which he presented both in Hebrew and Yiddish. Our members made sure that there was always a supply of light refreshments they prepared themselves and contributed significantly to the pleasant atmosphere.

The Committee also dealt with many other varied issues such as obtaining necessary authorization and documentary proofs of their claim to reparations from Germany and the discovery of documents and details for the investigation into Nazi war–crimes by the Israeli Police. The Committee also managed and organized the day–to–day administrative work, fees, treasury and correspondence, etc., and indeed achieved much progress in these activities during the period. Nevertheless, the main focus of the Association's effort was the production of the Book of Remembrance (see page 291).

C. The Benevolent Society named for Yehuda Zelmanowicz (Z"L)

Among the activities of the Association the establishment of a Benevolent Society in the name of Yehuda Zelmanowicz (Z"L), is worth noting.

Co-workers of the Association had for some time been contemplating the idea of founding a benevolent society in order to assist members in their hour of need with small loans at no interest. They recalled the example that had existed when they were active in our communities in the period between the two World Wars. The drive to give action to the idea became practicable in 1964 when a donation of $1,000 was received from the Association of Miechów Survivors in America. The donors expressed the wish to commemorate the name of their member, Yehuda Zelmanowicz (Z"L), by naming the fund after him. And indeed at the annual General Meeting of 1965 it was decided to name the Society after Yehuda Zelmanowicz. The family of the departed, his friends and work-colleagues from "Koor" donated additional amounts to the fund and thus the society came into being.

On 28th February, 1966 there was a celebratory party at Koor Industry's meeting hall and a Founding Scroll of the Benevolent Society was read and signed (see photograph).

Signatories to the Scroll were members of the Association's Presidium, representatives of the Association's members and colleagues from Koor and family members and friends of the departed.

From that day until today the Society has functioned according to the mandate outlined in the Scroll. The amount standing to the Society's credit at this time is above 7000 N.I.S.

Details of donations made to the Benevolent Society:

Donated by the members of the Society in the U.S.A.	2936.– N.I.S.
Donated by work colleagues	2781 N.I.S.
Donated by family members of the departed	700 N.I.S.
Donated by an Association member	500 N.I.S.
Interest from investments and Bank interest	244 N.I.S.
Total	7161 N.I.S.

From 1964 until 1970 26 loans were dispensed totaling approximately 16,170 N.I.S.

[Page 290]

ארגון עולי מיחוב חרשניצה וקשוינז בישראל

קופת גמילות חסדים
ע"ש יהודה זלמנוביץ ז"ל

מגילת יסוד

אנו החותמים מטה חברי הועד הארצי והמועצה של ארגון עולי מיחוב, חרשניצה וקשוינז בישראל, חבריו לעבודה בסולכור, בני משפחתו וידידיו ומוקיריו התאספנו כאן באולם הישיבות של בנין כור בתל אביב ומכריזים בזה חגיגית על יסוד של:

קופת גמילות חסדים של ארגון עולי מיחוב חרשניצה וקשוינז בישראל

ע"ש יהודה זלמנוביץ ז"ל

וזאת בהתאם להחלטת האסיפה הכללית של הארגון שהתקיימה אור לט"ו באלול התשכ"ד (23 לאוגוסט 1964) בתור יסוד לקופה ישמשו הכספים שנתרמו על ידי יוצאי עירנו בארצות הברית, חבריו לעבודה בסולכור, בני משפחתו וידידיו וכן הכספים שיתקבלו בעתיד.

כספי הקופה ישמשו לעזרה לנצרכים חברי הארגון. ההלואות תנתנה בלי רבית ובתנאים שיחליט עליהם מדי פעם בפעם הועד המנהל של הקופה, שירכב מחברי הועד הארצי של הארגון או באי כוח שיתמנו על ידו וכן באי כח של עובדי סולכור. הקופה תתנהל על פי תקנות שיתקבלו על ידי הועד המנהל. הועד המנהל יהיה אחראי לנהול תקין של הקופה על פי תקנותיה.

רוחו האצילה וכוונתו לעזור לזולת בעת צרה של יהודה זלמנוביץ ז"ל אשר על שמו תיקרא הקופה, תהיה נר לרגלי החברים שיעמדו בראשה. בתקוה כי הקופה תמלא את יעודה בנאמנות ותעמוד לימין החבר הנזקק לה.

אנו חותמים בחתימת ידינו לעדות על מגילת יסוד זו בעיר תל אביב היום הזה אור לט' אדר התשכ"ו (28 לפבריאר 1966).

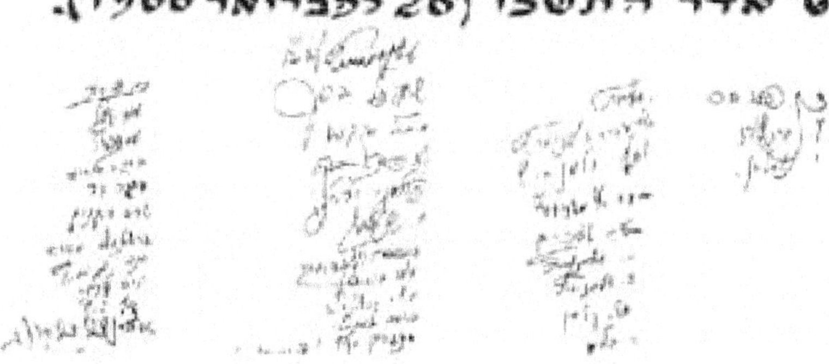

The Association of Immigrants from Miechów, Charsznica and Ksiaz in Israel Yehuda Zelmanowicz Benevolent Society Founding Scroll of Incorporation

We, the Undersigned, Members of the National Council and Committee of the Association of Immigrants from Miechów, Charsznica and Ksiaz in Israel, work–colleagues from Solkoor, His Family Members and Friends from his Youth, have Gathered here today in the Company Meeting Room of the Koor Building in Tel Aviv and hereby Solemnly Declare and Celebrate the Founding of :

The Yehuda Zelmanowicz Benevolent Society of the Organization of the Association of Immigrants from Miechów, Charsznica and Ksiaz in Israel.

And that in Accordance with the Decision taken at the Annual General Meeting of the Association which took place on the Morning of 23rd (Twenty–Third) of August 1964, has Established the above Association and that the funds of the Society Donated by the Survivors of our Towns Residing in The United States of America, Work Colleagues of Solkoor, Family Members of the Deceased and his Friends; it being understood that any such Monies that may be Accrued in the Future by the Society will be used to Assist Members of the Association under Stress at no Interest, under Conditions Decided upon from time to time by the Council managing the Fund, which will be Constituted by Members of the National Council, or Person or Persons holding Authorized Power of Attorney under the Auspices of Solkoor Workers. The Fund will be managed according to the Protocols received from the Managing Council. The Managing Council will be Responsible for the correct functioning and operation of the Fund According to its Protocols and Constitution.

The Noble Spirit and Qualities of Yehuda Zelmanowicz (Z"L), whose name the Fund bears, to come to the Assistance of the individual in need, will be a Guiding Lamp for the Members who will stand at its Head, in the hope that the Fund will Fulfill its Objectives Faithfully and will stand Purposefully at the Right Hand of the Needy and Distressed.

We, the undersigned, give our hand in Witness on 28th February 1966. (36 {Thirty–six} Illegible hand–written signatures in Hebrew script)

[Page 291]

The Process of Publishing the Memorial Book of the Miechów, Charsznica, Ksiaz Communities

by Shmuel Berger

Translated by Selwyn Rose

Our Association was constituted immediately with the cessation of the Second World War that is in 1945, and from its inception had, within its very soul, as a guiding "pillar of fire", the goal to memorialize the fallen of our communities in a Memorial Book. Nevertheless the project did not come to fruition until 1962. During that period hundreds of Memorial Books by community survivors' committees and organizations were published, most of them found in Israel and indeed, the name of our Association was to be found among them.

Although on several occasions at our Annual General Memorial Meetings the project was raised and spoken of we never got to the stage of translating the idea into a practical result and eventually we ceased discussing it. There was a real danger that the matter would be completely forgotten and a Memorial Book not materialize.

The matter touched me deeply and my conscience gave me no rest. Although I was not active in the work of the Association I decided to do something to bring idea of the book to fruition. At the Annual General Meeting that took place on 19th October 1962, when I saw that there was no mention brought to the table concerning a Memorial Book, I asked for the floor and from the rostrum I pled vigorously on behalf of the martyrs of our communities for a Memorial Book to be given consideration. – "To what have we come," I asked, "that the memory of our parents, our brothers and sisters and all our perished Brethren, should be forgotten? Is all the past history of our community, in which we ourselves grew up and lived, to be forgotten? Not many years will pass and there will be no one left to write about our community especially since we ourselves have little or no documentation; everything will come from our memory. Who will carry the burden of the responsibility of that outcome if not we, ourselves, now?"

My fervent and impassioned plea to the gathered members bore fruit and a Committee was instantly formed on whom fell the burden of carrying the idea forward to its early fruition and its members were: Shmuel Berger, Avraham Bryn, Moshe Spiegel and Ya'acov Wolbromsky.

With the election of the committee I left the meeting much encouraged in the hope that eventually we would have our own Memorial Book. And indeed the committee immediately began to work actively towards that end and with our first meeting which took place in my house with all three members, including a guest from America – Mr. Mitzenmacher, a member of the Association of Miechów Survivors in America. It was decided to send out a circular to all the members in Israel and abroad, outlining in general terms the proposed contents and to call everyone in the Association to harness themselves to the project. The circular was published early in November 1962.

The circular said, among other things: "...Every single survivor of our above communities should see himself as a partner in the general wish and a mutual obligation in erecting a Memorial to our beloved ones, our Martyrs (May G–d avenge their blood), and everyone fulfill this obligation, encourage and urge his friends and relations to fulfill this Holy Mitzvah..." After sending out the circular we began to receive a stream of material of all sorts – lists of names, articles and photographs. I can say with real happiness that we made contact for the first time with members of our community abroad, especially in America, something that had not happened until then. The entire Association came to life and a new spirit began to move within it. The majority of the members joined the sacred project – production of a Memorial Book.

Nevertheless, a mountain of problems now began to pile up and accumulate, mainly, however, two: the problem of editing the book and preparing it for publication, and financing the entire project as a whole. The financial problem solved itself slowly but surely with donations from abroad and members of the Association, each according to his possibilities. More problematic was the editing of the book and its readiness for publication. We had no one qualified or of a professional standard for such work and also everyone was engaged in their own day–to–day occupations. We thought originally, that perhaps we could engage a known editor or historian but the idea was abandoned as soon as we became aware of the cost. We decided, therefore, to approach Yad Va–Shem who took upon themselves the cost. In February 1964 there was the first meeting with representatives of the Institution and after several contacts during which questions concerning editing and printing the book were debated, an agreement was signed between the Association and Yad Va–Shem and in December 1965. The editing was assigned to Mr. N. Blumenthal.

[Page 292]

Nevertheless, the problems did not cease with the signing of the agreement. The collection and sorting of all the additional material coming to hand was more than we had anticipated and most of the burden fell on me, together with a small group of friends who gave as much assistance as they could. Also the management and organization of the cash–donations that were coming to hand still had no final arrangement and continued to take up our time and energies. But we didn't despair and continued with our efforts to fulfill the task we had taken upon ourselves.

We produced further circulars to members in Israel and abroad with a combined request and demand to fill a questionnaire, to search out material and to make every effort so that we could publish the book as soon as possible.

Our efforts bore fruit and again material began to arrive until in the end we were forced to shorten some material because of budgetary concerns and to further sort material to prevent unnecessary repetitiveness. Most of that critical work was performed by the late Mr. Yerushalmi who worked on the material assiduously and made many important and constructive observations.

Now is the time to mark the most welcome work of our President Mr. Eliezer Lavie (Yaskirowitz), who composed a comprehensive article on the Jewish community of Miechów and its different institutions and also described the activities of the people who strove for the public welfare. Our heartfelt thanks go to him with the deepest gratitude for the time and effort he devoted to the article.

After much toil and effort most of the material and photographs came to hand and we passed it all on to Yad Va–Shem. At that stage Yad Va–Shem passed the material to Mrs. Aviva Ben–Azar to assist in editing the material in readiness for publication. From that point on, things moved quickly. Mrs. Ben–Azar re–assessed all the material most of which was incomplete and un–worked, styling and preparing it for printing.

May this book be a continuation of the hundreds of Memorial Books already before the public which together constitute an everlasting memorial to the thousands of communities of the Children of Israel in their countries of dispersion and exile, extinguished by the hand of the oppressor.

[Page 295]

Miechów Martyrs

Transliterated by Selwyn Rose

ABRAMOWITZ	Elimelech	BERGER	Moshe & Family
ABRAMCZYK	Bryndl	BERGER	Shlomo
ABRAMCZYK	Haim	BERGER	Shlomo & Family
ABRAMCZYK	Leah	BERGER	Simha (Sela)
ABRAMCZYK	Ya'acov	BERGMANN	Yeshiyahu
ABRAMCZYK	Yisroel	BERMAN	Avraham
ABRAMCZYK	Zisl	BERMAN	Hertsl
ABRAMOWITZ	Yechiel-Shmuel	BERMAN	Miriam
ABUSZEWICZ	Dina	BIDNEY	Hertsl
ABUSZEWICZ	Haim	BLADY	Avshalom
ABUSZEWICZ	Leah	BLADY	Chaya
ABUSZEWICZ	Sheindl	BLADY	Tova
ABUSZEWICZ	Yechiel	BLADY	Wolf
ADLIST	Hertsl	BLATT	Brayndl
ADLIST	Shmuel-Leib	BLATT	Elimelech
AOIZD	David	BLATT	Yosef
AOIZD	Ephraim	BLEIER	Lona
AOIZD	Golda	BLEIER	Max
AOIZD	Rivka	BLUM	Rosa
AOIZD	Yocheved	BLUM	Tamar
AOIZD	Yosef	BLUM	Ya'acov
APELBOIM	Feygl	BLUM	Yermiyahu

APELBOIM	Yeshiya-Moshe	BORNSTEIN	Brayndl
ASPIS	Leah	BORNSTEIN	David
ASPIS	Mordecai	BORNSTEIN	Eliezer
ASPIS	Reyzl	BORNSTEIN	Esther
ASPIS	Shlomo	BORNSTEIN	Feygl
BACHMAIER	Berish	BORNSTEIN	Fishl
BAKALARZ	Wolf	BORNSTEIN	Freydl
BANEK	Yitzhak	BORNSTEIN	Haim
BENET	Eli	BORNSTEIN	Hanoch
BERGER	Aharon	BORNSTEIN	Maltshe

[Page 296]

BORNSTEIN	Ozer	CHMIELEWSKI	Pinhas
BORNSTEIN	Perla	CHMIELEWSKI	Sarah
BORNSTEIN	Reyle	CHMIELEWSKI	Yudl
BORNSTEIN	Sheyndl	CYMERMAN	Bluma
BORNSTEIN	Shlomo	CYMERMAN	Sheyndl
BORNSTEIN	Yiske	CYMERMAN	Yosef
BORNSTEIN	Yosef	CZAJKOWSKI	
BRAMACZYK(?)		CZAJKOWSKI	Haim
BRANDSTADTER	Fayvel	CZAJKOWSKI	Herschel
BRANDSTADTER	Yudle	CZAJKOWSKI	Shprintse
BRENNER	Abba	CZAJKOWSKI	Yitzhak
BRENNER	Aharon	CZERNIE	Isaac
BRENNER	Liber	DANZYGER	Feivel
BRENNER	Wolf	DANZYGER	Shprintse
BRUKNER	Blumer	DREZNER	Bezalel

BRUKNER	Chaya	DREZNER	Herschel
BRUKNER	Payle	DREZNER	Meir
BRUKNER	Reyzl	DREZNER	Melech
BRUMER	Faybish	DREZNER	Miriam
BRUMER	Mindl	DREZNER	Mordecai
BRUMER	Ya'acov	DREZNER	Pinhas
BURSTEIN	Chaya	DREZNER	Sarah
BURSTEIN	Elimelech	EHRLICH	Alter
BURSTEIN	Leah	EHRLICH	Haim
BURSTEIN	Sheve	EISENBERG	Haim
BURSTEIN	Yeshiya	EISENBERG	Hanna
BURSTEIN	Yisroel-David (Shochet)	EISENBERG	Lazar Yosef
CHARMETZ	Bezalel	EISENBERG	Shmerl
CHERNY		EISENFELD	Lemel
CHMIELEWSKI	Abba	EISENFELD	Moshe
CHMIELEWSKI	Bendit	EISENFELD	Wolf
CHMIELEWSKI	David	EISENSTEIN	Feygl

[Page 297]

EISENSTEIN	Motel	FRIEDMAN	Dr.
EISENSTEIN	Reyzl	FRIEDRICH	Avraham
EISENSTEIN	Ya'acov	FRIEDRICH	Elimelech
FAIVELOWICZ	Altar	FRIEDRICH	Gitl
FEIGENBUM	Elimelech	FRIEDRICH	Yosef
FEIGENBUM	Esther	FRUCHT	Abba
FEIGENBUM	Miriam	FRYSZER	Aharon
FEIGENBUM	Moshe	FRYSZER	Reyzl

FEIGENBUM	Pesle	FUCHSENBRUMER	David
FEIGENBUM	Rahel	FUCHSENBRUMER	Hanya
FEIGENBUM	Shlomo	GARNCARSKA	Yechiel
FEIGENBUM	Ya'acov	GASTFRAJND	Avraham
FEUREISEN	Haim	GASTFRAJND	Motel
FEUREISEN	Hava	GASTFRAJND	Rosa
FEUREISEN	Leibl	GASTFRAJND	Ya'acov
FEUREISEN	Mindl	GERSHTENFELD	Avraham
FEUREISEN	Pinhas	GERSHTENFELD	Bilha
FEUREISEN	Wolf	GERSHTENFELD	Esther
FEUREISEN	Yoske	GERSHTENFELD	Etl
FINKELSTEIN	Akiva	GERSHTENFELD	Haya
FINKELSTEIN	Berish	GERSHTENFELD	Hirsch-Leib
FISCH	Meir	GERSHTENFELD	Meir
FOGEL	Devora	GERSHTENFELD	Reuven
FOGEL	Moshe	GERSHTENFELD	Sarah
FOGEL	Shmuel	GERSHTENFELD	Yantshe
FRANKEL	Berish	GERSHTENFELD	Yitzhak
FRANKEL	Gutsya	GERSZONOWICZ	Yoske
FRANKEL	Hinda	GERTLER	Isaac
FRANKEL	Rahel	GERTLER	Melech
FRAUER	Yudl	GERTLER	Zalman
FRIEDENBERG	Natan	GIMALKHAWYCZ(?)	Aharon-Shmuel
FRIEDENBERG	Shmuel	GITLER	Berl

[Page 298]

GITLER	Fischl	GRUNDMANN	Ya'acov

GITLER	Hertsl	GRUNDMANN	Yitzhak
GITLER	Leib	GRUSZKA	Aharon
GITLER	Moshe	GRYNBOIM	Baruch
GOLDBERG	Avraham	GRYNBOIM	Bella
GOLDBERG	Dova	GRYNBOIM	Ben-Zion
GOLDBERG	Mendel	GRYNBOIM	Bezalel
GOLDBERG	Miriam	GRYNBOIM	Faygl
GOLDBERG	Mirl	GRYNBOIM	Fischl
GOLDBERG	Tsirel	GRYNBOIM	Haya
GOLDBERG	Yehoshua	GRYNBOIM	Hertsl
GOLDFARB	Eda	GRYNBOIM	Leibl
GOLDFARB	Haynrikh	GRYNBOIM	Monye
GOLDFARB	Yitzhak	GRYNBOIM	Sarah
GOLDFREUND	Netta	GRYNBOIM	Zala
GOLDFREUND	Nukha	GRYNWEL	Gitl
GOLDFREUND	Reuven	GRYNWEL	Kalman
GOLDKORN	Dov	GRYNWEL	Shalom-Meir
GOLDKORN	Haynrikh	GRYNWEL	Sheva
GOLDKORN	Malka	HEFTER	Binye
GOLDKORN	Shmuel	HEFTER	Moshe
GOLODNY	Leib	HEFTER	Pinhas
GOTTFRIED	Elie	HEFTER	Roza
GOTTFRIED	Micha'el	HEFTER	Sheyndl
GOTTFRIED	Natan	HEFTER	Simha
GROSS	Simha	HEFTER	Ze'ev

GROSS	Yosef	HERSZENHORN	Hanna-Leah
GROSSFELD	Hertsl	HERSZENHORN	Haya
GRUNDMANN	Aharon	HERSZENHORN	Leybush
GRUNDMANN	Esther	HERSZENHORN	Sarah
GRUNDMANN	Freydl	HERSZENHORN	Simha
GRUNDMANN	Moshe	HERSZENHORN	Yeshia-Shmuel

[Page 299]

HERSZLIKOWICZ	Miriam	JACOBSON	Sarah
HERSZLIKOWICZ	Shmuel	JACOBSON	Sheyndl
HERSZLIKOWICZ	Simha	JAMA	Meir
HERSZLIKOWICZ	Yisroel	JAMA	Shlomo
HERSZLIKOWICZ	Yitzhak	JAMA	Tsile
HERZIG	Esther	JASKIEL	Levi
HERZIG	Kalman	JASKIEL	Yosef
HOROWITZ	Avraham-Mordecai	JOSKOWICZ	David
HOROWITZ	Beynish	JOSKOWICZ	Esther
HOROWITZ	Hanna	JOSKOWICZ	Hirsh-Isa
HOROWITZ	Haya	JOSKOWICZ	Nahum
HOROWITZ	Hendl	JOSKOWICZ	Reuven
HOROWITZ	Hertsl	JUDKIEWICZ	
HOROWITZ	Leah	JZRAELOWICZ	Moshe-David
HOROWITZ	Micha'el	JZRAELOWICZ	Yeshiya-Moshe
HOROWITZ	Rahel	KAIZER	Hava

HOROWITZ	Ruhama	KAIZER	Wolf-Ber
HOROWITZ	Sarah	KAMINSKI	Avraham
HOROWITZ	Sheyndl	KAMINSKI	Avraham
HUBSCHER	David	KAMINSKI	Esther-Rahel
ITZKOWITZ	Feivel	KAMINSKI	Gitl
ITZKOWITZ	Haim	KAMINSKI	Leah
ITZKOWITZ	Hinda	KAMINSKI	Mira
ITZKOWITZ	Isaac	KAMINSKI	Rivka
JACOBOVITCH	David	KAMINSKI	Shifra
JACOBSON	Hanna	KAMINSKI	Shmuel
JACOBSON	Isaac	KAMINSKI	Wolf
JACOBSON	Lazar	KAMINSKI	Yokl
JACOBSON	Mania	KAMINSKI	Yosef
JACOBSON	Nahum	KAPELMEISTER	Yeshiya
JACOBSON	Perl	KATOLIK	Adina
JACOBSON	Rahel	KATOLIK	Bilha

[Page 300]

KATOLIK	Frimet	KORENBRUT	Mischa
KATOLIK	Leah	KORN	Pesah
KATOLIK	Miriam	KORNFELD	Netta
KATOLIK	Moshe	KORNFELD	Ya'acov
KATOLIK	Ruhama	KRAKOWSKI	Reyzl
KATOLIK	Shlomo	KRYMOLOWSKI	Yisroel-Eli
KATOLIK	Tsvi	KRZESIWO	Bluma
KATOLIK	Yosef	KRZESIWO	Eidl
KATZENGOLD	Moshe	KRZESIWO	Feygl

KATZENGOLD	Shlomo	KRZESIWO	Haya
KAZIMIERSKI	Meir	KRZESIWO	Tova
KLEINER	Faygl	KRZESIWO	Yeshiya
KLEINER	Hinda	KUSZER	David
KLEINER	Leibl	KUSZER	Moshe
KLEINER	Mila	KUSZER	Ya'acov
KLEINER	Netta	LANDSCHAFT	Haim
KLEINER	Rivka	LANDSCHAFT	shmuel
KLEINER	Tova	LANGER	Bluma
KLEINER	Ya'acov-Simha	LANGER	Mordecai
KLEINER	Yosef	LANGER	Sheyndl
KLEINPLATZ	Hirtsl	LANGER	Yoel
KLEINPLATZ	Yocheved	LANZBERG	Kalman
KNOBLER	Bluma	LANZBERG	Motel
KNOBLER	Feyvl	LANZBERG	Shmuel-Yosef
KNOBLER	Netl	LANZBERG	Wolf
KOPLOWITZ	Enzil	LANZBERG	Ya'acov
KOPLOWITZ	Frieda	LANZBERG	Yosef
KOPLOWITZ	Moshe	LAZAR	Dr.
KOPLOWITZ	Yehoshua	LEDERMAN	Baruch
KOPLOWITZ	Yeshiya	LEDERMAN	Bluma
KOPLOWITZ	Yitzhak	LEDERMAN	Bluma-Hanna
KORENBRUT (FRIEDRICH)	Mania	LEDERMAN	Haim

[Page 301]

LEDERMAN	Leibl	LIEBERMAN	Tsvi

LEDERMAN	Malka	LISS	Hanna
LEDERMAN	Nehemia	LISS	Peretz
LEDERMAN	Sarah	LISS	Tovia
LEDERMAN	Shmuel	LUBATCZI(?)	Kalman
LEISCHE	Hirtsl	LUBATCZI(?)	Roza
LEISCHE	Ya'acov	LUBATCZI(?)	Shmuel
LEJZOREK	Avraham-Ber	LUCKAY	Feivel
LEJZOREK	David	LUCKAY	Haim
LEJZOREK	David-Mordecai	LUCKAY	Libtshe
LEJZOREK	Feigl-Hendl	LUCKAY	Sarah
LEJZOREK	Lazar	LUCKAY	Shalom
LEJZOREK	Mendel	LUCKAY	Tova
LEJZOREK	Peretz	LUCKAY	Tsina
LEJZOREK	Sheyndl-Laeh	MAJTLIS	Boniak(?)
LEJZOREK	Yitzhak-Hirsch	MAJTLIS	Devora
LEWIT	Abba	MAJTLIS	Yisroel
LEWIT	Abba	MAMOR	Hirstl
LEWIT	Avraham	MANASSE	Doctor and Lawyer
LEWIT	Haim	MANDELOWITZ	Tova
LEWIT	Leah	MARMOR	Mordecai
LEWIT	Leibish	MATUSHINSKI	Mates
LEWIT	Lola	MATUSHINSKI	Rivka
LEWIT	Mani	MATUSHINSKI	Yitzhak

LEWIT	Meir	MILLMAN	Moshe-Avraham
LEWIT	Moshe	MINTZ	Avraham-Ber
LEWIT	Rivka	MINTZ	David
LEWIT	Rivka-Leah	MINTZ	Feigl-Hendl
LEWIT	Royzl	MINTZ	Leib-Hirsh
LEWIT	Yechiel	MINTZ	Lippa
LIEBER	Bruntshe(?)	MINTZ	Tuvia
LIEBERMAN	Hannia	MLINARSKI	Baruch

[Page 302]

MLINARSKI	Bat-Sheva	OLSHEWSKI	Ronye
MLINARSKI	Berl	OLSHEWSKI	Shmuel
MLINARSKI	Feitl	PASTERNAK	Avraham
MLINARSKI	Haim-Ber	PASTERNAK	Yitzhak
MLINARSKI	Hanna-Rahel	PERGRICHT	Gershon
MLINARSKI	Leibl	PERGRICHT	Yekutiel
MLINARSKI	Mania	PINCZEWSKI	Altar-Yehiel
MLINARSKI	Regina	PINCZEWSKI	Avraham
MLINARSKI	Reyzl	PINCZEWSKI	Benjamin
MLINARSKI	Rivka	PINCZEWSKI	David
MLINARSKI	Sheyndl	PINCZEWSKI	David-Yehuda
MLINARSKI	Zalman	PINCZEWSKI	Gershon
MLINARSKI	Zisskind	PINCZEWSKI	Haim

MULSTEIN	Avraham	PINCZEWSKI	Itzik
MULSTEIN	David	PINCZEWSKI	Moshe
MULSTEIN	Hela-Sheni	PINCZEWSKI	Sarah
MULSTEIN	Moshe	PINCZEWSKI	Yosef-Shmuel
MULSTEIN	Yitzhak	PLATKIEWICZ	Hanna
MUNCZNIK	Moshe	PLATKIEWICZ	Yonatan
NAYBERG	Avraham-Ya'acov	POLIWODA	
NAYBERG	Meir	POREMBA	Faygl
NEUFELD	Moshe-Mendel	POREMBA	Haim
NIEGUSLAWSKI(?)	Haim	POREMBA	Moshe
OLMER	Feivel	POREMBA	Natan
OLMER	Reuven	POREMBA	Reyzl
OLMER	Shmuel	POREMBA	Shaul
OLMER	Yosef	POSKBITOWSKI	Simha
OLSHEWSKI	Alter	POSKEVITOWSKI	David
OLSHEWSKI	Alter-Yosef	POSLUSHNY	David
OLSHEWSKI	Frumat	POSLUSHNY	Faybush-David
OLSHEWSKI	Malka	POSLUSHNY	Fraydl
OLSHEWSKI	Mordecai-Leib	POSLUSHNY	Hanna

[Page 303]

POSLUSHNY	Hillel	REINSTEIN	Aharon
POSLUSHNY	Hirtski	REINSTEIN	Bluma
POSLUSHNY	Hirtski	ROGOWSKI	Aharon

POSLUSHNY	Liber	ROGOWSKI	Devora
POSLUSHNY	Meir	ROGOWSKI	Leybush
POSLUSHNY	Mindl	ROGOWSKI	Mendel
POSLUSHNY	Pesl	ROGOWSKI	Miriam
POSLUSHNY	Shmuel	ROGOWSKI	Perl
POSLUSHNY	Wolf	ROGOWSKI	Rahel
POSLUSHNY	Ya'acov	ROGOWSKI	Roza
POSLUSHNY	Ya'acov	ROSEN	Leibl
POSLUSHNY	Yehuda-Leib	ROSEN	Yehezkiel
POSLUSHNY	Yitzhak	ROSEN	Yosef-Mordecai
POZNER	Dina	ROSENBAUM	Adolf
POZNER	Leah	ROSENBAUM	Hertsl
POZNER	Shmuel	ROSENBAUM	Leybush
PRAJS	Haim	ROSENBAUM	Moshe-Mordecai
PRZEWOZNIK	Avraham	ROSENBAUM	Pela
PSHECHAZKI	Isaac	ROSENBAUM	Rikl
PSHECHAZKI	Leah	ROSENBAUM	Tuvtche
PSHECHAZKI	Malka	ROTENBERG	Golda
PSHECHAZKI	Miriam	ROTENBERG	Mordecai
PSHECHAZKI	Rahel	ROTENBERG	Ya'acov the ADMOR
PTASZNIK	Kalman	ROTNER	Shmuel
PULASKI	Shmuel	ROZENBERG	Altar
PULASKI	Yosef	ROZENBERG	Koppel
RABINOWITZ	Leybush	ROZENBERG	Shlomo

RAFELOWICZ	Feyvl	ROZENBERG	Shmuel-Zanbil
RAFELOWICZ	Mordecai	ROZENKRANC	Asher
RAFELOWICZ	Pinhas	ROZENKRANC	Faygl
RAPOPORT	Reyzl	ROZENKRANC	Gitl
REDLICH	Yehezkiel	ROZENKRANC	Hava

[Page 304]

ROZENKRANC	Leah	SCHEINFRUCHT	Basha
ROZENKRANC	Leml	SCHEINFRUCHT	Koppel
ROZENKRANC	Rahel	SCHEINFRUCHT	Malka
ROZENKRANC	Raphael	SCHEINFRUCHT	Rabbi Hanoch
ROZENKRANC	Rivka	SCHEINFRUCHT	Rahel
ROZENKRANC	Sheva	SCHEINFRUCHT	Yeshiya
ROZENKRANC	Yakl	SCHEINFRUCHT	Yitzhak
SALTZBERG	David	SCHEINOLD	Barish
SALTZBERG	Esther	SCHEINOLD	Elimelech
SALTZBERG	Etil	SCHEINOLD	Haya
SALTZBERG	Fischl	SCHENKER	Tova
SALTZBERG	Haim	SCHENKER	Gala
SALTZBERG	Haim	SCHENKER	Mendl
SALTZBERG	Hanna	SCHENKER	Yitzhak
SALTZBERG	Hanna	SCHENKER	Ziskind
SALTZBERG	Hertsle	SCHMUCKLER	Mendl
SALTZBERG	Hinda-Rivka	SCHONTHAL	Baltchia
SALTZBERG	Malka	SCHONTHAL	David
SALTZBERG	Meir	SCHONTHAL	Shlomo

SALTZBERG	Miriam	SCHONTHAL	Tova
SALTZBERG	Monik	SCHONTHAL	Herschel
SALTZBERG	Motta	SCHONTHAL	Wolf
SALTZBERG	Noami	SCHWAJCER	Aharon
SALTZBERG	Pinhas	SCHWAJCER	Leah
SALTZBERG	Sarah	SEBERSKY	Yitzhak
SALTZBERG	Sarah	SERCAZ	Avraham
SALTZBERG	Sheyndl	SERCAZ	Motel
SALTZBERG	Shifra	SERCAZ	Rivka
SALTZBERG	Tsilke	SHMULEWICZ	Ya'acov
SALTZBERG	Yitzhak	SILVERBERG	Berl
SALTZBERG	Yoel	SILVERBERG	Shlomo
SCHEINFRUCHT	Shlomo-Meir	SILVERBERG	Yoel

[Page 305]

SINGER	Basye	SUKENIK	Shmuel
SINGER	Yerakhmiel	SULTANIK	Avraham
SKOWRON	Haya	SULTANIK	Gittel
SKOWRON	Hela	SULTANIK	Golda
SKOWRON	Micha'el	SULTANIK	Leibush
SKOWRON	Roza	SULTANIK	Lola
SOLNI	Feigl	SULTANIK	Malka
SOLNI	Leibl	SULTANIK	Mordecai
SOLNI	Paula	SULTANIK	Roza
SOLNIK	Haim	SULTANIK	Sarah
SOLOWICZ	Hirstl	SULTANIK	Shmuel
SOLOWICZ	Yehezkiel	SULTANIK	Yael

SOLOWICZ	Yisroel	SZANIECZKI	Abba
SOSNOWSKI	Elimelech	SZANIECZKI	Moshe-David
SOSNOWSKI	Haim	SZANIECZKI	Motel
SOSNOWSKI	Menasseh	SZANIECZKI	Reuven
SOSNOWSKI	Miriam	SZANIECZKI	Ya'acov
SOSNOWSKI	Moshe	SZPIEGEL	Anschel
STEIN	Devora	SZPIEGEL	Avraham
STEIN	Sender	SZPIEGEL	Baruch
STEIN	Ya'acov-Yehoshua	SZPIEGEL	David
STEINITZ	Hirstl	SZPIEGEL	Elimelech
STERN	Bine	SZPIEGEL	Freydl
STERN	Bluma	SZPIEGEL	Gala-Gitl
STERN	Mordecai	SZPIEGEL	Genandl
STERN	Yosef	SZPIEGEL	Leybush
STOLEK	Leibl	SZPIEGEL	Miriam
STOLEK	Moshe	SZPIEGEL	Moshe-Yosef
SUKENIK (KLURMAN)	Sarah	SZPIEGEL	Rahel
SUKENIK	David	SZPIEGEL	Reyzl-Tamril
SUKENIK	Moshe	SZPIEGEL	Sara-Sima
SUKENIK	Relye	SZPIEGEL	Ya'acov

[Page 306]

SZPIEGEL	Yidzia(?)	VANCHADLOVSKI	Golda
SZPIEGEL	Yisroel	VANCHADLOVSKI	Sarah

SZPIEGEL	Yitzhak	VISHLITZKI	Elimelech
SZPIEGEL	Yona	VISHLITZKI	Gedalye
SZPIEGEL	Yosef	VISHLITZKI	Yosef
SZPIEGEL	Zisla	WAJCHSELFISH	Avraham
TARNOWSKI	Moshe	WALBERG	Bunem
TATARKA	Avner	WALBERG	Hendl
TATARKA	Lazar	WALBERG	Yisroel
TATARKA	Shlomo	WALDLIWRAND	Yosef
TENNENWURCEL	Feivel	WARSZAWSKI	Miriam
TENNENWURCEL	Haim	WARSZAWSKI	Rahel-Leah
TENNENWURCEL	Yitzhak	WARSZAWSKI	Rivka
TSITERMANN	Pessah	WAXBERG	Netta
TSITERMANN	Reuven	WDOWINSKI	Avraham
TSITERMANN	Sarah	WDOWINSKI	Esther
TSITERMANN	Shmuel	WDOWINSKI	Lazar
TSITERMANN	Shprintse	WDOWINSKI	Mendel
TSITERMANN	Yosef	WDOWINSKI	Paula
TZIRBONHIGODA	Eli	WEGA	Natan
TZIRBONHIGODA	Haim	WEIL	Anshil
UNGER	Basye	WEIL	David Yedidye
UNGER	Blumer	WEINRIB	Ephraim
UNGER	David	WEINRIB	Hertske
UNGER	Eydle	WEINRIB	Leybe
UNGER	Feigel Malka	WEINRIB	Tova
UNGER	Roza	WEINSTEIN	David

UNGER	Sarah	WEINSTOCK	David
UNGER	Tamara	WEINTRAUB	Hava
UNGER	Yehonatan	WEINTRAUB	Moshe
VANCHADLOVSKI	Abba	WEITZMAN	Bezalel
VANCHADLOVSKI	Baruch	WEITZMAN	Bluma

[Page 307]

WEITZMAN	Bracha	ZINDER	Hanna
WEITZMAN	Freida	ZINDER	Leah
WEITZMAN	Haim	ZINDER	Mindl
WEITZMAN	Haya-Rivka	ZINDER	Miriam
WEITZMAN	Moshe	ZINDER	Moshe
WEITZMAN	Shlomo	ZINDER	Shmuel
WEITZMAN	Yisroel	ZLOTNIK	Moshe
WEITZMAN	Yocheved	ZLOTNIK	Yechiel
WELTFREUND	Basya	ZUCKERMAN	Avraham
WELTFREUND	Yisroel	ZUCKERMAN	Berl
WEXLER	Micha'el	ZUCKERMAN	David
ZELIKOWITZ	Kalman	ZUCKERMAN	Leib
ZELIKOWITZ	Ya'acov-Natan	ZUCKERMAN	Rahel
ZELIKOWITZ	Yeshia	ZUCKERMAN	Ya'acov
ZELIKOWITZ	Yosef		
ZELMANOWICZ	Bluma		
ZELMANOWICZ	Fraydl		
ZELMANOWICZ	Hendl		
ZELMANOWICZ	shmuel		
ZELMANOWICZ	Tova		

ZIBENBERG	Adam		
ZIBENBERG	Esther		
ZIBENBERG	Selah		
ZIEGLER	Gitl		
ZIEGLER	Haim		
ZIEGLER	Herschel		
ZIEGLER	Moshe		
ZIEGLER	Natan		
ZIEGLER	Simha		
ZILONIDZHEVO	Ber		
ZILONIDZHEVO	Melech		
ZINDER	Esther		

[Pages 307-308]

Charsznica Martyrs

Transliterated by Beryl Baleson

Note that the page numbers in the right column are page numbers in the original Yizkor Book and not the page numbers in this translation.

Family name	First name	M/F	Remarks	Page
א Alef				
AVIAZED	Hayyim ber	M		307
AVIAZED	David	M		307
AVIAZED	Rivka	F		307
AVIAZED	Roza	F		307
ULMER	Itcha	M		307
ULMER	Baril	M		307
ULMER		M	In list written "DER SHISTER"	307
ULMER	Herzl	M		307
AIBSHITZ	Yehiel	M		307
AIBSHITZ	Shaindel	F		307
AIBSHITZ		F	First daughter of three girls	307
AIBSHITZ		F	Second daughter of three girls	307
AIBSHITZ		F	Third daughter of three girls	307
ALBER	Rachel Leah	F		307
ANGELRED	Isaac Meir	M		307
ASELKA	Kalman	M		307
ASELKA	Abraham David	M		307

ASELKA	Hana	F		307
ASELKA	Esther	F		307
ASELKA	Joseph	M		307
ב Bet				
BLADI	Wolf	M		307
BRAINDEL	Hana	F		307
BRIN	Rabbi Hagaon Shlomo	M	Rabbi	307
BRIN	Rabanit Esther	F		307
BRIN	Pinchas Joseph	M		307
BRIN	Nehama	F		307
ג Gimmel				
GOLDKORN	Dov	M		307
GOLDKORN	Malka	F		307
GOLDKORN	Hershel	M		307
GOLDKORN	Ida	F		307
GOLDSTEIN	Joseph	M		307
GOLDSTEIN		F		307
GOLDSTEIN		F	First daughter of three girls	307
GOLDSTEIN		F	Second daughter of three girls	307
GOLDSTEIN		F	Third daughter of three girls	307
GERTLER	Abraham	M		307

GERTLER	Bella	F		307
GERTLER	Nahum	M		307
GERTLER	Ella	F		307
GERTLER	Yonah	M		307
GERTLER	Esther	F		307
GRAITZER	Mordechai	M		307
GRAITZER	Rivka	F		307
ד Dalet				
DRAILICH	Abraham	M		307
DERKSLER	Abraham	M		307
ה Hey				
HOROWITZ	Hirsh Lev	M		307
HOROWITZ	Billa	F		307
HOROWITZ	Yetel	F		307
HOROWITZ	Reuben	M		307
HIRSH	Shmuel	M		307
ו Vav				
WEITZMAN	Baruch	M		307
WEKSLER	Mechal	M		307
WEKSLER	Bluma	F		307
WEKSLER	Joel	M		307
WEKSLER	Asher	M		307
ז Zayin				
ZILBERBERG	Mendel	M		307
ZILBERBERG	Ezra	F		307

ZILBERBERG	Simcha	M		307
ZILBERBERG	Shoshana	F		307
	Moshe David	M	Son in law of SHOSHANA ZILBERBERG	307
	Hendel	F	ZILBERBERG	307
ZILBERBERG	Melech	M		307
ZELTZBERG			Not certain if it refers to single or family	307
ZACKS	Baila	F		307
ZSHERNOVITZKY	Joseph	M		307
י Yod				
YOSKOVITZ		M	Father in law of JOSEPH TZIMMERMAN	307
YNOVSKY			Not certain if it refers to single or family	307
ל Lamed				
LEDERMAN		M		308
LEVINZON	Mordechai	M		308
LOSTMAN		M	Son in law of MOSHE SHNOVSKY	308
LIBERMAN	Yacov Joseph	M		308
מ Mem				
MATOSHINSKY	Faivel	M		308
MATOSHINSKY	Shlomo	M		308
MATOSHINSKY	Yochevet	F		308
MATOSHINSKY	Yokil	M		308
MATOSHINSKY	Abraham	M		308

MATOSHINSKY	Miriam Roza	F		308
MATOSHINSKY	Gitela	F		308
MATOSHINSKY	Yosela	M		308
MATOSHINSKY	Mendela	M		308
MATOSHINSKY	Meir	M		308
ס Samech				
SALAT	Dov	M		308
פ Peh				
FOKAS	David	M		308
FOKAS	Moshe	M		308
FAIGENBOIM			No certain if it refers to a single or family	308
FAIGENBLAT	Moshe	M		308
FILA	Kalman	M		308
PALMENBOIM	Simcha	M		308
FRIZER	Aharon	M		308
FRIZER		F		308
PRAIS	Itcha	M	Son in law of YISHAYAHU LUBLINER	308
PERLGRICHT	Yeshiya	M		308
PASHEVOZNIK	Isaac	M		308
צ Tzadik				
TZUKER	Mordechai	M		308
TZUKER	Aharon	M		308
TZUKERMAN	David	M		308
TZUKERMAN	Yacov	M		308

TZIGLER	Hershel	M		308
TZIGLER	Sincha	M		308
TZIGLER	Moshe Nathan	M		308
TZIGLER	Leah	F		308
TZIMMERMAN	Joseph	M		308
TZIMMERMAN	Bluma	F		308
ק Kof				
KAZOVSKY	Mordechai	M		308
KLAIZNER	Israel Shmuel	M		308
KLAIZNER	Mendel David	M		308
KLAIZNER	Pinchas	M		308
KAMINSKY		M		308
ר Resh				
ROGOVSKY	Shlomo	M		308
ROGOVSKY	Mendel	M		308
ROGOVSKY	Shmuel	M		308
ROGOVSKY	Hava	F		308
ROGOVSKY	Reuben	M		308
ROGOVSKY	Baila	F		308
ROGOVSKY	Faigela	F		308
ROGOVSKY	Rachela	F		308
ROGOVSKY	Aharon	M		308
ROGOVSKY	Riva	F		308
ROGOVSKY	Moshe Joseph	M		308

ROZEN	Velvel	M		308
ROZENBERG	Shlomo	M		308
RAINHARTZ	Abraham Moshe	M		308
RAINHARTZ	Baruch Joseph	M		308
RAINHARTZ	Yudel	M		308
RAINHARTZ	Hershel	M		308
ש Shin				
SHVARTZ	Moshe	M		308
SHTEINBERG	Mottel	M		308
SHALDOVSKY	Shmuel	M		308
SHALDOVSKY	Shprintza	F		308
SHALDOVSKY	Mindeniya	F		308
SHNIOAVSKY	Moshe	M		308
SHNIOAVSKY	Shmerel	M		308
SHNIOAVSKY	Zalman	M		308
SHNIOAVSKY	Baril	M		308
SHNIOAVSKY	Isaac	M		308
SHTAIR	Wolf	M		308

[Pages 309-314]

Książ Wielki Martyrs

Transliterated by Beryl Baleson

Note that the page numbers in the right column are the page numbers in the original Yizkor Book and not this translation.

Family name	First name	M/F	Remarks	Page
א Alef				
AVRAMTZIK	Abraham Shmuel	M		309
AVRAMTZIK	Mindel	F		309
AVRAMTZIK	Hayyim Yacov	M		309
AVRAMTZIK	Isaac Yehuda	M		309
AVRAMTZIK	Shalom	M		309
AVRAMTZIK	Moshe Shlomo	M		309
AVRAMTZIK	Yacov	M		309
AVRAMTZIK	Ephraim	M		309
AVRAMTZIK	Hana Roiza	F		309
AVRAMTZIK	Abraham Lev	M		309
AVRAMTZIK	Mordechai	M		309
AVRAMTZIK	Hersh Wolf	M		309
AVRAMTZIK	Meir Nachman	M		309
AVRAMTZIK	Simcha	M		309
AVRAMTZIK	Shmuel	M		309
ADELIST	Hershel	M		309
ADELIST	Shlomo	M		309
ADELIST	Nathan	M		309
ADELIST	Hinda	F		309
ADELIST	Joseph	M		309
ADELIST	Golda Ita	F		309
ADELIST	Meltziya	F		309

AVERBACH	Hana	F		309
AVERBACH	Raizel	F		309
AIZOVITZ	Lemel	M		309
AIZOVITZ	Leah Basha	F		309
AIZOVITZ	Joseph Faivel	M		309
AIZKOVITZ	Tzilka	F		309
AIZKOVITZ	Hana Haya	F		309
AIZKOVITZ	Abraham	M		309
AIZKOVITZ	Wolf David	M		309
ANGELSHTEIN	Benjamin Laivish	M		309
ANGELSHTEIN	Mirl	F		309
ARLICH	Yacov	M		309
ARLICH	Miriam	F		309
ARLICH	Raizel	F		309
ARLICH	Yishaya	M		309
ב Bet				
BORNSHTEIN	Melech	M		309
BORNSHTEIN	Pearl	F		309
BORNSHTEIN	Traindel	F		309
BORNSHTEIN	Yacov	M		309
BORNSHTEIN	Shmuel	M		309
BORNSHTEIN	Deshva	F		309
BORNSHTEIN	Roiza Malka	F		309
BORNSHTEIN	Rivka	F		309
BORNSHTEIN	Kayla	F		309
BORNSHTEIN	Mordechai	M		309
BORNSHTEIN	Gittel	F		309
BORNSHTEIN	Melech	M		309
BORNSHTEIN	Yudel	M		309

BORNSHTEIN	Gershon	M		309
BORNSHTEIN	Hershel	M		309
BORNSHTEIN	Fromatziya	F		309
BIRENBAUM	David	M		309
BIRENBAUM	Tova	F		309
BIRENBAUM	Pesel	F		309
BIRENBAUM	Yerachmiel	M		309
BLADI	Kalman	M		309
BLADI	Rivka	F		309
BLADI	Faigela	F		309
BLADI	Fraindel	F		309
BLADI	Wolf Ber	M		310
BLADI	Idel	F		310
BERDIN	Shlomo	M		310
BERDIN	Kayla	F		310
BERDIN	Laivish Meir	M		310
BERDIN	Rivka	F		310
BERDIN	Baila Rachel	F		310
BERDIN	Yacov Ber	M		310
BERDIN	Moshe	M		310
ג Gimmel				
GVIRTZMAN	Hershel Laivish	M		310
GVIRTZMAN	Hava	F		310
GLASTER	Hayyim Shraga	M	Slaughterer and examiner	310
GERBERSKY	Nathan	M		310
GERBERSKY	Rivka	F		310
GERBERSKY	Darzil	F		310
GERBERSKY	Hershel	M		310
GERBERSKY	Kalman	M		310

GERBERSKY	Faivel	M		310
ד Dalet				
DERBINOVSKY	Hershel	M		310
DERBINOVSKY	Ethel	F		310
DERBINOVSKY	Neir	M		310
DERBINOVSKY	Raizel	F		310
DERBINOVSKY	Sima	F		310
ה Hey				
HOROVITZ	Hayyim	M		310
HOROVITZ	Hendel	F		310
HOROVITZ	Joseph	M		310
HOROVITZ	Haya	F		310
HOROVITZ	Ethel	F		310
HERSHKOVITZ	Shlomo	M		310
HERSHKOVITZ	Wolf	M		310
HERSHKOVITZ	Hinda	F		310
HERSHKOVITZ	Isaac	M		310
HERSHKOVITZ	Deborah Braindel	F		310
HERSHKOVITZ	Aharon Noah	M		310
HERSHKOVITZ	Meir	M		310
HERSHKOVITZ	Yedis	F		310
HERSHKOVITZ	Shmuel	M		310
HERSHKOVITZ	Yehoshua	M		310
ו Vav				
VELBEROMSKY	David	M		310
VELBEROMSKY	Faigel	F		310
VELBEROMSKY	Aharon	M		310
VELBEROMSKY	Tzirel	F		310
VELBEROMSKY	Shifra Leah	F		310

VELBEROMSKY	Tzarka	F		310
VELBEROMSKY	Sarah Ruchama	F		310
WEINBERG	Wolf	M		310
WEINBERG	Leah	F		310
WEINBERG	Shertza Ruchama	F		310
WEINBERG	Yerachmiel	M		310
WEINBERG	Tzipora	F		310
WEINBERG	Hershel	M		310
WEINBERG	Yochevet	F		310
WEINTRAUB	Isaac	M		310
WEINTRAUB	Hillel	M		310
WEINTRAUB	Hinda Leah	F		310
WEINTRAUB	Abraham	M		310
WEINTRAUB	Haya	F		310
WEINTRAUB	Yacov	M		310
WEINTRAUB	Michael	M		310
WEINTRAUB	Leah	F		310
VISHELITZKY	Mordechai Eliezer	M		310
VISHELITZKY		F		310
VISHELITZKY	Yacov	M		310
VELTZKOVSKY	Shmuel Zainbel	M		310
VELTZKOVSKY	Shva	F		310
VELTZKOVSKY	Shlomo Mendel	M		310
VELTZKOVSKY	Joseph Baruch	M		310
VELTZKOVSKY	Moshe Nathan	M		310
VELTZKOVSKY	Esther Hana	F		310
VIRZA	Joseph	M		311
VIRZA	Rachela	F		311

VIRZA	Laivish	M		311
VIRZA	Raizel	F		311
VIRZA	Gittel	F		311
VIRZA	Berel	M		311
WEINSHTOK	Eli Simcha	M		311
WEINSHTOK	Rochetza	F		311
WEINSHTOK	Udel	F		311
WEINSHTOK	David	M		311
WENDERSMAN	Kalman	M		311
WENDERSMAN	Joseph	M		311
WENDERSMAN	Roiza	F		311
WENDERSMAN	Eli	M		311
WENDERSMAN	Hershel	M		311
WENDERSMAN	Golda	F		311
WENDERSMAN	Laivish Mendel	M		311
WENDERSMAN	Malka	F		311
WENDERSMAN	Aharon	M		311
WENDERSMAN	Raizel	F		311
WENDERSMAN	Hanoch	M		311
WENDERSMAN	Fraida	F		311
WENDERSMAN	Rivka	F		311
WENDERSMAN	Bluma	F		311
WENDERSMAN	Necha	F		311
WENDERSMAN	Israel Shmuel	M		311
WENDERSMAN	Leah Natal	F		311
WENDERSMAN	David	M		311
VETZERINSKY	Bluma	F		311
VETZERINSKY	Hana	F		311
VETZERINSKY	Shaindel	F		311
VETZERINSKY	Reuben	M		311

VETZERINSKY	Mendel	M		311
ז Zayin				
ZAGENILIK	Mendil	M		311
ZAGENILIK	Zalman	M		311
ZAGENILIK	Hodis	F		311
ZAGENILIK	Laizer	M		311
ZAGENILIK	Gittel	F		311
ZAGENILIK	Kalman	M		311
ZAGENILIK	Roza	F		311
ZILBERBERG	Moshe Yacov	M		311
ZILBERBERG	Hayyim David	M		311
ZILBERBERG	Berel	M		311
ZILBERBERG	Shabati	M		311
ZILBERBERG	Elka	F		311
ZILBERBERG	Miriam Haya	F		311
ZINGER	Rabbi Abraham	M	Rabbi	311
ZINGER	Rabbanit Rivka	F		311
ZINGER	Hana Gittel	F		311
ZLOTNIK	Laivish	M		311
ZLOTNIK	Yehoshua	M		311
ZLOTNIK	Malka	F		311
ZLIGFELD	Shmuel David	M		311
ZLIGFELD	Faigel	F		311
ZLIGFELD	Israel	M		311
ZLIGFELD	Meir	M		311
ZLIGFELD	Gittel	F		311
ZLIGFELD	Mala	F		311
ZLICKOVITZ	Joseph	M		311
ZLICKOVITZ	Masha	F		311

ZALTZBERG	David	M		311
ZALTZBERG	Hayyim	M		311
ZALTZBERG	Moshe	M		311
ZALTZBERG	Rivka	F		311
ZALTZBERG	Roza	F		311
ZALTZBERG	Sarah	F		311
ZERNOVITZKY	Kayla	F		311
ZERNOVITZKY	David	M	In list family name written "ZERNOIVETZKY" apparently in error	311
ZERNOVITZKY	Itsha	M		311
ח Chet				
CHANTZINSKY	Moshe David	M		311
CHANTZINSKY	Shifra Leah	F		311
CHANTZINSKY	Zissel	F		311
CHANTZINSKY	Liba	F		312
CHANKIS	Ozer	M		312
CHANKIS	Gershon	M		312
CHANKIS	Yonah	M		312
CHANKIS	Moshe	M		312
ט Tet				
TEITELBAUM	Laibel	M		312
TEITELBAUM	Hana	F		312
י Yod				
YORISTA	Laivish David	M		312
YORISTA	Promat	F		312
YORISTA	Deborah	F		312
YORISTA	Fraida	F		312
YORISTA	Hana	F		312

YORISTA	Leah Netta	F		312
YORISTA	Pinchas Mordechai	M		312
YESKEL	Faigel	M		312
YESKEL	Esther Rivka	F		312
YESKEL	Wolf	M		312
YESKEL	Shlomo	M		312
YESKEL	Golda	F		312
YESKEL	Mottel	M		312
YESKEL	Braindel	F		312
YESKEL	Abraham	M		312
YESKEL	Hana	F		312
ל Lamed				
LEVKOVITZ	Fishel	M		312
LEVKOVITZ	Joseph	M		312
LEVKOVITZ	Raizel	F		312
LOPET	Israel	M		312
LOPET	Haya	F		312
LOPET	Bluma	F		312
LOPET	Rachela	F		312
LOPET	Yerachmiel	M		312
LOPET	Akiva	M		312
LOPET	Tzirel	F		312
LIZORK	Israel	M		312
LIZORK	Esther	F		312
LIZORK	Mendel	M		312
LIZORK	Abraham	M		312
LIZORK	Toiva	F		312
LIZORK	Yehiel	M		312
LIZORK	Basha	F		312

LIZORK	Hana	F		312
LERER	Golda	F		312
LERER	Fraida	F		312
מ Mem				
MONTA	Simcha	M		312
MONTA	Dina	F		312
MONTA	Leah	F		312
MONTA	Shaya	M		312
MONTA	Yakil	M		312
MOR	Moshe	M		312
MOR	Zissel	F		312
MOR	Sarah	F		312
MOR	David	M		312
MATOSHINSKY	Mendel	M		312
MATOSHINSKY	Rachela	F		312
MATOSHINSKY	Pessel	F		312
MATOSHINSKY	Meir	M		312
MATOSHINSKY	Rivka	F		312
MATOSHINSKY	Hana	F		312
MATOSHINSKY	Joseph	M		312
MATOSHINSKY	Malka	F		312
MATOSHINSKY	Wolf	M		312
MATOSHINSKY	Yacov	M		312
MATOSHINSKY	Gendel	F		312
MILLER	Oron	M		312
MILLER	Gissel	F		312
MINDEZIGORSKY	Sarah	F		312
MINDEZIGORSKY	Yetka	F		312
MINDEZIGORSKY	Israel	M		312

MINDEZIGORSKY	Hana	F		312
MINDEZIGORSKY	Aba	M		312
MINDEZIGORSKY	Simcha	M		313
MELINERSKY	Handel	F		313
MELINERSKY	Deborah	F		313
MELINERSKY	Baruch	M		313
MELINERSKY	Hana	F		313
MERKOVITZ	Barish	M		313
MERKOVITZ	Gittel	F		313
MERKOVITZ	Moshe Isaac	M		313
MERKOVITZ	Haya	F		313
MERKOVITZ	Sarah	F		313
MERKOVITZ	Matil			313
נ Nun				
NORDIN	Meir	M		313
NORDIN	Malka	F		313
NORDIN	Abraham	M		313
NORDIN	Haya	F		313
NORDIN	Rivka	F		313
NORDIN	Avigdor	M		313
NORDIN	Shaindel	F		313
ס Samech				
SULTENIK	Yacov	M		313
SULTENIK	Handel	F		313
SULTENIK	Jonathan	M		313
SULTENIK	Zissa	F		313
SULTENIK	Henich	M		313
SULTENIK	David	M		313
SULTENIK	Esther Rachel	F		313

SULTENIK	Shimshon	M		313
SULTENIK	Joel	M		313
SULTENIK	Yehiel	M		313
SULTENIK	Hinda	F		313
SULTENIK	Hirsh Lev	M		313
SULTENIK	Tova	F		313
SULTENIK	Rachel	F		313
SOLNIK	Yehoshua	M		313
SOLNIK	Hana	F		313
SOLNIK	David	M		313
SOLNIK	Haya Ethel	F		313
SOLNIK	Deborah	F		313
SOLNIK	Meir Shmuel	M		313
SOLNIK	Kalman	M		313
פ Peh				
PULNIKEVIAT	Laibka	M		313
PULNIKEVIAT	Hana Gila	F		313
PULNIKEVIAT	Baltsha	F		313
PULNIKEVIAT	Shlomo	M		313
PULNIKEVIAT	Haya Sarah	F		313
PULNIKEVIAT	Esther	F		313
PULNIKEVIAT	Moshe	M		313
PULNIKEVIAT	Hava	F		313
PINTSHEVSKY	Pessel	F		313
PINTSHEVSKY	Mottel	M		313
PINTSHEVSKY	Laivish	M		313
PINTSHEVSKY	Shalom	M		313
PINTSHEVSKY	Bracha	F		313
PINTSHEVSKY	Yacov	M		313

PINTSHEVSKY	Blatsha	F		313
PELKOVITZ	Sincha	M		313
PELKOVITZ	Sarah Ita	F		313
PELKOVITZ	Jonathan	M		313
PELKOVITZ	Nechemiya	M		313
PELKOVITZ	Moshe	M		313
PELKOVITZ	Hendel	F		313
FRIDBERG	Shalom	M		313
FRIDBERG	Ita	F		313
FRIDBERG	Miriam Hana	F		313
FRIDBERG	Baila	F		313
FRIDBERG	Deborah	F		313
FRIDBERG	Yochevet	F		313
FRIDBERG	Itsha	M		313
FRIDBERG	Yishaya Ze'ev	M		313
FRIDBERG	Leah	F		313
FRIDBERG	Hirsh Lev	M		313
FRIDBERG	Ruchama	F		313
FRIDBERG	Yerachmiel Israel Isaac	M		314
FRIDBERG	Abraham	M		314
FRIDBERG	Alter	M		314
FRIDBERG	Nachman David	M		314
FRIDBERG	Tova	F		314
FRIDBERG	Hayyim	M		314
FRIDBERG	Hana	F		314
FRIDBERG	Alter	M		314
FRIDBERG	Brish	M		314
FRIDBERG	Yerachmiel	M		314
FRIDBERG	Pearl	F		314

FRIDBERG	Yochevet	F		314
FRIDBERG	Yehiel	M		314
FRIDBERG	Elka	F		314
FRIDBERG	Wolf	M		314
FRIDBERG	Moshe	M		314
FRIDBERG	Meir	M		314
צ Tzadik				
TZITRON	Tzirel	F		314
ק Kof				
KAVELOTER	Itsha	M		314
KAVELOTER	Esther	F		314
KORTZOLD	Abraham	M		314
KORTZOLD	Rivka	F		314
KORTZOLD	Miriam Leah	F		314
KORTZOLD	Faigel	F		314
KORTZOLD	Moshe	M		314
KORTZOLD	Joseph Kalman	M		314
KLEIN	Joseph Isaac	M		314
KLEIN	Hana Kayla	F		314
KLEIN	Liba	F		314
KLEIN	Sarah	F		314
KLEIN	Abraham Yacov	M		314
KLEIN	Eli	M		314
KLEIN	Paitsha	F		314
ר Resh				
ROGOVSKY	Miriam	F		314
ROGOVSKY	Akiva	M		314
ROGOVSKY	Fraidel	F		314

ROZEMAITI	Abraham	M		314
ROZEMAITI	Haika	F		314
ROZEMAITI	Yacov	M		314
ROZEMAITI	Hayyim Shmuel	M		314
ROZEMAITI	Abraham Meir	M		314
ROZEMAITI	Tzvia	F		314
ROZEMAITI	Joseph	M		314
ROZEMAITI	Leah	F		314
ROZEMAITI	Yehiel	M		314
ROZEMAITI	Akiva	M		314
ROZEMAITI	Miriam	F		314
ROZEMAITI	Ethel	F		314
ROZEMAITI	Shaindel	F		314
ROZEMAITI	Tzirel	F		314
ROZEMAITI	Eliezer	M		314
ROZENTZVAIG	Hayyim	M		314
ROZENTZVAIG	Hana Rachel	F		314
ROZENTZVAIG	Zissel	F		314
ROZENTZVAIG	Yacov	M		314
ROZENTZVAIG	Laibel	M		314
ROZENTZVAIG	Raizel	F		314
ש Shin				
SHVARTZBOIM	Yehiel	M		314
SHVARTZBOIM	Shprintza	F		314
SHVARTZBOIM	Gutsha	F		314
SHVARTZBOIM	Golda	F		314
SHALMOVITZ	Joseph	M		314
SHALMOVITZ	Pearl	F		314
SHAPIRA	Rabbanit Rachel	F		314

SHAPIRA	Braindel Leah	F		314
SHAK	Chone	M		314
SHAK	Mendil	M		314

[Pages 318-315]

My Hometown – Miechov

Miechov was founded in the 13th century around a monastery that was erected there by monks of the order of the Holy Sepulchre (the Bozhogrovites). Up until 1819, the monastery retained the ownership of most of the land in the area and Jews were not allowed to settle there.

The Jewish settlement in Miechov started to develop in the years 1862–1863 after the great reform of the Polish Congress in which the prohibition on settlement by Jews in the region was abolished. By 1897, there were already 1,436 Jews in Miechov, representing one–third of the population. In 1921, their number reached 2,383, more than 40% of the total population.

The flow of Jews to the place was influenced indirectly also by the pogroms that took place in those years in the surrounding towns. Miechov, as the county–town, attracted Jews seeking shelter. The Jews for their part contributed much to the development of the town and fertilized her economic and cultural life.

The Jews of Miechov were mainly tradesmen and craftsmen and not a few of them were members of the free professions. They set up flour mills, electrical mills and many other enterprises. The Polish tradesmen tried to restrict their activities and did this by the establishment of trade associations only for Poles, putting a boycott on Jewish shops, levying high taxes, and so on. The status of the Jewish tradesman fell considerably in comparison with that of his Polish counterpart and it became increasingly difficult to keep going. Nevertheless, the Jews did not despair; they established their own associations, founded a co–operative bank and established funds for helping the needy.

Education of the very young children was put in the hands of teachers in the Mizrachi and Agudat Israel "Chadarim". The older ones attended the state primary school – boys and girls separate – since there was no Jewish school in the town. In the Polish school, the Jewish pupils received scripture lessons from a Jewish teacher. When the "Mizrachi school" was founded, the majority of the boys transferred to it, and next to it was then established a Jewish school for girls.

In the Polish state secondary school in Miechov there existed a "numerous clausus" with regard to Jews. Only a few Jewish children were allowed to continue their studies there. The children of Jews who wanted to obtain higher education were forced to move to other towns. For all that, there was a high percentage of people with higher education; lawyers, teachers and doctors.

[Page 317]

Two libraries operated in the town: the "Hazamir" for adults and the "Dror" for the youth. The former served also as a cultural centre and evening courses were held there. There was also a dramatics group and a sports club.

The economic foundations that the Jews established in Miechov have already been mentioned; the most important of these were the co–operative bank, founded by the craftsmen's association and the trade bank set up by the tradesmen's association. These two foundations provided economic support for the Jews of the town. Also of note were the activities of the various mutual aid philanthropic societies which gave much help to the needy. Among them may be recalled the "Achiazar" Association which served as a charity organization and the "Bikur Cholim" society which aided poor people when they were ill.

In the revival of independent Poland, Miechov played a distinguished role; there, was set up the staff of General Pilsudski – later to be the first marshal of Poland. And yet, the Jews of Miechov who had taken an active part in the uprising, suffered hardships after the liberation; in particular, the soldiers of General Haller (the "Hallerchicks") assaulted them and together with the farmers in the surrounding areas, made pogroms against the Jews, holding them in fear for a long time. These events left their imprint on the Jews of the town and they find their expression in some of the stories in this book.

During the period between the two World Wars, the town developed both economically and culturally and the Jews adapted themselves to this development. The community was not conservative and its members were open to progress and learning. In this period, 90% of the Jews of the town were Zionists, both in theory and in practice.

The political life of the town was very active and each of the important Jewish parties had a branch in the place. The Zionist Party had the greatest number of supporters followed by the "Mizrachi" movement and that of "Hashomer Hatzair". A small minority belonged to the "Agudat Israel" and to the "Betar" movements.

Parallel with these movements, there operated also youth organizations of which the largest and most important was "Hashomer HaLeumi" (afterwards called "HaNoar HaZioni"), founded by the General Zionist Organization.

Following them in importance was the "Betar" movement and "HaShomer Hadati" founded by the Mizrachi and finally, "Zeiray Agudat Israel" which did not take part in Zionist activities. All the organizations and movements engaged in lively and widespread activity and especially did much for the Keren Kayemet. They organized "flower days", shows and bazaars in which produce from the Land of Israel was sold. At all events and at every opportunity, the "Blue Box" was prominent as a sign and symbol of national revival and of longing for the homeland.

[Page 316]

Many members of the youth organizations left for pioneer training ("Hachsharah Chalutzit") in various parts of the land and awaited their turn for Aliyah to the Land of Israel despite the many difficulties in obtaining certificates.

The extent to which the Jews of Miechov took an interest in Hebrew culture may be gauged from the fact that on the day that the Hebrew University was opened on Mount Scopus in April, 1925, the whole town celebrated. The event left its imprint for a long while and contributed much to the spirit of national pride.

The Jews were active also in local councils and were even elected to the administration. The chairman of the congregation who served in that capacity for many years was also a member of the town council. The secretary of the congregation, Mr. Eliezer Lavie, in his foreword to this book, gives a detailed list of the heads of the congregation and prominent figures (see page 17). The first Rav of the Miechov community was Rabbi Yeshayahu Scheinfrucht who served there for 40 years from 1882 until his death in 1922. He was succeeded by his son, Rabbi Hanoch Haaneach Scheinfrucht who was beloved by all and who took an active part also in the social life of the town. He was also one of the founders of the "Mizrachi" school. In World War II, he refused to leave his congregation and perished in the Holocaust.

In the winter of 1938/39, there was an outbreak of typhus among the Jewish population of Miechov that took a heavy toll of life.

In World War II, Miechov was gradually invaded by Nazism: First, the civil German government took over with Dr. Hans Frauch as General Governor. Then, on September 6th, 1939, Miechov was conquered by the Germans. A month later, the city became attached to the Krakau district and the regional "Kraushauptmanschaft" was established there. At that time, all key positions were naturally held by Germans and the Jews, who were concentrated in the ghetto, suffered from incessant humiliation and maltreatment. During the German conquest, synagogues were ravaged and the Jews of Miechov witnessed Torah scrolls set on fire. They could not help when seeing that fearful sight, uttering the words of the famous chant 'Vetaher Libenu'. They did not, however, wait passively for their tragic fate. The Jewish community was quick to establish welfare agencies which were responsible for the regular supply of drugs, soap and basic food substances. The Jewish commissar appointed, distributed the products among the families and everyday administrative matters were well organized by the Judenrat. The conditions, however, were constantly deteriorating. In 1941, Miechov suffered another typhus plague and the Jewish population was nearly the victim of total starvation. Then, in June –, 1942, another humiliating edict worsened the status of the Jews in the region. Jews were compelled to live within the boundaries of the Jadischer Wohnbezirk (the quarter allotted to Jews by the regime). The edict was signed by Kelpers of the Police department. Naturally, the Judenrat could not avoid this edict but there were repeated attempts to avoid final expulsion by paying a heavy ransom. There were vague rumours of concentration camps and the Jewish population sought ways of survival. The ransom proved ineffective and in September, 1942, the Jews of Miechov were expelled from the entire region. The young and healthy were sent to labour camps, the rest to concentration camps in Belzits.

[Page 315]

Several youngsters tried to escape camp Prokocheim and found shelter among the labour groups at Miechov but soon after, in November 1943, they were killed together with the healthy youth of Miechov. Only 34 Jews survived from this holy community. Some of them had joined the partisans, others succeeded in escaping to the free countries. A few survived the camps.

There were some examples of heroism and bravery.

Magnified and Sanctified be His Great Name

INDEX

This index is for the main book. It does not include the names of martyrs on pages 416 – 456. Therefore when searching for family names, please also review those lists.

F

G

H

I

J

L

M

N

O

P

R

S

Y

Z

www.ingramcontent.com/pod-product-compliance
Lightning Source LLC
Chambersburg PA
CBHW082006150426
42814CB00005BA/246

* 9 7 8 1 9 3 9 5 6 1 7 9 4 *